TO BE
INDIAN

Portrait of Arthur Caswell Parker, 1918,
at the time he wrote *The Life of General Ely S. Parker.*

TO BE INDIAN

THE LIFE OF IROQUOIS-SENECA
Arthur Caswell Parker

JOY PORTER

Foreword by William N. Fenton

UNIVERSITY OF
OKLAHOMA
PRESS · NORMAN

Library of Congress Cataloging-in-Publication Data

Porter, Joy, 1967–
    To be Indian : the life of Iroquois-Seneca Arthur Caswell Parker /
Joy Porter.
        p.   cm.
    Includes bibliographical references and index.
    ISBN 0-8061-3317-1 (alk. paper)
    1. Parker, Arthur Caswell, 1881–1955.   2. Seneca Indians—
Biography.   3. Iroquois Indians—Mixed descent.   4. Anthropolo-
gists—United States—Biography.   I. Title.

E99.S3 P67 2001
974.7004 9755 0092—dc21
[B]

                                                        2001027420

1   2   3   4   5   6   7   8   9   10

For Ross,
without whom this book
would not have been written.

When I Read the Book

When I read the book, the biography famous,
And is this then (said I) what the author calls a man's life?
And so will some one when I am dead and gone write my life?
(As if any man really knew aught of my life,
Why even I myself I often think know little or nothing of my real life,
Only a few hints, a few diffused faint clews and indirections
I seek for my own use to trace out here.)

WALT WHITMAN
Leaves of Grass, 1871

Contents

Illustrations

Foreword

Arthur Parker was at home on either side of the "buckskin curtain" that separated the two cultures in which he lived. When I came to know him in the 1930s, he was the distinguished director of the Rochester Museum & Science Center. But busy as he was, he paused to suggest leads to my first fieldwork among the Senecas. No other American Indian savant had covered as broad a spectrum of achievement: folklorist, ethnologist, first New York State Archaeologist, museologist (a word that he coined), genius behind the much-loved "Indian Groups" (a set of dioramas in the New York State Museum, 1916–77, depicting Iroquois life). Besides, he had contributed the first broad study of maize subsistence in North America, which gave rise to a whole genre of later studies. And as a writer of children's books, he attained a style admired by Edmund Wilson in his later years.

One might ask how Parker found a biographer in Cambridge, England. Joy Porter, who teaches American history at Anglia Polytechnic University, is a native of Northern Ireland, and as such may feel some empathy toward American Indians. Having mastered the printed sources on Parker, she came to upstate New York, sought out persons whose lives and careers had touched Parker's career, learned to interview oral sources by asking direct questions, and befriended Parker's daughter Martha, who granted access to Parker's scrapbooks and personal papers unused by other scholars. Porter has thus approached her research in a systematic way, and she writes with a felicity that recalls the Dublin literati of the twentieth century. She has caught the spirit of the man and, for one who knew him, brings him to life. Her treatment of Parker as anthropologist and museologist hits the mark. Although it is hard for me to understand Parker's prolonged effort to bring American Indians into the mainstream of American life, Porter has done an admirable job explaining what motivated him.

Parker earned his living on the "white" side of the buckskin curtain, but the Indian side was always available to him. Dr. William A. Ritchie, whom Parker trained at Rochester, before acceding to Parker's early title as New York State Archeologist, accompanied me to Rochester to attend Parker's funeral. Parker had risen to the highest degree of Masonic orders, and fellow Masons said their rites at his service. But his native Senecas spoke last, as is their way—with solemn words of condolence to lift up the minds of the mourners—before repatriating the bundle of the Little Water Medicine that Parker had held since 1906. In a way, he never left his native Cattaraugus.

William N. Fenton

Slingerlands, New York

Preface

How did a scholar from the Northern Ireland find herself writing about an American Indian intellectual who lived and wrote in New York at the beginning of the twentieth century? What drew her to documenting his life? As a postgraduate student in 1989 at the University of Nottingham, England, I chose as a dissertation topic the work of the famous Lewis Henry Morgan, foremost early anthropologist of the Iroquois peoples of the northeastern United States. Through this early research, I glimpsed something of his American Indian informant, Ely S. Parker. Curious, I soon found that Ely was perhaps even more interesting than Morgan. I set out to learn what I could about him, and inevitably came across his greatest and most laudatory biographer, his great-nephew Arthur Caswell Parker. Not long thereafter, Arthur Parker became an ongoing fascination. Recording and evaluating his experiences as a nonenrolled Indian promised to reveal something of significance about modern Indian identity, and perhaps something about modern American identity as well.

No doubt cultural critics who concern themselves with issues of positionality would suggest other motives for writing this book. They would speak, perhaps, of deeper correspondences between the life experiences of Arthur Parker and my own. Certainly, although separated in time, there are connections between the larger cultural and political contexts surrounding my life and Parker's, and both of us have a cross-cultural heritage. The Irish, like American Indians, are a group of "tribal" peoples who have been misrepresented and stereotyped by a colonizing and dominant power.[1] The people of the six counties of the North live with the complexity of being in an environment where there are several traditions in conflict: Protestant, Catholic, British Loyalist, and Irish Nationalist. Like the six nations of the Iroquois League, they have had to interact for generations with a dominant and colonizing power. This has produced individuals, like Arthur Parker and myself, who are the product of two traditions, two often conflicting cultures. This is perhaps why both the writer and the subject of this biographical study share a fascination with the processes of mediation between one culture and another.

Yet even for someone with a personal interest in the issues involved, piecing together and analyzing aspects of Parker's life has been a tantalizing and frustrating task. Tantalizing, because so much about his circumstances connects powerfully with so many disciplines and areas of debate. Frustrating, because the painstaking business of plotting the development of his life has inevitable limitations. For example, even when published and archival sources are complemented by his personal scrapbooks and by the remembrances of his relatives and associates, it has not always been possible with any certainty to record what Parker was doing at any one time or to paint his picture vividly for the reader. This is especially true of his early life on the reservation and of the years before he achieved his first professional position at the New York State Museum in Albany.

This is therefore a very different study from, for example, Dorothy Parker's analysis of the great Indian novelist, Bureau of Indian Affairs (BIA) administrator, and professor of anthropology D'Arcy McNickle, and not just because of the nature of the available sources. Born twenty-three years after Parker, McNickle grew up far from Seneca Iroquois country, on the Flathead Indian Reservation in western Montana. Unlike Parker, he benefited financially and educationally from being an enrolled member of his "tribe." McNickle is resented by some Iroquois because of his association with John Collier, who as commissioner of Indian Affairs tried to implement New Deal reforms in Iroquoia, whereas Parker is to this day fondly remembered among a great many of his own people.[2]

But of course there are clear similarities between these figures. Both were of perhaps one-quarter Indian extraction. Both were plagued by an unease over never quite managing to gain higher educational degrees, though each was eminently capable of doing so and each gained valuable anthropological training outside of the universities. Both stayed aloof from much of the specifics of their tribal affairs, but in important ways their "Indianness" was what allowed them to get ahead. Each man put tireless effort into his work, and each devoted specific attention to Indian community projects. Both had literary aspirations: Parker, to write history or stories for young adults; McNickle, to write a great novel. Throughout their lives, each worked hard to ensure some form of Indian cultural continuity and to mediate to good effect between Indian and non-Indian worlds.

Whatever the similarities and differences, Parker has clearly generated a different kind of commentary and debate than McNickle. This is perhaps because of his varied personal and professional involvements. As an intellectual of Seneca-Iroquois extraction, he became a significant New York State archaeologist, anthropologist, Indian spokesperson, and museum professional; therefore he has inevitably been subject to several differing interpretations. Some have criticized his assimilationist stance on Indian issues and bemoaned his removal of many Iroquois artifacts from the soil so that they might form part of the extensive collections held by the state's museums. Still others wish he had pushed Iroquois land claims. They accuse him of trying to extend New York State criminal jurisdiction into Iroquois lands and of using Works Progress Administration (WPA) funds to re-create sacred Iroquois objects. But these complaints pale in comparison with the high esteem that most Iroquois retain for Parker. They recognize and applaud, along with much else, his scholarship on behalf of Iroquois culture, his valuable community work, his quiet generosity, and his robust, untiringly pro-Indian stance.

What was Parker like? He was a hardworking, pipe-smoking, well-tailored, and distinguished man whose accent, it is said, "retained the resonance of Iroquoian languages."[3] Although not tall, at perhaps five feet six inches, he cut a dignified figure in his smart clothes with his dark hair and hazel eyes winking out from under his trademark fedora. Some thought he looked quintessentially "Indian"; others thought of him as "white." However they encountered him, people seem to have warmed to Parker because of his skill at putting them at ease. A lover of puns and word games, he was friendly, with a charming sense of humor. What is more, he appreciated people for what they knew and took an interest in what interested them. When he encountered new people, they often ended up feeling important, as if they had a new friend for life who would not forget them or what they cared about. Somehow, people felt that what they had to say to him deeply mattered. They were also left with an abiding sense of his diligent and committed approach.

According to his secretary late in life, he had a soft voice but was a strong person who was tolerant and dedicated, with little interest in putting people down. "He would accept people as they were," she maintains, and even if he got angry would not show it. In her opinion, he succeeded because he "led by example, never expecting more from anyone than himself."[4] Intelligent, with a good memory, when he spoke in public, which was fairly often, he did so forcefully and with clarity. Like the great Seneca orator Red Jacket, whom he claimed as an ancestor, he brought forward his ideas with tact and diplomacy.[5] Many people considered him extremely generous, not just with his time but with his money and possessions, a trait said to be characteristically Iroquoian.[6]

Parker achieved recognized success within the dominant Euro-American culture, but he was never entirely at ease with his position as assimilated Indian. He registered a deep frustration at continually having, as he put it, "to play Indian in order to be Indian."[7] In voicing this frustration, he identified and articulated a key element of the twentieth-century Indian condition: that is, the necessity of negotiating

A modern Indian intent on success regards the camera.
This favored photograph was given to the
University of Rochester by its subject, Arthur Caswell Parker.

Courtesy of the University of Rochester

around imposed stereotypes and of finding a way of living beyond powerful definitions of "Indianness" articulated by non-Indian voices. Very little has changed since Parker made his remark. Modern Indians today continue to register the same irritation at having to "play Indian" and express the same weariness over the persistence of inaccurate and long-superseded notions of Indian character and potential.

It is a situation Indian spokeswoman Susan Harjo summed up with particular force in 1988. She testified before the U.S. Civil Rights Commission, describing how Indian peoples were "mocked, dehumanized, cartooned, stereotyped," and decrying that "everyone has that same old movie running through their heads, and Indians are identified as an era, not as a people." Contemporary Indian artists repeatedly return to the same theme, using their skills to attack the complex hypocrisies of Indian representation in the modern world. Many spend a disproportionate amount of their time reminding us that, contrary to the narrative of Hollywood Westerns, Indian peoples did not disappear with the close of the frontier and in fact remain a vibrant and strong component of the modern world.[8]

All this makes one wonder, just as Parker did, why mainstream American culture remains so at ease with the idea of the Indian as a tragic figure *of the past*. Why is the dominant American culture so resistant to replacing that identity with a new understanding of Indian survival into the present? Why must modern Indian peoples remain saddled with the image of the noble but doomed warrior, as victim of westward expansion, with an unchanging role as the elegiac "vanishing American"? Why did Parker, and why do so many Indian peoples today, have to "play Indian" in order to "be Indian"?

The reason may have to do with a problem within non-Indians, a disjuncture in the non-Indian image of self. Mainstream American culture has identified the Indian as a character at a certain stage within its own national history; so that culture has found it impossible to allow that character to develop. Too much is at stake. Acknowledgment of the actuality of Indian survival and success into and beyond the twentieth century has the power to disrupt accepted notions of how America came to be and therefore what it has become.

Vine Deloria, Jr., put this argument more succinctly in 1990 when he said, "Whites have a psychological problem with regard to their own authenticity." Phil Deloria unpacked the phenomenon further in a penetrating study published in 1998. In *Playing Indian* he explored how Indian people haunt the "long night of American dreams." They do so, he tells us, because American identity remains both powerful, creative, and yet achingly unfinished.[9] However it is ultimately theorized, the gap persists between the historical reality of Indian lives and non-Indian representation and understanding of that reality. It is a disjuncture Parker recognized, and in a fascinating way he succeeded as a twentieth-century Indian figure both because and in spite of it.

This book is therefore about the ways in which Parker "played Indian" and to what effect. It investigates his life, his work, his published texts, his speeches, personal records, and papers to uncover how he shaped a career at the heart of American life. We learn how a child, born on a New York reservation in 1881, came to develop and control a significant New York State museum; help form and direct the first modern nationally recognized "pan-Indian" organization; gain high rank within American Freemasonry; and, among other achievements, add his voice to a series of significant national debates.

It is a story that highlights new aspects of the ethnic history of early-twentieth-century America, stimulated by Parker's perspectives on concepts such as democracy, propriety, freedom, and patriotism. The reader learns something of what it means for an individual who was the product of two divided and complex societies to not just survive in an industrializing America, but to prosper against the odds. This first book-length body of research on Arthur Caswell Parker adds to the record of Iroquois leadership and individual achievement, developing and extending existing work that has considered aspects of his life selectively, be it his pioneering work within American museums, his anthropology, his work as a historian, as a "pan-Indianist," or as a leading Indian intellectual.[10]

Although Parker fits into all of these categories, the breadth and scope of his output and achievement defy any single or tidy description. This is evident from the great volume and range of material he published. In addition to work in archaeology, ethnology, and anthropology, he produced a series of newspaper and journal articles on the "Indian problem" and Indian assimilation and wrote extensively on museums and museum practice. Although described as author of "over 300 publications," in fact Parker produced some 440 separate books, articles, and addresses in addition to at least 32 published newspaper articles and at least 45 unpublished articles, speeches, and plays.[11] He also edited 5 periodicals, at times simultaneously, from 1913 to 1944, a total of 129 issues. He produced 28 radio scripts sponsored by the Rochester Museum of Arts and Sciences between 1937 and 1938 and 86 that were broadcast for the Rochester War Council Speaker's Bureau between 1942 and 1943. Clearly Parker was an exceptionally prolific writer, his writing being simply one aspect of his efforts. As those who knew him have repeatedly pointed out, today he would be considered a workaholic.[12]

He reached maturity early in the twentieth century at a time when the large-scale physical conflicts between American Indian peoples and the dominant Euro-American culture had just ended. He was part of the first Indian generation to reach adulthood after the official closing of the frontier in 1890. As he grew up, he quickly learned that his most powerful attributes in the modern world were his intellect and his industry. He wanted not just to survive but to excel within modern America, and he was determined to integrate fully within American society, even at some personal and symbolic cost.

In choosing structural assimilation as a life path, Parker was taking a stand in relation to a long-running dialogue between American Indian nations and the United States. He was responding to America's "final promise" to American Indians, a treaty in rhetoric put forward by politicians and intellectuals from the time of the nation's founding.[13] This promise offered a basic deal to Indian peoples. In exchange for their subjugation and submission to colonial military domination, they would one day be allowed to participate fully in the nation's institutions. If Indians traded the characteristics non-Indians perceived as "savage" for the characteristics concordant with Christian "civilization," they would enjoy full access to the dominant culture. This promise of compensation helped justify the process of warfare and systematic destruction of Indian environments whose final phase coincided with the time of Parker's birth.

A national Indian assimilation campaign with two distinct phases dominated the political and social contexts of Parker's life. The first, from the aftermath of the Civil War to the early decades of the twentieth century, saw a political and reforming crusade to transform and "civilize" the Indian, to pulverize the tribal mass and incorporate American Indians into the national population. The second phase witnessed a redefinition in national politics and a significant falling away of belief in the potential of Indians for transformation. As the new century progressed, Indians were assigned a marginal role within an evolving industrial hierarchy. By 1920, when Parker was thirty-nine, they were expected to accept not full incorporation, but rather a peripheral role within national life, a status comparable to that of other subaltern nonwhite peoples. Parker resisted this. He demanded, like his fur-trading ancestors, "full measure" in this long, biased exchange between nations. In each of his public roles, he required of the dominant culture something it was not always able or willing to provide—equality of opportunity and a chance for him to succeed as an assimilated Indian American.

The difficulty lay with the fact that creating and developing an identity that drew on both white and Indian cultures was messy and complex. To some extent, this was why Parker gained experience within such a broad range of overlapping professional and cultural registers. As a consequence, his life history is diverse and a challenging subject for a historian. It resists the formulation of any simple record of events. In fact, to set about ordering the multiple engagements of Parker's life in strict chronological sequence would eliminate clarity and lose the reader in a maze of separate concerns. Chronology is important to this study, but so too is analysis, and where necessary, a thematic approach has been taken. Certain topics or aspects of Parker's personal and professional life have been grouped and discussed as a whole. This has created space for considering why Parker made the choices he did and the impact of larger forces within modern America. Thus this book follows a basic chronological pattern but also deals with aspects of his life and work in discrete units. Where it is helpful, chapters are cross-referenced to make the reader aware of significant simultaneous events.

After an introductory overview of Parker's contributions, beliefs, and ethnic status, the book begins with something of the history of the great Iroquois group of nations, the tribal significance of Parker's ancestry, and his childhood. The following chapter considers Parker's guiding non-Indian and Indian influences. Chapter 3 continues the story of his development, discussing his early career and his work as archaeologist. From this point, Parker's life becomes increasingly multifaceted. So chapter 4 looks only at his work as an anthropologist, from 1905 to 1916. Chapter 5 returns to 1911 to begin its evaluation of Parker's role as national spokesman within the Society of American Indians, concluding the discussion as the 1920s begin. Chapter 6 again takes the reader back, this time as far as 1907, when Parker first became a Freemason, so as to assess his long-term role as fraternal member and American Freemason. The book then resumes a basic chronological pattern. Beginning in 1924, chapter 7 charts his mature museum work up until 1935. Chapter 8 analyzes his achievements during the New Deal and war years, from 1935 to his retirement in 1946. Chapter 9 discusses his retirement, his children's writing, the response to his death in 1955, and his legacy to us all.

Acknowledgments

My sincere thanks to the scholars from the United States whose guidance and encouragement helped this book toward completion: in particular, Distinguished Professor Emeritus William N. Fenton, Professor Laurence M. Hauptman, Professor Emerita Elizabeth Tooker, and Professor Dean R. Snow. Discussions with Professors Hauptman and Fenton during the spring of 1992 provided key initial insights, and their subsequent remarks oriented and broadened my knowledge of Parker immeasurably. Along with Professor Tooker, Distinguished Professor Fenton gave vital suggestions for improvement, and Professor Snow was kind enough to do the same for the initial chapter. This book owes another significant debt—to Hazel W. Hertzberg, now sadly deceased. Her work on Parker and Indian identity provided a basis for much of what follows.

Thanks are also due to Dr. Dave Murray of the Department of American Studies, University of Nottingham, who guided an early version through the British Ph.D. process. Dr. Murray first sparked my interest in anthropology and in native informants, and I wrote this book in an attempt to emulate something of his brand of acuity about the meanings behind aspects of Indian affairs.

Thanks too to Dr. Terry Zeller of Northern Illinois University; Arnold Krupat of Sarah Lawrence College, New York; Professor Phil Deloria of the University of Colorado at Boulder; Jim Bradley of Massachusetts; George Hammel and Jim Hogan at the State Education Department in Albany, New York; Taiaiake Alfred, director of the Indigenous Governance Program at the University of Victoria; and to friends made at the Rensselaersville Conference on Iroquois Research, Rensselaersville, New York, especially Dr. Randolph Lewis, George Abrams, and Art Einhorn.

I owe a great debt to a number of extremely competent and good-natured librarians: Karl Kabelac of the Department of Rare Books and Special Collections, Rush Rhees Library, University of Rochester; Charles F. Hayes III, Leatrice M. Kemp, and Jaré Cardinale of the Rochester Museum & Science Center; Mary Davis at the Museum of the American Indian Library at Huntington Free Library and Reading Room, New York; Ms. Rita Dockery and the library staff of the American Philosophical Society, Philadelphia; Patricia M. Virgil at the Buffalo and Erie County Historical Society; the staff of the Cultural Education Center, State Education Department, Albany; and Jane McCarren, faculty librarian, Anglia Polytechnic University. Thanks go also to Jeff Burnham and Alice Stanton at the University of Oklahoma Press and to the kind and extremely capable copyeditor John Mulvihill.

Special thanks also to dear friends Mrs. Pat B. Webster of the New York State Education Department, Albany; Ms. Mary Daley also of the New York State Education Department; Nancy and Larry Jessup of Rochester; and to Carol Kearney of Buffalo; Sarah Carlson of New York; Dr. John Cooley of Attleborough, Massachusetts, the inhabitants of Alpha Cottage, Cambridge, England; and to Alison Hancock and Mic McCann of Derry, in the North of Ireland.

Those who knew Arthur Parker, or who had direct experience of his legacy, have been kind enough to provide me with a number of insights into his life. My thanks in this respect go to Esther Parker Blueye of Basom, New York; Mrs. Ramona Charles at the Tonawanda Indian Community House, Akron, New York; Ray and John Fadden and family, at the unique Six Nations Indian Museum, Onchiota, New York; Miss Mabel Smith of Canandaigua; director emeritus of the Rochester Museum & Science Center W. Stephen Thomas; Lester Hochgraf of Tucson, Arizona; Arleigh Hill of Rochester, New York; and the late Dr. William A. Ritchie, state archaeologist emeritus.

Kindest of all, and a person to whom my deepest thanks and respect are extended, is Martha Anne Parker. She has generously allowed access to her father's personal papers, photographs, scrapbooks, and published works, thus bringing a wholly new set of materials connected to her father and his milieu into scholarly view.

A final heartfelt and sincere acknowledgment is owed to Ross Tomlinson, whose research assistance in the field, editorial commentary, patience, and love brought this challenging project to completion.

TO BE INDIAN

Introduction

Arthur Caswell Parker, Gáwasowaneh ("Big Snow Snake") or "the Chief" as he was affectionately known by museum colleagues and friends, was born on the Cattaraugus Indian Reservation of the Seneca Nation of Indians in western New York State on April 5, 1881.[1] By the time of his death on January 1, 1955, this learned, resourceful, and extremely energetic man had made his own significant contributions to American archaeology, folklore, ethnography, and anthropology. As an Indian intellectual he had published extensively and achieved prominence as a reforming spokesman and leader within the inter-tribal Society of American Indians. He had become a top-ranking Freemason, a thriving New Dealer, and, most enduringly, an innovative, enterprising, and influential New York State museum man.

By the time he retired in 1946 because of ill health, he had been instrumental in turning what was once a small New York State museum into a flourishing center of national significance. The Rochester Museum and Science Center, where he was director, has increasingly become a testimony to the vision he espoused of museums as "the university of the common man." Simultaneously, Parker won deserved respect on New York reservations, within Indian politics, and within the Indian reform movement of his day. The depth of his contribution to Indian life cannot be expressed just by listing his formal achievements, but it is useful to know that he served formally as state commissioner on Indian Affairs from 1919 to 1922, that he was appointed by the secretary of the interior to chair the 1923 Committee of One Hundred, and that, as he put it, he served as "Consultant on American Indian legislation and social amelioration to Theodore Roosevelt, Calvin Coolidge, Howard Taft and Woodrow Wilson."[2]

His diligence and determination to foster positive change made him an inveterate joiner and doer and brought him prestige within a broad range of organizations and fraternities. His various successes invariably captured the attention of the local and sometimes national press, as he won membership in learned societies and various accolades and awards. An incredibly busy and productive man, he was at the same time a complex mixture of sometimes conflicting impulses and beliefs. He was a Republican and a great patriot, something of a feminist, an ardent rambler and outdoors man, a firm believer in progress, democracy, citizenship, and the idea of just reward for hard work, and a conscientious and respected public servant. He was also at points an abject self-promoter and self-publicist, an undisciplined scholar, and

Arthur Caswell Parker surrounded, characteristically,
by a deluge of paperwork.

Courtesy of Rochester Museum & Science Center

someone who embraced the kind of eugenicist thinking that is now irrevocably bound up with and compromised by the Nazi political doctrines of World War II. In great part, however, he was simply a man of his time, seeking opportunities that were denied to his Indian generation. He tried something that many might say is impossible—to retain an Indian identity while constantly striving toward full integration within American society. Throughout his life, this complicated and sophisticated son of a nonenrolled Seneca Iroquois father and Scots-English mother worked to reconcile and manipulate the multiple loyalties and conflicting forces that surrounded his plural heritage.

Parker's professional and personal development owed a great deal to the specifics of his descent, and it is with this we must begin. Although born on the reservation to a prominent Seneca Iroquois family, he was in fact one-quarter Seneca and three-quarters white. Also, because his mother was white and the Seneca practice matrilineal descent, he was ineligible to be enrolled as a Seneca Indian. White blood through his mother made him one of the "outside people." It limited his political and social role on the reservation and excluded him from birthright membership in clan and tribe. One scholar has suggested that he resented his white mother over this, since he made scant reference to her in his writings, while writing warmly of many other female relatives, including his white paternal grandmother.[3] Parker's nonenrolled Seneca status was not mitigated until sometime around 1903, when he secured adoption into the Seneca Bear Clan and gained his ceremonial name, Gáwasowaneh. His father, Frederick, who also had a white mother, had had to go through a similar ceremonial adoption, a long-established Seneca custom toward significant whites.

Parker's status within the Seneca Iroquois Indian Nation was therefore circumscribed and ambiguous. So too was his status within the dominant American culture. He was non-Seneca and therefore non-Indian in terms of Seneca descent, reckoned through the mother's line. Yet in the eyes of the dominant culture, where descent is reckoned through the father's line, he was Indian, not least because of his physical appearance and the fact that he grew up on a reservation. Indians, then as now, had a contested legal status. The Seneca were not universally U.S. citizens until the Indian Citizenship Act of 1924, when Congress decreed that all Indians were citizens, but subject to wardship status. Even then, most Iroquois rejected citizenship, because they considered it a compromise to their own national sovereignty.[4] All this made life problematic and complex for Parker. Both as an Indian and therefore noncitizen and as a nonenrolled Seneca, he occupied a liminal position within white and Indian society. He was therefore, truly, a person in between.

Regardless of how Parker was perceived in legal, tribal, or social terms, he knew that his Indian heritage was both distinguished and important. He wrote biographies of his Indian relatives, collected details of his family tree, and tirelessly spread the message of how ancient Indian and Iroquois values could inform modern life. Although probably exaggerating the prominence of his lineage, he maintained that his Indian ancestry included some of the most illustrious figures within Iroquois history. By connecting himself to the history of Indian leadership in this way, he linked his twentieth-century attempt at integration to a long, extraordinary, and powerfully symbolic past. To attempt to understand Parker, it is essential that we gain an understanding of that past and of the Iroquois legacy of which he was so proud.

Beginnings

The Iroquois may have occupied a limited and fragmented land base during Parker's lifetime, but as late as the eighteenth century they were indisputably the preeminent power of the northeastern portion of the continent. Their geographical and historical significance has made them a much studied and written about composite group of nations, today comprising the Mohawk, Oneida, Onondaga, Cayuga, Seneca, and Tuscarora. Although the Iroquois have lived since the mid-twentieth century primarily in Ontario, Quebec, New York, Oklahoma, and Wisconsin, their related languages once spread to over 90,000 people in what is now New York, southern Ontario, and adjacent parts of Pennsylvania, Ohio, and Quebec. Their cultural roots have been traced back to about A.D. 900 and the Late Woodland Owasco cultural tradition.[1] Successful subsistence centered around horticulture, specifically the cultivation of what the Iroquois call the "three sisters"—maize, beans, and squash—and included intense intercommunity warfare. These provided the pattern of life in Iroquoia that Europeans encountered on contact.[2]

The Owasco cultural tradition also included the longhouse, the settlement structure that became synonymous with the Iroquois, who today still refer to themselves as Ho-dé-no-sau-nee, the People of the Longhouse. The origin of the more pervasive name, Iroquois, is difficult to pinpoint with certainty, since it has likely been heavily mediated by repeated cross-cultural translation, as has so much of the Indian record. Some commentators concur on a Basque etymology for the word "Iroquois," while another author simply describes the term as "a word of uncertain definition derived from one of the languages of the Algonquian family."[3] It is probable that Europeans accepted the name given to the Iroquois by their rivals the Algonquian, who lived along the northeast coast. They spoke of *Hilokoa*, "the killer people," in a Basque/Algonquian trading jargon developed from early-sixteenth-century contact. Yet "Iroquois" has also been connected to an Algonquian translation meaning "real adder," with a French suffix. Whatever the case, by around the end of the sixteenth century, the French had shaped the term finally to "Iroquois."

Also by this time, an alliance of five nations to constitute an Iroquois League (Confederacy) had occurred. The famous league, possibly complete by as early as 1525, stretched from the east to the west of modern-day upstate New York, between the Mohawk River and the Genesee River valleys. Through fostering spiritual unity and nonaggression, it facilitated the exploitation of its members' key geographical, cultural, and military advantages so that they held the balance of power in the northeastern region. Separate Iroquois nations came to be strategically housed within a metaphorical longhouse. The Seneca guarded the western door, while the Mohawk guarded the east. This league's formation also went some way toward addressing the endemic warfare and spiritual and demographic change that had by that stage developed within an expanding Iroquoia. A new intensity of European contact had led to epidemics that brought on an era of Iroquois population decline, tipping the population balance in favor of the colonists. In fact, from around 1633, diseases such as measles and smallpox wreaked physical and social havoc. Yet the Seneca Iroquois were able to maintain their population at around four thousand, where it remained throughout the latter part of the seventeenth century, apparently through absorbing many outsiders.[4] Even though its members were increasingly economically dependent on their trade relationship with Europeans, the league as a symbolic entity was a force for stability that began to flourish by the seventeenth century.

European powers were bringing constant and unstoppable change to the Northeast. After the Second Anglo-Dutch War ended in 1667, Beveryck was renamed Albany and the province of New Netherland became New York. By this time the Iroquois were finally at peace with the French, and a cultural reciprocity between the two peoples came to full flower in what has been termed the "Middle Ground."[5] Now Métis peoples, the products of Indian-French marriages, were trading using the peace pipe, or calumet. However, this Middle Ground was a realm more amenable to the Northern Algonquian, and their neighbors, the Iroquois, were to develop firmer ties with the English rather than with the French. After a meeting called in Albany in April 1677, the agreement between the English and the Iroquois known as the Covenant

Chain was founded. For the Iroquois, it was a diplomatic structure to encourage the fostering of a relationship analogous to a metaphoric linking of arms. But the English chose to view it as an agreement between empires, so that it offered the opportunity for overall appropriation of all those Indian nations deemed to be subordinate to the Iroquois. The alliance between the five nations of the Iroquois League had now broadened: from relative autonomy in which peace and spiritual unity were fostered, to true confederacy with an emphasis on political, military, and diplomatic unity.[6] After the 1690s, sacred and hereditary league men gave way to village headmen who, like modern diplomats, would effectively treat with increasingly significant foreign powers.

However, the league could not prevent foreign influence from progressively disrupting the social fabric of Iroquois life. By 1700 the longhouse as a settlement structure was being foreshortened, with some Seneca even living in individual houses. The middle of the century saw most Iroquois occupying cabins rather than longhouses. Clan matrons no longer organized large cooperative groups of women in the fields. Traditional headmen lost respect as talented men were given positions as "Pine Tree Chiefs" irrespective of their lineage or traditional position. Around 1722 the Tuscarora, emigrants from today's North Carolina, joined as the sixth nation of the league.[7] Along with the Oneida and Cayuga, they became "younger brothers" to "elder" league brothers the Seneca, Onondaga, and Mohawk.

During the eighteenth century, the league chose a strategy of aggressive neutrality in the face of colonial conflict, through mutual alliance with both the French and the English. Although politically weakened, the Iroquois did at points gain controlling influence by playing the two off each other. However, with English victory at the end of the Seven Years' War in 1763, the Iroquois unequivocally lost this leverage. The league had become a house divided, and political factionalism was increasingly unresolvable by traditional methods. In a series of coordinated frontier uprisings against the English beginning in 1763, known as Pontiac's Rebellion, the Seneca had struck some of the heaviest blows; but their contribution could not avert an eventual reassertion of the dominance of King George and the further weakening of league alliances. The American Revolution beginning in 1775 was the conflict that would unambiguously tear the league apart. The council fire at Onondaga was covered in 1777, symbolically suspending league affairs and confederate Iroquois consensus.[8]

Today the role and significance of the Iroquois League, described as "the oldest continuously functioning democratic constitution," retains an ongoing fascination. Commentators debate connections between the league, the development of Western democracy, and, specifically, the American governmental system. For example, one examination of "the red roots of European peace and freedom" finds American democracy to be in fact "a synthesis of Native American and European political theories," while another considers the making of such connections simply part of a short-term political fad.[9] In whatever fashion the Iroquois connected to the formation of that larger federation, the United States, events pushed most of them over to the British side and left the Longhouse in ruins.

The Revolutionary years saw an end to the Iroquois League, but they also brought about the birth of the Parker family name. According to Parker, an American officer taken captive by the Seneca during the conflict bestowed his surname on Parker's great-great-grandfather during an exchange of names following the officer's adoption into the Seneca Hawk Clan. Although Parker's relative Joy-e-sey never used this English name, it was passed down to his three sons, Samuel, Henry, and William. The notes Parker kept for a biography of his father tell the story of how his family came to adopt the Parker name:

> As the missionaries came in from New England many of the Indians embraced Christianity. One of these families was the descendants of the King-Jikonsaseh stock. During the Revolutionary War this family had captured an American officer and taken great pains to be kind to him, so much so that when he was to be taken to Niagara for exchange he suggested that the Indian family adopt his name in exchange for the Indian name it had bestowed upon him. This was agreed and so the Gayen-qwatoh (King) family became known as the Parker family. All the grown suns [sic] took Christian names. . . . It has kept the name ever since. Though friends of the British in the Revolutionary war the family soon became convinced of its error in listing [sic] to British counsel. By 1812 it was solidly patriot and all the Parkers joined the colors fighting in every battle on the Niagara frontier under Gen. Peter A. Porter and General Winfield Scott.[10]

Regardless of the specifics of the Parker family's political alliance, the Seneca, along with the Onondaga, Cayuga, and certain Mohawk, by and large supported the English. The Seneca in particular suffered terribly under the destructive campaign of American General John Sullivan in 1779. Raids by Sullivan and James Clinton had effects that were felt for generations among the western Iroquois, whom they attempted to burn out and destroy. Unsurprisingly, the Seneca and the other New York Iroquois who had supported the British found themselves in an extremely poor bargaining position at the 1784 Treaty of Fort Stanwix. The Iroquois, having suffered severe population loss, had little military influence and were facing a new phase of attacks on their land base and sovereignty. The Seneca, however, did at least manage to preserve a sizable proportion of their tribal lands, even though everything east of the Genesee River was lost. Although they were successful in having the federal government recognize their land in western New York at the 1794 Pickering (Canandaigua) Treaty, selling land became their most available means of immediate self-support in this period. In 1797 they sold a large proportion of their land in New York for $100,000 at the Treaty of Big Tree near Geneseo, reserving only 310 square miles in eleven tracts. Cattaraugus, where Arthur Parker would be born less than a century later, became one of their four largest reserved areas, along with land at Tonawanda, Buffalo Creek, and Allegany. Thus the Iroquois were the first Indians to experience the reservation system. As the eighteenth century came to a close, most found themselves living in small cabins on fragmented reserved land. For the Seneca nation, it was the end of an era of power and prosperity.

The enclosed reservation system forced the Iroquois to adopt plough agriculture and domesticated animals that could provide fertilizer. Traditional societal roles, involving men hunting and women farming, disintegrated, as did the system of reciprocal condolence and the traditional linkages between matrilineal households. Although U.S. policy of the time stressed the promotion of Indian civilization, the reservation environment itself stifled autonomy in such a way as to preclude the optimal implementation of either Indian or white ways. Iroquois culture now spiraled toward fatal decline, spurred by old fears of witchcraft and by the effects of pervasive alcoholism. At this grave moment in Iroquois history, in the years around 1800, a prophet arose. One man, Handsome Lake (Skanyadariyoh), conveyed to the people a code: the Gai'wiio', or "The Good Message." This new form of faith brought about a religious renaissance, revitalizing Iroquois culture with a mix of Christian and ancient tradition that is still practiced today. Handsome Lake helped the Iroquois to adapt to reservation life, not least through advocating an end to further land sales and affirming the validity of the nuclear family unit at the cost of the traditional quasi-matriarchal system. Religious and social reform, coupled with Quaker advice and technology, further helped to spur the transition to Euro-American–style farming.

In 1812, the United States was again at war with the English. Parker tells us that his great-grandfather, William Parker (1793–1864), also known as Jo-no-acé-doe-wah or Dragonfly, served on the American side. Afterward, he erected a mill on the Tonawanda Reservation at Indian Falls on Tonawanda Creek, thus becoming one of the first millers in the area.[11] Through taking up settled farming and hunting, William developed "one of the best farms along the [Genesee] valley." His great-grandson characterized him as both an American patriot and an early Indian assimilationist, writing, "Whatever may have been William's early training he now resolved that the old days had passed and that neither he nor his nation could live on memories or succeed by lamenting the events that had gone by." Adoption of white ways caused resentment among William's peers, who "affected to despise him and looked with jealousy upon his cleared fields with their winding rail fences," but at the same time, "the example of industry that he taught inspired many of the young men, who like him had fought in the war."[12]

Sometime around 1821 William Parker married Elizabeth Johnson, who Parker claimed was both a direct descendant of Handsome Lake and a great-niece of the famous Seneca Pine Tree Chief and orator Red Jacket. Elizabeth spoke little English, and Parker wrote of her as being "rare" and "a woman of considerable vision."[13] She and her husband were "progressives" and followers of the Handsome Lake faith with its strong Christian influences. Their union marked the amalgamation of distinguished Seneca Iroquois descent with a white name and white influences. According to Parker, the couple controlled more than one thousand acres. William, described as both a Baptist deacon and a miller, in spite of a crippled hand ended up owning his own sawmill and a gristmill. In time the Parkers' marriage produced seven children: Spencer Houghton Cone, Nicholson, Levi, Caroline (Carrie), Newton, Ely, and Solomon.[14] The children, according to Parker, "though reservation Indians . . . were industrious and valued education. All obtained excellent schooling, including some technical instruction."[15] The family's two-story farmhouse became a meeting place for both whites and Indians across generations: "Scientists such as John Wesley Powell, Lewis H. Morgan and Henry Schoolcraft frequently visited this home to find there historians and foreign savants engaged in conversation." It was only a small exaggeration when Parker wrote that the homestead was "in a measure the spot where a new American science was born," a circumstance that explained why, he claimed, his family "has ever felt responsible for recording and preserving the fame of its race." The family's connection to the beginnings of anthropology as a science through their association and friendship with such notable non-Indian authorities as Lewis Henry Morgan was significant. Specifically, Parker's great-uncle Ely was to grow up to be Morgan's principal informant and collaborator on the ground-breaking ethnography *The League of the Ho-dé-no-sau-nee, or Iroquois,* a classic published in 1851. His sister Caroline would even make the costume she was to model on the frontispiece engraving for Book II of *The League*.[16]

Although the family enjoyed an intellectual and privileged relationship with certain significant whites, and their home was a center on the reservation for resisting fraudulent treaties, the larger picture was of a still further reduction of Iroquois sovereignty and their land base as the nineteenth century progressed. Buckling under external pressure, the Seneca sold most of their remaining territory at the 1826 Buffalo Creek Treaty, leaving the four large reservations and a tiny reservation at Oil Spring. As a result, by 1826 they had lost their sovereignty over more than 3 million acres, and their remaining reservation land base, which totaled around fourteen square miles, was itself under threat from a land company. Then, in 1842, they were forced to make a poor compromise deal after having been sold out by a section of the traditional sachems in a second Buffalo Creek Treaty in 1838. This 1838 fraudulent attempt to gain land by the Ogden Land Company required the Seneca to abandon their reserved land and move to Kansas within five years. The subsequent compromise deal struck in 1842 still required that they relinquish both the Tonawanda and the Buffalo Creek Reservations. All this was too much for certain young Christian Seneca who had been educated by missionaries, the Reverend Asher Wright, M.D. (1803–76), and Mrs. Laura Sheldon Wright (1809–86). The Wrights had brought literacy to the reservation and had set up a printing press from which they published teaching material in the Seneca language. After enduring the ignominy of removal from Buffalo Creek, the missionary-educated young Seneca rebelled against the traditional form of government, "de-horned" the tribe's life chiefs, and set up a constitutional democracy in an attempt to avert further disastrous loss of land.

At Allegany and Cattaraugus, a convention was held that, on December 5, 1848, voted to abolish government by traditional sachems and chiefs and to substitute an elective council. Eventually sixteen elected chiefs governed what was now named the Seneca Nation of Indians. However, the Seneca band at the Tonawanda Reservation, some fifty miles from Cattaraugus, did not take part because they were then in the middle of a long battle to retain their reservation. Eventually they were able to buy back part of their reservation in 1857. Irrespective of this, the Seneca's revolutionary change away from tribal government was significant, a development that allowed Parker to state proudly: "The Seneca nation, be it known, is a republic, self-governing and recognized by the State of New York and by the United States. It had revolted from the 'chiefs' government' in 1848 and set itself up as a democratic state. However, the older system of aristocracy continued as an undercurrent."[17] The "aristocracy" to which Parker referred were the "dehorned" life chiefs.

Events surrounding the 1838 treaty produced a casualty within the Parker family, turning the eldest child, Spencer Houghton Cone, into a black sheep. He alone in the family approved of the treaty of 1838, and according to Parker, "He vacillated between duty and the promise of reward, and so flagrant was his initial insincerity that his family forbade him to use the name Parker, and he was most frequently addressed as Spencer Cone." Spencer was not cast out by the family, just forbidden to use its name. It seems likely that he was given his new name by a missionary at the nearby Baptist school. In supporting the forces pushing for Seneca emigration, he had committed a great political error that rankled within the family for generations. In fact his father was still praying for his wayward son ten years after the 1838 treaty, by which time he had become a Christian along with his wife and daughter Caroline.[18] Even after the 1857 land buyback, the Parkers were still adversely affected by the threat to Tonawanda, which added further acrimony to the situation. William Parker's family was eventually forced to move across the stream to a less desirable location, even if it did still overlook a gorge into a rugged streambed. At least the move brought a form of conclusion to what had been almost a generation of turmoil.

The reforming young Christians who had been instrumental in the genesis of a written constitution and republican democratic government for the Seneca had benefited crucially from the influence of the Reverend and Mrs. Wright. So too had Spencer's brother, Parker's paternal grandfather, Nicholson Henry Parker (1819–92). Nicholson was a successful Cattaraugus Reservation farmer who also served as a U.S. Indian interpreter. Parker proudly wrote of him: "Nicholson, or 'Nick' as grandfather was known to his intimate friends, passed the greater part of his life on the Cattaraugus reservation. He was a man of great energy, and worked with method and regularity. He never allowed Sunday work on his farm and never would permit a drop of liquor on his premises. He was a true 'son of the prophet' in this respect." A graduate in 1854 of Albany Normal School, a respected teachers college, "his contacts had been wide, while his ability as an orator placed him in great demand for patriotic meetings."[19] Parker boasted that his grandfather had been "clerk of the [Seneca] nation, United States interpreter, census agent, marshal of the nation, orator, agriculturalist and civil engineer."[20] Apparently Nicholson was exemplary in conduct, "ever proud of his blood and ancestry," a dignified and cultured man who employed a "coloured coachman" to care for the horses he bred. He was "ever a pioneer of progress among his people," had "an eye for business," and owned the blacksmith's shop adjoining the fairgrounds near the reservation. He helped to form a stock company and was the first on the reservation to acquire "all the best farm machinery." Nicholson married a white woman, Martha Hoyt, a teacher and the niece of Mrs. Wright. She descended from a family that at Deerfield, Massachusetts, had survived a conflict with the Algonquian, a quirk of history that led her grandson to quip in print, "I suppose it's a bit ironical that a descendant of a survivor of that horrible massacre two hundred years later married into a western New York Indian family."[21] Martha met Nicholson at the Congregationalist mission where he was getting paid to translate the Bible. Initially they lived in the mission house, and there their six children were born: Frank Spencer, Frederick Ely, Albert Henry, Sherman, Ulysses Grant, and Minnie Clark.[22]

Although Nicholson often proudly wore the costume that accompanied his role as Seneca chief, he nonetheless felt the pressure that accompanied crossing the boundaries between Indian and white cultures. Parker's description of his grandfather's character could very easily stand as an explanation of his own ambivalent position as acculturated modern Indian:

> Like his brother Ely, he never could completely accept civilization's teachings or wholly neglect the philosophy of his fathers. Seeing true virtue in each, according to his mood he argued for each. Many Indians have this same characteristic and often appear vacillating and uncertain in judgment when in reality the quality is merely the involuntary mental struggle between hereditary impressions and proclivities and those acquired. Until civilization crushes out all of the old instincts, or wisdom brings with it a strongly balanced judgement, Indians will ever be at moral sea; for character, point of view, methods and philosophy, like religion, may be historical and ethnic. . . .
> . . . There ever will be confusion, until in the course of cosmic alchemy all bloods revert to an original strain, like Darwin's pigeons [sic]. How dreary and hideously uniform the world will be then! There will be no mental flint and steel. It will be all flint or all steel.[23]

Although Nicholson would greatly influence his grandson, it was his brother Ely who would make a name for himself during and after the

Civil War, providing Parker with his most illustrious and famous recent relative. The Civil War found certain Iroquois ready for voluntary service and prepared to lobby the government for the opportunity to fight. Although Indians were not drafted, heavy Union losses at Shiloh and First Manassas prompted the government eventually to allow them to enlist, and various Iroquois fought in nearly every battle after March 1862 within the U.S. cavalry and infantry, receiving the same pay as their non-Indian comrades. The best known of their number remains Parker's great-uncle Ely, who rose to the rank of brigadier general. As Grant's scribe, he drew up the terms of surrender that secured the end of the conflict on April 9, 1865.[24] Throughout the war, Ely's old friend and collaborator on Iroquois history, Lewis Henry Morgan, kept up his connection with the Parker family and even wrote letters of recommendation on Ely's behalf to his military superiors.[25] After the war was over, Ely was appointed commissioner of Indian Affairs by his friend, the new president Ulysses S. Grant, becoming the first American Indian to hold that position. By comparison, Nicholson spent the war years serving as clerk at Cattaraugus and dealing with local and Iroquois concerns. We know little of how he spent his time exactly, but his manuscript of the minutes of the Council of the Six Nations when they met on December 1, 1862, gives some sense of what was going on around him. It registered past abuses by whites, described council concerns over the implementation of non-Indian law on Indian land, and called for new legislation "for the protection of timber."[26]

After the death of Rev. Wright in 1876, his wife moved into Nicholson and Martha Parker's nearby farmhouse, newly built by Nicholson and his sons using lumber sawed on the homestead. Like the Tonawanda farmhouse of William and Elizabeth Parker, Nicholson and Martha's commodious Cattaraugus home with its big kitchen table was a favored meeting place for both Indians and non-Indians. This mixing of both worlds was symbolically reflected in the decor, with one room containing Indian tools and heirlooms displayed alongside engravings from Bunyan's *Pilgrim's Progress*. Parker wrote glowingly of the house as a center for cultural exchange and progress for the Seneca, claiming that "it was to this farm that many distinguished men and women of a generation ago came—writers, scientists, missionaries, newspaper men, tourists, philanthropists. In this home and the Mission across the fence—in this family, of the grandfather generation—grew and were nursed the forces that did most to bring civilisation to the Senecas of New York and to save their lands from the spoiler's cunning."[27] Nicholson, as a ranking officer for the Seneca Indian Nation, played host to meetings between government officials and Indian leaders, and his home provided a place for discussion of ways to "undo the work of landgrabbers who tried to steal Indian land."[28]

Parker's father, Frederick (1857–1929), also benefited from this productive mixing of cultures. He first attended the reservation school and later a private school that his father, with missionary help, built for his sons and other children of the neighborhood. Frederick, along with his brothers, trained as a teacher at the Fredonia Normal School and graduated in 1878. He then began teaching in local schools and the following year married another teacher, Geneva Hortenese Griswold of Saybrook, Connecticut, "a member of an old Scotch-English-American family."[29] The couple would have three children in all: Arthur, Edna, and Dorothy. Edna would in 1927 marry an anthropologist, Dr. Mark Raymond Harrington, eventually curator of the Southwest Museum, Los Angeles, while Dorothy would remain with her father and look after him at their home in Peekskill, New York, after his wife's death in 1923.[30]

Frederick and Geneva's first child and only son, Arthur Caswell, was born on April 5, 1881, on the Cattaraugus Indian Reservation, in the township of Collins, Erie County, around thirty miles south of Buffalo. It was a year when events seemed symbolically to signal the end of the Wild West and the image of Indians that went with it. The Earp brothers of Tombstone won their final shoot-out at OK Corral; Billy the Kid was finally shot down by Sheriff Pat Garrett; barbed wire and protectionism at last made moving cattle along the Chisholm Trail to Dodge City obsolete, and Sitting Bull (Tatanka Yatanka) finally surrendered at Fort Bulford. Capitalizing on the focus on change in the West, Helen Hunt Jackson sensitized the nation to the Indian situation with her bestseller *A Century of Dishonor.* A national Friends of the Indian Movement took shape amid a new focus on what was habitually referred to as the "Indian problem."

The young Arthur Parker began life in the homestead built by his grandfather Nicholson. It was part of a nucleus of minority Christian timber homes in and around the mission school and church, and it was surrounded by a majority of "pagan" or "longhouse" homes. In total, around 1,500 Seneca lived on the reservation, most of whom spoke Seneca and/or a mixture of Iroquois and English called "Reservation English" or "Asylum-geh."[31] Because he had an English-speaking mother and grandmother, Parker learned English as his first language, but he also early in life acquired a serviceable command of Seneca, the language of his childhood friends.[32] He grew up in a privileged position since the Parkers were a leading extended reservation family. His aunt Caroline Parker Mountpleasant was married to a Tuscarora chief on the Tuscarora Indian Reservation near Niagara Falls, and several of what he called the "grandfather generation" lived at Tonawanda where his uncle Ely was a life chief.

Contemporary Parker family significance was by no means all. As Parker grew up, he could not but be aware of the local and wider importance of his heritage. After all, the family house was decorated with artifacts laden with tribal history: "The old tomahawk, scalping-knife and flint-lock, the beaded sashes and feather cap all hung in the big sitting-room and helped the children imagine wonderful things when grandfather told his evening story about 'old times.' Oh those grandfather tales, of legends of his hunting, of traditions of his boyhood days! Those tales helped to mold the minds of his grandchildren."[33] Amid the war clubs, bows and arrows, and skins of wolves, wildcats, and bears, the young Parker would sit wide-eyed, listening to stories told by "visitors who lived back in the woods or on the hill where the long-house people dwelt, they who followed the old Indian customs and had grotesque masks and dances and who wore feathers and buck-skins." After supper, as they smoked to keep out the winter chill, older Seneca who were famous within the tribe for their storytelling abilities told him fantastic tales about fairies called Jung-ga-on and about other, nonhuman kinds of people who lived at the wood's edge.[34]

At his grandfather's fireside, the young boy learned with fascination of a family history filled with accounts of leadership and virtue going back generations, peopled by individuals of supreme religious and political significance to Seneca and Iroquois history. He heard amazing tales of his great-grandmother, the Peace Queen of the Neutral Nation, of how she, with the great Hiawatha and Deganawida, founded the Iroquois League. He marveled at stories about his ancestor Old Smoke, or Gaiengwatoh, who six generations before had led the Senecas at the Battle of Wyoming, Pennsylvania. He heard still more incredible stories of his connection by blood to the Seneca prophet Handsome Lake, and of how Handsome Lake had led those who first carried the Parker name to settle at the Tonawanda site, which had been revealed to the prophet in dreams. He heard tell too of family connections to the eighteenth-century leader Cornplanter, half-brother of Handsome Lake, and to Red Jacket, whom George Washington himself had honored with a large silver medal.[35] This evocative history gained from his grandparents filled Parker with inspiration, a sense of romantic possibility, and the desire to live up to the glories of the past.

But not only family history was learned at his grandfather's knee. By the same cheerful fire in the big kitchen, Nicholson, a great reader, would read aloud to his grandson. He read Milton's *Paradise Lost* and Shakespeare's *King Lear* and *A Midsummer Night's Dream* to him before he was nine. There was rivalry between the grandparents over Parker's early home curriculum, with Nicholson favoring the classics and algebra and Martha favoring common sense books. Both grandparents, however, made sure he had a firm grounding in the Bible, and they gave him a Presbyterian background that valued hard work, temperance, and self-improvement.[36] With his head full of Indian lore and imbued with the Protestant work ethic, Parker grew up determined to live up to the heroic achievements of his family history.

He developed into a healthy and active child with an inquiring mind and a readiness to learn. In fact, because he jumped around so much, he was given the name Skoak, meaning Frog.[37] The name is suggestive of the love of the outdoors that he developed from a early age through exploring the environs of the family farm, which lay between two large creeks. It was "an ideal 'boy's' farm" with a good orchard and a brook to fish for trout. A stage route crossing the road that divided the farm, allowed access to the government medical dispensary, the Seneca national fairground, the Thomas Indian School, the mission house, and the tribal cemetery. This appealed to Parker because, he said, "Members of the family by this rare situation get the daily paper; can be married and preached to, attend the fair, get sick, call a doctor, die and be buried, with all the rites of the church, without even leaving the neighborhood,—so 'civilized' has the reservation become."[38] The farm was close to reservation amenities, but at least as important, it was also a base from which father and son could explore the woods and fields of Erie County. Parker's father took pains to introduce his son to the great outdoors and, through it, to the Indian past. His careful efforts much later led Parker to dedicate a popular illustrated book on Indian lore to him: "TO MY FATHER, Whose loving hand first gave me guidance to the wonders of the woodland, glen and glade, and whose knowledge of the red race through ancestral inheritance gave me a sympathetic understanding of its history and culture."[39] By all accounts, therefore, Parker had a loving and stimulating childhood where he was encouraged to appreciate nature and to value his family heritage.

For generations, the Parker family had been structural models of the kind of Indian assimilation sought by the dominant piece of legislation of the time, the 1887 General Allotment Act, or Dawes Act. The new act required Indians to accept an allotment of tribal land according to status, with remaining unallotted tribal lands to be sold and the money used for Indian education. Those Indians who accepted allotted land under the provisions of the act were awarded American citizenship.[40] The idea was to foster ideally Christian, English-speaking nuclear family farms in the Euro-American tradition. Essentially, the act was a Draconian attempt to impose state law, individualized self-sufficiency, and non-Indian concepts of thrift, work, and relationship to the land. Its primary practical effect was to break up tribally owned land and assimilate to white ownership close to two-thirds of it nationally, an estimated 86 million acres by 1934 when policy changed. The opportunities offered to Indians by the Dawes Act to enjoy the rights and responsibilities of civilized citizenship in fact masked a scheme to assimilate Indian land primarily, and Indians themselves only secondarily, into the American mainstream. Looked at in terms of Seneca national interest, the act was clearly a poor deal, and along with certain other named tribes, the Seneca secured exclusion.[41]

The year after the act was passed, Frederick Parker, now with two children to support—Arthur, aged seven, and Edna, aged about five—gave up teaching to go work for the railroad at Gowanda.[42] This happened around the time Parker had his first encounter with his famous great-uncle Ely. Rushing into the family sitting room, to his embarrassment he mistook Ely for his grandfather Nicholson because the two looked so alike. In awe of his famous relative, the young boy would always remember the moment and remember how each of Ely's visits was inevitably something of an occasion at his grandfather's house. Ely would bring presents for everyone, and as Parker described it, "While our distinguished uncle was there, all the Indians of note would come to greet him. Then there would be a time of story-telling and reminiscences."[43] Through Ely and other connections off-reservation, the family was increasingly exposed to the trappings and conveniences of modern living, many of which were in extremely short supply on the reservation. At school, the young Parker was even able to trade things like wheat bread, roast beef, jelly cake, and cookies with his Indian schoolmates for traditional Indian foods such as corn bread and hulled corn hominy. The Parkers lived in a style that combined both Indian and non-Indian elements in a unique fashion. It produced a child who was accustomed to moving with ease between these worlds. Before he was nine, for example, he had developed his lifelong interest in natural history by collecting bird eggs and Devonian fossils, probably so he could add them to the cabinet of curiosities in his grandfather's home. But at the same time, he was accompanying medicine men and women when they traveled into the deep woods around the reservation looking for medicinal plants. All his life, he would retain fond memories of rising early and feeling the crispness in the autumnal air before setting out with them to hunt for plants.[44]

Eventually, the well-connected Ely secured Parker's father a more promising position as clerk with the New York Central Railroad in 1891.

Being a railroad man suited Frederick, and he was to serve for many years as a committed, even passionate, member of a railroad patriotic fraternity, the Junior Order of United American Mechanics. He became known as someone who delivered stirring patriotic addresses throughout New York State and as someone keen on restricting immigration. He passed on a pride in a specific American heritage to his son, who was to write admiringly of how his father's "ancestral background gave him the fire of conviction and the courage to express it. His older American blood came from a famous line; on his mother's side his New England blood was that of the earliest families, dating back to 1628. His Indian ancestors had helped Sir William Johnson break the power of New France in the New World. They were the stalwart champions of an English speaking civilization. They were the friends of the settlers and often gave asylum to the needy."[45]

When Frederick's job caused the family to relocate to the suburb of White Plains, New York, the halcyon security of reservation life for Arthur and his sister came to an end. The Parker children were enrolled in local public schools. Up to this point, it is likely that they were educated at the reservation school and at home. There was talk of Parker attending the best off-reservation boarding school of the time, Carlisle in Pennsylvania, but its founder, Richard Henry Pratt, "refused to entertain" his application and advised Frederick that no Indian school could possibly reach the same results as a public school and a college education.[46] Aged eleven, Parker moved away from "colic; green apples; fights; lickings; Indian district school; hookey; bow and arrow hunts; fishing and swimming; visits to old warriors in the woods; visits of 'the big white chiefs from Washington'"; and permanent reservation life.[47] Any distress he felt at leaving it behind could only have been augmented by the loss of his beloved grandfather and his great-aunt Caroline the same year. This left only Ely surviving from what Parker always affectionately called "the grandfather generation."[48]

The move brought Parker toward a realization of the nature of his position as Indian within the dominant culture. Now he lost the relatively privileged context of family life centered around the mission at Cattaraugus and became instead the Indian boy living in the New York suburb of White Plains. On the reservation his family had real influence over the development of Seneca and Iroquois affairs, and they were in a position to control their interaction with selected whites. Life in a New York suburb by comparison was vastly different, and it must have led Parker to consider things from the perspective of his new childhood peers. Their Indian knowledge would have owed much more to the dime novel and nickel library Western than to the kind of heroic tales of proud survival he had learned from his grandfather. Buffalo Bill's Wild West show had opened in 1884, bringing stereotyped "wild" Indians to the paying public and promulgating the same representation of "vanishing" Indians that was also the stock-in-trade of contemporary photographer Edward S. Curtis. The shock of life in a suburb of the great metropolis after growing up in the cultural security of the reservation may have been what kindled Parker's unending desire to interpret one way of life to the other. At any rate, he must have keenly felt the difference between White Plains and the rural reservation to which he frequently returned, probably using the free railroad passes that were a perquisite of his father's job. He would be drawn back to the environs of his childhood periodically for one reason or another, but inevitably it became harder to find time. He nonetheless made a point of sending back presents to the old storytellers who had so enchanted him with tales passed down from the days of the ancient league, so as to keep alive his relationship with them.[49]

While at White Plains he developed his interest in natural history and collecting. He visited the Museum of Natural History and networked there with luminaries who would later aid his progress within anthropology and museum work. His scientific interest was stimulated during the early 1890s as he browsed "in the laboratories of the great New York physician, Dr Salisbury, looking at his skulls and other anatomical specimens, wondering what caused man to have such strange fragments in his framework." Later he met other professional men such as "the awesome Gratacap, Bogoras and Boas, the obliging Dr. Allen and Frank Chapman, the friendly Dr. Putnam and the genial Bumpus," who were all impressed no doubt by the young boy's seriousness, quick mind, and sharp memory. They were "never too busy to identify pottery, fossils or birds' eggs brought in by a wandering youth," and Parker became enthralled by the museum, absorbed by "a thrilling world back of the scenes" that smelt of "spicy dust and moth balls, but mostly mystery and greatness." He was able to debate these new interests at the "salon" of Harriet Maxwell Converse and her husband Frank. Mrs. Converse was a journalist and poet whose work on Indian issues had facilitated her adoption by the Seneca. At "Aunt Hattie's" and "Uncle Frank's," Parker met with like-minded Indians and whites and was to make at least two lifelong friends, the anthropologist Mark R. Harrington and the cartoonist Joseph Keppler. Aside from all this, his childhood interest in walking and the outdoors solidified during the White Plains years. It would later develop into a love of organized hiking and scouting. At this stage, however, Parker simply "assisted in organizing a group of boys who explored the fields and woods and then returned to the home of their Sunday school teacher, Miss Evangeline Slosson, to read papers or to discuss what they saw in the out-of-doors."[50]

Parker's reservation education and family tutoring gave him a good springboard for success at the local school. Prior to his graduation from White Plains High School in 1897, his local Presbyterian minister, who had known him several years, recommended him as "one of the best lads I have known. He is a good student, fond of reading the more valuable books, conscientious, faithful steadily [*sic*] to the duties of any position where he may be placed."[51] Parker would have encountered a very different educational environment had he ended up in a government Indian school, but it seems little could have deterred him from self-improvement. "I had to earn my way wherever I went" he wrote later; "I was too far ahead for a government school and too poor to go to college. I worked my way through the rudiments of an education and when I was through school I realized that my education had just begun. I studied faithfully ever since, laying out a course of study for myself every year."[52] He was acquiring the quietly diligent, studious, and, most of all, hardworking demeanor for which he would be remembered.

The adolescent Parker, with his open, intelligent face and great shock of black hair, was highly recommendable but by no means sure of the specific direction of his future career. He entered the coeducational Centenary Collegiate Institute in Hacketstown, New Jersey, in the autumn of 1899 but left soon after. Before the year was out he had enrolled to study for the ministry at Dickinson Seminary at Williamsport, Pennsylvania. Characteristically, while there he found time to do more than solely study for the ministry. He wrote as "associate editor" for the student paper under the pen name Moonstone.[53] At this stage, though, apart from one story revealing an early but enduring concern with women's rights, little of lasting interest flowed from the Parker pen.[54] Seminary life did not prevent him from deepening his contacts at the American Museum of Natural History and at "Aunt Hattie's" salon. As time went by, he was increasingly distracted by such secular interests. Museums absolutely fascinated him, and he was in regular correspondence with Dr. Putnam at the Museum of Natural History, who was subsidizing his school attendance and encouraging his efforts to produce an article on archaeology. "These were the years of the sinking in of ideas, of the loding of a career which was much tinctured by philosophical as well as scientific thought," he was to reminisce many years later. "But, for a while philosophical considerations swept me from my future course, I investigated philosophy and religion and soon

A dapper and professional image of Arthur Caswell Parker
as he began his museum career.

Courtesy of Rochester Museum & Science Center

began to wonder why the pursuit of pure truth should not be enough,
with all labels and departmentalized names stripped away."[55]

Soon, events would force him to choose finally between the religious career on which he was already embarked and the possibility of
making a living from the personal scientific interests that had so captured his imagination.[56] As he approached manhood, the new century
was just about to begin, and in an increasingly complex world Parker
looked for ways of constructing both an identity and a career. All the
great Indian stories he had heard in his youth drew him toward formal
study of the Indian past. Such study, after all, had so often been the
springboard for interaction between his family and important figures
within the dominant culture. If he was to carry on the tradition of

intercultural mediation and achievement that characterized his lineage, he would have to abandon the seminary and set about the kind of work that had occupied the two great men he had been brought up to so respect, the famous anthropologist Lewis Henry Morgan and Morgan's Indian friend, his own great-uncle Ely. These two central figures in his life are the focus of the next chapter. The narrative of Parker's life will be suspended momentarily, as we consider the broader context of his loyalty to them and the differing ideas about ethnicity that had currency as his life progressed.

CHAPTER 2

Contemporary Thought and Influences

Parker never hid the fact that, as he put it, "the influence of Morgan and my great uncle have been with me since childhood and their example has been a tradition that has spurred me to carry on where they left off." Lewis Henry Morgan and Ely S. Parker were not only significant role models for Parker, but powerful figures whose influence extended well beyond Parker's family. Morgan, whose Presbyterian ancestors settled Iroquois land after the Revolution, was a pioneer figure within American ethnology and often is cited as the "father" of American anthropology. His gift to Parker was a conceptual framework that Parker referred to throughout his life. The attraction of Morgan's social evolutionary ideas for Parker was that they described human development across time through stages of savagery and barbarism to civilization. This schema allowed Parker to think of assimilated Indians like himself as progressive, as people in advance of their contemporaries. It was a positive way of seeing "Indianness" and Indian culture.

Parker's intellectual life was guided by Morgan, whose stature was heightened further by his connections with the "grandfather generation." The romance surrounding great-uncle Ely was just as powerful. Parker was fascinated by the very idea of him even before the two met. Ely quickly became an example of someone who had successfully crossed the boundaries between Euro-American and Indian culture and achieved respect and acclaim from each. Not only was Ely a life chief on the reservation, he had served as a brigadier general under President Grant, had transcribed the articles of surrender at Appomattox, and subsequently been appointed commissioner of Indian Affairs. He was the last of the "grandfather generation" to pass away, and Parker's enduring respect for him knew almost no bounds. His biography of the great man opened with this remark: "There is a sense in which he was the first American of his time and an embodiment of all the heroic ideals that enter into our conception of American manhood."[1]

Praise indeed. But such individual influences close to home must be considered against a wider backdrop. Parker's relationship to Morgan and Ely needs to be understood in the context of ideas developing at the time about the appropriate role of ethnic groups such as Indians within mainstream American society. To understand why Parker both empathized with and respected these men, we must be aware of the attitudes and affiliations available to and surrounding him as industrial America took shape.

· · ·

As the twentieth century began, Parker pursued his interests in philosophy and religion at Dickinson Seminary. While he mulled over the merits of a theological versus scientific career, old and new thinking about assimilating minorities jostled for position within the dominant culture. Ideas about national identity and about how each ethnic group connected to that identity affected both how Parker was perceived from without and how he thought about himself as Indian, from within.

The American public's adjustment to the realization that Indians now constituted a new minority had begun around the time of Parker's birth in 1881. During that decade, large-scale military conflict on the Plains ended. The idea of a frontier of settlement was declared defunct by the superintendent of the census in 1890, and three years later the young historian Frederick Jackson Turner argued that the closing of the frontier marked the end of the first period of American history.[2] Those who put their minds to the issue in the late nineteenth century generally retained a belief that American Indians could be transformed into "civilized" citizens, and that it was possible for them to achieve full incorporation into the fabric of American society if only they abandoned their "primitive" condition. This belief was epitomized by the assimilationist thinking underpinning the Dawes Act of 1887. The act attempted to create "civilized" Indians worthy of citizenship within a single generation. Its rhetoric invoked the old bargain used to rationalize colonization of Indian lands in the eighteenth and nineteenth centuries—the promise of full membership within a "civilized" nation for those American Indians willing and able to conform to the norms of the dominant culture. In sum, U.S. social policy required both

Indians and immigrants to conform to Anglo-Saxon culture, such that they surrendered or lost every vestige of their traditional culture. The more popular name that reformers gave to the allotment process and Dawes Act—the "vanishing policy"—was telling. At this time, Indian culture was perceived as having so little value that when Commissioner of Indian Affairs Thomas J. Morgan issued instructions in December 1889, he not only made explicit that "the Indians are destined to become absorbed into the national life, not as Indians, but as Americans," but also recommended that Indian identity be ignored altogether. Teachers of Indian pupils "should carefully avoid any unnecessary reference to the fact that they are Indians."[3] Indianness and Indian culture was deemed to have no viable role in the American future.

However, by the early twentieth century a new concept was in vogue, an idea that seemed to offer scope for the incorporation of some of the best attributes of Indian culture within American society. Indian intellectuals like Parker used it to argue for the policy changes they considered necessary to ensure full Indian assimilation. The concept was of an American "melting pot."

Although the idea goes back as far as Crèvecoeur's *Letters from an American Farmer,* published in 1782, it is usually held to have originated with the play *The Melting Pot,* produced in 1908 by an English writer of Russian Jewish extraction named Israel Zangwill. Zangwill suggested that through the fusion of America's divergent immigrant nations a new superior being would come into existence-the American. America was "stirring and seething" with "Celt, Latin, Slav and Teuton, Greek and Syrian, black and yellow," "Jews and Gentiles."[4]

Several things about this melting pot metaphor attracted Parker and his contemporaries. First, the idea allowed for diversity, both within the dominant culture and within Indian culture. Essentially, it was a description of an ongoing process in America. It allowed for a glorious Indian past, and at the same time, seemingly, allowed continuity and status for Indian characteristics in the future. Like the American Dream, the melting pot concept was concerned with the individual rather than the group. Therefore, the success of individuals like Parker was not necessarily affected by limitations placed on their ethnic group. The idea meant Indian intellectuals could flatter themselves that they were part of a vanguard close to "melting" completely and becoming the new, true patriots. All this was usefully vague; no one very closely analyzed how the "melting" process came about, or at what pace. Overall, the process's great attraction was that it allowed for a rosier future, a future where America's constituent groups "melted" and thus brought constant national renewal.

Nevertheless, it must be pointed out that in Zangwill's play, and in the public mind, the melting pot metaphor did not include or even consider the American Indian. The Indian was not thought of as a contributor to the new mixing of European nations that was now to constitute the United States. Yet, for a decade or more, this did not stop Parker and others from using the idea to further Indian integration within the dominant culture. He abandoned faith in the concept in 1922, at a time when the idea of an ethnically unified America was under attack. He took refuge then in a form of eugenicist thinking on race and race relations. He joined those for whom a single Anglo-Saxon norm was the national imperative, those who saw America and its future as fundamentally Anglo-Saxon or Anglo-American. There were those who spoke against "hyphenated Americans" and demanded, like Theodore Roosevelt at the New York Republican state convention of 1906, "There can be no fifty-fifty Americanism in this country. There is room here for only 100 per cent. Americanism, only for those who are Americans and nothing else."[5]

In adopting the idea that the human race could be improved in form, mind, and behavior through hereditary manipulation, Parker was following a new and dangerous trend that would peak in several countries during the first half of the century, culminating in the eugenicist atrocities of World War II. Equally fashionable in the United States was its corollary—the fear that the country was fostering dysgenics, an increase in negative hereditary characteristics in the population. This fear, and the eugenicist's obsession generally with biological distinctions, centered around the many recent, mostly Catholic and Jewish immigrants from eastern and southern Europe who were making their presence felt in America. Eugenic enthusiasts, by comparison, were the more established immigrants who were largely upper to middle class, educated, white, Anglo-Saxon, and Protestant.[6] Parker associated himself with this powerful group when he adopted their language and shared their nativist concern with restricting immigration so as to reduce the proportion of the "less fit" in society. We should not overlook connections between American eugenics and the German counterpart. In the 1930s, German eugenicists described the debt they owed to American precedent—for example, the use of IQ tests to isolate the "feeble-minded" and the passage in several states of eugenic sterilization laws. This is not to say that American eugenics was directly analogous to that within Nazi Germany, but it does give the phenomena context.

In one sense, eugenicist thinking was a natural intellectual refuge for Parker. Although the movement had been spurred by the advent of Mendelian genetics in 1900, a basis for eugenicist thinking had been created by social Darwinism, which used natural selection to explain social phenomenon and was closely allied to many of Lewis Henry Morgan's ideas. Looked at more broadly, Parker was simply following a fashion. Racist and anti-immigrant arguments were relatively commonplace around the turn of the century, particularly during the 1920s. Eminent men and women echoed the anti-immigrant prejudice of popular nativism and eugenics. For example, as early as the 1880s, Woodrow Wilson expressed his fear of "foreign blood" from southern and eastern Europe, and the famous frontier historian Frederick Jackson Turner fretted over what he perceived as a specific threat from Jewish immigration. Turner's concerns were repeated by Henry Adams and Henry James. As an undergraduate, F. Scott Fitzgerald wrote the song "Love or Eugenics" for the 1914 Princeton Triangle Show. Vice President Calvin Coolidge wrote in 1922 of how biology necessitated a deterioration within Nordics who intermarried with other races, and after signing the 1924 Immigration Act, remarked, "America must be kept American."[7] Local eugenics groups met throughout the United States. These included the Galton Society, which regularly gathered at the American Museum of Natural History, New York, which Parker frequented. The American Eugenics Society, a national organization, came into being in 1923. Although membership remained limited, funds reached forty thousand dollars by 1930, after gifts from John D. Rockefeller, Jr., and George Eastman of the Eastman Kodak Company.

Parker may well have read *The Passing of the Great Race,* by the Park Avenue socialist and eugenicist Madison Grant. The book served as a model for many of the racist books and articles that succeeded it, even though it did not have mass appeal. First published in 1916, its prophecy of race disaster was particularly popular during the 1920s. It expressed a concern that Parker came to share about "mongrelization," which resulted from the cream of the white race—the Nordics—marrying the lesser biological orders.

According to Grant's text, and in the understanding of many eugenicists, Parker, as the product of a Nordic and American Indian union, was tainted by biological association with an inferior race. In fact, Grant explicitly stated that the Indian "half-breed" "will play no very important role in future combinations of race on this continent."[8] Theodore Roosevelt expressed a similar concern when he called for America to bolster its production of the right "stock." On the specific topic of Indians he admitted: "I don't go so far as to think that the only good Indians are the dead Indians, but I believe nine out of every ten are, and I shouldn't inquire too closely into the case of the tenth."[9] Yet

Parker, especially around 1922, chose to ignore all this and to adopt the language of the dominant group to which he aspired.

But even in 1922, older biologistic paradigms and the racial assumptions behind eugenicist, Spencerist, and social Darwinist thinking were under attack, from men like Horace Kallen and Franz Boas. Parker remained resistant to their ideas. But in time they became constitutive of the major alternative view of American nationality.

As early as 1915, Kallen had published his essay "Democracy versus the Melting Pot" and coined the now ubiquitous term "cultural pluralism."[10] He argued that ethnicity was a fundamental and necessary way for peoples to define themselves and that the United States should stop requiring all its peoples to conform to a single normative standard. Instead, he talked of "a multiplicity in a unity, an orchestration of mankind."[11] In Kallen's analysis, the melting pot was unnecessary and the idea of a single "American race" a fiction. Instead, cultural pluralism would allow the perfection of the democratic ideals of the Declaration of Independence and Constitution by allowing people to perfect themselves according to their own ethnic group. Instead of "melting," a number of distinct nationalities would continue to self-perpetuate within the American political state. English would remain the public national tongue, with ethnic languages continuing inside specific communities. Thus the insurgent ideal in the second decade of the twentieth century was not concerned with melting away difference but with valuing ethnicity. Rather than urging minority groups within the United States to abandon their origins, this new wave of theory stressed the desirability of growth stemming from ethnic "roots."

The idea that race determines mentality and temperament was attacked further by those in the social and behavioral sciences. Within anthropology, the main assault was led by Franz Boas (1858–1942) at Columbia University and his disciples. Boas was a German-Jewish immigrant who came to the United States during the peak of the immigration period, and he spoke up repeatedly against racist anti-Semites like Madison Grant and the idea that somehow superior Nordic traits could be lost through intermarriage with other groups.[12] Boas knew that Grant and his ilk could not prove their conviction that hereditary, racially specific mental or behavioral traits existed. There was no simple correlation between "race" and culture, and the various cultures simply could not be judged by the same criteria.

Therefore, during the first decades of the twentieth century, Boas and his school attacked the evolutionary schemes that dominated anthropological thought. These ideas, based upon an overarching idea of progress, had found their most extensive and renowned U.S.

exegesis in Lewis Henry Morgan's description of inevitable human development through stages of savagery and barbarism to the condition of civilization.[13] To Boas and his stable of anthropological professionals, such a social evolutionary approach was generalizing and ethnocentric. They wanted it replaced with a scientific concern for objectivity and were keen on the meticulous recording of data on "primitive" cultures. This detailed knowledge of communities revealed a close connection between ideas and customs and highlighted the severe limitations of interpreting any society in terms of racial inheritance. Because these "primitive" cultures were assumed to be rapidly vanishing, what became known as "salvage anthropology" made it an imperative to gather information on them immediately. The new idea, cultural relativism, in which each culture was considered valid in its own terms, began to replace the idea of progress, which had been at the heart of evolutionary theories like Morgan's.

There were reasons why an acculturated, middle-class figure such as Parker would remain resistant to Boas's new approach to social science. The early anthropologists had provided an explanation of both the past and present relationship of Indians to the dominant culture. Those Indians most acculturated, those whose lifestyles compared favorably with the "civilized" condition of the dominant society were seen as having progressed to a higher position on the scale of human development. Social evolutionary schemata could therefore be used to justify reform that encouraged Indian progression from the "savage" or "barbarous" condition to that of civilization. Such thinking was, in the main, rooted in a respect for Indians as noble examples of stages within the history of human progress. By comparison, cultural relativism did not easily lend itself to applied Indian reform, or even coherently address the contemporary relationship of Indians to the dominant society. There was little purchase for Parker in the idea. He was angling for tangible advance for himself and for what he called the Indian "race." By comparison, the new professionals concerned themselves with vigorously attacking the concept of race as a suitable category for understanding individual mental and emotional characteristics.[14]

Even though the direction of Boas's work was to separate race, language, and culture into specific and independent categories, his school did consider the biological mixings of human groups. This was limited and mostly to do with immigrants; but people like Parker, the progeny of Indian-white intermarriage, were discussed. One example is Boas's chapter "The Indian Half-Blood," in *Race, Language and Culture,* which presented evidence to contradict the view that "half-bloods" were less fertile and of persistently smaller stature than "full-blood" Indians.[15] Therefore, in a small way, cultural relativism validated the identity of Indians like Parker, but it did not investigate in depth the relationship of Indians, acculturated or otherwise, to modern America. The absence of scientific anthropological investigation in the twentieth century on this topic left the modern acculturated Indian essentially in a nonrelationship to the dominant culture. More significant was the fact that salvage anthropology and cultural relativism tended to assume that what was most nonacculturated and most "primitive" was also, by implication, the most "Indian." By definition, development in Indian culture meant an erosion of Indian cultural essence. Boasian anthropology simply did not offer a sufficiently sophisticated set of concepts to encompass the realities of Parker's life. Instead, he found most leverage and potential in Morgan's ideas.

Parker, and the Parker family, had a fascinating relationship to Lewis Henry Morgan (1818–81). The Iroquois, and specifically the "grandfather generation" of the Parker family, intimately connect to Morgan and his anthropology, not least because a friendship with Ely S. Parker began Morgan's serious study of the subject. Ely introduced Morgan to the Seneca, structured his initial fieldwork experiences, and in all served as his interpreter and collaborator for six years. Perhaps surprisingly, the forum that facilitated their connection was a local fraternal organization that at first used Greek culture as the club theme. As one scholar put it: "Who would have guessed that out of the Greek revival in upstate New York at the mid-nineteenth century would have come the science of anthropology?"[16]

Morgan was twenty-four in 1842 when he found himself unable to begin practice as a qualified attorney because of the business depression after the Panic of 1837. His attention turned to a young men's literary club known as the Order of the Gordian Knot, organized at Cayuga Academy, Cayuga County, New York. The order was failing because of lack of interest, prompting its members to consider reforming to become an "Indian society." Its revitalization was spurred by Morgan's chance meeting with Ely in an Albany bookshop in April 1844. Soon Morgan initiated his new teenage friend as an honorary elected member, and the group's organization and character began to change.[17] Morgan got Ely to lecture the group on Indian life and persuaded ethnologist Henry Rowe Schoolcraft (1793–1864) to come to Aurora and do the same in August 1845. Called the Grand Order of the Iroquois, and sometimes the New Confederacy of the Iroquois by its members, the society prospered, eventually organizing chapters elsewhere in western New York and as far east as Utica. Modeled as closely as possible on the ancient Iroquois League, it survived about six years.[18]

It was symptomatic of the nationalism of the day, which glibly adopted Indian symbolism to signal independence from an English past.

Morgan became the organization's "Supreme Chieftain" and dominant spirit, with the club "warrior" name of "Skenandoah," supposedly the name of an ancient Iroquois chief.[19] Members attended "secret" meetings at the Masonic Lodge building or outdoors in full Indian regalia, with chaplets of eagle feathers, "Indian" tunics, scarlet leggings, and decorated moccasins.[20] Morgan made up new rules, ceremonies, and regulations, including an elaborate initiation ceremony known as "InIndianation."[21] For most of the club's young male members, the organization's main purpose was decidedly social. However, for Morgan, the fraternity marked the genesis of a genuine interest in Indian culture that eventually made him famous. As he wrote in 1859, "whatever interest I have since taken in Indian studies was awakened through my connection with this Indian fraternity." Morgan's developing relationship with Ely and the Seneca kindled a concern for the protection of Seneca lands. He wrote in his journal: "As we hoped at that time to found a permanent order, with a charitable as well as literary basis, we connected with it the idea of protecting, so far as it lay in our power, the remainder of the Iroquois living in this State; and particularly the band of Senecas at Tonawanda who then and since the year 1838 had been beset and hunted by the Ogden Land Company, to despoil them of their remaining lands."[22]

According to Arthur Parker, "the members of the Grand Order of the Iroquois . . . did much to defeat the crooked schemes of the land sharks." Morgan traveled with Ely to Washington to defend the Tonawanda Seneca's right to their land and was "widely hailed as a champion of the Iroquois."[23] Overall, Parker has left us with a picture of happy reciprocity and understanding between the fraternity, Morgan, and the Seneca. For example, when adopted into the Seneca Hawk Clan on October 31, 1847, Morgan took on a name meaning "One Lying Across," or "Bridging the Gap," which "referred to him as a bridge over the differences that lay between the Indian and the white man." The same year, he began publishing articles on the Iroquois in the *American Whig Review*. The next year he was able to send material to the New York State (Cabinet) Museum, before going on to make his major collecting efforts in 1849 and 1850. Almost the whole Parker extended family got involved in helping him compile information on the Iroquois, with the Parker house serving as his collecting headquarters. Ely, besides acting as interpreter, was Morgan's "constant companion" and Ely's parents, William and Elizabeth, his "principal informants."[24] In return, Morgan and his Grand Order helped get Ely's brothers Nick and Newton and his sister Carrie to the State Normal School in Albany, Morgan having introduced in the state legislature in 1849 a bill for the support and education of Indian students there.[25] To Morgan, the Parker family were extraordinary and fascinating, "the most talented Indian family of the Iroquois stock."[26]

Morgan spent the Christmas of 1850 with the William Parkers at Tonawanda, as he had the previous year, gleaning information and insight on Iroquois life. He had been commissioned by the regents of the University of the State of New York to create a collection of Iroquois material culture for the State Museum in Albany. Because of the Parkers, he was able to amass a large collection and get extensive information on the use and significance of some objects. "Many of the choicest heirlooms of the Iroquois," Arthur Parker wrote, "were procured for the State Museum of New York by Ely Parker and turned over to Morgan."[27] Morgan and William Parker are known to have exchanged gifts, but the bulk of their transactions concerning Iroquois material culture and its interpretation involved money. The Parker family received most of the $215 that the State Museum allotted for this piece of salvage anthropology, intended by the regents of the state to create "a full exhibition of the manufactures of the Indian tribes still remaining within our State, and thus to show, as it were, their transition condition, in the union of their ancient and rude constructions, with the improvements received through the whites." In all, from 1848 to 1850, Morgan obtained around five hundred objects, creating by far the largest collection from a single Indian group of the time.[28] In Morgan's opinion, this transaction was highly appropriate, material culture being a significant addition to ethnographic knowledge—in fact, an access point to the intellect of a people. As he pointed out in the 1851 publication that resulted from his collaboration with Ely: "The fabrics of a people unlock their social history. They speak a language which is silent, but yet more eloquent than the printed page."[29]

This praise for the interpretative importance of material culture appeared in Morgan's *The League of the Ho-dé-no-sau-nee, or Iroquois*, a description of ancient Iroquois social and political structure that quickly became a classic of American ethnology. Major John Wesley Powell, chief of the Bureau of American Ethnology, described it as the "first scientific account of an Indian tribe ever given to the world," and as late as 1922, Alexander Goldenweiser, a respected anthropologist of the Iroquois, commented that "the best general treatise on the Iroquois still remains Lewis H. Morgan's *The League of the Iroquois*.[30] To his credit, Morgan made no bones about where his information originated, dedicating his text to "Ely S. Parker, Ha-sa-no-an-da, an educated

Seneca Indian," and describing it as "the fruit of our joint researches." Ely's "intelligence and accurate knowledge of the institutions of his forefathers have made his friendly services a peculiar privilege."[31] The presence of Carrie G. Parker, Ely's sister, modeling traditional Seneca costume in an engraving reproduced in the text, was further evidence of Morgan's intimate relationship with the family. Morgan had actually made only a few trips to reservation sites, but in the mid-nineteenth century the very idea of fieldwork as a means of writing about "primitive" peoples was fairly new. Instead Ely, as interpreter and go-between, had given him access to knowledge of Iroquois kinship and ancient political and social structure.[32]

Because of how his understanding of Iroquois history, society, and politics came about, Morgan's anthropology tended to characterize the Seneca as representative Iroquois and the Iroquois as representative of all American Indians. As the respected scholar of the Iroquois William Fenton explains, "as the result of intensive collaboration with Parker, Morgan viewed the Iroquois through Seneca eyes, just as he incorporated the Iroquois into his world view as the first Americans."[33] Many now consider the ancient Iroquois League to have been primarily a ritualistic rather than political social organization as Morgan was led to understand. Nevertheless, Fenton's summative evaluation of Morgan's book still stands: "Short on history, but long on social organization and the mechanics of a kinship state, the *League* grasped the concept of a whole culture. Its approach was functional and comparative and not historical. Though not entirely free of the ideas of savagism and primitivism, from which his predecessors never escaped, Morgan sought to describe the Iroquois in their own terms and fairly succeeded."[34]

Morgan's views on Indians were symptomatic of his time, combining paternalism with respect for noble examples of a previous stage of human development.[35] He described a democratic Indian society where blood relationships provided the fundamental scheme of government and American ideals of liberty and autonomy flourished. Morgan wrote: "It would be difficult to describe any political society in which there was less oppression and discontent, more of individual independence and boundless freedom."[36] Echoing his former fraternal allegiances, he connected the individual freedom and personal dignity of ancient Iroquois government to that of the ancient Greeks. However, convinced that an Indian "residue" was unreclaimable, he predicted that with their decline, what was distinctively Indian would ultimately vanish.[37]

Although the book's reception was favorable, it seemed to mark the end of Morgan's career in Indian research. He abandoned his interest in Indian ethnology and devoted himself instead to his professional life as an attorney and businessman. He married his cousin in August 1851, and from 1850 until the summer of 1857 did no research work.[38] Morgan achieved relative success in both business and politics, but from the date of his meeting with Ely he kept up an ongoing concern for Indian welfare. He wrote to President Lincoln about the "Indian problem" after the president's 1862 annual message to Congress. He made a set of suggestions to improve conditions for Indians within the United States, including return of the Indian Bureau from its position within the Department of the Interior to the War Department, strictures to end fraud and exploitation, and the creation of two self-governing Indian states within the Union where Indians could develop their own farming economy. He wanted to see an attempt "to save a portion of the Indian family" whom he knew had the potential to become "a prosperous pastoral people."[39] He concluded: "A more fatal mistake was never made than to suppose the Indian deficient in brains. He is as sound headed as any species of man on the earth. His notions of the objects and ends of life are different from ours. This is the principal fact we have occasion to recognize, and we must deal with him accordingly."[40]

When Morgan once again took up ethnographic study in 1857, he began broad-based comparative research to explain the terminology surrounding kinship and the nature of clan organization. In investigating human kinship systems and collecting a vast record to substantiate his conclusions on the topic, he truly pioneered the field. In May 1859, he set out from Rochester on an extended field trip west to Kansas and Nebraska and discovered that many other Indian groups had kinship systems similar to the Seneca. Elected Republican assemblyman for Rochester in 1861, Morgan's success as a lawyer and businessman made him a small fortune, allowing him in 1862 to devote himself more fully to scholarship.[41]

His huge 1871 publication, *Systems of Consanguinity and Affinity of the Human Family,* the founding study of kinship, extended his earlier ideas. Morgan described the aboriginal use of what he termed the "classificatory" system of kinship and social organization, which, in contrast to the "descriptive" system within the Aryan-Semitic historical sphere, called collateral and lineal kin by the same name. Collateral kin denoted general types of social standing, lineal kin only true, genetic relationships. In "primitive" classificatory systems, just prior to the classificatory system Morgan found within the Seneca, generally all male relatives in a person's parental generation were called by the same term as a person's genetic father, and all female relatives in the parental generation were called mother. Own generation relatives were all classed brothers and sisters, and all relatives of the next generation were considered a person's sons and daughters. The Iroquois system of naming kin was, in Morgan's analysis, more advanced than this, because among the Iroquois a person would call his genetic mother and all her classificatory sisters "mother," but, unlike earlier systems, would call all classificatory brothers by some other term, equivalent to "uncle."

All this led Morgan to propose an original ancient "consanguine family," where all brothers as a group shared sexual relations with all sisters as a group. The earliest human societies he suggested, were "promiscuous hordes" within which no marriage customs were practiced at all. There is little evidence in modern anthropology to support this idea, and even at the time Morgan's critics disparaged it, referring to "a thousand miles of wives."[42] Essentially, he was fantasizing a lost stage of human sexual abandon. However, his conclusions also allowed him to later contrast "primitive" societies, organized around kinship relations, with modern societies organized around property relations. He also used his research to argue for Asiatic as opposed to indigenous origins for the American Indian, an issue much debated in the mid-nineteenth century and still in debate today.[43]

By 1877, Morgan had published his magnum opus, *Ancient Society, or Researches in the Lines of Human Progress from Savagery through Barbarism to Civilization.* It remains his most influential work, although it was in essence an extension and development of his earlier theories. In it, Morgan presented nothing less than a complete theory of social evolution from the beginning of time, which rejected the Danish archaeological classification of a Stone, Bronze, and Iron Age.[44] He isolated successive stages through which humankind the world over progressed—lower, middle, and upper savagery; lower, middle, and upper barbarism; and civilization, ancient and modern. Each "ethnical period" was characterized by indicators of mental and moral development. Knowledge was somehow somatically stored and transmitted from generation to generation, with both human intelligence and morality progressing geometrically through time. Through the accumulation of human experiential knowledge, the brain gradually enlarged and humans progressed.[45]

One of the most interesting things about *Ancient Society* is that after Karl Marx's death, Friedrich Engels used Marx's notes on Morgan's book as a springboard for *The Origin of the Family, Private Property and the State* (1884). "Morgan," Engels wrote in the preface to the first edition, "in his own way had discovered afresh in America the materialistic conception of history discovered by Marx . . . and in his comparison of barbarism and civilization it had led him, in the main points, to the same conclusions as Marx." It had been Marx's intention "to present the results of Morgan's researches in the light of the conclusions of his own—within certain limits may I say our—materialistic conception of history, and thus to make clear their full significance."[46] Thus, a "Yankee Republican" whose Indian interests began with dressing up as part of a young men's fraternity ended up a source for a socialist classic. Perhaps stranger still, because *Ancient Society* seems to offer a transcultural explanation of sexual subordination, it has also now become popular with feminist anthropologists.[47]

Whatever impact the book has had on left-wing thought and feminism, its publication in 1877 developed and contextualized Indian status within history. *Ancient Society* brought Indians more firmly into the human family, showing that they were subject to the same forces and influences as other peoples. God or "the Supreme Intelligence" had originally created humans, but humankind had a single, common origin and had developed in parallel the world over.[48] This at least denied the notion, commonly held at that time, of an innate degeneracy or sinfulness within "savage" peoples, even if it did characterize them as inferior to "civilized" societies. The "marvelous fact" of civilization, characterized by the development of a phonetic alphabet and the beginnings of commerce, had begun with the Semitic and Aryan family types, as Morgan made clear: "The Aryan family represents the central stream of human progress because it produced the highest type of mankind, and because it has proved its intrinsic superiority by gradually assuming the control of the earth."

To be specific, white nineteenth-century America was at the forefront of human development, while American Indians were examples of the "Middle Status of Barbarism." As such they had a considerable amount of catching up to do "in the race of progress."[49] Indians lagged behind, but they had made vital contributions to the civilization that was most advanced. Nineteenth-century democracy, Morgan claimed, had its roots in the clan, or gens—the form of kin-based social organization he found within the Iroquois. This gentile tradition deserved respect, because "out of the ancient council of chiefs came the modern senate; out of the ancient assembly of the people came the modern representative assembly." In essence, as one modern scholar puts it, he made the U.S. Constitution itself "the logical and natural flower of the ancient order of the gens."[50]

Parker was able to use Morgan's validation and explanation of Iroquois and Indian culture as "scientific" support for his own acculturated position; but his relationship to Morgan went much deeper.

He saw his own professional career as an extension and development of Morgan's; he greatly admired Morgan and often discussed his work. At age thirty-eight, he delivered the presentation speech at the 1919 unveiling of the Morgan Tablet by the New York State Archaeological Association. Here he claimed, half in jest, that Morgan was his relative, before describing the hospitality Morgan had received at his great-grandmother's table and his gift to her of her first set of china dishes. He said Morgan was a brilliant and gifted thinker but that he would improve on his work, taking particular issue with Morgan's characterization of primal society as a "promiscuous horde."[51] In November 1928, Parker delivered another speech on Morgan before the Rochester Labor Forum. He compared him to Copernicus, Galileo, Edison, and Columbus. Morgan had disseminated a broader and more complex understanding of American Indian culture, given Indians a position within a developmental scale that included all humankind, and highlighted the different characteristics and accomplishments of various tribes. *The League of the Iroquois,* Parker said, had proven that Indians "were indeed organized and had rigid social laws" and were "far from being anarchistic hoardes [sic] without complex government, or . . . groups under the despotic rule of ferocious chiefs." *Ancient Society* was a "marvelous work," and "in the main Morgan was right." He had begun the new science of anthropology and was "the bridge or the chain that bridged the gap between the two races." His speech concluded with a heartfelt testimony to Morgan's great impact on his own life:

> Morgan died on December 17, 1881. This was the year that I was born. The closest friend of Morgan among the Indian people was my great uncle Gen. Ely S. Parker who introduced Morgan to the fascination of Indian history. The *influence of Morgan and my great uncle have been with me since childhood and their example has been a tradition that has spurred me to carry on where they left off.* I placed a wreath on Morgan's tomb under the auspices of the Morgan Chapter 10 years ago, I assisted in designing his memorial tablet and unveiled it on the occasion of his 100th anniversary at Wells College, and now I feel honored indeed in speaking before a group of his admirers on this 110th anniversary of his birth.[52]

In 1935, Parker wrote an unpublished eight-page discussion of "Iroquois Studies since Morgan's Investigations" for the Russian Academy of Science. He repeated many of Morgan's themes, making clear that change and development characterized the Iroquois across time and that therefore they were capable of advance on Morgan's scale of human progress.[53] At age fifty-nine, on January 22, 1940, he delivered a paper before the Rochester Philosophical Society. Entitled "Lewis Henry Morgan, Social Philosopher," it was subsequently published by his own institution at that time, the Rochester Museum & Science Center. By 1940, although Parker still retained respect and admiration for Morgan and his anthropology, his opinion had modified. He quoted extensively from Stern, Morgan's earliest biographer, and agreed with Stern that a general scheme of social evolution was unsustainable. Using the keyword of the new anthropology, he acknowledged that "Morgan's scheme must be revised if we are to understand the march of culture." He also dismissed Morgan's thesis that humankind was at first promiscuous and the idea that the family was unique to the latter stages of human development.[54]

However, Morgan was still Parker's intellectual hero. Morgan's theories of social evolution had framed his professional life and work. It had given him a clearly defined status and an acceptable position on a linear scale of human development. Besides validating Indian peoples, their societies, and systems, it placed a special emphasis on the Iroquois and owed a central debt to the Parker family, particularly to its leading name, Ely.

Ely's achievements and example were just as significant as Morgan's in how Parker understood his position as an assimilated Indian. After all, it was Ely's chance encounter with Morgan that advanced Morgan's interest in, and access to, Indian society. It was Ely who gave Morgan the opportunity to take his knowledge of Indian life beyond the level of the limited and superficial. He was the shining example of family success with which Parker grew up. An impressive and formidable individual, Ely not only played a pivotal role in the genesis of American ethnology, he secured, from 1869 to 1871, one of the most powerful administrative positions affecting Indian interests, the commissionership of Indian Affairs. Arthur Parker thought of his own aspirations as an extension and development in the twentieth century of Ely's social and political enterprise in the nineteenth. In Ely he had a model of successful accommodation to the white world and a touchstone against which to measure his own experience.

• • •

Ely S. Parker achieved prominence during and after the Civil War, when American Indian integration within the United States was viewed differently than in the early decades of the twentieth century. Ely's achievements within both white and Indian cultures were commendable, but his great-nephew's reverence for him had as much to do with the scale of opportunities available to educated, assimilated Indians during his time as it did with the specifics of Ely's personal success. When Arthur Parker praised his great-uncle, as he did often, he was really paying homage to a lost era. Then, it seemed, a richer, fuller, more honorable Indian integration was possible, and status and merit within Indian life translated more directly to the dominant culture. Pride in his great-uncle's achievements brought Parker hope and bolstered the whole edifice of ideas that supported his engagement in the non-Indian world. Patriotism, inherited status, and talent justly rewarded surrounded Ely and became part of Parker's understanding of the path to success. As important, Ely's story also allowed Parker access to his own inner turmoil over being "in two camps," a chance to locate and articulate an unease about the assimilative process that he knew was not easily resolved.

Parker's version of Ely's life is well worth reading. Like so many heroes, Ely was marked out as special from the time of his birth; his life was accurately prophesied in a dream of his mother's. He would be a peacemaker, "a wise white man," who would "never desert his Indian people nor 'lay down his horns' (sachem's title) as a great Iroquois chief."[55] Encouraged by his parents to study, he attended school at the reservation Baptist mission, but then at twelve ran away to Canada to be an army mule driver. Returning, he went back to school. He entered Cayuga Academy, in Aurora, New York, in 1845; went on to take a course in civil engineering at Rensselaer Polytechnic Institute, Troy, New York; and then became, as one twentieth-century biographer has remarked, "conspicuously successful, holding various important posts."[56] Aside from his structural success in the non-Indian world, in 1851 this great-nephew of the renowned Iroquois orator Red Jacket inherited the grand sachem title Do-ne-ho-ga-wa, Keeper of the Western Door of the Iroquois Confederacy.[57] Thus at only twenty-three, he took on a primary leadership role within Iroquois society.

In the mid-1800s, Ely's abilities as public speaker, interpreter, and scribe were essential to the Tonawanda Seneca's fight to retain their land. He met with presidents and pursued the Seneca case in the state and federal supreme courts and on one visit to Albany met Morgan. He had studied to become an attorney but found that he could not be admitted to the bar because, as an Indian, he was not a citizen. Undeterred, he then worked his way up the ranks to become a successful civil engineer, finally receiving several commissions to supervise the construction of canals, hospitals, and customhouses. While supervising government works at Galena, Illinois, he made another highly influential friendship, this time with Ulysses S. Grant, then working as a clerk in a leather store.[58] Ely secured a commission with the Union army in 1863, and the following year he became military secretary to his friend within weeks of Grant being catapulted to the rank of general with command of the entire Union army. His duties as secretary included transcribing the official copies of the articles of surrender that ended the Civil War, because "his handwriting presented a better appearance than that of any one else on the staff."[59] Some representation of Ely with Grant at Appomattox, either a Matthew Brady photograph or a sketch reproduction, is common in books about the Civil War. Continuing his military career after the war, in 1867 he gained the rank of brevet brigadier general of volunteers at age thirty-nine. His social standing and influence was advanced further the same year by his marriage to Minnie Orton Sackett, a white, eighteen-year-old Washington socialite. Grant, soon to be the Republican nominee for the presidency of the United States, was best man.

As president, Grant made Ely the first Indian commissioner of Indian Affairs in 1869. Although he resigned in 1871 under a cloud, critics have generally been kind about his achievements within Grant's notoriously corrupt administration. Ely saw his commissionership as a chance to bring conciliation and accord and as an opportunity to ease Indian tribes toward the "civilized" condition. He made early moves toward allotment, attempted to garner support for the idea of making Indian Territory self-governing, and encouraged a new role for religious bodies, especially the Quakers, in the administration of Indian affairs. He was also prepared to discipline Indian groups by withholding their rations. Essentially, the first Indian commissioner did little that can be identified as action taken from a specifically Indian perspective. His primary achievement in office was the implementation of Grant's so-called peace policy and the continuation of the fight to end the treaty-making system. In fact, as scholar Henry Waltmann put it, "Much of the time Parker's administration was indistinguishable from that of a paternalistic, though stern, white official."[60]

Nevertheless, Ely was always proud of the fact that the country had not been forced to finance expensive Indian wars in the West during his time in office. His reputation was irreparably tarnished in 1870, however, when accusations of fraud and improvidence were investigated by the House Committee on Appropriations. The whole experience embittered him against the government. He was eventually acquitted of the charges, with only supplementary references made to "errors of judgment."[61] Overall, as Waltmann's analysis shows, Ely's "commonly underestimated contributions to Grant's Peace Policy stemmed from a conviction that frontier tribes had more to lose by resisting than by accepting socio-economic change. And, in part, his resignation on July 24, 1871, showed the inherent difficulties of advancing such a program when most reformers were less concerned about the Indians' dignity and self-determination than their submissiveness and social conformity."[62]

At the time, Ely privately blamed Grant for his political problems. Perhaps by that stage he also had come to resent the distance he had traveled from Seneca tradition. In any case, events surrounding the investigation spoiled forever any pleasure he might have taken from office: "They made their onslaught on my poor innocent head and made the air foul with their malicious and poisonous accusations. They were defeated, but it was no longer a pleasure to discharge patriotic duties in the face of foul slander and abuse."[63] After leaving office, he went on to make and lose more than one small fortune, and eventually he gave up business altogether to work out his life as a supply clerk for the New York City Police Department. He died in 1895, two years after the traumatic deaths of his sister and two brothers, when Arthur Parker was around fourteen. Sadly, although he had once moved in the best Washington circles, in his later years Ely survived "largely through the favors and handouts from military colleagues on General Grant's staff."[64]

Yet to Parker, Ely was always the embodiment of assimilated Indian achievement. He spent twenty years compiling the data for his laudatory biography of his great-uncle. It was a tale of the American Dream, not dissimilar in tone to the inspirational novels produced by Horatio Alger after the Civil War. The subject is born to humble origins and through education, self-improvement, and endeavor rises to fame and fortune. As Parker put it, it was "the story of a man's struggle against adversity—of an effort to achieve." The central point of the biography was to make clear that Parker's great-uncle deserved the "special honor" of being "the only American Indian who rose to national distinction and who could trace his lineage back for generations to the Stone Age and to the days of Hiawatha."

Parker was sensitive to the dislocation that he knew accompanied his great-uncle's success within white and Indian cultures. He presented Ely as a quintessentially Indian hero who tragically suffered from an identity crisis caused by the psychological stress of straddling two worlds. Beginning the biography with an in-depth discussion of the issue, he described how a sculptor, working on a bust of Ely, had once remarked the following to his subject:

You are a man who has "pierced the enemy's lines." You have torn yourself from one environment and made yourself the master of another. In this you have done more for your people than any other Indian who ever lived. Had you remained with your people, and of your people alone, you might have been a Red Jacket, a Brant or a Tecumseh, but by going out and away from them you added to the honor that you already had and won equal, if not greater, honors among the white people. You proved what an Indian of capacity could be in the white man's world.

Ely's reported reply pointed both to his modesty and to the impossibility of judging how successfully or otherwise he bridged the gap between cultures: "That may be true, but why should you test the capacity of the red man's mind in measures that may have an improper scale?"

Parker's biography also selectively quoted from a private letter sent by Ely to Harriet Maxwell Converse, the white woman who had been adopted by the Seneca and who had gained the position of chief at Tonawanda in 1891.[65] Mrs. Converse was an exceptional woman, who formed a close bond with many Seneca traditionalists, especially at Cattaraugus where she was admitted to ceremonies, given objects, and told creation stories and myths. "Aunt Hattie" was a great friend to both Ely and Arthur, although the really intimate friendship was with Ely, her contemporary. Nevertheless, Arthur was a regular visitor to her salon from the time he was enrolled at Dickinson Seminary. Through her, he made key friendships that developed his interest in science and anthropology. After her death, he would refer to her to his friend Joseph Keppler as "our friend who did so much to make our lives broader and better."[66] Harriet Converse, therefore, had a valued and empathetic relationship with both generations of Parkers, which was steadfastly maintained. The prose from Ely and Harriet's correspondence that Arthur Parker chose for his biography of Ely highlighted the stress that came from success in both worlds, what he later called "the cost of assimilation." Thus he published Ely writing to Harriet: "I am credited or charged by you with being 'great,' 'powerful,' and finally crowned as 'good.' Oh, my guardian genius, why should I be so burdened with what I am not now and never expect to be! *All my life I have occupied a false position. I have lost my identity and look about me in vain for my original being.*"[67]

Parker devoted a whole chapter of the biography to the friendship, from 1881 on, between Ely and Mrs. Converse. They spent time "confessing and confiding to each other the innermost secrets of their souls." Her interest made Ely think "about his real self" and share what

Arthur Parker felt was "the true General Parker." On December 7, 1886, Ely pondered the direction and meaning of his life in a letter to the woman he called "the little Snipe":

> Do you know or can you believe that sometimes the idea obtrudes itself into my obtuse and lethargic brain, whether it has been well that I have sought civilization with its bothersome concomitants and whether it would not be better even now (being convinced by my weakness and failure to continue in the gladiatorial contest of modern life) to return to the darkness and most sacred wilds (if any such can be found) of our country and there to vegetate and expire silently, happily and forgotten as do the birds of the air and the beasts of the field.[68]

Writing Ely's biography offered Parker a unique chance to explore the phenomenon of a dual heritage and the angst of assimilation. He had ample opportunity to discuss it all with "Aunt Hattie" at her salon, where there was an open forum for discussion of pressing issues of acculturation. Ely was an inspiring model of the successful, educated Indian, respected by powerful and significant whites and Indians alike. This was exactly the standing Parker wished for himself, and it precisely reflected his personal and professional aspirations. Like Morgan and Ely, he wanted to cross the boundaries between white and Indian worlds and to powerfully interpret and re-present the Iroquois to the dominant culture.

Entering the World of American Museums: Parker's Early Work as Ethnologist and Archaeologist

Perhaps inevitably, while still at Dickinson Seminary, Parker began to reconsider his decision to undertake a career as a minister. Now in his early twenties, he seriously contemplated devoting his energies to science rather than to religion. Surely, the world of American science was a better platform from which to act as a successful Indian statesman like his great-uncle Ely, and to develop and extend the intellectual legacy of the man he so revered, Lewis Henry Morgan?

In many ways, science was an intelligent choice for a young man selecting a profession at the turn of the century. The scientific world was alight with innovation, and recent developments in technology and medicine seemed nothing short of miraculous. Already electricity and the telephone had transformed daily life. The Wright brothers had begun building their own gliders, prototypes for the first flight in 1903, the same year Henry Ford would begin a revolution in urban transportation with the sale of his first Model A. Science and the scientist looked like the nation's best hope as the United States began to address the problems created by the rampant industrialization of the latter half of the previous century. According to the reforming ethos of the time, the direction for future progress was to come, not from government, but, broadly speaking, from the ordered world of science and its experts. With its help, it was thought, conditions could be changed to facilitate a change in people also. Science, moral virtue, and positive social development were all linked in the minds of the young, well-educated, urban middle-class to which Parker aspired. Scientific careers satisfied the social service evangelism of the day; they offered the opportunity for unselfish contribution to the wider society.

Science was popular, but at the most basic level, Parker's new outlook stemmed from his exposure to a series of potent museum influences in New York City and at the Converses' salon. Already the city had yielded at least one powerful museum friend, Frederick Ward Putnam. Putnam, a key influence on the fledgling anthropological discipline, had formed a friendship with Parker during Parker's visits to New York's American Museum of Natural History (AMNH) when still at high school. Parker loved being exposed to professional scientists and the romance of the distant past. When still "stringy as a rawhide strap," he had been able to "rub elbows with explorers and museum men," had "helped boil heads from Mexico," had "unpacked vile smelling hides from the Arctic and washed bushels of specimens, some of which I catalogued with a hand more accustomed to a spade than to a pen."[1] Putnam had warmed to the young man of Indian extraction, giving him advice on a proposed archaeological publication and even offering to help with his educational expenses.[2]

Aside from his curatorships, Putnam wore another hat—that of professor of American archaeology and ethnology at America's oldest university, Harvard. His disciples liked to get together and enjoy the genial atmosphere at the Converses' salon. Young anthropologists like Mark R. Harrington, Alanson B. Skinner, and Frank G. Speck all met Parker for the first time there, as did the artist and teacher John W. Fenton and Parker's great friend Joseph Keppler, cartoonist for *Puck*.[3] The Converses enjoyed the vibrant and intelligent conversation of Indians and friends of the Indian at their home. The salon allowed Mrs. Converse to pick up information on Iroquois folklore, the basis of the romantic poetry she published in newspapers and journals. She and the young Parker had a warm relationship. Perhaps she saw in him some of the same fire and passion that had once attracted her to his great-uncle Ely. Certainly, they shared a romantic vision of the Indian past, evident in the ironized "Indian" language of the letters he sent to her while still at Dickinson. "My appetit [*sic*] for knowledge is very sharp and I intend to eat all I can while I have the opportunity, for what is life unless we constantly learn?" he wrote "Aunt Hattie." He continued: "Beauty, beauty everywhere, but where, Oh, where is the Red Man who ownes [*sic*] it? and who are these userpers [*sic*] I see? I have scratched these few signs on the birch bark to let the GREAT CHIEF know that I am still on the warpath and not scalped by the pale-faces as yet."[4]

Those who gathered at the Converse home had a great deal to talk about in the early 1900s, because it was a transitional period in the development of the anthropological discipline in the United States. The old museum-based focus of anthropology was giving way to an incipient professionalization within a new forum, the university. Anthropology's emphasis on evolutionary stages that could be compared within the museum was being replaced by a new concern in the university with the concept of culture. "American anthropology in 1901," it has been noted, "was turning the corner from the Museum period of converted naturalists represented by Putnam, from the romantic view of the Indian's literature and music, epitomized by Mrs. Converse, to folklore, to the rigorous training of ethnologists in the universities, a tradition that Boas brought from Germany."[5] Although the museum would remain the primary locus for anthropology until the 1920s, the university-trained professional was steadily replacing the self-taught field-worker.

Parker's friend Putnam belonged with the best exemplars of the older type, men like Lewis Henry Morgan, J. N. B. Hewitt, James Mooney, and Frank Cushing.[6] In fact, until 1875 and his appointment as curator of the first major American anthropological museum, the Peabody Museum of American Archaeology and Ethnology at Harvard, Putnam was primarily a zoologist who specialized in ichthyology.[7] Today he is best remembered as a pioneer in the process of museums becoming viable scientific institutions and as an innovator in museum method. For example, he advocated that instead of simply buying existing collections, representatives be sent out to collect material culture in the field. He had followed his own route to prominence within the discipline, teaching and practicing anthropology for years before Harvard awarded him a bachelor's degree. After studying under the renowned Swiss geologist Louis Agassiz in the 1850s, he corresponded with Morgan, who became a friend, and then in the mid-1860s led the rebellion of Agassiz's students against their mentor's resistance to Darwinian evolution.[8] Morgan's brand of cultural evolutionary thinking was very evident in the Peabody's Indian collection put together by Putnam and viewed by Parker. But even though Putnam was of the old school, by the 1890s he was aware of the new trend toward professionalization. In 1891, he started a three-year research course based at the Peabody Museum, and in 1894 his student George Dorsey received the very first American doctorate in archaeology.

Whatever advice Parker may have received from Putnam, Harrington, or others at the salon, he left Dickinson early in 1903, without graduating but having studied for perhaps three years. Having turned away from the cloth, he may have worked as an archaeological assistant or tutor at the American Museum for a spell before he turned his hand to a potentially more lucrative occupation, journalism.[9] Working as a reporter and feature writer for the *New York Sun* might have been just a stopgap to make ends meet while he waited for a firmer opening in science, but it undoubtedly developed his writing ability. It has often been suggested as the source of the expressive writing style he retained throughout his life.[10] Parker later talked about "a few months of exciting work on a New York newspaper," where, he said, "I got the worst assignments and the best experience."[11] His tendency to write without editing or revision could well have been a result of the rigors, early in his career, of producing regular newspaper copy. One museum colleague wrote of Parker's time with the *Sun*: "Here he developed his amazing facility of writing quickly and to the point. All through his life people marveled at his tremendous literary output and the ease and quickness with which he composed, very seldom making corrections after his first draft."[12] He also developed a gift for writing in editorial style, using an event or idea as a springboard for philosophical reflections geared to the interests of the average reader. Although he was inclined to flowery expressions, his compositions always made easy reading. So, Parker's brief stint as a newspaperman honed his writing skills and gave him a valuable understanding of the mechanics of publication. "Each writer should know exactly, even to a line, how much space he has available," he later said in print, adding, "He should then learn how to write this copy for space to a dot."[13] Also significant, the Sun gave Parker an understanding of the power and influence that could be wielded through promotion and publicity, and a nose for discerning the needs and interests of the public. He drew on these skills to great effect for the rest of his life.

Having studied for the ministry and having flirted with journalism, during the summers of 1903 and 1904 his contacts with Putnam and the salon at last brought him his first formal taste of field archaeology. The experience whetted his appetite for more such work and severed, finally, his ties with the seminary. When he later recalled how this first job had come about, he wrote as if he had been enticed away directly from his religious studies by his museum contacts: "a young man of remarkable talents whom I had learned to admire immensely called me into conference. 'Would I forget Greek and Hebrew and the origin of the decalogue for a few weeks and undertake an expedition with him?'"[14] The young man was Mark R. Harrington, a Putnam disciple and salon associate who was conducting an archaeological survey for the Peabody at Cattaraugus Reservation. Since Parker had grown up there, Harrington selected him as his field assistant, and he spent time from that summer to the next assisting on several expeditions in southwestern New York for the Peabody and the AMNH, all under Putnam's overall direction.

Working with Harrington paid very little, but it allowed Parker to return to his childhood home under the banner of archaeological science and to hear again the folktales and legends of his youth. He later reminisced: "To our camp came many Indian friends who sought to instruct Mr. Harrington and myself in the lore of the ancients. We were regaled with stories of the false-faces, of the whirl-winds, of the creation of man, of the death panther, and of the legends of the great bear, but in particular we were blessed with an ample store of tales of vampire skeletons, of witches and of folk-beasts, all of whom had a special appetite for young men who dug in the ground for the buried relics of the 'old-time folks.'"[15] The ancient stories Parker heard from base camp at the old Silverheels farm were to stay in his memory for many years.

Admittedly, at the time there was other useful work a young, educated part-Seneca like Parker could have been doing on the reservation. After all, Cattaraugus was still engaged in a long-term battle against allotment of its 21,000 acres, which was not to subside until after 1906. Parker could have chosen to pit his talents in some way against the various interests supporting Republican congressman and president of the Salamanca National Bank Edward B. Vreeland, who persisted in attempts to permanently allot Seneca lands and to gain title for his constituency of non-Indians leasing reservation lands.[16] However, this was not something Parker concerned himself with, maybe because he felt allotment would ultimately speed necessary and inevitable Seneca assimilation or because he felt the work of salvaging the Iroquois past was itself more important. Whatever the case, Parker very much enjoyed his first experience of work involving liaison between the two cultures, not least because many who came to tell stories to him and Harrington around their campfire were relatives or old friends and acquaintances. The stories and folktales he collected would eventually be published by the State Museum; and even though some would be lost in the 1911 fire in Albany, Parker would use his original notes dating from 1903 to produce his *Seneca Myths and Folktales* some twenty years later. Overall, this first excursion into the field as a scientist was an enjoyable and valuable building block for the rest of his career.

Another benefit was that around this time Parker was able to make a new and significant tie with the Iroquois. He was adopted into the Seneca Bear Clan and given one of the "free" names within the clan set. This kind of clan adoption remains a long-established Indian custom, and it happens to most ethnologists who work among the Iroquois. The name Parker was given, Gáwasowaneh, meaning "Big

Snow Snake," was ceremonial and bore no specific personal reference. It was simply "a typical adult male's name of distinction."[17] Although on occasion in later years Parker would make much of his Indian descent and often sign his publications with his clan name, he rarely made explicit that it was given through adoption. This was probably because adoption served to both affirm and deny his Indian status. Prior to it he had considered himself truly Indian; yet adoption was necessary to his further integration within Iroquois culture because Iroquois Indian status is reckoned through the mother's line and Parker's mother was non-Indian.

There is no substantial data on the specifics of Parker's adoption ceremony, but likely it was similar to others he knew of. When Harriet Converse was adopted at Cattaraugus for the second time in April 1890, she was led up and down between two lines of "braves," her conductor "chanting a weird but solemn air (of the long, long ago) while the Indian spectators sounded . . . a wild whoop." Afterward a "royal feast" was laid on, and "Seneca maidens smilingly served the guests." Most important: "Many beautiful and valuable presents were made by the adopted, to their relatives, and were on exhibition to the guests in a side room of the house."[18] Similarly, when Governor Arthur H. James of Pennsylvania became a "blood brother" to Chief Cornplanter, he too was placed in the center of a group of "braves" while the adoption drama was enacted. The governor was treated as "a traveler arriving at the camp of the Indians." The Seneca then greeted the traveler "with a question as to where he is going and what he is going to do." The adoptee, in role, replied by promising the group he would do "many, many things for your people." After conference, the clan decided against scalping the governor and instead lifted him from the blanket on which he had been seated. He then exchanged gifts with the clan mother, received his adopted name and a scroll, the adoption song was sung, and he joined in an adoption dance.[19]

Adoption was a professional boon, since it developed Parker's bond to his ethnographic subjects. This was probably why Putnam wrote to congratulate him about it.[20] The ceremony also created another social and structural link to his native roots, something he perhaps needed more than ever now that the salon in New York was winding down. During the winter following the 1903 expedition at Cattaraugus, Frank Converse died, followed a few weeks later by his wife. This loss of members by extension of the "grandfather generation" pained Parker very deeply.[21] He had, after all, sat with Mrs. Converse in the medicine lodge while they both witnessed, in full, secret Seneca medicine society ceremonies.[22] Their mutual friend, the cartoonist Joseph Keppler, eventually took over Mrs. Converse's position as honorary Seneca chief and, with Parker, became her literary executor. Parker eventually fulfilled this responsibility to "Aunt Hattie" when he edited *Myths and Legends of the New York State Iroquois, By Harriet Maxwell Converse (Ya-ie-wa-noh)* for publication in 1908.[23]

· · ·

Events had pushed Parker toward scientific work. With the seminary firmly behind him, he now faced another significant choice. Sometime in 1904, he was taken by the young anthropologist Frank Speck to meet Franz Boas, at that time curator at the AMNH. Like Putnam, Boas was interested in Parker. He encouraged him to enroll at Columbia University to study anthropology under him. Parker must have been thinking seriously about the offer, because Putnam wrote to advise him, "I think this is a good step, and you will have my sincere wishes for your success."[24] Instead, however, Parker chose to continue his informal education with Putnam and thus effectively closed off the avenue of a structured academic career within the developing field of anthropology. This was a decision of great significance, because Boas was offering Parker a golden opportunity to join the first group of modern university-trained professional anthropologists. Boas would leave the AMNH the year following his meeting with Parker and continue his work as professor in the Department of Anthropology at Columbia until his death in 1942. During this time he would train some of the central figures in twentieth-century American anthropology, including Alfred Kroeber (who in 1901 had received the first anthropology doctorate at Columbia), Alexander Goldenweiser, Clark Wissler, Robert Lowie, Edward Sapir, Margaret Mead, Ruth Benedict, Ruth Bunzel, and Paul Radin.[25] Unlike Parker, fellow salon associates Speck and Harrington did choose to study under Boas. Speck subsequently became professor of anthropology at the University of Pennsylvania, and Harrington, who married Parker's sister Edna in 1927, went on to curate the Southwest Museum, Los Angeles, California.[26]

Parker's decision to eschew structured anthropological study and instead pursue archaeology meant Putnam rather than Boas became his primary early professional influence. It was a choice that shaped his whole professional approach. As he later admitted to Putnam: "The character of my work has been the result of carrying out the methods which you have taught and which I have gleaned from your papers and addresses and from the advice and criticism which you gave me in New York."[27] Aside from turning Putnam into his primary professional mentor, his decision not to enroll for a Ph.D. at Columbia meant he did not achieve an anthropology doctorate early in his career. This would hamper some of his professional relationships. William Fenton, who knew him, has argued that "the decision to turn his back on the doctorate in anthropology would haunt his professional career, for it was an achievement he very much coveted and envied in others, allowing himself to be called "Doctor" Parker for years before Union College sanctioned the long usage with an honorary degree in 1940."[28]

Why, given that Parker had the institutional contacts and ability to pursue an academic career within anthropology, did he choose to focus his professional development within the confines of the museum? There are several possible answers, including the argument that the academic route to professional status was simply too long and arduous because he was "always in somewhat of a hurry" and "needed to get ahead quickly with marriage and a career." Besides, he "could not know for sure in the early 1900s that anthropology had decisively entered a new professionalized phase."[29] There is some truth in this. Parker married Beulah Tahamont (Dark Cloud), an enrolled Abenaki, on April 23, 1904, which placed him in urgent need of a salary. Beulah was the daughter of Chief Elijah Tahamont of the Abenaki Nation of Canada, ironically, ancient enemies of the Iroquois. A newspaper report of the time described her parents, who were considerable landowners in Canada, like this: "The mother is a woman of exceeding beauty, is a full-blood Abenaki, and her husband is of the same tribe and a well-educated Indian who during the summer 'lectures' for medicine companies." Like her new husband, Beulah had benefited from an association with Harriet Converse, who had used her influence to secure a public school education for her at sixteen and for her sister, Bessie, at six.[30] Beulah had studied at Sabrevois College in Montreal before Converse, sometime around 1900, helped make the two young Dark Cloud girls the first Indian children to attend a New York public school. Beulah's marriage to Parker was to produce two children, Melvil A. and Bertha A. Parker.

However, it must also be remembered that Putnam, archaeology, and the museum context had much to offer a young Seneca of plural descent that was not available from the study of anthropology within the university under Boas. After all, Putnam was a disciple of Lewis Henry Morgan, and archaeology and ethnographic collection within the museum fitted well with the material representation of social evolution according to Morgan's schema. By comparison, Morgan was irrelevant even to the disciplinary attack on cultural evolution that Boas was to spearhead, something Parker must have sensed. Instead, Boas was to focus his assault on Morgan's British contemporary,

Edward B. Tylor. Unlike social evolutionary thinking, Boas's theoretical approach did not lend itself directly to Indian reform, and it did not significantly impact the concern so central to Parker, Indian assimilation. Even though Boas would reject the idea of innate inferiority in any one culture or race, this rejection in itself did not facilitate Indian assimilation into the dominant society. Rather, a pluralistic and relativistic approach to culture complicated the issue. Whereas Morgan's evolutionary analysis marked out clear stages of human development through which it was possible to pass in a generation, Boas's work would reinforce the significance of culture as the ultimate determinant of individual personality, and it could not, therefore, be used to argue for rapid and easy Indian assimilative change. The complexities of assimilation and acculturation were never in themselves central to Boas's anthropology. As Herskovits has pointed out about Boas: "the consistent contrast he drew in his writing between 'primitive' nonliterate, and historic societies, suggests that he never resolved for himself the question of values involved in comparing these types of civilizations, certainly not to any degree approaching the clarity of his resolution of the question of racial differences in endowment."[31] By comparison, cultural evolution's focus on change from one developmental stage to another could directly inform political and social attitudes to Indian integration. Ironically, as has been pointed out, "In this period it was not the apostle of cultural relativism or his students who sought to improve public attitudes towards Indians or to reform Indian policy, but rather these tasks were undertaken by the cultural evolutionists whose views Boas opposed."[32]

So, from Parker's perspective, cultural evolution, the convivial Putnam, and the ordered confines of the museum offered much more than Boas and the complexity of his theory. Aside from all this, it is probable that Boas's personality influenced Parker's decision. Late in life, Parker described him as "awesome" compared with the other museum men he met at the AMNH whom he found "obliging" and "friendly."[33] But centrally, had Parker chosen to study anthropology under Boas, he would have been forced to question cultural evolution. Thus he would also have had to reconsider Morgan and Morgan's sanguine approach to the status and potential within white culture of "civilized" Indians like Parker himself.

Aged twenty-three, Parker had chosen between two of the most powerful figures in the early development of the anthropological discipline and its associated sciences. With hindsight, it is easy to suggest that he backed the wrong horse. After all, the man who would reorient anthropological thinking and direct future development was Boas, and that reorientation would occur within the context of the university rather than the museum. The awareness Boas would foster of the limitations of the museum and its collections in anthropological exegesis heralded the ultimate decline of museum anthropology in the twentieth century.

Of course, all this would not have been obvious to Parker, especially since Boas's career up to that point had been facilitated by Putnam within American museums. In fact, with Boas as his assistant, Putnam had been responsible for introducing anthropology as a new discipline to the public back in 1893. When Boas was within the Department of Psychology at Clark University in 1891, Putnam had appointed him his chief assistant and head of the physical anthropology and ethnology section of the anthropology division of the World's Columbian Exposition at Chicago. Putnam intended the exposition's ethnographic exhibits to represent evolutionary "stages of the development of man on the American continent . . . spread out as an open book from which all could read." They were strictly "scientific" and discrete from the other depiction of Indians by the Interior Department's Indian Bureau. "The great object of our Department," Putnam said, "is to illustrate the Indian in his primitive condition," whereas "the Government proposes to show the Indian on his road to civilization." As far as Putnam was concerned, his work in 1893 was an uncomplicated attempt to display materially the Indian as an example of the "primitive" stage of human development. He even tried to have Indians from British Columbia transported to the exposition as living exhibits, rather than as fare-paying individuals.[34]

At that stage Boas was continuing with the museum method of anthropology. In 1896, Putnam further facilitated his career by appointing him curator in charge of ethnology and somatology at the AMNH, the same time that he first became affiliated with Columbia College. But soon Boas advocated emphasis on artifacts' meaning rather than their external form, an approach demanding change in the way exhibits were customarily displayed. Eventually, conflict over this and what has been described as "a bitter dispute over the subordination of the Museum's research to public entertainment" culminated in Boas's 1905 resignation.[35] By 1907, Boas would be explicit in print about what he felt were the limitations of the museum method of anthropology, arguing that "the psychological as well as the historical relations of cultures, which are the only objects of anthropological inquiry, can not be expressed by any arrangement based on so small a portion of the manifestation of ethnic life as is presented by specimens."[36] This dissatisfaction marked a fundamental divide between the interests of the museum and those of the anthropological discipline. Henceforth anthropology would develop primarily within the university. Parker did not share either Boas's concern over the limitations of the museum method or his reticence about allowing ethnographic collection to become entertainingly accessible to the public. While Boas and his disciples would direct the development of anthropology in the succeeding decades within the university, Parker would be at the forefront of a movement within the museum world to foster greater awareness of the public and the community.

• • •

The same year that he rejected Boas and the university, in 1904, Parker gained his first firm foothold in a museum, securing a temporary position as ethnographic field-worker for the New York State Library and State Museum. He later remembered coming to Albany to be interviewed by the commissioner of the State Education Department, who had said, "Son, so you want a chance to be an archeologist. Don't you know you'll starve to death?" He had replied, "Not if you'll allow me to make archeology what I think it is!"[37] He found the job both stimulating and appropriate to his background and talents. His remit was to procure for the state of New York "all possible information concerning the history, customs, ceremonies, festivals, songs, traditions, etc. . . . of the tribes constituting the Iroquois Confederacy"; collect "any articles of dress, household goods or utensils, implements" and all "indicative of the manner and life and habits of the Indian people." It was the perfect opportunity to capitalize on his Indian connections while developing his interests within a respected profession.

Several factors helped him get the job. Before her death, "Aunt Hattie" had brought his name to the attention of Melvil Dewey, secretary of the Board of Regents and state librarian. Dewey was in charge of developing the Indian Museum in the state capitol, which originated with materials Morgan had collected for the regents of the university from 1848 to 1850. With Mrs. Converse's help, by 1898 Dewey had been able to purchase the colorful Iroquois wampum belts said to have originated as a memory aid of Hiawatha. Such belts had played a significant role in seventeenth-century diplomacy and trade relations, and they were much sought after.[38] It had been Dewey who convinced the new commissioner of education, Andrew S. Draper, of the need for someone to carry out local ethnographic fieldwork. Getting his name mentioned to the right people helped Parker get hired, but so did his Iroquois heritage. Thus when Draper produced a document to facilitate Parker's work among the tribes, he not only testified to Parker's integrity but also made a direct appeal to the Iroquois to welcome "a young man of Indian descent."[39] For his part, Parker was delighted to have secured a position at the museum that held Morgan's famous Iroquois collection, and to be charged with the task of collecting information and artifacts from the very same reservations where the father of American anthropology had conducted his original fieldwork.

The enthusiasm and alacrity with which he approached his first job made 1905 and 1906 the most productive years of his career in terms of fieldwork. As he said himself over a decade later, during 1906 he set about planning the first systematic archaeological survey of the state and "conducted excavations and researches not hitherto equaled by one tenth by any other investigator." In one four-month period alone, he collected "aboriginal pottery and other ancient remains" that he valued for the state at ten thousand dollars.[40] The museum paid him according to the quality of collected information and artifacts, reimbursing him when he presented receipts. Thus he became a sort of intermediary, making deals with Indian contacts on the museum's behalf. Careful about securing a good price, he would tell Keppler how he put in a strategic "by the way" with the Indians regarding some brooches at around seed-buying time, when he could negotiate a lower price.[41] Other times, he would alert his friends to materials for sale on the reservation. For example, he wrote to Keppler: "perhaps you or Mr. Heye would like a wampum string. It is a double string of 54 beads attached to a notched stick and is a New Years notification to delegates from other reservations. Delos has it and wants $25 for it." He was careful to protect his market, telling Keppler, "Regarding commissions, etc, I think that 20% on matters over $20.00 is right and 25% on things under that amount to be about the proper figure, at any rate I want to satisfy the purchaser—and although I must live, I don't want to be a leech."[42] At the time, he was known to most of the collectors of Indian material in the state. Even when he couldn't buy a collection, such as the one owned by William T. Fenton on the Fenton family farm, he would visit and talk about it for his own reference.[43]

Aside from trading in Indian materials, he was getting valuable information. In accordance with the state commissioner's wishes, he worked on gaining the confidence of the Iroquois longhouse leaders and eventually was allowed access to hitherto obscure secret medicine societies at the Cattaraugus Reservation. His work was facilitated by his wife, who helped him forge a relationship with the Keepers of the Faith in the Newtown Longhouse. Her help meant he was able to "discover" and report on the rites of the Seneca Little Water Medicine Society and False Face Company, and collect speeches, song cycles, and associated artifacts.[44] Aside from amassing a great deal of general information on tribal life, during this time Parker also began his work creating a translation of the "Code" of the Iroquois prophet Handsome Lake.

Aware of a historic significance to his efforts at salvaging the Iroquois past, he approached the work with gravitas. He wrote to Keppler in 1905: "A friend of mine here is providing a phonograph and I hope to make records of a few permitted things. The sacred I will not profane upon a cylinder of wax, that putty [*sic*] substitute for a man's brain and fit emblem of many men's minds!"[45] But this respect for the task at hand, and even the awareness of Indian ways that he carried with him from his childhood, did not make access to information on the reservations easy. His "outsider" status had to be overcome, as he confided to Dewey:

> It takes a long time for the Indians to give their confidence to anyone and for some time, although they accepted my statements and gave me preveleges [*sic*], I was conscious of a certain reserve on their part. The trouble was the fact that I was brought up under mission influence and the "pagans" are always more or less suspicious of such a person's motives. I have therefore, sought in every way to remove all obstacles that would cause the people to withhold information from me. I was much gratified, therefore, when the council of chiefs assured me through their chairman that after watching my movements and noting my methods they would give me their complete confidence in all matters and give me a place that only Mrs. Converse had enjoyed. My work immediately became much easier and I am admitted to secret ceremonies that I was formerly barred from and this with the full knowledge that I am taking notes for publication. . . . I am just beginning to appreciate my people myself.[46]

It is perhaps ironic that he had to work hard to achieve the confidence of his forefather's people, something the non-Indian Mrs. Converse had enjoyed for many years.

Parker used his new Indian name when he sent letters to Keppler, which reverberated with his excitement at becoming an ethnographer. "I am exuberant in my work—It thrills me," he wrote, admitting elsewhere, "it seems to me a sin to secure a salary for becoming educated."[47] The pleasure he took seems to have outweighed any hardship caused by his small income. After all, he was acquiring an education that would lead to professional status and that satisfied a personal need to retain an Indian association. Even though he ran up personal debts, as a scientist he was achieving a very great deal. Up to the spring of 1906, he was "a real ethnologist," deserving specific credit. In this period he discovered Jesse Cornplanter, the Seneca boy artist whom he would help toward fame by using Cornplanter's drawings to illustrate his monographs. Another coup was gaining "the last dog pole," an artifact he found in the attic of the Newtown Longhouse, "for preservation by the State." Pleased with this acquisition, he wrote at the time: "The pagans do not easily part with the treasured rites of their ancestors and have long guarded them from publicity."[48]

• • •

His success led to promotion in 1906, when Parker was offered the new position of archaeologist within the Science Division of the State Museum on a temporary basis, pending the result of a qualifying civil service examination. He feared that "the quarter-blood Indian . . . may not come up to the mark and capture the . . . prize," but, with direction and recommendation from Putnam, in fact he did extremely well in the examination against, he said, "a swarm of angling college men eager for the position."[49] When he first met with the state administration—that is, with Commissioner Draper, Assistant Commissioner Rogers, Dr. Dewey, and Director Clark of the State Museum—he later confessed, "They flattered me a great deal," and Draper promised him, "I will take care of you."[50] He was so excited at the prospect of his first scientific job, that when he got the letter telling him he was hired he "emitted several war yells and offered tobacco to my great clan totem."[51]

His success secured a salary of $900 a year, which he was expected to supplement with an income from publications. This was one of the long-term drawbacks to the archaeologist job, which he considered "a stepping stone to greater things."[52] When he was hired, he was led to believe that legislation would soon be passed to increase his salary. But in fact, during the eighteen years he was to spend at the State Museum, he never felt properly financially rewarded for his work. When he finally left, he would claim that the only reason he had stayed so long, in the face of higher-paying job offers, was because he considered his work in itself to be so important. At the very beginning of his State Museum period, however, he was delighted with his new professional advance and very hopeful of what he might achieve. He received many letters of congratulation, the most gratifying probably being the one from Putnam. "From what you have done in the past," wrote the great man, "I am sure you will do credit to the State, and in realizing your own ambitions you have brought about the consummation of my hopes for you."[53]

Putnam was part of the problem Parker had with the other major drawback to the new job, his boss. His immediate superior, John Mason Clarke (1857–1925), director of the Division of Science, state geologist, and state paleontologist, had his own professional imperatives, which sometimes frustrated Parker's determination to promote a program for the Science Division somewhat in Putnam's style. In Clarke's defense, from the beginning Parker had firm, set ideas about how the museum should operate.[54] As time went on, he fleshed out his vision, imagining his department as a future amalgam of the university and the museum, with separate sections for archaeology, ethnology, folklore, philology, and physical anthropology. But Clarke, as director, favored archaeology alone and was primarily concerned with getting exhibit cases filled on budget. He wanted to extract what remained unexcavated within the state forthwith, at least in part so that he could fill the collection areas created by the museum's relocation from Geological Hall and the capitol to the planned new State Education Building.

Almost immediately after Parker was hired, Clarke suggested that Parker switch his efforts from ethnographic collection to archaeological excavation. Then he began to find fault with operations at one of Parker's earliest jobs as salaried archaeologist, the excavation from June 1 to October 1, 1906, of an Iroquois village and burial site at Ripley, Chautauqua County.[55] At Ripley, working conditions were very basic. According to one of Parker's field hands, "the State was so stingy that Parker had to buy most of the equipment himself. He supplied the typewriter, the surveying outfit, some of the chemicals, and for us he had a large phonograph with a case of cylinder records. Food wasn't any too plentiful." But Parker made sure there were adequate stocks of smokes, ginger ale, cookies, and candy when Alanson B. Skinner came up to give support. This incidentally, is evidence, of Parker's innate generosity, a characteristic often stressed in accounts. It also indicates that by this time he had probably begun to smoke, a habit that, in the form of a pipe, became a trademark of his later in life.

Skinner told jokes and caroused into the night until Blue Sky, a Seneca field hand, shoved Skinner's tent and its occupants over a bank into a creek.[56] High jinks aside, Ripley was an important site, teeming with new material. "I am having the most astonishing luck I ever had in my life," Parker told Keppler at the time. "My trowel and shovel are veritable magnets—The most unique and beautiful things in clay and bone and stone were drawn from the ground to them. You see the Great Spirit is giving me success." Excited, he told his friend another time, "I know of no other systematic exploration in N.Y. that has yielded the treasure this expedition has and I hope to profit in reputation by it."[57] The excavation of over one hundred graves and Parker's resulting report did indeed "make his reputation as an archeologist," constituting, William Fenton tells us, "a landmark in the history of American archeology since it represents one of the first attempts to describe the complete excavation of a large site and then interpret the results as the description of a local culture."[58] Aside from the many human skeletons Parker and his coworkers found buried, as if asleep, with their knees drawn up to one side, there were also several thousand other artifacts, including perfect pots, pitchers, and pipes with bowls made in the shape of human heads. Clarke, however, was never entirely satisfied with the haul from Ripley, even though it must have represented a valuable accession to the State Museum's collections.[59] He had fretted that Parker's crew worked unsupervised while Parker was off doing ethnology, and felt Parker should have known exactly where to dig. It would have been much cheaper, he was convinced, to purchase collections directly from amateurs instead.

Given the respect Parker now commands because of his archaeology, Clarke's misgivings seem petty. Beginning with Ripley, he would make valid and lasting contributions to the archaeology of New York State and conduct an extensive amount of collecting, recording, publishing, and promotion of the discipline. From 1911, he would excavate further east, at sites in the Seneca and Finger Lakes area, such as Richmond Mills and Broughton Hill in Ontario County, the Tram Site in Livingston County, and the Lake Side Park Site in Cayuga County. In the 1920s, he would work in the Catskills, at Four Mile Point Site in Greene County, and help lead a campaign to preserve the Flint Mine Hill Site, also in Greene County.[60] According to a record he compiled for his state superiors to make a case for a greater salary, during the overall period Parker spent working on the state's behalf, he built up the Department of Archeology and Ethnology's collections "from almost nothing to . . . more than $200,000."[61] Ripley was the opening piece of work in a prolific and creative period of research and writing over the following twenty years. During that time, Parker produced a total of eight major monographic works, as well as 132 papers, addresses, articles, biographies, essays, and other writings.[62]

Parker was an early practitioner of the direct historical approach, whose principles dictate that it is possible to reconstruct past cultures by working back into prehistoric time from the historic record.[63] This is still used today in Iroquoian archaeology, given that "the goal of much research is to link the ethnographic accounts with the archaeology."[64] Although his archaeological interpretation was not particularly original for the time, the views he adopted on methodology and professionalism were.[65] Thus his book *Method in Archaeology* would stress the more progressive, Boasian ideal of attention to context and demand, in which only trained professionals would be allowed to carry out the historically significant work of excavation. In fact, unlike Clarke, Parker felt private collectors should be forbidden by law from doing "any excavating whatsoever," since they were much more interested in extracting artifacts than in reconstructing past life.[66] He felt that "for the 'pot hunter' to loot . . . sites is like having an untrained person perform a major operation upon a human body."[67] Today, Parker's name remains well known among archaeologists working in New York, who are said to refer to sites of unsure location or existence as "Parker sites." This harks back to his efforts to inventory New York sites while relying mostly on local informants and artifact collectors.[68]

An "Indian" identity never seemed to limit Parker's work or inhibit his enthusiasm for excavation. He had no qualms about disturbing the sanctity of Indian graves and displayed a particular insensitivity to the mechanics of excavating Indian remains. In one letter to a white associate, he wrote of digging up "50 good Indians." In another he wrote: "We have been digging up old Indians for the last six weeks and are having great luck. We find lots of 'em too. Rate of ten a week. They are good injuns too, for you know that they say the only good Indian is a dead one."[69] This may have been ironic, but lack of concern for the sanctity of the graves of ancient Indians would recur in an appendix to another book of his, *A Manual for History Museums*. What mattered to Parker was the preservation of "the record . . . for the interpretation of the trained expert," because he felt one of the greatest "moral crimes" perpetuated against American Indians was not interference with the remains of their dead, but rather the destruction of their material record. Even though he referred to an "invisible empire of the dead," any reverence for it was effaced by a larger imperative to reconstruct the American ethnographic past.[70]

It does seem, however, that on at least one occasion he encountered resistance to his excavation from Indians living on the reservations. He was told to stop and warned that should he persist, a spell would be put on him. He would be "witched." In response, as Parker later described it, he simply laughed at the sorcery and outwitted his challengers with a few practical tricks. He added, however, that even though this was exactly what the wisest old chiefs would recommend, they also warned that "to outwit a witch is to get the whole company of evil doers on one's track, seeking revenge."[71]

Witches were irrelevant to the real object of archaeology as Parker understood it—to further understanding of all aspects of the human species within the social evolutionary framework. Although concerned to present the Iroquois as exemplars of "racial genius," his general aim was always to demonstrate evolutionary change through time. For example, in his article "The Amazing Iroquois" (1927), he would present an ancient, noble, freedom-loving, and warlike people who were also patriotic proto-Americans enthused with "moral energy." He also praised contemporary Iroquois who now understood how "assimilation is but an economic measure, and that for Indians to seek economic separation is suicide."[72] Similarly, the intellectual orientation of his two-volume *Archaeological History of New York,* published in 1920, owed a great deal to Morgan's evolutionary analysis of human development. "Morgan's work was ethnological rather than archaeological," he wrote in the introduction, "but as the two sciences are interrelated and coordinated, Morgan must be recognized as the father of New York archaeological science."[73] In fact, most of what Parker was doing at this time, he apparently saw as a direct extension of the work of his hero, Morgan. Even the book he conceived on Seneca ethnology, he intended as something that would "greatly suppliment [sic] Morgan's work and present a vast amount of hitherto unknown material."[74]

At the Ripley site, he wanted to use his work to present the Iroquois very much as Morgan had understood them. His report described them as a people in transition, about to divest themselves entirely of a savage past, making the task of ethnological and archaeological fieldwork even more vital. Potentially, fieldwork could make the State Museum's collections into more than what Morgan first thought, simply "a memento [sic] to the red race." The Iroquois past needed to be properly reconstructed before it was too late, since the Iroquois were fast becoming "anglicized." He wrote: "It is late, far too near the hour when a new epoch will dawn and there will be no more red men as such. Yet in the short time that remains it is our purpose to save at least a part of the tattered fringe of the ancient fabric that was, and from this small part learn something of its entirety."[75]

He signed his report on Ripley, "Arthur C. Parker, Archeologist," but elsewhere caused conflict by his persistent use of the statutory title "state archaeologist," an aggrandizement of his job that the state commissioner called to Clarke's attention. At least the young Parker looked the part. Well-built and generally well presented in formal professional clothes, he sported tall, crisp white collars and an impressive wide-brimmed hat over his dark, well-cropped hair. With his erect posture, intelligent open face, and soft, proudly Indian features, he looked every bit the up-and-coming professional. By now he had been accepted as a Freemason, something that would augment his professional image and allow him to network with those in a position to develop his career. Yes, he had adopted the name "state archaeologist," which he did not deserve, but around the same time, perhaps to make up for it, he gave Clarke the opportunity to be given his own ceremonial clan name by the Seneca. In 1908, Clarke permitted official funds to be used when Parker organized a naming ceremony for him as representative of the state of New York, justified by the fact that the state now held the prized Iroquois Confederacy wampum belts. This was a chance for Parker to ingratiate himself with his boss, who by all accounts was a strict, formidable administrator.[76] Clarke got the name Ho-sen-na-geh-teh, which Parker told him meant "He carries the name" or "The name bearer." Once more, adoption served as a useful public-relations tool between a powerful non-Indian and a group of Indian peoples.

A new Indian name did not, however, blind Clarke to the labor hours needed for Parker's next innovation, the creation of a series of six Iroquois life groups, or dioramas, "authentically" characteristic of the aboriginal past. These were three-dimensional, life-size replicas, or casts, of Indian figures set against various traditional backgrounds. According to Parker's record, he alone planned the construction of all six groups and supervised the whole project from its inception in 1906 to final installation in 1915. The finished dioramas were "recognized as the finest exhibits of their kind in America," attracting over 200,000 visitors a year. Paid for by private funds secured by Clarke, Parker estimated they had "a value of $75,000 or more."[77] The background work necessitated that time be spent in the field, allowing Parker to maintain his contacts with the Iroquois.

He employed Indians from New York and Canada to carefully reproduce clothing and artifacts and used sculptors and painters to create mannequins for each specific group. He bought braided mats and wooden benches from the Tonawanda and Cattaraugus Reservations and was especially careful about seeking out models "whose figures and facial characteristics conform best to the Seneca type." He had to travel to the Ontario Six Nations of the Grand River Reserve to find "good Oneida types," since he felt that the Oneida of New York State were "too few and too white, though they may serve as body models." The quill and moose-hair embroidery needed was produced at the Huron Lorette settlement in Ontario and in upstate New York because Parker "much prefer[red] to have Indian women do it."

Clarke griped about "unsatisfactory experiences" as a result of "irresponsibility and lack of supervision" in employing Indian people to make costumes. But, perhaps because of this use of native craftspeople and the careful attention to detail, the State Museum's life models were popular among museum professionals. Museum planners and representatives from other states and abroad started to seek Parker's advice about diorama construction. Eventually the Illinois State Museum director asked him to create seven or eight life group figures, "ethnologically correct" artifacts, and an appropriate habitat setting, all for the considerable sum of $2,500. In all, dioramas served to make Parker a recognized authority and to solidify his reputation as museum innovator.

For his part, Clarke remained concerned about the expense of the life groups even though they were to be good value for the State Museum right from the planning stage in 1908 until another new museum building was opened in 1976.[78] He balked at the number of life casts and at such things as Parker's insistence that new deerskin, which he had had tanned "by Iroquois methods," be used on the Seneca group tanning frame on display. After all, Parker said, "Indians had new things." When Clarke suggested paint and canvas rather than selected elm and cedar bark for the bark house from the Wisconsin Menominee reservation, Parker replied: "We must . . . keep in mind that the exhibit is primarily ethnological . . . whenever possible actual objects must be used and that art must be called into play when we find it not feasible to produce the actual object. . . . To have constructed the bark cabin of canvas and paint would have been absolutely absured [sic]."[79] He pointed out to Clarke that the main concerns should be "Ethnological Accuracy," then "Natural Consistency," and lastly "Artistic Harmony."

The life groups were to serve as vivid, mimetic illustrations of the stages described by cultural evolutionary theory. Their job was to represent the narrative of cultural evolution as accurately as possible. Therefore, Parker would inform Clarke that, for one group, fabric would be used instead of deerskins for aboriginal dress because "the idea is to show the evolution of the costume after the European period. This will give us room for beadworking so characteristic of the Indians of the Colonial period."[80] He paid the same kind of attention to detail in the making of the life casts' wigs, sending the manufacturers drawings and returning wigs that he felt inappropriate.[81] Even the backgrounds he had constructed were based on artists' impressions of actual archaeological sites.

Parker likely got the life group idea from the systematic and synoptic exhibits of Northwest Coast Indians installed under Boas's direction at the AMNH. In fact, one of the earliest uses of the ethnological life group had been under Boas's direction at the World's Columbian Exposition in Chicago back in 1893. In itself the phenomenon was an interesting application of certain Boasian ideas, but this was not what particularly attracted Parker to it, or what made him develop it as his own. It was not the life group's synoptic nature or what it implied about culture that attracted him; it was its sensory appeal to the public, its ability to "free the imagination" in a way shelves of artifacts never could. He preferred life groups dramatically lit within a darkened hall with painted panoramic backgrounds. Aware that "we like to look at things that we are not quite sure about," he felt that in the Seneca display "the value of the darkened portion in the immediate foreground is considerable. It gives the necessary distance and atmosphere."[82]

The life group was much more appealing psychologically to the museum visitor than artifacts presented within cases in rows. It was "the most effective method of staging and of interesting and teaching the public." "There is a psychological value," Parker wrote, "in getting people to talk about the exhibit. The imagination is busy and without being aware of it, they are being instructed."[83] He would remain firmly committed to the importance of psychology in getting maximum educational purchase from museum exhibits throughout his life. In 1943, he was still arguing eloquently: "People want to be entertained by exhibits, sights and sounds. They want sensory stimulation. They want to be thrilled by what they experience in a museum, not merely bored by long labels and crowded cases. People want to painlessly absorb stimulating knowledge, a knowledge that makes them talk about it. . . . They want a feeling of personal contact."[84]

To his mind, dioramas were an obvious improvement because the public "prefers to see and get the subject for itself in a 'nut shell.'"[85] Such attention to the psychology of the museum visitor was never at the heart of the Boasian life group. Boas designed his AMNH groups to be seen from all sides, but Parker's dioramas, as one commentator put it, "were laid out more like a film script than a scholarly monograph." By comparison, Boas was to resist the movement within museums toward using mannequins that were particularly realistic, objecting to "the ghastly impression such as we notice in wax-figures" and to displays showing figures in arrested motion.[86]

Parker's fundamental idea was to make education within the museum enjoyable, because he felt people went "not to *consult* but to be *interested* without effort or fatigue."[87] This was all part of a democratic, interactive attitude to the museum as a social phenomenon— ideas that, for the time and in that context, were extremely progressive.

Not until the 1930s did psychologists at Yale repeat many of the ideas Parker practiced in the first decades of the twentieth century and advocate their museum implementation.[88] For his part, Parker wanted only for his work to have real impact and for it to connect directly with the present. He produced a wealth of important research, but what mattered to him was to be of contemporary value as a professional. Thus he wrote: "An archeologist is supposed to be a backward-sighted person whose life is devoted to the study of antiquity. In real life an archeologist is a person who, having a knowledge of the past, applies it to real human needs of today."[89] It was a progressive, inclusive vision that he would later bring to even fuller expression.

Even though the comparative, synoptic exhibits were extremely attractive to the public, Parker did not envisage them having any specific educational role for Indians. Rather, their function was to educate the wider public on the Indian's role within the American past. They were a message to the dominant culture, a vivid representation of Indian society as a particular stage in human evolution. Museums as institutions were a bulwark against the degeneracy of the urban present, he felt, and a place where the past informed and guided current values and attitudes. Museums "link life with living values, they entuse [sic], they inspire, they promote patriotism and international understanding, and they symbolize the community's understanding of itself. . . . [T]he museum stands for a nation's culture and pictures its progress."[90]

But if museums did serve as a force for social uplift, they did so as sites where America trumpeted its global positioning and worldwide cultural dominance.[91] Within their walls, American status was carefully fixed by comparison with other "races" and animals from across the globe. An appropriated "primitive" past was on display from which the "civilized" present could draw strength and direction. In a very real sense, Parker's life groups were comparable to the taxidermic dioramas of African primates, created from animals that Carl Akeley (1864–1926) shot on safari and stuffed for the AMNH. Both Akeley's primates and Parker's Indians were frozen in a single realist pose forever, noble specimens caught close to the moment of first encounter. The carefully constructed museum re-presentation of both African primates and Indian peoples served the same purpose—they testified to the resounding triumph of American civilization.

At the time, the same desire to conceptualize the United States as naturally globally preeminent was being successfully articulated by the nation's president, Theodore Roosevelt. In office from 1901 to 1909, Roosevelt sought to embody just the kind of virile American prowess conjured by museum display. He was the "patron saint for the museum and its task of regeneration of a miscellaneous, incoherent urban public threatened with genetic and social decadence, threatened with the prolific bodies of new immigrants, threatened with the failure of manhood," and he caught the spirit of the age.[92] After his defeat in the 1912 election, he could not resist the opportunity to explore an Amazonian tributary for the AMNH and the Brazilian government, an expedition the president-who-never-grew-up described as his "last chance to be a boy." The triumphalism that both the museum and Roosevelt expressed served an important function: it helped unify a divergent nation and confirm America's adopted role as global leader.

Museum work allowed Parker to prove himself an excellent cultural mediator. Solid effort had brought him the respect of fellow archaeologists, and his commitment to innovation and to public education had impressed his peers within the museum world. Turning thirty as the second decade of the twentieth century began, Parker must have felt that the fulfillment of his childhood dreams was eminently possible. After all, he had found a niche that allowed him to combine a love of his people, the Iroquois, with status within the Euro-American, professional class.

With his diorama work still being developed, with a growing museum reputation, Parker plunged into research publication within anthropology in an attempt to capitalize on his specialized knowledge of the field and to advance his career. The topics he chose were ambitious in scope probably because Parker wanted his publications to reflect very positively on his department. In fact, the studies he produced and the responses they provoked from within the discipline were to do something more significant. They brought him a new understanding of his professional status and pushed him closer to a new professional direction and the work for which he became best known.

CHAPTER 4

The Limitations of Parker's Anthropology

While planning and creating Indian life groups, purchasing and bartering for ethnographic material, and fulfilling his administrative duties for the museum, Parker carried out anthropological fieldwork. This was published as a series of valuable anthropological studies that Parker thought of as extensions and developments of Morgan's own. His interpretations repeatedly stressed connections between the Indian past and the values and mores of contemporary America. In essence, he used anthropology to present the Iroquois as a people whose history made them acceptable Americans, worthy of assimilation.

As Parker moved through his thirties, anthropology brought significant recognition and laid the bedrock of his professional status. However, Parker's anthropology also embodied all the ambiguities and limitations accompanying his position as both Indian and scientific scholar choosing to remain outside the academy. Eventually, the approach he adopted to the data he collected on the Iroquois raised eyebrows among his disciplinary peers. They did not share his specific Indian connections, and they were not subject, as he was, to the pressures and perplexities inherent in interpreting the past of one's own people to a larger, dominant culture. Anthropology gave Parker a productive forum within which the specifics of his birth were an advantage, but, as will become clear, it also brought him closer to a new comprehension of the gap between his own ideas of Indian potential and those of the larger society.

· · ·

The first anthropological study with which he was connected was a fulfillment of the role he had been given five years earlier as literary executor to "Aunt Hattie." Parker had been pleased when Melvil Dewey snapped up Mrs. Converse's writings for $10.00 on behalf of the state in October 1905.[1] But it seems Dewey resigned too soon afterward to carry out his promise to secure speedy publication, and Parker had to wait until the winter of 1907 to ask again that they be published and to negotiate for "a personal appropriation for 100 copies," which he wanted "to sell to form a nucleus for the $150.00 of her grave."[2] Ensuring publication was an important personal responsibility. He told Keppler, Converse's other literary executor: "Indeed we do owe our most solemn obligation to our friend who did so much to make our lives broader and better. Yiewanoh's [Converse's Indian title by adoption] inspiration lives with me and I hope one day—not far distant— to do a small but abiding duty which yet remains for her friends to carry out."[3] Producing the text was also valuable museum work that would promote the department, especially since Parker had been able to revisit Converse's sources and double the length of the manuscript with new material. These additions, he assured Clarke, negated any prior publication claim from Dewey and the State Library. In the event, the text materialized successfully as "strictly an affair of the adopted Iroquois," based on material originally collected by the adopted poetess, augmented and introduced by Parker. In the preface, which he signed using his own new Indian title, Clarke said Parker had been motivated to do the work by "the piety and inspiration of inheritance."[4]

Myths and Legends of the New York State Iroquois, By Harriet Maxwell Converse (Ya-ié-wa-noh), was given to the museum for publication in late May 1908. Pleased with this first, sizable manuscript printed under his name, Parker wrote disarmingly to Keppler: "I have finished Yiewanoh's book.... I hope you will like it as much as it comes forth and if not I will be a sick moose with a heavy head, and live on old pine cones for twenty moons. I reasoned out an introduction of some length which the Director brands as a most philosophical treatise."[5] His introduction to the Converse study was indeed philosophical and soaked in the evolutionary language of Morgan's *Ancient Society*. It explained to the reader that although Indian myth might "appear as a worthless fancy or a child's tale," in fact, "deeper study . . . reveals within it the beginnings of physics, philosophy and theology." If the rational reader was puzzled, he should recall that "the minds of men, through the varying grades of culture, from lower savagery to civilization, are characterized by wide differences," differences that in the present day were "illustrated by groups of living peoples." Myth was in fact "a primitive theory, a rude attempt to reach truth, a tentative hypothesis upon which to fasten one's belief, for one must believe something." Religion itself was composed simply from older myths circulating within a culture, and, Parker argued, as time passed newer myths simply became "the science of the day."

Daring as such theorizing was, the most unusual arguments put forward in his introduction concerned folklore's collection and presentation. He recommended an innovative and individualized method involving a fundamental interpretative freedom with primary data. This brought no academic censure at this stage, but it was symptomatic of a creative attitude that would eventually conflict with notions of scientific objectivity held by his peers. He had brought into play a wholly new approach to represent the folklore of the Iroquois, "the Indians of Indians," "the most splendid of barbaric men." Rather than merely "satisfy strictly scientific requirements" through using the phonetic style favored by institutions like the Smithsonian, he tried to preserve his material's "native beauty." He felt that to simply record it as told, "in the broken English of its narrator," sometimes produced "grotesque caricature," when in fact "it is the impression, its form, its spirit that we wish to apprehend." Many had tried "recasting primitive ideas in their own thought molds," but this had "produced a mass of florid, ocherous, recast and garbled folklore." Instead, like "Aunt Hattie," he favored combining elements of other approaches so as to reproduce in English the transcendent essence of the myth.

Parker advocated a technique whereby "the transcriber attempts to assimilate the ideas of the myth tale as he hears it, seeks to become imbued with the spirit of its characters, and, shutting out from his mind all thought of his own culture, and momentarily transforming himself into the culture of the myth teller, records his impressions as he recalls the story. His object is to produce the same emotions in the mind of civilized man which is produced in the primitive mind, which entertains the myth without destroying the native style or warping the facts of the narrative." However, he recommended that the method should be honestly followed only "by one familiar with all the incidents of the culture which produced the tale, by one who is familiar with the language, life and psychology of the myth maker." Thus the reader of the Converse manuscript was given the opportunity to "feel all that the red man felt when he listened to the ancient stories of his forefathers."[6]

The same approach was applied to an account appended to the text describing the Little Water Medicine Society, the shamanistic Iroquois group to which Parker, like Mrs. Converse, had gained full membership. The following year he extended this work to include descriptions of the workings of other hitherto unknown societies and published it under the title "Secret Medicine Societies of the Seneca" in *American*

Anthropologist. It was valuable, original work at a time when the topic was hot among ethnologists. It nicely coincided with similar studies being done under the aegis of the American Museum, and it "projected Parker into the mainstream of ethnology."[7] It is possible, if not probable, that he overemphasized the "secret" nature of these medicine societies, but the work was nevertheless new, worthwhile, and well received.[8]

Clarke was no doubt pleased with this publishing success. "We must," he reminded Parker by letter in 1909, "keep our Department as much in the foreground as possible."[9] For his part, Parker was worried that other work would prevent him doing the fieldwork and writing necessary to continue to capitalize on his specialized knowledge of the Iroquois and their folklore. He had written to Clarke in April of his concerns about being scooped in this respect, hoping that "other ethnologists will out of courtesy keep out of my territory."[10] By June such worries had been put to one side. He was so excited about the caliber of what he could publish, he told Clarke, "My summer plans include further ethnological studies . . . that I am vain enough to hope will out-Morgan Morgan. I have a large amount of data now."[11] He was also pleased to be attracting more attention from local bodies in need of a worthwhile speaker and to have his name appearing with greater regularity in the local and state press. He made good copy in January 1910, for example, when he secured from Seneca sources a Ga-no-da flute and water drum, reportedly used by secret medicine societies, for the State Museum.[12] By now, he was much more at ease about the future direction of his life's work, writing to a reservation acquaintance: "My first duty is to the State and to the Indian study to which I have intended to devote my life."[13]

· · ·

Such commitment paid inevitable dividends, and Parker was indeed able to "out-Morgan Morgan" on the single topic of Iroquois subsistence with *Iroquois Uses of Maize and Other Food Plants,* submitted for publication in April 1910. An extensive illustrated description of the history and significance of foods central to Iroquois culture, detailing their influence on cooking, eating habits, ceremony, and language, it "put ethnology at the State Museum and Parker on the scientific map."[14] It stands today as his finest single piece of ethnology, the result, like the work on medicine societies, of systematic field study. "Purely original enquiry," he told his readers, had been conducted "during a period of 10 years, while the writer has been officially concerned with the archaeology and ethnology of the New York Iroquois and their kindred in

Canada." A serviceable understanding of the Seneca language and many family ties on Iroquois reservations enabled him to probe "scores of Indians" on "many interesting facts . . . brought out from almost hidden recesses of their minds." All this allowed him to build on Morgan's *League of the Iroquois,* contradicting some of Morgan's findings and exemplifying others.[15] An example was the evidence he unearthed of ancient Iroquois corn cultivation. This upset Morgan's characterization of the Iroquois as a people in the "Lower Status of Barbarism" and improved their position within the social evolutionary scale of development.[16] Even so, *Iroquois Uses* had something of the developing Boasian approach in its attempt to describe Iroquois culture through meticulous attention to small detail.

Fairly general in scope, the text placed intriguing detail within an immediate and meaningful cultural context. It went far beyond a simple listing of the uses of maize, beans, and squash, the "three sisters" of Iroquois subsistence. From discussion of the gendered division of labor among the early Iroquois to stories about the mythological "tall slender maiden" said to appear to men and to embody the spirit of the corn, there was something to interest almost every reader. How to prepare succotash the old Indian way, how to make leaf bread tamales, tasty hominy, and dumplings. How to use corn to stop a nose bleed, make rope, and even how to ease the delivery of a child using partridge berries. The myriad uses of squashes, beans, fruits, berries, and food nuts were described. Specifically, Parker dwelt on the joys of the first fruit of the year, the wild strawberry, an Iroquois "symbol of the Creator's renewed promise of beneficence." He also listed the range of foods that can be made from sap, bark, and roots, giving his readers a charming description of exquisite maple sap, "the wholesomest Drink in the World."[17]

Aside from this wealth of detail, Parker stressed the importance of maize to the early English colonists, and by implication the significance of the Iroquois to the very existence of a Euro-American United States. Maize was "the bridge over which English civilization crept, tremblingly and uncertainly, at first, then boldly and surely to a foothold and a permanent occupation of America." In fact, he argued: "Had it not been for the corn of the Indians the stories of Jamestown and Plymouth instead of being stirring accounts of perseverance and endurance might have been brief and melancholy tragedies. The settlement and development of the New World would have been delayed for years."[18]

His efforts brought praise and commendation from old friend and contemporary Frank G. Speck in a review for the *American Anthropologist*:

In this paper we have a most careful and detailed study of an important topic in the ethnology of the Iroquois. The author is in a particularly favorable position to investigate these important tribes which have for so long remained in a state of neglect on the part of the trained ethnologists. The esoterism of the Iroquois has no doubt been responsible for this. Mr. Parker, however, in a series of systematic studies which it is hoped will soon appear, possesses unusual advantages with the Iroquois and if the other sides of their culture are treated in the same critical manner as that shown in his recent papers we shall have a comprehensive library on the life of these Indians.[19]

Iroquois Uses was indeed an excellent contribution to the field. It developed work published two years previously by Parker's future brother-in-law, Mark Harrington, and was not surpassed until 1916 when *Iroquois Foods and Food Preparation* was published by F. W. Waugh.[20] As late as 1917, Clark Wissler would refer to it as one of the few existent field studies "approaching a satisfactory standard."[21] However, when William Fenton introduced the 1968 reprint of the text, he devoted a section to Parker's technical errors of scholarship in terms of spelling, grammar, syntax, and referencing. He confessed this was "nit-picking," but his point was that "Parker, in representing himself as a scholar to the learned world, took some shortcuts and never got caught." Had he chosen an academic context within which to produce a work of this length, "Parker would have been sent back to the library."[22]

Soon after submitting his manuscript, Parker went not to the library, but to Canada, to the Six Nations Reserve, Brant County, Ontario, where Iroquois were in revolt against their traditional nonelective system of government. Although he was there simply to study and secure models for the life groups to be exhibited at the new State Education Building, he weighed in on the debate in the *Daily Record*. He vented his displeasure at the system of matrilineal descent, which supported traditional politics and which had been a barrier to his own integration within Iroquois culture: "Legalists point out that only animals, slaves and some Indians, among them the Iroquois of New York, take their descent from the female line." Calling for no less than the intercession of the state to sort out the debate at the Grand River Reserve, Parker claimed, "The fact that the Canadian Iroquois have abandoned the ancient system of descent as a thing no longer necessary and have become a stronger and more intelligent people than their New York brothers, ought to be an object lesson [*sic*] to the lawmakers that watch over State Indian matters."[23]

Such strong words revealed a fundamental irritation over his status as an adopted but nonenrolled Seneca, an ambivalent position that may have fuelled his desire to have a significant impact on scholarship on the Iroquois. However, misfortune struck before he could see his next anthropological text in print. On March 29, 1911, fire swept through the west end of the Albany state capitol and State Library, devouring over two-thirds of the ethnographic collections, including material collected by Morgan, some of the Converse collection, and two hundred of the almost three hundred separate objects Parker had collected himself. State funds had to be diverted away from publication.

A local paper carried Parker's letter to his father describing the fire: "It was after the great roar of flame had swept through that my assistant and I got in and amid the crashing walls, burning cases and clouds of smoke, rescued much of great value in the Archaeological and Ethnological exhibits. All of the Morgan fabrics went up in smoke, as did as many relics that can never be replaced. All the fruit of my six years' work was destroyed with the exception of the Ripley 1906 collection, which I got out of danger intact." Although not physically hurt, the newspaper noted that "the shock following the news of the destruction of the Indian relics caused temporary breakdown in his health," and Parker "was sick abed for several days afterward."[24] He had used the Cornplanter tomahawk as his "fire axe and mascot," he told Keppler, while "Stones fell to the right, fire bellowed to the left etc. . . . but nothing touched me." At one point it seemed "Hell broke loose," but he felt his "manitou" was with him as protection. Parker was especially thankful that at least the Iroquois wampum belts and the Converse silver had somehow remained safe.[25]

Clarke shared his distress, stating in print that only $1,500 worth out of the $30,000 Indian collection held at the capitol had been saved. He took his responsibility as adopted keeper of the wampum belts very seriously, seeing it as a distinguished role the State Museum had taken over from the Onondaga. "There are about twenty," he wrote, "and on the market today they would probably be worth $2,000 apiece. If these were lost I would never be able to look an Iroquois Indian in the face again." Fortunately, around three years before the fire he had sensibly had them removed from the State Library and put in a safe deposit vault.[26] Parker, too, had withdrawn around half of his manuscripts from the State Library and put them in his office in Geological Hall.[27] Even so, up to a month later, Parker was still affected, writing: "The memory of those things which shriveled almost before my eyes still lingers to shock me. I was truly heart sick." But by this stage he was already imagining the wonders of the planned new Iroquois museum, about which he could not "enthuse too much." Nevertheless, he had learned a lesson and was determined to avoid the havoc of another fire. "All my new cases for which I hope to secure $35,000 to build will be *steel*," he wrote. "No more fire for me. I could not live through another."[28] His emotional reaction reveals how deeply engaged Parker was with his work and that he cherished the artifacts and material for which he and his institution were responsible.

However, the fire was not the only thing on Parker's mind that month. He had become interested in forming a national organization to represent Indian interests, composed of the foremost Indian spokespeople. He was soon to join the educated group who met in Ohio that April to discuss the formation of what eventually became the Society of American Indians. His passionate involvement with that organization will be considered separately in the next chapter.

· · ·

By September, thoughts of fire had been put to one side. Refreshed by time spent in the field, Parker was once more extremely positive about prospects for his Iroquois scholarship. His mind was filled with the data for his next publication, *The Code of Handsome Lake, the Seneca Prophet,* since he had just completed visits to all the key sites "to get local color and feeling." Ethnology now dominated his concerns, and he was eager to see all his material and ideas in print. "Work surrounds and nearly consumes me there is so much," he wrote to Keppler, "and I'm glad because of it. Sometimes however I feel that something may come up to stop it all and thus leave all my precious Iroquois documents a mass of shapeless notes but I hope not." However much he immersed himself in his research, there was something he could no longer deny to his friend—his concern over the well-being of his wife. An isolated paragraph in the same letter expressed his fears in two sentences: "I write confidentially when I say that I sometimes fear for Beulah's mental health and I am never very sure what she may do to herself or to the rest of us. Last winter I had her in the hospital for some time."

Compounding such serious domestic worries was the fact that his salary, now $1200 per annum, simply did not meet family expenses, let alone cover his habit of being generous financially, as in other ways, to deserving cases from the reservations. Therefore he grumbled about how he was treated at the State Museum, telling Keppler, "they know an archeologist works harder and has better results—and can be paid in press notices instead of ducats." All he could do was to continue his research and the work creating the new Indian groups for the State

Museum while supplementing his income when he could with outside lecturing and publishing. He may not have been getting paid enough, but he still loved his work and the opportunity it offered to preserve the cultural history of the Iroquois: "Midnight gas, and a pen save the day, however—and now and then a few lectures. But I like it. Wouldn't take a different profession for greater inducements. Queer how love of work fills a fellow with ambition."[29]

The Code was published by the State Museum in 1913. It did not bring Parker exactly the kind of personal and professional response he expected, but it was nonetheless a significant and important addition to the Iroquois record and to Iroquois culture. From the preparation stage he had hoped that his translation of the moral code Gai'wiio', or "The Good Message," of Handsome Lake, would prove "of some psychological as well as sociological interest." After all, as he acknowledged, "It was Handsome Lake who revolutionized in 16 years the disintegrating Seneca and Onondaga tribes and recrystallized their native beliefs. This was accomplished at the critical moment in [their] history—immediately after the Revolutionary War, when the Iroquois League was broken and disheartened. Handsome Lake's teaching gave new life and new hope."[30] He was right. Handsome Lake's teachings have had a tremendous impact on Iroquois religious life, and the faith is still practiced by the New York Iroquois today. Despite the fact that his account enjoyed only one printing of two thousand copies, it became "for want of anything better . . . the Bible of the 'new religion,'" that is, the Longhouse religion: Gai'wiio' or "The Good Word."[31]

The bible Parker produced would also be the basis of the nationalist movement at the core of Edmund Wilson's well-known 1960 text *Apologies to the Iroquois.* Divergent traditions and versions have since been recognized, but Parker's remains the best single early record.[32] Also, it agreed remarkably well with the versions recorded by Ely S. Parker in 1845 and 1848, which were used as the basis for Morgan's own 1851 account.[33] Given the significance of such a work, it is perhaps surprising that although Parker referred to his great-uncle, he did not mention his familial relationship to Ely, whom he considered the maternal great-great-grandson of Handsome Lake. This is a noticeable omission, since he would have been well aware of the connection since childhood, and had even reminded Keppler when the book was in preparation, "You know he was my grandfather's great-great grandfather—vide Morgan."[34] But within *The Code* he neither spelled out his connection to the prophet nor made any reference to his own Indian identity. Rather, his focus was on the unique value of the version of the faith he was making public and on what it said about the special identity of the Iroquois and their social cohesion as a proud American minority.

His source had been the Seneca Chief Edward Cornplanter, or Sosondó:wa, one of six authorized "holders" of the Gai'wiio' at Cattaraugus Reservation. Cornplanter had begun writing down the code in the Seneca dialect in 1903, fearing that the original form of the faith might be lost. Parker had somehow managed to persuade him to finish writing and to entrust the document to the State Museum. *The Code*'s introduction told how "he [Cornplanter] was at first reluctant, fearing criticism, but after a council with the leading men he consented to do so. He became greatly interested in the progress of the translation, eager for all white men to have the privilege of reading the 'wonderful message' of the great prophet." Even more remarkable was the fact that Parker got Cornplanter to accept "William Bluesky, the native lay preacher of the Baptist church," as translator. Parker wrote, "It was a lesson in religious toleration to see the Christian preacher and the "Instructor of the Gai'wiio' side by side working over the sections of the code, for beyond a few smiles at certain passages, in which Chief Cornplanter himself shared, Mr. Bluesky never showed but that he reverenced every message and revelation." In all likelihood, "Cornplanter read from his minute book or recited from memory, Bluesky rendered it into English, and Parker wrote it down." The result has been authoritatively described as "a remarkable job of translation" within which Parker's role was central.[35]

The Code's subject, Handsome Lake, had experienced the first of a series of visions in 1799, at age sixty-four, and had preached to the Iroquois about them until his death in 1815. *The Code* described how he had fallen into a catatonic state before receiving the supernatural revelations. Four celestial messengers appeared to bring him to repentance and to deliver a message for him to proclaim that revealed all forms of evil within Iroquois society. Handsome Lake was taken on a divine journey, a kind of Pilgrim's Progress, where he was led by a guide dressed in sky-blue clothes. On "The Journey over the Great Sky-road," he met none other than George Washington, a figure generally well thought of by the Iroquois because he had "allowed" them to retain their land after the Revolution. After seeing Washington occupying a privileged supernatural residence near the new world of the "Creator," Handsome Lake was given a tour of the infernal world of a devil-like figure, complete with horns, tail, and cloven hoof, named Ganos'ge', the "punisher." The fiery world of Ganos'ge' was peopled with unrepentant Indian sinners suffering ironic punishments for their sins. After traveling, like Dante in the *Inferno*, through this underworld,

Handsome Lake visited "heaven" where he found "delicious looking fruits" and "beautiful things . . . on every hand."

These experiences caused him to describe four "words" that told "a great story of wrong" and summarized the practices that made the Creator sad and angry. These involved whiskey, witchcraft, love magic, abortion, and sterility medicine. Alcohol, Handsome Lake proclaimed, was a tool of the Evil Spirit, as were its associated vices: insanity, nudity, vandalism, laziness, depopulation, murder, and accidental death. He made further injunctions against wife-beating, quarreling in marriage, sexual promiscuity, fiddle playing and card playing, failure to keep promises, failure to repent, and lack of belief in the "Good Message" itself. He admonished gossip, vanity, and pride while advocating filial obedience. Significantly, Handsome Lake also required a redefinition of the Iroquois attitude toward their ancestors. A ban was placed on traditional medicine societies and totem worship because the worship of individual animal spirits displeased the Creator and provided an opportunity for illicit drinking. The remaining older dances and rituals still deemed appropriate were carefully stipulated. The Iroquois ancestors, it was explained, had no bearing on the Creator's precepts. Unlike comparable Indian faiths, such as the essentially restorative Ghost Dance, the ancestors were vaguely placed, not in heaven, but elsewhere "in a place separate and unknown to us, we think, enjoying themselves."[36] After the record of Handsome Lake's visions, *The Code*'s main section concluded with a description of the circumstances of his death at Onondaga.

Alongside the Cornplanter version, Parker reprinted two articles he had published previously, together with his field notes on funeral rites, ceremonies, and legends. A discussion of Iroquois sun myths was included together with "Secret Medicine Societies of the Seneca," describing the fraternities that had gone underground with the growth of the Handsome Lake faith. The reprint brought his earlier work to a wider audience and reminded his readership of how, with the assistance of his wife, he had gained access to societies that the great Iroquois scholar Morgan had previously written off as lost.[37]

What was most striking about the monograph in total, however, was the absence of any analysis of the obvious way in which Handsome Lake's doctrine very closely resembled the formal millennial teaching of orthodox Christianity. After all, Handsome Lake had even made a call for essential repentance before the end of the world in 2100. From a scientific and comparative point of view, the faith was clearly an Indian appropriation of Christian teaching, given its adoption of the idea of a single omniscient Creator and the inclusion of concepts such as the soul, afterlife, sin, repentance, self-sacrifice, and heaven and hell. This last was perhaps the greatest cosmological innovation to Iroquois theology introduced by Handsome Lake, together with his stress on what were in fact white standards of morality. However, to Parker, what mattered most was that the phenomenon had served to "crystallize the Iroquois as a distinct social group" and that it had "created a revolution in Iroquois religious life." In fact, he felt that the reservations where Handsome Lake did not preach, such as Tuscarora, Oneida, and St. Regis, became somehow less Indian. By comparison, he maintained, contemporary adherents to the Handsome Lake faith lived in poverty in accordance with their religion. As a social unit, they were "at variance with the social and accepted economic systems of the white communities about them" and therefore retained more of the essence of Indian identity.

81

THE LIMITATIONS
OF PARKER'S
ANTHROPOLOGY

Parker's close relationship with his ethnographic subjects made him avoid comparative, systematic, or searching analysis of Handsome Lake. Instead, he stressed only the essentially Indian nature of the faith and maintained a romantic reverence for the habits of a people he considered to be of another time:

> The writer of this sketch has no complaint against the simple folk who have long been his friends. For a greater portion of his lifetime he has mingled with them, lived in their homes and received many honors from them. . . . There is virtue in their hearts and a sincerity and frankness that is refreshing. If only there was no engulfing "new way" and no modern rush, no need for progress, there could scarcely be a better devised system than theirs.
>
> Asked about the clothes they wear, the houses they live in, the long house they worship in, they reply, "All these things may be made of the white man's material but they are outside things. Our religion is not one of paint or feathers; it is a thing of the heart." That is the answer; it is a thing of the heart—who can change it?[38]

Parker avoided discussing the validity of the prophet's message, and the analytical comments he did provide were carefully prefaced by statements such as, "His message, whether false or true" or "Whatever may be the merits of the prophet's teachings." Similarly, he made no attempt to place Handsome Lake within the broader context of other Indian messianic movements. Neither was any reference made to the fact that the visions reflected many of the prophet's own personal concerns such as his fervent wish to beat an addiction to alcohol, his alienation from his family, and loss of his niece. Further, there was no mention of the dictatorial aspects of Handsome Lake's teaching, even though the prophet declared himself divine around 1800 and had undertaken an extensive witch hunt that led to several deaths.[39] He had also negotiated with the U.S. government so that he could own his own personal estate, the Oil Creek Reservation, and had engaged in a fair amount of political maneuvering to ensure supremacy over his main political rival, Red Jacket. However, Parker highlighted only that Handsome Lake helped define Indians as Indian within the dominant culture. Centrally, the faith was "a creation of their own," affording "a nucleus about which they could cluster themselves and fasten their hopes."[40] Parker's background and the personal relationships he formed with Handsome Lake adherents in the course of his research had made him reluctant to publish "objective" or comparative conclusions. Instead, he focused on the specificity of the Iroquois and their faith.

Research published since 1913 suggests that Handsome Lake's teachings should be viewed as an accommodative response to political and economic circumstances in the aftermath of the Revolution. They served to consolidate practices and sanctions already put forward within Iroquois society while incorporating selected white ways.[41] Handsome Lake encouraged Indian attendance at white schools and, although not opposed to profitable exchanges of land, demanded an end to extensive land cessions, prophesying doom to those who would "consent to the sale of Indian reservations" and "hardship for those who part with their lands for money or trade."[42] He envisioned an autonomous reservation community for his followers, which retained an Indian identity, rejected social evils and the white private profit motive, but which also adopted useful aspects of white culture. In essence, his teachings promised salvation through preservation of biological and cultural integrity.

There is, of course, debate over specifics. Most contemporary scholars see the Handsome Lake faith as an example of adaptive change and as a response to the breakdown in social order as a result of land fraud and military defeat. But others have suggested that this view oversimplifies the phenomenon.[43] Commentators have emphasized psychological needs (for conformity and control within a disorganized, or "irresponsible," sociocultural system), but also the idea that Handsome Lake was not so much attempting to control disorganization as to instill values consistent with the economic system introduced at the time involving the adoption of the plough and the move toward fixed agriculture.[44] All this explains why the faith's strictures encouraged a shift toward reduced individual autonomy and restraint in social affairs.[45]

The idea that the faith was in essence an accommodative response to removal and cultural disintegration is supported by the sanction the

faith received from prominent whites. In part, Handsome Lake's credibility stemmed from his correspondence with President Thomas
Jefferson. On March 10, 1802, the Senecas' "father and good friend, the
President of the United States" had his secretary of war, Henry
Dearborn, write: "Brothers—If all the red people follow the advice of
your friend and teacher, the Handsome Lake, and in future will be
sober, honest, industrious and good, there can be no doubt that the
Great Spirit will take care of you and make you happy."[46] Such correspondence was treasured and displayed by the Seneca and was "of
supreme importance to Handsome Lake and to his followers, for it
proved the sanction of his mission by the highest authorities of the
land."[47] A copy of the president's commendations was held by all the
chiefs of the Six Nations and was taken at the time as virtually a license
to teach and minister the new faith. The faith must therefore ultimately
be considered "an aid in the accommodation of the Iroquois Indian
peoples to life as a dominated minority."[48]

Although all the limitations of Parker's analysis were spelled out in
review, the response overall was commendatory. Alanson B. Skinner
for the *American Anthropologist* described it as "a translation of one of
the most remarkable documents of modern Indian propaganda."
Unlike Parker, he was at pains to point out the structural similarities of
the Handsome Lake faith to other Indian religions and to highlight
missionary influence on its form:

> One point which Mr. Parker does not mention is this: Almost
> since our first contact with the Indians of North America there
> has been a constant succession of Messianic or revealed religions
> outcropping sporadically among all the tribes south of the
> Canadian line. That of Tenskwatawa and Handsome Lake in the
> East, and the Dream Dance, Ghost Dance and Peyote, in the west,
> being perhaps the best known. In almost every one of these the
> half-digested teachings of the missionary have been apparent.
> The white man's theory of morality and justice, if rarely seen in
> practice, was highly appreciated by the Indian, and the idea of a
> revealed religion was nothing new to him.

Skinner specifically compared the Handsome Lake religion to the then
especially contentious peyote faith: "The Peyote teachings have been
far more prosperous and popular than the Code of Handsome Lake,
having spread like wild-fire over many of the tribes of the West, and are
now working eastward and northward, while that of Handsome Lake
has always been confined to the Iroquois." He went on to compare
Handsome Lake to his contemporary Tenskwatawa (The Prophet), the

Shawnee leader and twin brother to the Indian nationalist Tecumseh. Like Handsome Lake, Tenskwatawa believed he had a divine mission, but unlike the Seneca prophet, he had preached war and hatred against whites and advocated a return to ancient customs and traditions. He had promised immunity to Indians in battle against whites after the fashion of Wovoka, the prophet of the Ghost Dance religion.

Skinner made clear that "the Code is preeminently one of submission to the inevitable, and it is remarkable that it was endorsed by some of those same white officials of high authority who ordered the troops to advance against Tecumseh and Tenskwatawa." In conclusion, he very appropriately praised Parker's achievement in gathering the text's material: "Only an intimate knowledge of the people, combined with tact and genuine sympathy for their viewpoint, can bring it out. It is not to be bought for money alone." Even so, he added, "the reader may feel disappointed that Mr. Parker has given us none of his own conclusions on the subjects which he presented, since, from his intimate knowledge of the Iroquois, and particularly of the Seneca, he is well qualified to do so." He then tempered his remarks with, "The writer, however, through his personal acquaintance with Mr. Parker, realizes the many difficulties which surrounded and hampered the publication of this paper."[49]

$\cdot \quad \cdot \quad \cdot$

If Parker's first two major anthropological studies largely escaped damaging criticism, this was not to be the case with *The Constitution of the Five Nations,* published in 1916. It consisted of a series of documents describing the Deganawida and Hiawatha legends on the founding of the ancient Iroquois Confederacy—essentially attempts to codify custom law hitherto transmitted orally. Parker took a much stronger editorial role in this text's production than with the previous two, and he made a series of specific claims about the material. Once again he presented his work as a development of Morgan's, noting that although both Morgan and Hale knew of an Iroquois constitution, "neither seems to have been able to make a transcript and translation of it." But all this was secondary to his desire to present the Iroquois as a special, superior group with a proto-American constitutional governing structure, which had allowed them to successfully absorb other tribes and ensure survival of their unique identity.

The Iroquois had devised a governmental system "almost ideal . . . for the stage of culture with which it was designed to cope," he argued, "the greatest ever devised by barbaric man on any continent." Their civic structure had brought peace and "political coherence." The intertribal unity bred by their "constitution" and their leadership by a government of noble "'lords' or civil chiefs," with an associate membership of "men of worth," had ensured that they became "the dominant native power east of the Mississippi." They had been superior and advanced in relation to other American Indians and all "barbaric men." Thus the Iroquois Five Nations had called themselves "Ongweoweh, Original Men, a term that implied their racial superiority." In tangled prose, Parker described how their "constitution" had "produced leaders and finally the great lawgiver who should bring about peace and unity and make the Iroquois the 'Indians of Indian,' the 'Romans of the New World.'" Adoption and absorption of other tribes had meant they "became an ethnic group of composite elements."

As well as being ancient practitioners of a sort of Indian melting pot, the Iroquois had a "constitution," it seems, that incorporated much of the reform ethos of the Progressive period. The Iroquois war chief had been "a sort of aboriginal public service commissioner who had authority to voice their will before the council." Also, the constitutional structure had allowed for a kind of associate membership within the governing council, so that "men of worth who had won their way into the hearts of the people were elected pine tree chiefs with voice but no vote in the governing body." With all this in mind, Parker was able to conclude: "Here, then, we find the right of popular nomination, the right of recall and of woman suffrage, all flourishing in the old America of the Red Man and centuries before it became the clamor of the new America of the white invader. Who now shall call Indians and Iroquois savages!" Because of the "constitution" and the heroes it produced, both Iroquois numbers and identity had been preserved across time.[50]

Such grand claims led to close scrutiny of the provenance of the two principal manuscripts. Parker claimed to have "found" the material for the first around 1911 at the Six Nations Reserve at Grand River, Ontario, after meeting a native scribe named Seth Newhouse and finding ancient rites and ceremonies practiced there as if the Iroquois League still operated.[51] "This material," he explained in his introduction, "has been brought together by Seth Newhouse, a Mohawk, who has expended a large amount of time and given the subject a lengthy study. His account written in English was submitted to Albert Cusick, a New York Onondaga-Tuscarora, for review and criticism. . . . Mr. Cusick was employed for more than a month in correcting the Newhouse manuscript until he believed the form in which it is now presented fairly correct and at least as accurate as a free translation could be made."[52] Parker said little about the second manuscript other than that it had been produced by the chiefs of the Six Nations Council. He avoided mentioning that Newhouse for many years had been in conflict with them because he wanted to reform the system of hereditary chiefs. In fact, what had moved the chiefs to produce their version had been dissatisfaction with the one produced by Newhouse.[53]

This failure to adequately contextualize sources earned the particular ire of fellow ethnologist of the Iroquois J. N. B. Hewitt of the Bureau of American Ethnology at the Smithsonian. Himself of partial Tuscarora descent, Hewitt was an established and respected scholar, working on the Six Nations Reserve, who had already rejected some of the sources Parker brought together and edited. His review critique of *The Constitution* carried in the *American Anthropologist* held very little back. It stressed the text's "untrustworthy character" and bemoaned Parker's failure "to point out the value of either manuscript, or to explain the serious conflict of statements of essential facts or events between the two." The reader "should have been told the essential fact that the document prepared by the Committee of Chiefs of the Six Nations was prepared as a substitute for the Newhouse document, which the chiefs had thrice rejected as faulty in arrangement and erroneous or spurious in many of its statements." Hewitt also attacked Parker for claiming that he had "discovered" both manuscripts in 1910, given that they had both been known to ethnologists like himself since 1880 and 1900.[54]

Furthermore, the chiefs' version had already been published in 1912 by Duncan Campbell Scott through the Royal Society of Canada, something Parker never mentioned.[55] He claimed a "free translation" had been made of the Newhouse version, incorporating Mr. Cusick's corrections. Hewitt found this "contrary to the facts," since every version of the Newhouse manuscript "were one and all originally recorded in the English language making the concept of a 'free translation' redundant." As if this were not enough, Hewitt pursued various "serious blunders in translation and statement" and highlighted a conspicuous lack of evidence for "any notion of peculiar 'originality' of descent or of 'superiority' of race" among the Iroquois. His review concluded, savaging Parker in a tone of irritated resignation: "But to enumerate the redundancies, the contradictions, and the misconceptions in Mr. Parker's *Bulletin* would require a volume larger than the publication in question. It is most unfortunate for the cause of historical truth that great institutions insist on publication at the expense of study and accuracy. . . . I have purposely not given out this unfavorable estimate of Mr. Parker's recent work until it had been reviewed by one whose motive Mr. Parker might not question."[56]

The unbiased reviewer referred to, Alexander A. Goldenweiser, was another ethnologist acquainted with the sources in question. Like Hewitt, he attacked Parker's scholarly integrity and, if anything, was even more scathing. He began his review by dismissing the ethnographic information in Parker's appendices as "of so superficial and fragmentary a character that the printing or reprinting of it could hardly be regarded as justifiable." Next, referring to the Newhouse version as MS 1, and the manuscript compiled by chiefs of the Six Nations Council as MS 2, he noted with surprise that Parker failed to discuss the fact that MS 2 had appeared in print previously, archly surmising that, "As Mr. Scott's publication could not have escaped the notice of Mr. Parker the absence of any reference must be due to a regrettable oversight." There could be "no doubt that MS 1 reflects Iroquois society at a much later stage in its development than is the case in MS 2." The Newhouse version reflected "ancient Iroquois society distorted by abnormal social conditions and the intrusion of modern traits." It had value as "material for a study of the breakdown of a highly complex and coherent socio-political system, under the stress of modern conditions," but properly, it was not a "genuine native product." In his opinion, it was "a figment." Native material had been "welded into a highly formal and rationalized document, the product of a sophisticated mind," and, as such, it was "conspicuously un-Indian in character."

Although Goldenweiser's implication that what is Indian cannot also be formal or sophisticated is obviously spurious, his larger points concerning Parker's scholarship cannot be ignored. Parker had represented the second, Council of Chiefs' document as though he had himself "discovered" it; he had presented the Newhouse manuscript in a way that, although not altogether a lie, was not true either. It rehistoricized the Iroquois as reform-oriented democrats and created a "Constitution" when, in Goldenweiser's view, "apart from the legend of Deganawidah, the Indians of the Iroquois League had no constitution, either written or unwritten."[57]

Of course, Parker fought back in print, writing a trenchant reply to both critics for the *American Anthropologist*. He began by thanking Hewitt for pointing out "both the faults of the native authorities who supplied my information and the errors in editing." This was hardly the case. Hewitt's primary criticism had centered on Parker's use and presentation of material, not the material itself. Parker seemed offended that any scholarly criticism should have appeared at all, writing, "In the light of the conditions under which the bulletin under discussion was presented, a compilation of native documents, criticism seems gratuitous." He continued: "Especially significant is Mr. Hewitt's attempt to controvert [*sic*] my statement of Mr. Cusick's help. One would almost suspect this to be designed to impute a falsehood, but in the light of Mr. Cusick's assistance, this imputation would seem to fall little short of maliciousness through probably not so intended." Clearly ruffled, he tried to explain his claim to having made a "free translation" with the lofty remark, "no presentation in English can gracefully and fluently express the Iroquoian idiom." He continued: "The lack of accuracy, consistency and forethought on the part of the authors of the manuscripts is to be deplored but even though these Indian annalists wrote clumsily it did not occur to me that of my own initiative I should alter their writings, even for the sake of presenting them as I personally desired to see them."[58]

He misunderstood or avoided the thrust of Goldenweiser and Hewitt's criticisms throughout. Rather than address accusations that he was a poor scholar who had misrepresented ethnographic material, he belabored the fact that the manuscripts were written in the best English his sources could achieve. Instead of reevaluating his approach, he insisted that "we do not believe that in presenting the Indian manuscripts, we should eliminate their crudity and naiveté from consideration, even to satisfy those who possess other versions of these Iroquois codes and legends." Even this was a gloss on the exact nature of his editorial input in the production of Newhouse's manuscript, since he had written to Newhouse in 1911 after receiving the manuscript, informing him that he had "made a codified version of the Constitution for comparative purposes and placed similar articles together regardless of the original form." He had, in fact, changed the language "just as a barrister would do" to make the style conform to "the Regents editing system" so that, he told Newhouse, "our readers may understand." Nevertheless, he assured him, the overall meaning remained unchanged.[59]

His formal reply attacked Hewitt as someone who "has had a large influence in directing the minds of his informants," accusing him of having written the introduction to the chiefs' version and sarcastically challenging him to produce his own record of the constitution. In conclusion, Parker distanced himself from both manuscripts, stating that "they do not necessarily represent what the present writer thinks accurate in detail or satisfactory," although this was exactly how he had presented them. As a finishing touch, he included, without irony, a quotation from Kipling: "There are nine and sixty ways of constructing tribal lays, And—every—single—one—of—them—is—right."[60]

Several points should be made to mitigate the accusations of Parker's critics. Although Hewitt referred to Parker, after *The Constitution* was published, as "a dear friend of mine," their relationship was not always entirely genial.[61] They had clashed over certain Indian reform issues, and Hewitt must have been irked because in publishing the manuscripts at the time and in the way he did, Parker had stolen his fire. Hewitt had been laboriously attempting for some time to get Newhouse to write in the original Mohawk and had been "badly scooped" by Parker.[62] His opinion of Parker would not mellow over time. Almost twenty years later, he would rail that "among the worst offenders among the Indians in general who dislike to admit that they do not know certain facts in the past experience of their people are the half-educated mixed bloods, who do not hesitate to spew out all manner of stupid guesses as alleged matters of fact." Parker was a key figure in this group, and *The Constitution* "a very storehouse of misinformation and idle bombast concerning the League of the Iroquois." In his opinion, Parker had produced "rotten work."

He confessed, "I must say that Dr. Parker is a past master at window-dressing, usually banking on the fact that the average person knows so little about Indian, especially Iroquois customs and manners. But I admire Dr Parker for accomplishing what he has in awakening an interest in Iroquoian matters. My only regret is that he tries to cover too much ground, and so has to do it superficially."[63] Also in Parker's defense is the fact that at the time the manuscripts were in preparation, he was under considerable pressure to cut corners. As he later recalled:

It was the frantic work of trying to create the Indian section of the State Museum, the horrible work of trying to re-catalog the material from the Capitol fire and the single-handed effort to keep the section administered that prevented my fuller attention to field work. Coupled with this was the insistent demands of the museum editor for "copy." Thus I had to let many things slide in order to have the great halls (a total of 680 feet) ready for the opening of the building. It was a time of mid-night work and no vacations, let alone a piled up desk. Still, I like to think about it. For a long time it was a one-man effort.[64]

There is little point in weighing up whether Parker or his critics were right. Fundamentally, the controversy surrounding Parker's two manuscript sources arose from the contemporary anthropological approach to the Indian. Parker had upset his fellow anthropologists by presenting a manuscript as essentially "Indian" when it had been heavily influenced by the dominant culture. His peers required that as a professional anthropologist, he should point out that the chiefs' version was more valid and more Indian because it showed less evidence of acculturation. Anthropology held that what was authentically Indian was unable, by definition, to incorporate what was "American." Parker had given each manuscript equal validity and contravened early-twentieth-century anthropology's project to isolate specifically Indian sets of material. Quite simply, his agenda had not been that of his peers. His primary desire had been to publish and to present the Indian, specifically the Iroquois, in a good light—as progressive, enlightened, and democratic early Americans.

Negative professional responses to *The Constitution* marked the end of his production of significant, primarily anthropological texts. His "Indianness" and concern to advance Iroquois culture had conflicted with the scientific and "objective" approach required by the discipline. But even if Parker had his fingers burned through his forays into anthropology, museum work overall still brought him a measure of success. It allowed him to prove himself a useful mediator between the Indian past and the economy of the museum, and his commitment to innovation and to public education was beginning to impress his peers within the white museum world. He had also developed his reputation as a publishing archaeologist, having, in 1916, organized the New York State Archeological Association and won an award for his research in Iroquoian ethnology, the Cornplanter Medal of the Cayuga County Historical Society.

Even though his anthropology had not brought him unreserved success, the fulfillment of childhood dreams still seemed eminently possible. In 1916 he was thirty-five. Since 1911 he had been getting more and more involved with a cross-tribal reform group. They were his Indian peers, a newly emergent, educated middle class keen to advance themselves and their people. He had taken up their reform banner just as his period of anthropological study in the field came to an end. Perhaps it seemed like a forum for the family talent for statesmanship and leadership to blossom in the twentieth century, as it had in past decades and centuries. It was certainly a broader platform from which to shine, and it offered the chance for resolution of some of the conflicts surrounding his choice to live and work as an assimilated Indian American. His engagement with the group, from its earliest beginnings, was heartfelt and profoundly sincere, but it probably brought him one of the greatest disappointments of his life.

A Leadership Role within the Society of American Indians, 1911–1920s

The Society of American Indians (SAI), a cross-tribal group that pushed for national Indian reform, was created on the tide of progressive feeling sweeping through American politics during the early decades of the twentieth century. Minority leadership seemed to have a golden opportunity to initiate and direct change in government policy. The moment seemed ripe for a broadening of popular understanding of Indian capabilities and potential. All this prompted Parker to become committed to this organization of primarily middle-class, educated Indians. He gave an inordinate amount of his attention and effort, becoming the organization's central supporting force, and eventually its president. His solid hands-on involvement persisted for about seven years, although he was also sometimes intensely involved from the group's inception in 1910 until well after it began to disintegrate during the early 1920s. Even after his ignominious departure in 1918, he always maintained that the group was a historic fraternity of the utmost significance to the development of the country's Indian peoples. Yet engagement with the SAI's affairs brought about an irreversible philosophical transformation, both in Parker's understanding of the character and potential of other Indians and in his self-identification in relation to the dominant culture.

The story behind Parker's journey, from firm believer in the SAI's potential to improve national Indian life to disgruntled and angry critic of the very idea of a viable intertribal consensus, tells us much about the limitations affecting America's new, educated Indian middle class during that time. Parker's gradual disillusionment with the vision of a modern, proud, and unified Indian elite spearheading full integration within the dominant culture was a sorry indicator of the failure of the inclusive dream at the core of American rhetoric.

• • •

The SAI was a unique manifestation of the political optimism of the time, and part of a tradition of intertribal unity and action. It was the most significant organized group based on an assumed common Indian interest and identity, with an agenda comparable to that of other groups already formed to further "race" interests, such as the National Association for the Advancement of Colored People (NAACP). The NAACP had been helped into being in 1909 by W. E. B. DuBois, the distinguished professor of sociology and history at Atlanta University. Like the SAI, the NAACP campaigned for legal and political recognition of its people and spread the word through its own journal. No doubt reform solidarity was what made DuBois venture to become an early associate SAI member, even though most of the leadership, including Parker, had expressed anti-black sentiments. The SAI drew on the legacy of Joseph Brant (Thayendanega), who had tried in the 1780s to unite the Indian nations of the Northwest in an "all of one mind–one heart" political and military confederacy. It also invoked Tecumseh, the leader of cross-tribal resistance to Anglo-American encroachment of the early nineteenth century. This history of effective indigenous action added credibility to the organization's quest to serve as the modern, united Indian representative body. It was able to develop alongside the religious intertribalism of the peyote faith and the Native American Church, which still endure today, but eventually it would be completely eclipsed by the city-based fraternal intertribalism that crystallized during the 1920s.

A specifically Indian identity made the SAI unique among the other bodies with a voice within Indian reform debates. Unlike existing defense organizations, such as the Indian Rights Association (IRA) and the Lake Mohonk Conference of the Friends of the Indian, it placed a definite value on and had a definite pride in an Indian heritage. It enjoyed strong white support, but was run by Indians.[1] It voiced Indian demands for reform, defined Indian responsibility for change, and articulated the conditions it alone considered necessary for full Indian integration. As one society publication put it, it was an association "of Indians, by Indians, and for Indians." That said, the SAI was always a complement to the non-Indian Indian reform organizations. After all, it shared their basic agenda: final detribalization and the individual absorption of Indians into American society as patriotic citizens.[2]

"Supposition and Reality," Society of American Indians cartoon, 1916.

Personal Papers of Arthur Caswell Parker, in author's posession

Core SAI leadership was always small in number, and when the group first came together, Parker, at twenty-nine, was almost the youngest. Certainly he was not the best known. Among its educated, established professionals from the law, medicine, the church, government, and education were national figures—men like Dr. Charles A. Eastman, the prominent physician, lecturer, and author, and Dr. Carlos Montezuma, perhaps at the time the most recognized Indian in the country.

Eastman and Montezuma had their own ideas about the best way forward for their people. Eastman, although he became president in 1919, was for most of the SAI's active years ambivalent about its agenda

INDIANS OF NEW YORK
YOU MUST REGISTER
As Required by the Provost Marshal General of the United States

In order that the loyalty of every Indian may be a matter of record the Questionnaire issued by the Provost Marshal General of the United States through the Draft Boards must be filled out by non-citizen Indians, as well as citizens and aliens.

Registration by non-citizen Indians does not mean that they will be drafted without their consent. Deferred classification or exemption may be claimed by them if they so desire. Voluntary enlistment of non-citizen Indians is welcomed, but a registered non-citizen Indian asserting his status will not be inducted into military duty.

Disloyal persons, whether citizen, alien or Indian, occupy a dangerous position and one contrary to the interests of the United States Government and its War Policy.

REGISTER NOW AS REQUIRED AND AVOID FUTURE CONSEQUENCES

The Adjutant General has especially provided for the registration of non-citizen Indians from this section, on   Any day up to and including

Date ___SEPTEMBER 12, 1918 Hours___ 7 A.M. to 9 P.M.

LOCAL BOARD OFFICE

Place ___

FAILURE TO REGISTER VIOLATES THE PLEDGES OF PEACE AND FRIENDSHIP MADE IN TREATIES BETWEEN THE SIX NATIONS AND THE UNITED STATES AND WILL BRING ALL THE PENALTIES PROVIDED BY LAW

Registration is a Record of Loyalty

CONSULT YOUR LOCAL BOARD

THE INDIAN AGENT OR REGSTRAR

OR SPECIAL ADVISORS

JULIUS HERNE AND

LOUIS BRUCE

This applies to males from 18 to 46 years old

"Indians of New York You Must Register," September 12, 1918, Regis Reservation, New York draft registration poster.

Personal Papers of Arthur Caswell Parker, in author's possession

and functioning. Montezuma, by comparison, got more actively engaged but became probably its strongest and most penetrating internal critic. This was largely because "Monty" (or to use his native name, "Wassaja") had listened carefully to General Richard Henry Pratt while enrolled at the Carlisle Indian School, Pennsylvania. This made him an advocate of instant assimilation, an ardent individualist, and a vociferous campaigner for the abolition of the Bureau of Indian Affairs (BIA). Pratt was a blunt and doctrinaire achiever, who founded Carlisle and the Indian Department at the Hampton Institute in Virginia. His slogan was "Kill the Indian and save the man!" and his impact on SAI affairs, although not obvious, was significant. An example was the correspondence he kept up with Parker, with whom he shared a mutual appreciation. Pratt once called him "the highest product of my idea," but Parker had a much broader understanding of the political complexities surrounding Indian matters than either Montezuma or his mentor.[3]

Given Pratt's antipathy to all forms of paternalism, it is not surprising that the then most powerful Indian executive within the BIA, Supervisor of Employment Charles E. Daganett, became the subject of Montezuma's ire. Daganett was in good company, since Montezuma also quarreled publicly with the Reverend Sherman Coolidge, the moderate and equable Episcopal minister whose SAI association was the most enduring. Yet another notable SAI moderate and minister was the young Presbyterian Henry Roe Cloud. A Yale graduate, his main concern was Indian education and, along with Parker, opposing the peyote faith. By contrast, the two Indian lawyers involved, Thomas L. Sloan and Hiram Chase, were firm advocates of peyote. Overall, the key voices were highly diverse, and each had an individual approach to the need to generate change.

Although the leadership, and Parker in particular, made an issue out of establishing the degree of Indian descent within the membership, perhaps a majority were themselves of mixed ancestry. In fact, many occupied as ambiguous a position in relation to their respective nations as Parker did. He may not have been aware of this initially, since he apologized about the caliber of his "Indian" credentials in an early letter to Elaine Goodale Eastman. She was the wife of the physician Charles Eastman, who called himself a "full-blooded" Sioux. When she asked for Parker's photograph and "native name, if any, proportion of Indian blood, where graduated, and any other facts of interest" to help illustrate "Indians of distinction" at the Universal Races Congress in London, he replied: "If I can find a suitable photograph, I shall be glad to send you one, though perhaps it may be best not to use it. At heart I am very much an Indian though in reality I am but a 'quarter blood.'... Possibly I talk, think and write Indian so much and allow my 'full-blooded' Indian heart to beat so strongly at times that the public gets the impression that I am more of an Indian by blood than a view of my ancestral tree will warrant." He concluded,

"After these confessions if you still wish the photograph you may have it."[4] He made no mention of his Indian name, "Gáwasowaneh," which he often used in private personal correspondence, and so avoided discussing his Seneca adoption.

The issue of "Indian blood" concerned him at this time. Without referring to his own descent, he discussed "half-breeds" at some length in the article "Albanian Working for Betterment of Indians; State Archaeologist Parker Tells of the Aims of the Society of Which He Is Secretary-Treasurer," printed soon after the first flurry of SAI activity during June 1911.[5] He said that the SAI was a vehicle to express "the thoughts and ideals of the race," requiring "a large membership of white Americans to stand as staunch supporters." He decried prejudice against Indian "mixed bloods" and complained about the way the "movie half-breed is always presented as a moral degenerate." Rather than blood quantum, "individual competence . . . should count in determining civic or social status."

But whatever he argued in newspaper copy, an explicit Indian identity was very important to what Parker understood the SAI to be about. It pleased him that the name was unmistakably Indian and that, like Indian assimilation itself, membership had an individual rather than tribal basis. It mattered to him that active members were supposed to be "persons of Indian blood only." In fact, the membership hierarchy divided into three: active, Indian associate, and associate. Actives could vote and hold office, were of "Indian blood," and resident in the United States; Indian associates were from other parts of the Americas and could vote only on issues related to their own tribal interests. When agreement was finally reached on a constitution during 1912, there were also "juniors" of "Indian blood" under age twenty-one and "honorary members." Full active membership was available solely to U.S. Indians on tribal rolls and to any Indian with more than one-sixteenth "Indian blood." The constitution made clear that the conference floor was for "active members and for authorized tribal delegates of Indian blood." Others were to speak only "on motion" or at special events, a stipulation Parker insisted on at least once.

In one sense, the SAI's careful categorizing was of little overall consequence, since the society would claim to represent a constituency its membership could never adequately encompass. At first, there was talk that the SAI could become a "representative government," but it became clear that a representative intertribal confederation was an impossibility at that time.[6] The SAI was "pan-Indian" only in the sense that it expressed an aspiration for, and the notion of, the political union of all Indians. What really united the group at the outset was an educational history within the Indian boarding schools of the East rather than any specific project to represent the concerns of the majority of Indian peoples, however defined. Their concern to foreground the idea of an intertribal Indian "race" was a symptom of the social evolutionary thinking characteristic of that background. Behind it lay the notion of "racial" progression through successive evolutionary stages toward "civilization," something made clear in the SAI's "objects" as an organisation.[7] As a consequence, like Parker, the SAI always valued the Indian past. However, it could never fully resolve the distinction between Indian tribal identity, some kind of pan-Indian "race consciousness," and how that identity might operate within the dominant culture.

Activity began in earnest in June 1911 after letters were sent out to "Persons of Indian Blood" from the "Temporary Executive Committee."[8] They had first come together that April at the behest of Professor Fayette A. McKenzie of Ohio State University, a non-Indian, progressive Christian reformer, educationalist, and sociologist. An idealist and civic reformer who sought to ease the process of "race transformation" from the tribal and less evolved to the civilized and Christian, McKenzie advocated clarification of Indian legal status, Indian education at all levels, and the establishment of self-supporting reservation industrial settlements. Parker was tied up sorting out the debris from the exhibits damaged in the fire in Albany's capitol building and couldn't attend the first meeting. Yet after the group created its pledge requiring members "to discourage and oppose all backward tendencies," he was the first person they thought of for the permanent committee.[9]

Happy to be called on, he readily took up the whole idea behind what was then called the American Indian Association. Almost immediately he began to put both effort and flair into its promotion. By September, he was able to report to Daganett that he had been publicizing the first conference, scheduled for October 12–15, 1911, in Columbus, Ohio; that he had "stirred up my people the Senecas" about it all; and that he had secured the interest of some of his "influential friends among the whites."[10]

As an ex-newspaper man, he knew how to get good copy and may well have been the source for the *New York Tribune* article entitled "Looking for an Indian Booker T. Washington to Lead Their People," which appeared around this time. It bemoaned the fact that "the reservation does not offer the opportunity for the use of that education that is to be found by the white man," and gave career synopses of those involved with the SAI's inception. Listing Thomas Sloan as an Indian congressional committee representative; the Reverend Frank Wright, preacher; Montezuma, instructor in the College of Physicians and

Surgeons, Chicago; Laura Cornelius, scholar and social worker; and the ethnologist Francis LaFlesche, it highlighted the "great powwow" they planned for Columbus to "discuss race needs and point the way to race progress."[11]

Parker very much wanted to be involved, although, as he said himself, there were "heavy demands" on his time. The fire had created a mass of work; he had his fieldwork on the Handsome Lake faith to write up; he was struggling to supplement his meager State Museum salary through lecturing; and he was busy dictating and signing several hundred State Museum letters a day from his office in Albany. Worst of all, his wife was once again "seriously ill." Still, he was determined not to miss the founding conference. He sensed that this was another pivotal juncture in Indian history, and whether or not influence or a leadership role beckoned, he very much wanted to add his voice and effort to the struggle. He could not hide his enthusiasm when he wrote to Keppler: "The Indian convention comes off in October and I am making great efforts to go. It is there our people are speaking for themselves. Manitou help us."[12]

The fact that there was now an Indian-run force for change excited Parker. In comparison, the other existent reform bodies served simply as adjuncts to the BIA or as religious or philanthropic agencies. The Lake Mohonk Conference of the Friends of the Indian was the forum for one such group. Participants met each autumn at the resort hotel in New York State at the expense of the Quaker Albert K. Smiley. He was on the U.S. Board of Indian Commissioners, a group of religious philanthropists who had first been authorized in 1869 to oversee, jointly with the secretary of the interior, the disbursement of Indian appropriations. They operated as an apolitical committee supervising Indian policy, and met in conjunction with the Mohonkists. Parker expected little from the commissioners and considered the Mohonkists ineffectual and exclusive. However, as his SAI involvement deepened, he would feel the need to court their support, even though his first instinct was always to promote Indian leadership and Indian input into policy development.

Somehow, in the run-up to the inaugural conference, he found time to pen the lengthy paper with which he opened its Friday afternoon session, "Educational Problems." Parker conceded that in 1492 the "so-called civilization of the whites was a distinct advance" and recommended the establishment of reservation "social betterment stations" in order to speed up Indian development. This was already old-style progressive welfare. As the elite of their race, the SAI wanted to foster the kind of Euro-American values they espoused. A practical application of the idea would eventually come about with SAI support in 1915 at a community center in Fort Duchesne, Utah. Its limited duration and influence would be symptomatic of the gap between the SAI's aspirations and its true ability to improve Indian conditions.

Overall, Parker's paper was a firm statement of his commitment to education as the path to Indian acculturation and elevation. This did not mean that Indians should lose all of their heritage. Education should not "make the Indian a white man, but simply a man normal to his environment." Like the immigrant, he had to assimilate, to learn "the necessary things of hygiene and industry," but at the same time he should retain something of what was best about his traditional culture. Citing Franz Boas, Parker said Indians had equal capacity for advancement when placed in a favorable environment, but the problem was that once advanced, the educated Indian was left isolated: "Progress cannot be made any faster than the majority or their ruling element are willing to make it. He who is in advance is alone, unprotected and despised." Even so, a developing Indian acceptance of education was, in his opinion, currently opening a window of hope.[13]

His paper successfully set the tone of race confidence and uplift through education that would characterize so much of the SAI's rhetoric as the decade progressed. His influence would keep educational issues at the fore and give the organization many of the trappings of a learned body, including an edited journal and published conference papers. He would favor academic settings for conferences, as he put it, "in order that our people may never lose sight of the fact that their salvation lies largely in obtaining higher education."[14] Educational, rather than, say, economic reform was always easy for SAI delegates to talk about.

The SAI committed itself to Indian citizenship, revealing both optimism and political naïveté. Despite its support, when a bill similar to its resolution was eventually put to the House of Representatives by the Indian Congressman Charles D. Carter on January 19, 1912, calling for a presidential commission of three men to review the legal status of the Indian, it had no significant impact. It would take until 1924 before a significant number of Indians had the right to vote, and even then those who did remained reticent or unprepared to for fear of losing their property rights.

But the SAI did achieve some notable public triumphs at the conference that could only have served to broaden popular understanding of Indian potential and patriotism. Held on the Ohio State University campus and at the Hartman Hotel, the whole style and tone of the event put Indians forward as individuals eminently ready for civic responsibility. Local people were given a chance to engage with the new kind of progressive Indian at the two fund-raiser talent concerts organized at the Memorial Hall, one of which reportedly attracted an audience "of about 600."[15]

The SAI also received a warm welcome from local dignitaries and from representatives of the more established bodies within Indian affairs. The local mayor, secretary of the chamber of commerce, and state university president all delivered addresses, as did then Commissioner of Indian Affairs, the Honorable Robert G. Valentine. Representatives from churches, the Indian Rights Association (IRA), and the Improved Order of Red Men (IORM) attended, with the latter hosting a dinner for nearly one hundred conference delegates at the Ohio Union. This was an especially patriotic event. The SAI emblem was a prehistoric thunderbird that greatly resembled the American eagle; each diner left with his or her own small silk U.S. flag; and the Ohio Daughters of Pocahontas took an automobile ride to a prehistoric mound, where they gave a rendition of "America the Beautiful."[16]

The IORM's dinner was probably the highlight of the inaugural conference, but in fact the two "Indian" groups had very little in common. The Red Men composed a "secret" fraternity formed in the 1830s, which, contrary to its title, was solely for "palefaces"—"white males 21 years or older of good character."[17] Concerned with the Indian only as a symbol of revolutionary patriotism, they excluded genuine "red" men. They had no qualms about denying membership to the SAI's first president, Sherman Coolidge, when he tried to join later in the 1920s. With their "Indian" costumes and rituals, the IORM wanted only to memorialize the ways of a people they considered "vanishing." The SAI, by comparison, was firmly wedded to the notion of a non-vanishing Indian race.[18]

Altogether, the first conference filled Parker with a sense of occasion and convinced him that the SAI could make a powerful long-term impact. He ended up staying at Columbus for two days longer than intended and came away satisfied about his inclusion at the heart of organization's affairs. He was elected to the executive committee, which gave itself the task of monitoring Indian legislation and communicating with the BIA "for the welfare of the Indians to the best of their ability."[19] For at least a year afterward he routinely referred to Columbus as "an epoch making event," and he made much of its symbolic significance to Keppler: "How proud I was to be in such company," he wrote. "Headquarters were at the most exclusive hotel in the city, and every Indian had money to burn and used it as cultured people would.

Columbus was discovered this time by the Indians and the town was surprised."[20]

But in truth, he was well aware of trouble brewing internally from the outset. Even though there had been much talk of a "new day in Indian affairs," attendance, at around fifty, was deemed to have been small, and there was talk of trying again in July or August.[21] There was also widespread internal dissent over the U.S. government and its potential power to control the group. According to one local press write-up, "The discussions were heated and showed much resentment on the part of the majority over the alleged ill-treatment of the red man."[22] There were even arguments over whether a permanent organization should be formed at all. The *Sunday Dispatch* detailed delegates' claims that the government was "secretly opposed to the work of the [SAI] congress, and that it will try to elect a reactionary ticket."[23] Because Eastman and Cornelius were intent on barring all government employees from officeholding, no consensus was reached about a constitution.[24] When Daganett was elected as secretary-treasurer, Cornelius threatened to withdraw from the committee completely.

Parker wrote to Fayette McKenzie immediately after returning to Albany: "I am not quite satisfied with the outcome of the Columbus meeting, nor do I yet quite comprehend the various motives which actuated some of our members." Parker summed it up ruefully to Daganett: "Our members at the conference seemed to have many views, many plans and all come to no plan." He would always be more aware of the dangers of factionalism than most of his committee peers, and he would always be pushing for joint action and sustained unity of purpose. In time he took on a clear role as arbiter and peacemaker. He was prepared to do so because he felt this was a golden chance for Indians to function politically as a "race" rather than as members of tribal groupings.[25]

Parker knew his enthusiasm for the SAI could alienate him from his own people, those who had to date been central to his research and professional development. He told Rosa B. LaFlesche:

Like you I occupy a peculiar position among my own tribe. My father is a citizen and a leader in great movements for patriotic work near N.Y. City. I am a citizen and without any tribal interests. In working for Indian betterment I expect no profit from it. I can only incur criticism, suspicion and unjust remarks. The Senecas of a certain class will think that I am working to make citizens of them and this they have protested for 60 years. They wish to remain as they are, and today the percentage of adult illiteracy in New York among the Indians is greater than in

Oklahoma. In a movement of this kind I am injuring myself in a field which must be my life's work. Someone must sacrifice however before any good can ever be done.[26]

It was heartfelt, but also very much the rhetoric of the time, invoking both the public service ideal and romantic individualism. In the words of better-known WASP reformer Jane Addams, Parker had fully adopted the "social ethic." His SAI letters and writings were grounded in the newly popular belief that all individuals were capable of remaking both themselves and their culture. Like so many others involved in the bureaucratization and professionalization processes of the Progressive years, he was claiming a moral benefit to his activities and those of his group.

Unfortunately, the rest of the membership did not quite share his commitment to service and sacrifice, and he heard complaints from each of the SAI factions as they developed. By early December, he was able to subdivide complainants into two overall classes: those who suspected government infiltration, and those who fretted over SAI sympathy toward the mescal-peyote element. Parker generally tempered his remarks about the government and came out against peyote only if pressed. He considered the drug's sole commendation to be that it cured alcohol dependence, but he avoided becoming vehement in his opposition to it lest he fuel the factionalism he so dreaded. "I can only make the plea for internal harmony," he would say, "as the means of inspiring external confidence."[27]

Since he heard every complaint, he told Daganett that two members in particular, Eastman and Cornelius, wanted Daganett to resign, and that someone had suggested that he, Parker, could take his place.[28] Soon after, when he wrote to McKenzie for advice on how to improve his "amateurish" methods in dealing with the politicians he needed on side to press for Indian bills, he brought the matter up once again. Before long, he was selected as the compromise candidate to replace Daganett when SAI headquarters opened in Washington, D.C., in January 1912.[29] He threw himself into what he saw as the secretary's duties with enthusiasm. He had put himself right at the center of the group through taking on the most practically powerful leadership role within it.

For his part, Parker had no overriding fear of government infiltration and every confidence in Daganett personally. However, he recognized that Daganett had to go, since the feelings of some SAI executive committee members against government employees simply echoed suspicions rife nationally on the reservations. He knew from personal experience that "a large portion, perhaps the majority, of reservation Indians tremble lest the federal agencies or bureaus get further control of them to their disadvantage."[30] An accomodationist, Parker wanted to engage with the governing system rather than turn away from it.

Very probably, he harbored hopes that he might someday become one of the three men "qualified by legal and sociological training" who, with a twenty thousand dollar budget and a secretary, were to carry out the dictates of the SAI-sponsored Carter Code Bill, should it make it through Congress. Certainly his SAI memoranda around this time urged a great push to favorably place the Carter Bill on the congressional agenda. Parker argued that without a certain legal position, "the ambitious Indian is almost compelled to be irregular in any endeavor to rise in the world," a theme he warmed to in greater depth in an article for *The Indian Leader*.[31] If only the SAI could show its deep commitment to the United States and an ability to cohere as a unified force, he was convinced, a new Indian leadership would be allowed a voice in shaping the Indian future. But even with so much at stake, he did not always find it easy to remain tolerant and calm. He felt his position was "difficult" and even though he knew it would "create more or less of a rupture," confessed, "I don't know how long I shall be able to hold it without giving my compeers the truth from the shoulder."[32]

Mulling things over in a letter to McKenzie, Parker even wondered whether a properly staffed Indian school or college might do more for the Indian than the SAI. A school, for example, could realize their shared dream of developing Indian literature. "Not necessarily the old," Parker wrote, "but also the new. The poems of Pauline Johnson, Alex Posy, the writings of Eastman, Simon Pokagon, Zitkalsa and others might be rescued from oblivion or popularized still further." He also let McKenzie know in confidence that his own "Indian improvement" work was disapproved of by Draper, his professional superior.[33]

Money was not only limiting the degree of Parker's involvement but motivating a great deal of SAI activity just then. Since the industrial barons of the late nineteenth century had already spectacularly endowed certain causes, it was not impossible that the SAI would receive a large injection of funds. After all, it had been partly the connection between Booker T. Washington and philanthropists like steel magnate Andrew Carnegie that had allowed Washington to do so much for his people and to become so personally powerful. "Wish some big man who has benefited much from this red man's America would endow us," Parker wrote to Keppler. "Am trying for it."[34]

Then, with press rumors in the air that a rival organization had been given $850,000 by Carnegie, a hurried meeting was called for January

25, 1912, to show SAI stability. A new version of the constitution was put together and a Legal Aid Division formulated. Since it was always hard to protect Indian clients from unscrupulous attorneys, the SAI stipulated that fees would be paid by their committee and were never to total more than 6 percent of the overall claim. The idea was a good one. As Parker put it in a letter to Eastman, the SAI was trying "to defeat the many schemes now afoot to still further 'bleed' Poor Lo." However, actually making Indian legal aid available was to prove problematic. From the outset, the issue of how much effort the SAI should exert on individual cases was never successfully resolved. Unsure about the option of giving up his State Museum job to work for the SAI, he told Eastman, "I only wish that someone else could have been found since I realize the peril and uncertainty that attends the giving up of a life position for one that depends upon the good will of the general public and the favor of the Society."[35]

A month into the secretary job, he was still sure that the SAI was destined for great things, but he also admitted his role had "meant so far only the sacrifice of many things of considerable importance to me." Such sacrifices had proved too much for the SAI's first administrator, who was by then leaving to return to the Indian Service. When Rosa LaFlesche left, she reminded Parker that he had a family to look after and he should not give up his Albany position before he could see money directly coming in from the SAI. Her warning should have rung alarm bells, since by February 23 he was personally responsible for three hundred dollars worth of SAI printing orders and having to write to Coolidge for a loan of seventy-five dollars to keep afloat. He told his president: "We have been devoting so much time and energy to discussing internal things that we have been letting the work of the society go to smash." Already he was feeling isolated in terms of the depth of his commitment. He told Coolidge: "I am willing to work and spend my money if I find someone else willing with me to do so for the good of the organization but I can not do so all alone nor can any one else." To McKenzie he was more forthright, telling him, "I sit chafing in my chair in restless anxiety for my collaborators to speak." Even so, outside SAI circles he stayed chipper, describing the society as "progressing splendidly in most ways."[36]

By March 5, 1912, he was anxiously sending out circulars asking for donations. He was trying to raise the three hundred dollars from the membership as a loan and was prepared to personally take care of a further two hundred dollars owed to printers. He complained in correspondence: "I am giving my time and money freely without hope of any return whatever, though I can ill afford it now, with many personal obligations pressing me. Will you help me work?" In the end he managed to get the report on the proceedings of the first conference, a particularly large document of over 185 pages, excluding plates, in press for the end of the month. It was an impressive achievement, appreciated by a membership now swollen to a hundred active and a hundred associate members, but it had cost him a lot of time and he had had to employ proofreaders, index experts, stenographers, and a clerk.[37]

The strain was beginning to tell, especially after a trip Parker made to Washington to speak before the House Indian Committee on the Indian Code Bill. When he wrote to tell McKenzie that there was no hope for it this session, he said: "I suspect a lot of political undercurrants [sic]. I did my best." It seems he had been working for eighteen hours a day for the previous two weeks. Nonetheless, in the days ahead he still found time to send out canvassing letters to "the thinking Indian." Fellow member Marie Baldwin soon heard of his new society motto: "Get a member! Then get another one." Bristling with frustration, he told her, "I should like every present member to get that humming round in his or her cerebellum and then act upon it."[38]

By April 21, SAI work had expanded to take up not only four or five hours of Parker's day but also much of the time of a special clerk brought in to help. It may be that Parker was putting in so much effort because life was difficult at home, as he alluded to McKenzie: "Sometimes intense work is the result of a desire to become completely absorbed in a certain line of thought to forget another less repellent." At least the visit he made around this time to hear Jacob Riis speak gave him some inspiration. Riis was the elderly *New York Tribune* journalist famous for his illustrated exposé *How the Other Half Lives,* which in 1889 had revealed the slum conditions of the Lower East Side. An old friend of his late great-uncle Ely, Riis would have been a stellar addition to the one thousand membership target Parker set for October 1, but he declined Parker's invitation to help.

Parker was unabashed. He joked that he had "sweat brain juice many a night keeping things going," and his financial losses were already "somewhat large for a poor anthropologist."[39] Plus, there seemed to be hope of personal advance through his SAI contacts. On June 13, he was offered a job as chief assistant supervisor under Daganett at the Indian Service in Washington at $1,400 a year, with occasional authorized field trips. He accepted of course, but the job failed to materialize and Parker continued as before.

Partly to foster unity and partly to encourage fund-raising, his next move was to begin talking up the idea of an SAI-sponsored national American Indian Day. This had the attraction of being an innovation unlikely to threaten the already fragile consensus holding the SAI together. It was symptomatic of how Parker wanted to represent the Indian to the dominant culture, since it was designed to associate the Indian with the great outdoors, invoke a glorious Indian past, and to bring together Indians and whites in patriotic celebration. He wanted Indians to be seen and treated as "an American people in America."[40] Perhaps curiously, it was to be primarily a spectacle for the benefit of non-Indians. Parker wanted the publicity generated to educate whites, reflect well on the SAI, help drum up activity, and generally excite reform spirit.

Indian Day was an acceptable alternative to the image of the "show-Indian," which had burgeoned with the success of Buffalo Bill's Wild West shows since 1883. Most educated Indians viewed these with distaste, because they presented the Indian as an unassimilated savage and because they put forward Plains tribes as the Indian model. The same problems persist today within popular entertainment, and some version of Plains costume is still the dress most easily identifiable as Indian by many non-Indians. Indian Day was at least a practical attempt to do something about this. Parker much preferred the image promoted by the 1911 SAI conference, of Indians as seemingly indistinguishable from other American middle-class professionals. He hoped an Indian "day" might educate the "Anglo-Agglomerated race," as he once described them to fellow anthropologist J. N. B. Hewitt, about Indian diversity and potential.

Indian Day was part of a more general SAI movement to alter the popular perception of Indians, including, for example, efforts to monitor and correct terms used to describe Indian peoples, especially within the BIA. Parker wrote as secretary several times to the BIA commissioner, criticizing the use of the word "squaw" by Indian school superintendents, a practice he described as "bad form." Eventually, Indian Day enjoyed sporadic observance, having its greatest impact within New York State mostly on the second Saturday in May each year.[41]

At the end of July 1912, the SAI's Washington office closed because conference headquarters were once again established at Columbus, Ohio.[42] By August, Parker was actually paying someone to do his own routine work so that he had "spare" time to devote to the SAI. He made no bones about telling Laura Kellogg (née Cornelius), "It is costing me some but I am not worrying about that either."[43] By September he was working "like the proverbial bee." In one personal letter, he said he had a clerk and two stenographers on the job, adding, "Most likely I shall swallow the bills and say nothing of this end."[44]

The hard work seemed worthwhile by the time of the second annual conference, which took place October 2–7, 1912. Parker billed the event as a "Great Council of Modern Redskins" in the *New York Times*: "Last year Columbus was taken by storm by these patriotic redskins—these university bred Americans, 'of the older families.' Did they call themselves 'the new Indian'? Not a bit of it. They proclaimed their Indian ancestry as the highest honor of which an American could boast, and said: 'We are not the new Indian: we are the same old Indian, with the same love of nature and the big open, only we have adjusted ourselves to modern environment.'" With the national reform ethos nearing its peak, the SAI's potential seemed stronger than ever. By now Dr. Montezuma was back in the fold, and there was talk of an SAI associate being considered to succeed Valentine as commissioner of Indian Affairs. This was wishful thinking, even though Valentine needed replacing given his poor policy and leadership.[45]

The hot issue at the 1912 gathering was the complex question of how to speed up the assimilative process on the reservations. Montezuma grew especially impassioned when Joseph Griffis (Tahan) asked delegates why they chose to "trail among the white people and live in the cities?" Why, he wondered, weren't they living on the reservations so as to tell their people the things they had learned? To Montezuma, reservations were prisons and instant integration with non-Indian culture was the only possible way forward. When Parker stood up to speak, he tried to move discussion beyond the ambivalent feelings stirred by this kind of talk and instead focus attention on self-help and the need to encourage change through accommodation. Rather than heated rhetoric, he wanted amelioration and constructive criticism. He told the delegates that their value did not lie in their "ability to kick"; rather, "I believe in the long run fair play and a square deal will come if the American people are once awakened, but we cannot get a square deal unless we tell them how to give it to us and then work to get it."[46] To his mind, the SAI had to cohere as an Indian body first and foremost, so as to prove Indian credentials for inclusion within the dominant culture.

He formed two fraternities at Columbus: the Loyal Order of Tecumseh, and the Descendants of the American Aborigines. The first allowed "associate" SAI members of less than one-sixteenth Indian "blood" and "active" SAI members to socialize and perform ritual. The two groups mixed Indian adoption, which Parker had already used to charm museum superiors, and fraternalism, which a developing Freemasonic involvement had taught him was a powerful vehicle for group activity. The two fraternities were also in keeping with the wider

SAI aim of redefining "Indianness," a way of capitalizing on Indian identity as a noble and patriotic "inner quality."

Parker was so convinced of the attractiveness of some kind of Indian ancestral connection that he wrote the next year to W. E. B. DuBois to inquire if he might like to join the Descendants of the American Aborigines.[47] Perhaps unsurprisingly, there is no evidence either that Parker's inner fraternities ever came to anything, or that DuBois took up his offer "to boast American descent" within them. Parker had miscalculated, but he and DuBois did have something in common. Both shared a vision of uplift spearheaded by a "talented tenth" of their "race." Each elite was to bring inspiration to their own people while seeking out the aid and support of powerful whites. DuBois, like Parker, had articulated the distress that went with finding oneself in two camps in terms of identity. He had written famously in 1903 of feeling a "two-ness," an internal angst at being "an American, a Negro; two souls, two thoughts, two unreconciled strivings."[48] Added to this, both men saw education as key to the way forward, and both had a romantic sense of racial pride.[49] However, in truth, Parker's only real concern through his subfraternities was for the SAI to broaden its constituency and increase its revenue through associations that tied the idea of being in some sense "Indian" with middle-class respectability and patriotism.[50]

Subfraternities were a side issue to the main conference job of agreeing on a platform. The principal planks agreed on concerned Indian education, specifically the improvement and standardization of state provision, along with calls for better health and sanitation.[51] The call to codify Indian status was endorsed, as well as a formal entreaty "that the Commissioner of Indian Affairs have as his primary object the advancement of the Indian" and that he allow capable and qualified Indians greater access to positions within the BIA. There was also a rather optimistic request that the president of the United States authorize the SAI president to investigate complaints "of wrongs perpetrated upon Indians who need aid or representation in adjusting their claims or righting their wrongs" and that investigations be conducted through public hearings.

This last issue took up a spiraling amount of Parker's time because he found it almost impossible to set aside pleas that he act or speak on behalf of fellow Indians ill-equipped to deal with various injustices. Uneducated reservation Indians sent him letters, often dictated or written through an interpreter, that needed much investigation in response. Most often, Parker's constituents, as it were, were making complaints against superintendents or seeking action on allotments. He would have to ascertain the facts and often carry out further research before bringing individual cases to the attention of the BIA, with whom he tried to maintain "cordial relations." He assured one New York chief: "When the American people are aroused to the idea that the Indian is desirous of standing on his own feet a free man and able to fight his way unhelped, then the Indian will have every right which any other man has in the United States and no man will ever think of denying him the justice which he claims."[52]

Events at the conference, at which he said he had found only "perfect harmony and uniformity of purpose," so convinced Parker that fundamental reform was within reach that he agreed to devote all his energies to the cause. "I am resigning my position as State Official in New York," he let it be known, "especially to undertake this great work for the uplift of the Indian people and the securing of a basic legislation upon which to build anew." His position as secretary-treasurer was made permanent, with a salary and a definite program for action. Parker was sure it was the right move. No doubt he also had the support and encouragement of his father, who had attended both conferences. Even so, after Columbus old fears soon returned about giving up a "comfortable berth" with the State Museum and about the warnings he had received about working solely for a fledgling reform group.[53]

In the end, he admitted in correspondence, "By a certain arrangement I am holding the Secretaryship of the Society and at the same time keeping my connection with the State." Leaving the State Museum would have meant the abandonment of four years' worth of anthropological work that he felt could not be finished by someone else. Although he carefully hedged his bets, he was nevertheless demonstrating a singular and wholehearted commitment to the SAI's cause. Developments from this point onward would be both a measure of the support of his fellow Indians and, as he put it, "a test of the ability of the White race to see things in a new light."[54]

Part of the program agreed on was for the new paid secretary to orchestrate "an active campaign for the enlisting of new members and for getting the objects of the organization before our people" first in Nebraska and South Dakota and then down into Oklahoma. Councils were planned for Santee, Winnebago, and Omaha country and at Pine Ridge and Rosebud. An extended trip West may well have seemed more attractive because of the strain Parker was experiencing just then at home. Although never explicit about his home life in any of the letters that survive, Parker told Mark Harrington that "things are with me just as they have been for some time,—in business very successful, in personal matters uncertain as ever." The same day he wrote to someone else: "I am practically alone in my home here. Bertha is in school in Ohio where I hope to see her occasionally. I have no idea that there is any remedy for my situation."[55] Heading West would at least allow him access to a bigger pool of potential membership and a chance to assess the true needs of the race on a local level. Equipped with buttons and emblems to dole out, he was "going out . . . to see whether I am really fighting for God and for race or merely ripping holes in the fans of windmills."

"Our expenses this year are up to $4000 or over," Parker calculated in correspondence; "this includes the cost of office hire in Washington, the salary of a clerk, my bread and butter, the publication of our annual report, the getting out of the Quarterly Journal, traveling and other expenses in the field to interest our Indian people and the precaution of our work to protect their rights in the best possible way." He was doing all he could to encourage activity and to bring errant contributors back into the fold. He asked Montezuma to contact Eastman, who had more or less abandoned the SAI once he had realized it would not be a representative Indian organization. Parker valued Eastman's opinion, but felt people like him were asking for too much too soon. As he reasonably pointed out, a voluntary body like the SAI could not at that time be more representative than its initial spread of volunteers.[56] He had a good point. Diversity of experience, of allotment, assimilation, and reform itself meant that a truly representative body did not exist until 1944, with the National Congress of American Indians.

In November 1912 the money making its way to SAI coffers was "just about enough." Disappointment began to make Parker doubt his own capacity for leadership. Weeks went by and the funding for his trip West still did not materialize. Quite candid about it all in one letter, he wrote, "had I cut off the sure income which comes from my connection with the State by this time I should have probably been slamming back yard gates for a hand-out."[57]

The SAI was not shaping up, financially or as a team. Yet Parker kept trying to encourage unity of purpose, this time writing to fellow Iroquois Laura Kellogg, vice president on education, in an attempt to establish common ground and to stem her worrisome inclination toward fomenting factionalism. He told Kellogg, who in the next year would fall away from SAI affairs and be arrested on charges of fraud and impersonation, "I believe that I myself must have some of the same Iroquois spirit which characterizes you in your thoughts and dreams of better and greater things."[58]

Another blow came in December, when Parker lost his assistant secretary. This pushed him to tell Daganett: "My present income has been entirely cut off and I am only depending upon the honorarium which comes to me as an Archeologist.... I do not know how this will affect my future success since the time I am giving the Society will make it impossible for me to receive the increase in salary which would be mine under normal circumstances." The SAI's financial standing had become "a source of considerable embarrassment." Besides money owed to him, outstanding bills by January 6 amounted to three hundred dollars, all pledged against his personal credit.[59] By any reckoning, this was sterling individual support for the reform cause at his direct expense and that of his family. Fortunately, at this stage he was still able to joke about it, describing himself in correspondence as "such an improvident fellow I can't even find the money to look after my own welfare."[60]

Parker was in a difficult position. He was extremely loyal to the State Museum, but his salary was not a living wage. He confessed to Keppler that he was doing his newspaper work "under a midnight lamp to secure clothing and medicine." He asked his friend's advice on whether he would be well advised to leave the State Museum for the SAI and told him of his big dreams for what the group could achieve. He imagined a small Indian college ahead and a paper and fine volumes and more. He mused, in something of a quandary: "Now can I abandon my N.Y. work (and starvation) for a larger and wider work (and perhaps starvation too)? Or is it my duty to plod on even though my children suffer."[61]

Whatever Keppler advised, soon afterward, from mid-January 1913, Parker managed to fund a sojourn for a month in Washington, where he had specific SAI instructions to "excite interest in the various bills which are endorsed or had their origin with this Association." Then, very probably using his own money, he visited as SAI secretary throughout the state of Oklahoma, a much-curtailed version of his planned trip West. He might have had to pay for it himself, but it was "a great trip" and he "saw heaps."[62]

By mid-March he was having to bargain with coworker Alice Denomie to get her to hang on in the Barrister Building at least until he could get out the first issue of the *Quarterly Journal*. He was convinced it would be "a bombshell." "We must send a copy to every member of the Lake Mohonk conference, the Indian Rights Association and the best people everywhere," he wrote to her. "It will go a long way to save us." It had the potential to communicate a new Indian identity to society at large. As he told one member, "The white people never knew we Indians could make such a magazine." The *Quarterly Journal* was the best method he could think of to focus Society discussion and dissipate internal dissent.[63]

The idea was a good one, but the struggle was already taking too heavy a toll. Although no longer in Washington very consistently, what he called his "productive time" had been so reduced that he half-joked, "I have just drawn on my last financial asset to keep afloat and when that is gone I'll have to stop eating." He told SAI vice president Sloan candidly that the secretary "can not do all," and went on: "As matters stand I do work eight hours a day and have totally abandoned all my literary and press work that formerly brought me a good many hundreds of dollars. After each days work for the State here I do Society work until 2 a.m. and also use holidays and Sundays. The correspondence is heavy and publicity work is exacting." Even when the *Quarterly Journal* was successfully published on April 15, it was, perhaps unsurprisingly, a personal disappointment. He said it was "the hurried work of a fatigued brain and shows it."[64] Publishing it, together with dealing with the great bulk of administrative duties that he took on as secretary, was a much greater sacrifice than he had ever imagined.

Parker was also concerned about the activities of rival Indian fraternities and acutely disappointed that sufficient monies had not materialized to fund the SAI's legal aid work. Calling their attention to the fact that he and his assistant had "given up high salaried positions in order to take up this work for you," he wrote to every active SAI member asking directly for donations. His greatest fear was that the SAI would fail to meet the challenge he perceived as having been set by the country. This was an increasingly likely scenario. Parker had had to reprimand Mrs. Kellogg; Daganett was now being hounded by various young women whom he had crossed; and poor Miss Denomie was resigning "on account of his [Daganett's] continued advances in the office." Public shame and organizational ruin was a worrying possibility.

Then, a piece of good fortune boosted flagging spirits and prompted the secretary even to hope that he might finally get paid for some of his hard work to date. Denver, the location of the next annual conference, granted the SAI two thousand dollars. Excitement at such a tangible vote of confidence made Parker worry to Coolidge whether they would rise to the occasion.[65] He also said one hundred dollars would be some recompense for his full-time work during October, November, and January, but he got nowhere with his request.

There was some consolation in the fact that the SAI going to Denver would be, as Parker put it, "something of an antidote against Buffalo Bill's $2000.00 Wild West Show which Denver is going to run during

1915 to capture the Panama visitors." He appreciated the idea of an educated Indian conference presenting a wholly separate image from stagecoaches, covered wagons, and "wild Indians." He wrote Pratt: "I am unalterably opposed to our connection with any Buffalo Bill event or circus Indian performance whatever. If the educated Indian or persons of Indian blood have no more stamina than to continue to play the carved wooden 'cigar store Indian' to sell tobacco for another man's profit—he is poorly educated indeed."

In one sense he need not have worried, since the heyday of the Wild West shows had already passed. Cody had begun a series of farewell performances as far back as 1910 to clear his debts and would die in Denver in 1917 at his sister's home. Yet in another sense, Parker was right to seize every opportunity to supplant older Indian stereotypes, because the image he found so distasteful was to be much more pervasively perpetuated when motion pictures developed in the 1920s.[66]

Parker did not benefit from Denver's largesse, and by that June his money worries were severe. He was busy compiling documents for the manuscript he had by now partially finished on the life of his great-uncle Ely, and was garnering support for the remarking of Ely's grave site.[67] He was forced to wind down the Washington office and clerk and instead concentrate SAI work in his own office in Albany.

There was little encouragement to be had the next month either, especially after fellow anthropologist J. N. B. Hewitt sent him a letter spelling out the inadequacies of the SAI as he saw them. He reminded Parker of some of the charges then being made against some of the SAI officers, including infractions of the Mann White Slave Law and, as Hewitt put it, "other equally vicious indulgences of evil habits." Society president Coolidge was, in his opinion, a "microbe of inertia" and the October 12 letter to the U.S. president "a masterpiece of aimless effort and bumptious flapdoodle." What could Parker say? In reply, he admitted to the lack of calm within internal SAI affairs and reminded Hewitt he was doing all he could:

> Nearly all of us have been accused of something which appears to make us unfit for service as officials: Dr. Coolidge is accused of being phlegmatic and lacking in initiative: I have been accused of knowing nothing about Indians and their real needs; Mr. Sloan has got many things filed against his character and business methods; Mr. Daganett is accused of immorality and drunkeness and inticing [sic] Indian girls to drink and lose their reputations; Mr. Dennison Wheelock is said to have once drunk too much liquor and fallen into the gutter and made it necessary for his wife to sell his clothes and bail him out of jail; Mrs. Laura

Kellogg is accused of impersonating federal officers, of being an actress, dancing almost nude and of swindling businessmen from Maine to California. Mrs. Kellogg practically hates Mr. Daganett and the dislike is mutual. Mrs. Kellogg also despises Dennison Wheelock: Mr. Sloan and Mrs. Kellogg cling together. Mr. Coolidge and I are compelled for the very honor of the society's existence to keep together, to simply do the best we can, though we are ignorant, in keeping things together and preventing an open rupture.[68]

He was feeling, as he described it, "almost entirely consumed" by the workload. He told Montezuma that nearly a thousand letters each month were dealt with in the SAI office, that he'd given the organization at least seven solid months of his time since the last conference, and that "many weeks have been spent in days of ten to twelve hours each and the numerous questions which have come in have entailed many hours of research." The pressure even made editing the *Quarterly Journal* unattractive, and Parker hoped someone else might take it over at Denver. By then he'd be claiming that the SAI had "settled many thousand dollars worth of claims for Indians, without charging a single penny," and that "50,000 pieces of mail had gone out from the central office and nearly 12,000 personal letters sent out to correspondents." Parker wanted Montezuma to be persuaded at Denver to take up the reins as president in order to inject dynamism.[69]

To his surprise, Parker's pre-conference worries proved to be unfounded. The 1913 Denver forum, nominally under the auspices of the University of Denver but with main meetings held at a hotel, was an overall success. A larger minority of reservation Indians was now participating, and the membership profile was more representative, having shifted west. Numbers peaked at over two hundred "actives," with Oklahoma, Montana, South Dakota, Nebraska, and New York as the main sources. It seemed Parker's conference invitation slogan, "Come to Denver and talk it over," had been heeded.[70]

Floor discussions were opened to the entire membership, and Parker made little fuss over the change.[71] In years to come, he would often refer to the "Denver Platform" as the high point of SAI thinking.[72] There was support, once again, for the Carter Code Bill to define Indian status; an amended Stephens Bill asking for the admission of Indian tribal claims directly to the federal courts of claims; and for the first time, expanded demands for education reform to include "the complete reorganization of the Indian school system." It was a set of requests well ahead of its time. In all, the Denver Platform antedated reforms of the thirties, forties, and twenties, respectively.

To Parker, Denver epitomized the apex of SAI cohesion and agreement over the path toward positive change. He wrote about it the next month in *The Red Man* as though some wondrous philosophical reorientation had occurred in the delegates. At the very least, the SAI had managed to avoid scandal. Neither Sloan nor Kellogg, of whom Parker said he'd been "humiliated and chagrined beyond expression from my dissolution of my original belief in her integrity," were reelected, and their names were carefully not mentioned on the floor.[73]

Parker left Denver "wonderfully strengthened," but he was still left with an impossible workload and no SAI salary. Soon the demands of his State Museum work made it seem as though "physically as well as mentally" he was risking a breakdown. He had a predilection for administration and organization, (once telling the press that his boyhood ambition was to be a mailman because he liked putting letters in boxes), but this was simply too much. On October 27, he wrote to let McKenzie know why he now wanted out: "My physical and financial condition is such that all this extra work, given, as I assume it, day by day is only drawing me closer to an ultimate collapse." He added ruefully, "As far as my personal assets go now, I have nothing to draw upon."[74] But no one took much notice, and his duties continued to grow as the SAI became better known.

The next month he asked Henry Roe Cloud if he could take over the burden of SAI secretaryship—to no avail. His depression was then lifted by a small piece of good news. He was made "curator" of archaeology and ethnology at the State Museum, which he said meant there was "now something for which to care" at the museum. But as the year drew to a close, Parker resigned himself to having to continue carrying out the lion's share of SAI work, even in the face of difficulties. He was distracted, he told McKenzie, both by business pressure and by "recent depressing personal matters."[75]

Disagreement and membership apathy worsened during the coming year. It began with the SAI owing five hundred dollars, along with advances Parker had made himself and monies owing for his time. Clearing the outstanding debt for which he was personally responsible became his main preoccupation, aside from keeping up the *Quarterly Journal,* which he felt had a "wholesome and dignified" influence. He spent mid-January at SAI headquarters in Washington and in February planned a series of local "get-together-and-get-acquainted" meetings.[76]

Next, a seemingly successful SAI banquet held in Philadelphia caused Parker to disappoint an old acquaintance from his days at "Aunt Hattie's" salon. Frank Speck, now an anthropologist at the University of Pennsylvania, was so displeased by SAI thinking that he refused to deliver his scheduled speech. He had taken the chance to study under Franz Boas at Columbia, and by now his opinions on Indian matters diverged fundamentally from those of his friend from late adolescence. He had little time for the banquet's naive emphasis on immediate assimilation and its concern that Indians abandon their cultural heritage.[77] Parker's overriding faith in the principle of disinterested public service and his lack of political finesse were also causing difficulty. For instance, through publishing an exposé of fraud in Oklahoma in the *Quarterly Journal*, he stepped on the toes of one Senator Owen, who threatened to withdraw his support for SAI bills before Congress. Yet more political flack came from the SAI's move to incorporate the Carter Bill into another proposed piece of legislation, the Robinson Bill, with the aim of securing the abolition of the BIA and of establishing an effective commission. All in all, as the Indian lawyer Henry Roe Cloud put it in personal correspondence, Indian affairs surrounding the SAI were now a "hodge-podge of politics and mud slinging."

As SAI secretary, Parker was still at sea. He was faced with the awkward task of explaining to creditors why the SAI was unable to meet its bills and was simply overrun with work. The *Quarterly Journal*, which went to both libraries and reservations, was a marvelous ongoing Indian achievement, but as Parker told Daganett, the "amount of thought effort" necessary to get it in shape took up his "entire mental operation." This was not surprising, since he was writing under his own name, under two pen names, and supplying all the editorials, reviews, and special notices. He had received only two hundred dollars in payment for his SAI work, and although he'd let Clarke, his State Museum superior, assume he was reasonably reimbursed so that it seemed he was using the time productively, in truth he found himself "in embarassing [*sic*] positions some times in both official capacities."

So far the State Museum had been "extremely lenient" about letting him devote time to his reform work, but he knew he had to make it a more manageable commitment. The problem was that he was consistently generous with his time, and there was always so much to do: helping individual Indian students cope with being educated far from home, dealing with land claims and even issues of probate, and then, the largest task of all, the countless mundane membership issues to deal with. It seems Parker made sure every subscription payment, query, and *Quarterly Journal* purchase was logged and replied to, a very sizable task at the time. As a capable Indian professional, he felt a duty to help the "race," but at the same time knew it was not possible to continue doing so and prosper. "If I leave," he admitted to Pratt, "I shall be accused of shirking a great duty—if I do not I shall go bankrupt and starve."[78]

In any case, the SAI's impetus seemed to be fading. In late June, he feared, "too much attention to routine and no meat, no ideas, and no accomplishment will only produce a thin cob covered by a thick husk." A month later he had hustled to plan the fourth annual conference at the University of Wisconsin at Madison and was at least able to put a brave face on it all to Pratt: "Our plans for the Madison Conference are maturing and all is splendid. We have the State and city officials, the best people in influential circles and many others are with us. Our welcome session will be in the State Capitol itself and the Governor will be there." Yet he could not hide his worry and isolation in the messages he sent out to the membership. In the early autumn of 1914, his letters to them bore an urgency and had an almost hectoring tone demanding action.[79]

His impending second marriage could only have added to the urgency Parker felt about the need for progress. He married his second wife, the young non-Indian woman, Anna Theresa Cooke, on September 17, 1914, at Whitehall, New York, a place where both had spent time growing up. Sixteen years Parker's junior and only seventeen when she married, Anna was to be his capable and loving companion until the day he died. An accomplished musician who had both charm and a commitment to community effort, she was to be a great boon to Parker personally and professionally. The couple shared mutual interests in the outdoors, in natural history, in skiing, in hiking, and of course, in education and the Indian past.

Anna had helped Parker at several archaeological digs, including those at Boughton Hill and Vine Valley in Yates County, and the relationship may well have solidified during the time when the Iroquois exhibits were being installed in Albany. It is hard to gauge exactly what she thought of Parker's SAI involvement, even though, at the very least, it affected family finances significantly. It is clear, however, that Anna had an abiding interest in Parker's work. Fourteen years after their marriage, he would facilitate her adoption into the Seneca Bear Clan when she took on the name "Yeiwano:t," meaning "Resting Voice."[80]

Perhaps marriage provided the last straw. Finally, in a letter written from his father's home in White Plains, he let it be known that he did not intend to go to Madison that October. He was distressed at the extent of SAI debt, at Daganett's resignation in the face of opposition to government employees, and fearful lest the meeting "degenerate into . . . merely talk." Probably, he hoped his absence would alert a few people to just how much work he was doing for so little reward. When

October came, the six days of conference deliberations did little to halt his suspicion that the SAI had begun to decline. The governor did not attend but sent a representative, and since the program had not been properly prepared, there was confusion and delay in getting started.[81]

The delegates at least dwelt on the need to pay the secretary-treasurer for the debts he had incurred. In fact, a general and sincere sense of regret was expressed when it was reported that Parker did not wish to be reelected, and McKenzie spoke at length in Parker's defense concerning the Owen affair:

> He has been obliged to keep his position in the state of New York in order to have some income and I know as a matter of fact that Mr. Parker has refused an increase in salary from the State of New York in order that he might continue this work. He has refused to write articles because he had no time. You know a man can be so tired that he can't think straight, he will seem to do the wrong things and it seems to me that if a man for two or three years has wanted to resign, and we objected, saying "we can't get along without you and so on," under that pressure he has broken.

In the end, the group decided unanimously to reelect Parker in absentia, and, feeling better appreciated, he accepted. Nevertheless, he made it clear that he wanted help.[82]

Parker may have chosen to sit out Madison, but he was happy to attend the Lake Mohonk Conference along with several other prominent SAI members, and to give a talk on Indian legal status. He put forward the SAI line on the issue and made a special point about reforming tribal politics, without of course referring directly to his own personal history. He was listened to politely, but "the peyote menace" was what most Mohonkists really wanted to hear and talk about. Suppressing peyote had become a major preoccupation of Indian reformers around this time, even though the faith was in fact accommodative in that it incorporated elements of Christianity. Peyote was to long outlast the reform fraternalism of the "red progressives" and eventually become central to a new form of intertribal fraternity in the 1920s; but at Mohonk in 1914, it was simply worrisome to Parker. He admitted he did not "know anything about this peculiar habit of eating mescal, buttons and having visions, etc.," but at the same time he sensed that it would be best to disapprove of it since it was a developing focus for dissent.[83]

Then, as the year approached its close, a small political coup came off. On Thursday, December 10, an SAI delegation met with President Wilson to present a memorial on Indian affairs. In the presence of

Parker's antagonist Senator Owen, over forty delegates, including Parker, each shook the president's hand. Parker was enthused and wrote to Keppler: "I wish you might have been in Washington at our meeting with Mr. Wilson and the Indian banquet. The big and great Indians of the land were there and every one was a red man sure!"[84] The president declared himself to be "very impressed" with those he met, but the meeting had no impact in terms of the SAI's main aim, to stimulate fundamental Indian legislative reform. The *Quarterly Journal*, of course, gave the occasion and its accompanying banquet a very positive write-up.

Parker tried to negotiate a way of separating his dual functions as secretary and treasurer and asked if there might be some way he could at least pass on the appeals for help to Wheelock. Neither attempt came too much. In a letter to Francis E. Leupp, who had been commissioner for Indian Affairs from 1905 to 1909, he shared his frustration over the time-consuming and complex problem of dealing with the heartfelt pleas for assistance from reservation Indians: "Any one who goes into Indian activities, especially one who desires to serve honestly as the intermediator between these natives and the interests that desire to exploit them, finds himself in a treacherous sea. Very often those who claim to be, and are the friends of the Indians, render conditions very difficult for an administrative to follow so that an air of suspicion constantly hovers over everything that is done and every act is questioned for a concealed motive that is ulterior."[85]

Parker was finding it impossible "to handle the whole business without occasioning the criticism that I am permanently neglecting the duties for which I am paid by the State." What he really wanted to do was complete his biography of his great-uncle, but there was just no time. At least his faltering campaign to institute an American Indian Day was receiving a boost, even if he was not sure its manner was appropriate. Montana rancher Red Fox James had ridden a pony into various state capitols and managed to collect the endorsements of several governors for the Indian Day, efforts that culminated in his own meeting with President Wilson, this time accompanied by the Boy Scouts.

Although Parker was continually calling for dynamism and action on the part of SAI members, he could not quite hide his concern when it finally materialized. Fearful that James had not fully grasped his idea, especially given the "show-Indian" character of James's publicizing, he wrote to him, "I am a little bit dubious about the amount of good that will be accomplished by holding general 'pow-wows,' as you call them." His concern was that they would be "seized upon for their advertising value" and that this "would not lend anything to the dignity which the original intention sought."[86] James carried on regardless, and by the second Saturday of May the next year made sure Indian Day enjoyed modest observance within New York State.

In the spring of 1915, Parker's workload lessened somewhat. Society finances were momentarily in better shape, and several of his more minor duties were taken over by Daganett. Encouraged, Parker decided to make yet further sacrifices to ensure that the organization stayed afloat. Now giving only four hours a day to the work, he chose not to claim his salary for the time being and instead began to campaign for membership loans. Inevitably, Daganett having greater input caused the anti-BIA forces within the SAI to fret, but Parker felt the situation could not be helped. He worked hard to placate Montezuma over the issue and, while he was at it, to convince him that instant abolition of the BIA was not feasible.[87] To Parker, fear of government domination came a distant second to the danger that the SAI might fail outright, probably because of a lack of finance.

One possible answer came when Daganett hit on the idea of an SAI "sales department," which could retail handicraft items picked up from the tribes. Although wary of the "show-Indian" image, Parker nevertheless recognized the power of the name "Indian" to make money and found Daganett's proposition "sufficiently attractive to make it worthy of very serious consideration." He thought it would be good to use the SAI eagle emblem as a trademark, above it placing the word "Guaranteed" and beneath it the word still today so powerfully associated with the Indian in advertising—"Genuine." He and Daganett were never able to make the idea come to anything, but future Commissioner of Indian Affairs John Collier would in 1930 float a proposal for an Indian arts and crafts corporation analogous to Daganett's "sales department." In the American Indian Defense Association newsletter, Collier would also suggest the setting up of retail shops where Indian goods could be sold, this time with government-issued certificates of genuineness.[88]

By late April it was clear that monies would have to be borrowed to proceed with preparations for the 1915 conference planned for Lawrence, Kansas. Parker proposed closing the Washington office and taking on full responsibility for the secretary-treasurer role from his Albany state office. Aside from this, his biggest contribution for the rest of the year was made through editorship of the *Quarterly Journal,* where he devoted the majority of copy space to reform of Indian vocational and industrial education. He shared Booker T. Washington's respect for industrial skills, calling for recognition of the true dignity of manual labor, because "the ditch-digger is as important a man as the law clerk, and entitled to as much respect and consideration."[89]

Washington's rhetoric reverberated through much of Parker's expressed faith in hard work, in minority self-help, and accommodation to the dominant society. "Work! Work Work! Be patient and win by superior service" had once been Washington's advice for the younger black generation, and the phrase also practically summarized Parker's reform philosophy. Yet at the same time, Parker felt that full liberal education should be available to promising Indian students in order to develop "race leadership." Although he selectively borrowed from Washington's rhetoric with its implied acceptance of "racial" civic inferiority, he believed, just like DuBois, that the elite should govern within any given group. Like DuBois, he wanted to foster a "talented tenth" to develop the movement for equality of opportunity.

As the 1915 conference approached, Parker was full of misplaced optimism, perhaps because he had got wind of a possible new appointment for which he was suitable.[90] He chose "Responsibility for the Red Man" as the theme of the conference, a title that smacked of a blinkered commitment to self-help as a panacea for all social ills. Irritated with what he felt was a language of dependency within Indian affairs and an emphasis on "the securing of rights," Parker wanted instead to talk up the concept of Indian self-reliance. The same lack of knowledge and understanding of the realities of reservation life characterized his writing around this time to agency superintendents, of whom he would sincerely inquire as "to what extent willful incompetency exists among the Indians?"[91] It was a simplistic, paternalistic approach to the cultural erosion, endemic poverty, and health problems resulting from the reservation system, symptomatic of the yawning gap that persisted between the SAI and their supposed constituents.

The fifth annual conference was marred by serious factional dispute, even though the choice of venue had itself been an attempt to bring factions together by allowing more reservation Indians to attend. Sessions, held at the University of Kansas and at what was now the leading non-reservation Indian boarding school, Haskell Institute, were disrupted by arguments over peyote and the BIA. Over twenty-five tribes were represented at the conference, and many came with the erroneous impression that it was a forum for the presentation of claims and complaints.

The largest party of all was from Oklahoma and included several important peyotists. By now Parker had developed strong views on the topic. Prior to the conference, he had written to one wavering Oklahoma Indian warning him not to "listen to what these smart Indians say about peyote," since "if they did know everything that was necessary they could make engines and flying machines and find ways to make wonderful things, but they never did." He told Henry Roman Nose that ingesting peyote was "a serious thing if you find that that herb makes you dream and see colors and different things." He advised rectitude, adding rather vaguely, "There is only one kind of man to be; it is not an Indian man nor a white man, but a real man."[92] Such fuzzy thinking no doubt contributed to the Lawrence conference not reaching a position on the issue. It managed only to reflect national prohibition sentiment in condemning "the liquor evil"; there would be further heated debate about the powerful psychedelic cactus.

The peyote issue was divisive but not nearly so damaging as the issue of relations with the BIA. Parker had always tried to remain detached, reassuring Pratt: "It has been my plan not to connect myself in any way with the Federal administration. I have desired to become rather the spokesman for the Indians purely in a social sense." But even his unbiased mediation could not prevent either the resounding impact of the address from Montezuma, which later became his polemical pamphlet calling for immediate abolition of the BIA, "Let My People Go," or the decision to replace Daganett as first vice president.

Exasperated, Parker wrote to Pratt about Montezuma's address to say he "wished most heartily that he had boiled it down to give it the virtue of constructive logic." As he pointed out in the *Quarterly Journal*, Montezuma had no viable alternative to the BIA, and in any case, his recommendation of immediate abolition had no hope of governmental sanction. "The fiery Apache wields a scalping knife in the sure hand of an experienced physician," wrote Parker, but for an Indian leader "to fail to provide adequate laws and regulations for the conservation of his heritage would be poor wisdom."[93] As for Daganett, he and Parker had crossed swords in the past, but Parker was well aware that his departure signaled a destructive hardening of attitudes toward the BIA that was unlikely to help the SAI advance. Furthermore, he happened to know that the key anti-BIA voices within the SAI each had "a special grouch" that was entirely personal.

The Lawrence conference might have been disheartening, but at least the Lake Mohonk Conference shortly afterward gave Parker, and no doubt his wife, Anne, who accompanied him, "a considerable thrill of pleasure." A good part of that stemmed from the attention he received from the commissioner of Indian Affairs. Cato Sells charmed him thoroughly, leaving him convinced of his own importance through the *Quarterly Journal* and with the false impression that fundamental reorganization of the school system along SAI lines was imminent. As a result, Parker became convinced that the SAI's power lay "in our logical appeal to the public and the facts we present in our Quarterly." Modifying his self-help agenda somewhat, he decided it would succeed "not so much in the actual things that it is able to do of itself but the justice and better things it is able to compel the delegated authorities to do." Since he felt the SAI's effectiveness now lay in its ability to appeal to an abstract sense of justice, he resolved to keep numbers low at next year's conference, not to encourage people with disputes to come, and instead simply to "get our thinking people together."[94]

Parker had been beguiled by Commissioner Sells, but he was still well aware that the SAI's campaigning power had severe political limitations. He knew it would never be easy to expose the graft and corruption rife within Indian affairs, or to garner support for targeted attacks on individuals, since SAI membership was "composed of persons whose interests are linked perhaps in some way directly or indirectly with the men we may attack. This has been demonstrated in the Owen matter as well as in several others."[95] The SAI's power to do good would always be limited by those charged with enforcing the will of the people. Perhaps inevitably, Parker began to view the way federal monies were administered as a barrier to Indian advance. Frustrated with the slow pace of change and frustrated that the "race" was not pushing for it with sufficient vigor through the SAI, he started to blame the BIA for perpetuating non-assimilating Indians. He developed the increasingly focused conviction that rapid assimilation was the only way forward and that citizenship and freedom from BIA subsidy and control should be extended to far greater numbers on the reservations.

The overarching desire to develop Indian "race competence" prompted him to apply ideas to the issue that owed much more to eugenics than to the progressive ideals of social welfare and social service: "I sometimes think," he said in correspondence, "that the Indian Bureau through its endeavors to give protection has so protected some classes of individuals that they and their progeny are physically unfit now or at any time to be anything but public charges. In normal citizenship the diseased and unfit die off as they naturally should in any healthy human community [sic]."[96] He had come to believe that "willful non-competence" in assimilation was an Indian racial aberration that should not be subsidized by the government. This was the nervous arrogance of a leader gradually having to face the fact that he did not have a cohesive racial group to lead. Too many of "his" people would not, or simply could not, assimilate.

For a while, he kept up the good work for the organization he had decided to think of as a kind of racial lobbying group. He said he "would actually prefer to be allowed to again enter the ranks of common membership," but was yet again reelected as national secretary. Sometimes he felt that some of the officers regarded him as "too active and as controlling too largely the funds, the policy and the chief position in the Society," but when the treasurer's job was given over to Marie Baldwin, such worries were put to one side and his old optimism returned.[97] Daganett, too, was optimistic, but that may have been partly because he was just then wooing the lady stenographer in the Washington SAI office, whom he would marry by the summer.

That November Parker decided to revamp the *Quarterly Journal* to broaden its potential sphere of influence. He asked the membership if he could change the name so as to "make a wider appeal to the general public and attract a news stand sale." His ultimate plan was to take the publication out of their hands entirely and then to contract with them for copies.

Duly in January 1916, the first issue of the rechristened *American Indian Magazine* appeared as "A JOURNAL OF RACE IDEALS Edited by Arthur C. Parker." Parker told the readership, "A Journal of a particular Society appears too clannish many times to the general reader."[98]

To emphasize that the SAI was capable of encompassing the whole spectrum of Indian debate, he made a point of printing a range of conflicting viewpoints in the first issue, including Montezuma's "Let My People Go." He also promoted the one activity that all could support and develop—American Indian Day on May 13. "Heretofore Indians have considered only tribe and reservation," he wrote. "To them the tribe was mankind and the tribal area the world. Today there is a growing consciousness of race existence. The Sioux is no longer a mere Sioux, or the Ojibway a mere Ojibway, the Iroquois a mere Iroquois. . . . [N]ow with a coming race-consciousness the American Indian seeks to go even further and say, 'I am not a red man only, I am an American in the truest sense, and a brother man to all human kind."[99] Indian Day turned out to be a minor success, with three states holding school celebrations; but it did not impress Montezuma, who denounced it in his own rival publication, *Wassaja,* as "a farce and the worst kind of fad." Parker's reply in *American Indian Magazine* was restrained, but privately he was concerned that Montezuma was a loose cannon capable of causing real damage.[100]

Soon, further conflict arose over bills in Congress that sought to replace the BIA with a system of agents nominated by tribes and bands themselves. Parker and Coolidge strongly opposed these moves, but others, like Sloan, supported them. Parker would have preferred for Sloan to concentrate on somehow creating the much-needed SAI legal department, because so many Indians were still making appeals and finding there was "no attorney to assist them and no funds to secure one."[101] But even this important work was less significant, in Parker's view, than the SAI's symbolic potential to change the Indian's outlook. After all, the SAI was "the spirit of the race, . . . its soul."[102]

It was the very argument Morgan had put forward years ago after carrying out his research with the Parker family. He too had concluded, back in 1851, that the "fatal deficiency of Indian society" was the "non-existence of the progressive spirit."[103] Parker, too, felt that if only the SAI could demonstrate its civilized nature through unified consensus, it would triumph in the end. After all, given the upcoming presidential election, true improvement in Indian matters might be just around the corner. "If a new administration comes into being," he told Pratt, "some of us can formulate the policy."[104] Such hopes, however, were soon dashed by the reelection that November of Woodrow Wilson, a Southern gentleman with no doubts as to the innate superiority of the white race and no enduring interest in Indian reform.

By the spring of 1916, Parker feared the outcome of the next conference, planned for Cedar Rapids, Iowa. He was ill over the summer, and this, coupled with finances preventing publicity at previous levels, resulted in low attendance. When the group photograph was taken, it was of a paltry twenty-eight delegates, including associates, and the hospitality was simply not on the same scale as before. Just as Parker suspected, infighting, mostly over BIA abolition and peyote, plagued most conference events. The founder of the SAI, Fayette McKenzie, did not attend, and without his calming influence, disorderly and confused debate had a free rein. In particular, Montezuma held little back, railing against the *American Indian Magazine,* Indian Day, and what he felt was the cowardly way the SAI was ducking out of taking radical action against the BIA. Unfortunately, the press got news of one incident where he ended up waving his arms wildly on the debating floor and shouting at President Coolidge, "I am an Apache, and you are an Arapahoe. I can lick you. My tribe has licked your tribe before." Fortunately Coolidge simply stood up, towered over the diminutive Montezuma, and said, "I'm from Missouri," raising a laugh and diffusing the tension.[105]

Overall, conference events were depressing. Since Mrs. Bonnin's community-center movement had never really gotten off the ground after being initiated at the last conference, it was now dismissed. Most of the rest of the decisions only further alienated vital sources of support. For example, the conference platform called on the government to "look to the closing of the Indian Bureau, so soon as trust funds, treaty rights and other just obligations can be individualized, fulfilled or paid." Once more peyote was linked to the "Liquor Evil," and the conference called "unequivocally upon Congress for the passage of the Gandy Bill to prohibit the commerce in and use of peyote among our people." Most of these decisions, along with the creeping sectarianism introduced with the prominence of Father Philip Gordon of Washington, served to heighten dissent.[106]

Almost nothing had been achieved toward getting either the Carter Code Bill or the amended Stephens Bill enacted. Now with McKenzie fading from the picture, even the strongest non-Indian voices within the organization were strongly partisan over key issues. Although General Pratt attended and spoke on the advance of the "negro race," the old spirit of the Carlisle Indian school no longer had the same strengthening pull, and shadows lay over its reputation. Even a "smoker" social session, planned for the Hotel Montrose, had to be canceled because the entertainment committee failed to function.

The wider political context offered little encouragement. The national progressive domestic reform dynamic was beginning to ebb. America was moving closer to war in Europe, and the issue of Indian uplift now had little political weight. Added to this, SAI members had proven themselves intent on carping from the sidelines rather than setting about implementing action based on an agreed set of principles. It was in this problematic context that Parker took on the presidency and the almost certainly impossible task of snatching success from the jaws of factionalism and financial decay.

Soon he was convinced he had taken the decision too hastily. In December he wrote to Bonnin, always an intelligent confidante and, incidentally, a former love interest of Montezuma: "It was a mistake to elect me the President. You should have continued as Community Center Superintendent and I as Secretary plus Treasurer. The only difficulty here is that my losses were so great that I could not continue to give my time to the work and survive."[107] He had always exerted a great deal of control, largely through doing so much of the work, but now he was required to take full public responsibility for the success or otherwise of all the SAI's aims and programs.

Bonnin's work had made him much more aware that conditions on the reservations were seriously awry, but he still could not understand why Indians opted to remain on them or why they failed to assimilate.[108] He voiced all this in what became his primary external action as president—a letter to Congress attacking Indian "segregation." He sketched a predictable SAI program of legislation designed to do away with tribes as "social, commercial and political entities" given the fact that "Indians must come into the nation as individual units." It was a reiteration of Dawes Act thinking at a time when the assimilationist assumptions underlying it were about to be challenged and reform was not foremost in representatives' minds. His specific legislative ideas had no hope of enactment and were therefore more or less ignored.[109]

Another significant early action for Parker as president was penning the article "Problems of Race Assimilation in America, with Special Reference to the American Indian," which was published in the 1916 October/December issue of the *American Indian Magazine.* Here, in much the same way as a child who is ignored invents his own conversation, Parker invented his own dialogue with his parent country, systematically comparing the conditions of assimilation operating for three groups of "potential Americans": European immigrants, American Negroes, and American Indians. He imagined the voice of America spelling out its feelings toward each in turn. It was, perhaps through desperation, a negative and racist attempt to distance the Indian from other American minorities.

What he imagined the United States saying to Indians was harsh. It demanded that they lose all previous culture, an "undeveloped form," now that they were exposed to "the full glare of twentieth century enlightenment." It concluded: "To the Indians we say, 'You were here first, that is true, and though we tried we could not kill you entirely. You have a great deal of land and mineral wealth and although we will try to protect you, our sharper citizens are going to try to get everything from you that they can. You'd better understand that first as last, because that is the way we do business. Listen to your friends and learn to live and think like us, or—well, you'll become extinct.'" To the European immigrant, whom Parker felt had demonstrated "moral energy" in choosing America, he imagined the nation extending a grudging invitation. To the "Negro," his "American" voice was a stern and less than accommodating master: "'We will tolerate you for after all you are a convenient laborer and may do even more for us, in time.'" The Chinese, as far as Parker was concerned, were unknowable, and therefore America rejected them as unassimilable.

However, once a minority possessed seven "Factors of Assimilation," including desire (to be American), ability to speak the language, education, religious tolerance, participation in "American" activities, and patriotic loyalty, then, he assured his readers, "we need have no fear of granting them political equality and the privilege of the ballot." "Negro"/white unions he dismissed as a distasteful impossibility, but intermarriage between Indians and whites was entirely positive. In fact, such unions were producing competent and industrious "half-bloods," presumably like himself, who somehow combined in their personalities the better traits of each parent. Overall, the article was a heady mixture of wishful thinking and prejudiced claptrap.

The article's prejudice against "Negroes" no doubt further alienated white friends of the SAI who believed in reform for both minorities, but this was not the president's main concern. His article was concerned fundamentally with restating the old bargain of the nineteenth century concerning assimilation at a time when it was becoming clear that compensation for Indians through full participation within American life was not forthcoming. To a lesser extent, it was also a personal statement about the psychic cost of the assimilative process. But regardless of how Parker articulated the situation on his country's behalf, the truth was that Americans were willing to grant Indians, along with certain other nonwhite peoples, only limited and partial access to the life of the nation.

The new century had seen a new hierarchy develop and with it an increasing consensus that minorities should serve only at the lower levels. Political or social equality for American Indian peoples in any way comparable to what Parker described was an impossibility at a time when black segregation, exclusion of Japanese and eastern European immigrants, and a possible suspension or reduction of the whole immigration process had popular approval. All Parker could do in his article was to issue a reminder of the compact at the heart of national assimilation policy and make much of the effort needed to fulfill the minority half of the bargain. Thus, he told his readers that the assimilative process "costs the other man something" and that "just what this cost is we should know." His arguments were after the fashion of social scientific analysis, but in truth they were an expression of his angst at not finding acceptance, both in terms of his ideas as voiced through the SAI and on a personal level.

The problem was that there was little support for his position and a great many problems surrounding it. Even American anthropology could no longer be relied on to provide it with any firm justification, because the old ideas of universal human progress were being replaced with a modern awareness of racial diversity. Culturally relativist thinking was casting doubt on the assimilationist program epitomized in the Dawes Act back in 1887, because the big new idea, that culture alone shaped identity, implied that full assimilative change within a generation was nearly impossible. The new orthodoxy suggested that Indians would find it extremely difficult to enter the modern, highly complex industrial world, since they belonged to cultures much more static and primitive. Any development on their part was considered an erosion from an unchanging cultural base.

Not that anyone was very interested in what Parker had to say in his article. The climate of opinion just then was not concerned with the complexities of minority experience in relation to the dominant culture. The push for domestic reform was receding in light of concerns over the external threat in Europe and the need to prepare to engage militarily. Nevertheless, Parker had applied himself to the thorny topic of Indian assimilation, put it into some kind of comparative context, and said something new about the pressures involved.

Montezuma had a field day with Parker's ideas. He disparaged the article in the January 1917 issue of *Wassaja* as "a choice selection of wide generalizations (not always true), meaningless conclusions, bad reasoning. It is . . . characterized by a lot of pretended philosophy, as senseless as it is shallow." Perhaps with a nod toward Parker's own rather patronizingly diplomatic editorial style in *American Indian Magazine,* he added that Parker's remarks had nonetheless been "well-meant, no doubt." Parker, however, thought his ideas on assimilation might interest Theodore Roosevelt, whom he had met at the opening of the new State Museum that December. He sent him a copy of his article with the comment, "I should be pleased to know that you had read at least the principal arguments in my thesis because my attitude on Indian matters has been largely influenced by your own utterances, one of which I took the liberty of re-publishing in the magazine."[110] It seems Roosevelt never replied.

Although unable to shake off the illness he'd contracted soon after taking office, Parker remained determined to continue as president as 1917 began. He was irritated at the fact that the secretary-treasurer role had been split, worried about money, and was suspicious of outside input, dramatically telling Secretary Bonnin: "I almost believe that there is undue external pressure at work to destroy the Society or at least to discredit the administration. I must have $350 at once to liquidate our indebtedness. Otherwise the Magazine will have to be eliminated." By March, he was also getting seriously irritated with both his secretary and treasurer, who were fighting because of religious rivalry and personal bad feeling.

Now there were absolutely no funds. Collectors for engraving companies and stationery printers had hounded his door until he had had to pay them out of the monies raised for *American Indian Magazine.* In desperation, he thought about abandoning the SAI in its present form altogether. Since he felt their real work was "a moral task which consisted of bringing about an awakening of the race from within," he suggested to the Coolidges that the SAI re-form from scratch. He also now recognized that the Legal Aid Division had been an unrealizable dream.

It dawned on Parker that he simply could not keep on trying to lead an organization beset by such a painful lack of cohesion. The best he could say was that the SAI was an "unfinished experiment," which had been "too optimistic and trustful of dangerous elements."[111] Very probably his depressed state was connected with his first wife, Beulah, and with his two children. Since he never mentioned his personal circumstances directly in surviving correspondence, it is possible that his SAI peers were unaware that familial stress compounded the organizational pressure he was under.

Next, he made a firm decision that the *American Indian Magazine* as an SAI publication must soon be suspended, although he thought it might be able serve the same purpose under the sponsorship of a different set of individuals. He told Bonnin, "If we can do nothing else we can publish a journal that will be independent and act as the voice of the red man crying manfully for justice and a man's part in the affairs of the nation." At least if it were a private enterprise, it would have steadfast support, and people like he and Bonnin would be able to "tell our story to our race and to the world un-hampered." Bonnin remained a confidante as Parker got more depressed. Beset by worries, ill, chronically underfunded, and in half a mind to quit altogether, he nonetheless stuck by the organization he had done so much to promote. Sitting gloomily in his Albany office and gazing out at the windswept street covered in ice and snow, he told Bonnin he was at least one hundred SAI letters behind, but since he had neither clerks nor funds, his hands were tied.[112]

Then, after the Coolidges had forwarded enough money to pay office expenses, he cheered up enough to write to her again: "I have been away on State duties but worried all the while by the condition of the Society. All my various organizations seem to flourish but the SAI whom of all I love most. The Philosophical Society of which I am president is solvent and in good working order and so is the State Archeological Society which takes its orders from me, but our beloved SAI is between the millstones of those who hear the Bureau and those who hate the Bureau. However, I shall arise and fight on."[113]

Parker brought out the *American Indian Magazine* on time, but, perhaps inescapably, it was full of unrestrained comment unlikely to dampen growing factional disputes. Ranting against "the peyote poison," the editorial proclaimed: "This is an age of enlightenment. Stupefying gases, narcotics and peyote must be banished. The God must be perceived by a clear, clean moral vision and not by a crazed dream of a drug eater's brain."[114] Just perhaps, Parker's revulsion against peyote came from having tried it. Years later, he would write:

I wish that I had time to describe its effects from personal experience. In passing, however, it may be said that it retards respiration, causes heart irregularity that brings about a choking feeling, and then induces the hallucination of revolving rainbows that finally pass and lead the drug-taker into a strange world of exaggerated dreams. From this comes a feeling of personal humility and a conviction of great sinfulness, leading the patient to cry out his infamy and desire to become forgiven. Out of this state grows a feeling of great personal importance and power, and then again the dreams.[115]

Aside from disparaging peyote, *American Indian Magazine* opposed legislative proposals that a separate Indian regiment be organized within the U.S. military fighting overseas. "Much of the clamor for a spectacular Indian regiment or battalion arises from the showman's brand of Indian as seen in the circus," it said, sentiments also put forward by Parker in a letter to the secretary of war in Washington.[116]

As 1917 progressed, the war and the Indian contribution to it took up more and more of Parker's time. By the summer, he was "as busy as can be . . . recruiting men for my company here." It seems he served as a private in the Tenth Regiment, Company A, of the New York State National Guard until May the next year. Through his Selective Service work, he helped secure almost total Indian registration in the state, while making efforts to change the wording of the registration questionnaires so that Indians did not have to claim exemption as "resident aliens," which he considered demeaning. The war was a convenient reason for the annual conference to be postponed indefinitely. In truth, the SAI might have imploded otherwise. At least postponement meant that the officers could retain titular control and continue with Parker's plan to make the SAI secondary to *American Indian Magazine.*

In any case, by that stage national service was taking up most of Parker's time. He told Baldwin that "between sitting with the Draft board and acting as recruiting officer and guarding state property,—together with managing the affairs of various associations keeps me busy for sure."[117] He was working for free as a draft board inspector and in total served in the National Guard for eight months.[118] Still, he was happy to keep up *American Indian Magazine* in preparation for a time when its message would be really listened to. To Parker, the war was a significant opportunity to speed Indian reform, especially if the public and their representatives were made aware of Indian patriotism. "With the enlistment of 5,000 Indians in the United States army," he wrote to remind one senator, "our country again is face to face with the question of ultimate citizenship for the Indian." Calling himself "a Seneca, but a citizen and a voter," he was using the war as a lever to again press for a bill to clarify Indian status. Of course, since Indian patriotism might spur reform, it was important that there be some record of it. This was why, even though he accepted that Indians had a right to exemption as what he called "non-citizen Indians," he was especially fervent in his efforts to secure mass Indian registration.[119]

Parker put all of his current philosophy into a New Year address to the Federated Conference of the Friends of the Indians in Philadelphia called "Making Democracy Safe for the Indians." The title applied President Wilson's description of the conflict as a "War to Make the World Safe for Democracy" directly to internal Indian policy. Parker argued that since America was "engaged in a gigantic world war over a theory—the theory of the right of the smaller peoples to determine how they shall live and be governed," it must therefore reconstruct its Indian administration and free the Indian from fraud and an autocratic BIA. Congress should immediately make "all Indians within the United States of America ... citizens or candidate citizens of the land." He concluded: "Our American Indians are today in France on the battle line, fighting that liberty, fraternity and equality of opportunity may prevail throughout the world. Are they to return and find that they alone of all human kind are denied these blood-bought privileges? We who remain here to labor, to think and to conserve true democracy are responsible for the answer!"[120]

Eventually around 15,000 Indians from across the nation would fight in World War I, with a significant number of Indian women serving in relief organizations like the Red Cross. Parker's demands for citizenship and BIA abolition had little hope of immediate implementation, but his argument that patriotic defense of the country deserved some form of political dividend was robust and timely. The same line of thinking was put forward by the leadership of several other U.S. minorities, and suffragists were to use it to great effect. Eventually, late in 1919, an act would be passed that gave citizenship to all Indian veterans of World War I, and it served as a catalyst for the more fundamental bestowal of citizenship for Indians in 1924.

As for the SAI, it was Bonnin, rather than Parker, who now took the most active role. Along with fellow Lakota and peyote advocate Charles Eastman, she had new ideas for the organization and its publication.

Her influence helped make the final 1917 issue of *American Indian Magazine* a "Sioux Number." By February 8, 1918, she was bold enough to take the initiative and call an SAI conference in Parker's name in Washington. Parker was pessimistic about the outcome, even before he got there. Afterward, the best he could say was that it allowed the two warring female officers, Bonnin and Baldwin, to iron out some of their difficulties through being brought to order in a public forum. About thirty Indians attended. The Lakota contingent's voice was reflected in the decision to plan the 1918 conference right in the heart of Lakota country, at Pierre, South Dakota. At least this was preferable to another suggestion, to hold it in Omaha, where Parker feared the divisive influence of "the large number of fairly 'well-off' peyote people in the neighborhood."

Squabbles over peyote were edging him closer to the end of his tether. He acknowledged to Pratt that month that "patience can become exhausted." Bonnin and Eastman had agreed to speak as the main Indian testimony in defense of peyote at hearings of the House Subcommittee of Indian Affairs during February and March. These were held in response to Representative Carl Hayden's Indian Bureau bill, which called for the suppression of most forms of intoxication, including liquor, cannabis, and peyote. The SAI associates, young lawyer Thomas L. Sloan, and Francis LaFlesche from the Bureau of American Ethnology also spoke to support peyote and to defend its appeal to younger and more educated Indians.

Parker, of course, was in the other camp—a supporter of both the Hayden Bill and the Indian Citizenship Bill proposed by Representative Charles D. Carter. His hope was that some combination of the two would get passed, even if this meant considerable suffering for many Indians. He acknowledged as much to Carter, writing that such legislation would "provide what the Society of American Indians has always contended as primary,—the even chance to struggle into the life of the Nation. No doubt many will suffer, be pillaged and be driven to the alms houses, but nothing radical and evolutionary ever takes place without loss of somekind."[121] As for peyote, even though prominent Indians and Commissioner Sells were anxious to see it curbed, it would not be possible to restrict its use given that its contents did not violate any existing law.

As the potential for intertribal unity seemed to irrevocably decline, Parker became more interested in Iroquois affairs. Strangely, he saw no contradiction in advising that they demand exemption from the policy initiatives he was supporting nationally. He warned Seneca leader Walter Kennedy about the Carter Bill making its way through the legislative process in Washington: it was "all right for western allotted Indians, but we must see that our people stand on their rights as an exception."[122] He suggested that the Seneca construct an independent declaration of war against Germany and Austro-Hungaria along the same lines as the one he had already drawn up for the Onondaga. He advised the Seneca to "establish your independent right to act as a Nation and not as a ward-bound tribe that had no powers of a Nation. The Senecas have lost none of their sovereignty since 1812 and a war declaration would serve to emphasize your status. The fighters could then enter the U.S. Army the same as now."[123]

The peyote furor eventually subsided, but SAI affairs remained as fragile as ever. Late that June Parker was again bemoaning that he had let his friends talk him into taking on the SAI presidency. He had no time to do justice to the role. What with war work, his State Museum duties, and the need to make up for the losses he had sustained over the last four or five years, now all he really wanted was to resign to a suitable successor. He told SAI associate and missionary Reverend Thomas Moffett: "I regret that I will be unable to go to the Conference, all my income, which has not had any war increases being tied up. I have given until I shall feel the giving for a long time to come."[124] Come September 25, 1918, the Pierre conference went ahead as scheduled without him. Eastman, who did not attend either, was elected president. Parker was offered the chance to continue as editor of *American Indian Magazine* but with the proviso that an appointed editorial board had veto powers. This didn't appeal to him, and Bonnin happily stepped into his shoes.[125] Thus he lost control of the publication he had created, and a central tie was severed between him and the group.

But in any case, after 1918 the SAI was no longer a worthwhile Indian reform vehicle in his eyes. With so many of the original stalwarts either out of favor or not in attendance and with only twenty-five or thirty people present, the conference agreed on a divisive, radical, and simplistic platform. Along with the planks put forward in previous years and a forceful statement in support of the war came a plea for immediate abolition of the BIA. Montezuma was delighted and the next month in *Wassaja* crowed about the change in philosophy, calling the new SAI officers the "most loyal of the Indian race." In truth they were a very select group who favored policies out of sync with the beliefs of the majority of middle-class Indians. For the national Indian reform body to formally embrace the idea of abolishing the BIA at a time when so few Indians were in a position to prosper without some form of federal protection was suicidal. It fundamentally alienated a wide band within the organization's constituency, both non-Indian and Indian.[126]

Parker had fostered a gradualist belief in change within what he believed to be a more or less inclusive and fair American system, but the new form of the SAI demanded instant answers from an America that it perceived as less than capable of bringing about productive change. To Parker, it was a sorry end to what he saw as the first great test of the caliber of the "race" in the twentieth century. He had given a great deal, risking his health through overwork and taking time and funds away from his family for little tangible gain. The SAI had brought about no reform, and now it would drift further and further from its original aims and emphases until it lost coherence. For a while, Woodrow Wilson's key idea, self-determination, was something of a unifying catchword, but it was never comprehensively defined. When invoked, the idea mostly involved full Indian citizenship, the chosen theme of the eighth annual conference held in Minneapolis in October 1919.

Parker felt much too hurt and annoyed to ever allow himself to become involved again. Before the Minnesota meeting, Reverend Moffett tried to get him to attend and reconnect, but he would have none of it. Admittedly, he was busy with State Museum work in Albany and with new projects, such as serving as secretary on the State Indian Commission, but in truth he felt that the "race" had failed him. It had failed itself, and he had failed to give enough to the cause.[127] In reply to Moffett's letter, he wrote: "From the time of the Lawrence conference until I withdrew my active participation I had less and less time to give. To me it was a tragedy for I saw what we all had hoped for slipping through our fingers."

Even though he wished the SAI well and hoped that "the best blood and the best minds" would prevail, he had finally had enough. Because he had decided to give his full attention to his work for the State Museum, his employer had given him the promotion due five years before, and he now felt it was "quite essential" that he make good.[128] He had finally decided to abandon the quest for reform through a national Indian group, and he had lost faith in the idea that an educated Indian community was capable of cohering sufficiently to work toward reform.

Meanwhile, the SAI continued its downward spiral. The 1919 conference was yet another revolutionary affair, with Sloan taking over the presidency and Eastman and Bonnin giving up for good. Delegates were unable to unite around the citizenship theme or a platform. New officers decided on a program that more or less reshaped the SAI into a political pressure group open to patronage. Along with a number of the older founding members, Parker was formally relegated to the advisory board. Just how jaded he had become at this stage with Indian reform is clear from the correspondence he kept up with one insider, the SAI's vice president for education, James Irving. Irving wrote to him in connection with the SAI's new dynamic—the campaign for an Indian as Indian commissioner. Correctly predicting a forthcoming Republican administration, he thought Parker might be worth the SAI supporting for commissioner. He wrote: "The Jews had their Moses; the negroes their Booker T. Washington. I believe it is now time to have a real Indian leader for the next Commissioner of Indian Affairs."

Parker was at the time New York State Indian commissioner. His reply was restrained. It said nothing about the SAI's previous commitment to remaining outside politics and noted, "under the circumstances the position of commissioner is one with so many difficulties that no one intimately acquainted with the work would care much to take it up."[129] In the end, President Sloan was the one the SAI decided to support, to little effect. The SAI's affairs were increasingly distasteful to Parker, who could only watch as, in his opinion, the group embarrassed the "race."

During the spring of 1920, he was so incensed at a proposal to change the name of *American Indian Magazine* that he told Irving: "The entire tone of the magazine is shoddy, and hysterical wailing of men who are supposed to be educated brings only discredit upon us. However, since I am not in a position to be of constructive service it ill becomes me to criticize."[130] By autumn 1920 the SAI had effectively become another lobbying group to Congress. Parker had resigned, even from the advisory board. He no doubt realized that the group had neither the cohesion nor backing to function successfully. How could it lobby when a majority of Indians were not enfranchised and when many of those who were did not wish to use their vote for fear of compromising their property rights and/or their tribal status?

Parker scaled down his Indian concerns to the New York Iroquois. He took on the presidency of the New York Indian Welfare Society and made another localized attempt to achieve the goals he felt had been lost within the larger group. With a very similar structure to the original SAI, the New York society had a distinguished white advisory board and met twice a year in places like the University of Rochester. He described it as "a small group of Iroquois Indians who will come to deliberate on the welfare of their people." When they met, he reminded an associate, they looked no more like blanket Indians than white men of the day resembled Elizabethan courtiers. He added tetchily, "Time changes everything except the white man's notion of an Indian."[131] The

SAI struggled on, but with time it made more and more concessions to exactly this, the white man's notion of the Indian.

A poor SAI conference was held in St. Louis that year, and then another in 1921 that even the secretary described as a "fiasco." It took the form of a "big Indian pow wow" in Detroit, billed as an "International Convention of the American Indians" with the idea of bringing together all the disparate groups in any sense involved with Indian life. Only eight active and associate members attended what became a campfire travesty of the older SAI ideals. Parker's despondency turned to explicit bitterness in a letter to his old SAI colleague Daganett. Further clumsy attempts to coax him back had simply infuriated him: "I never think of the Society without thinking also of the work you and I did in company with the hard heads that helped us. Then, thinking of the present state of things, I develop nausea. That bunch of bolshevists could never have started the Society; now they are living on the reputation we made for it." He said he would be happy to go to Detroit if he could place horseshoes in his mittens and if Daganett could just tell him what size gun to tote.[132]

His anger and disappointment, coupled no doubt with the mainstream hostility toward minorities rife during what has been termed the "tribal twenties," gave Parker a new, radical perspective on the whole project of Indian assimilation.[133] He accepted a new imperative—white cultural and racial perpetuation—and began to make it known. A few months after his "bunch of bolshevists" tirade, he made a speech to the Albany Philosophical Society where he described a future America without a single reference to any positive Indian contribution. Dismissing the idea of an American melting pot, he instead used eugenics to proselytize openly against both immigration and "racial blendings" and to argue for "the preservation of racial type—that of the Aryan white man."

It was a complete reversal from 1916. He now recognized that America had no place in the sun for its ethnic minorities and that a fundamental gap existed between the rhetoric and reality of American political, cultural, and social life. He said bitterly: "America, the *melting pot* of the world. What a beautiful simile . . . and yet there are some of us who are skeptical enough to think that the myth of the 'melting-pot' has all gone to pot." He went on to discuss the "national philosophy of the commonwealth, as expressed by our Nordic-Aryan forefathers of the colonial days," a philosophy he now knew demanded "the preservation of the physical type—that of the Aryan white man." Finally, he warned that "indiscriminate blood blending and inharmonious race contacts" would lead the nation to "blindness . . . palsy . . . leprosy and . . . death by fire upon a bed of scented silks."[134]

Gone was any previous stress on the importance of the desire of the noncitizen to be assimilated, together with any requirement of common association with the dominant culture. Parker had gone from an advocacy of integration, assimilation, and amalgamation for European immigrants and Native Americans in 1916, to a general advocacy of exclusion and preservation of the white race in 1922. The new science, eugenics, provided support for his fresh perspective, even though it disapproved of the kind of intermarriage across cultures within his own family background. Specifically in 1916 and certainly up until 1920, Parker had argued for special conditions for Indian assimilation and made much of the beneficial effects of Indian-white intermarriage. Now he was using eugenics to exclude the Indian along with most other non-Aryans from American society and stressing the detrimental effects of the majority of cross-cultural unions. For the first time, he put forward a vision of the United States where the Indian was a "blood stock" capable of contaminating the true America.

It is difficult to imagine where Parker placed himself within his own argument. It seems he was above the issue, in some transcendental analytical space where his own doctrine need not apply. Once the strongest support of the primary Indian organization working toward reform and assimilation at the beginning of the twentieth-century, he now advocated the exclusion of his own people from the future of his country. Where once he had used Morgan and evolution to foster Indian assimilation and what he called "amalgamation," he now used eugenics to rant against an inclusive America that he feared could become "a crazy-quilt nation full of racial patches, some black, some white, some yellow, some brown." His 1922 speech reflected disillusionment with both the SAI and its vision of a successful and fully integrated Indian minority. With that dream gone, he had retreated to the fashionable fears of the "older" American immigrants, the group with which he so much wanted to associate, middle- to upper-class, white, educated, Anglo-Saxon Protestants.

Meanwhile, the SAI struggled on without Parker, who started to develop his interests in radio scriptwriting and broadcasting.[135] Montezuma planned a convention for Chicago, but then contracted tuberculosis and returned with his wife to his home reservation in Arizona where he died on January 31, 1923. Committed to Indian uplift and to the Apache to the end, he made a white friend named Miss M. Stanley promise to organize the convention in his stead. Parker concerned himself with other things, but he defended the SAI in a letter to the editor of the *Christian Science Monitor*.[136] When Miss Stanley wrote that summer for advice on suitable conference speakers, he was sympathetic, telling her that although not an organizer, Montezuma had "had many lovable qualities." Still, he had no intention of getting involved again. He told her: "To go into the work too deeply only brings a heartache.... One must realize that there is no such being or race today in America as 'the Indian.' To the contrary, there are between 300,000 and 340,000 persons of more or less Indian blood, each one of which has his own vital individual interests. Few have any very deep interest based on the idea of race."[137]

Perhaps predictably, when finally organized, the Chicago gathering was noted for its "show-Indian" events rather than for any substantive plans for reinvigorating Indian affairs. For a few years more, the SAI limped on with Father Gordon as president, never making any further real impact.

By the mid-1920s, white intellectuals and those concerned with Indian reform had lost the kind of interest they once showed in educated Indians. The dynamic shifted once again to white-run organizations, and talk of an Indian "race" faded in place of concern for specific "traditional" tribal cultures. One such group was the Pueblo of New Mexico, who would have lost large segments of their land and water rights had the Bursam Bill of 1922 been allowed to go through. The whole affair made the Pueblo, along with other agricultural cultures in New Mexico and Arizona who had managed to escape the effects of allotment, something of a cause célèbre among contemporary intellectuals and reformers. They now saw in traditional cultures features that were lacking in the atomized individual competition of industrial America.

This thinking informed a coalition of Indian defense organizations, such as the Indian Rights Association and interested non-Indian groups, together with a selection of intellectuals, academics, and so on who were organized by sociologist and reformer John Collier into the influential American Indian Defense Association. With Collier providing leadership, the group played an important role as the movement for fundamental reformulation of Indian policy gained momentum. Thus it was a non-Indian vision of the Indian future that gained precedence as the 1920s progressed rather than any program put forward by educated Indians such as those who had toiled within the SAI.

Parker nevertheless had input into the shaping of the new agenda and a working relationship with Collier as the man spearheading the change. He and Parker probably met first in the autumn of 1923 when the new secretary of the interior, Hubert W. Work, brought together a distinguished group to advise on Indian affairs. The Committee of One Hundred, as they were called, met in Washington. They included nine eminent anthropologists, such notaries as William Jennings Bryan, General John J. Pershing, Matthew K. Sniffen, and Fayette McKenzie, together with much of the core membership of the early SAI: Roe Cloud, Coolidge, Eastman, Gordon, Sloan, and Wheelock. Parker had the honor of presiding over the committee sessions. Perhaps remarkably, they were able to agree on a series of resolutions generally similar to the SAI's early overall agenda.

In turn, this consensus fed into the Meriam Report, a much more thorough investigation begun in 1926 by members of the independent Brookings Institution research group, which included Roe Cloud and McKenzie, again at the request of the secretary of the interior.[138] The report, also known as *The Problem of Indian Administration,* was submitted in February 1928. In essence, it revealed in a politically significant way that government policy, including the General Allotment, or Dawes Act, had failed and in fact contributed to the desperate conditions—in health, economics, and education—then existing for so many Indian peoples. The report also helped fuel a general movement within Indian affairs, led by Collier, to revive tribalism and traditional cultures and to use social science to ease Indian integration within American society.

Popular dissatisfaction over specific injustices and the glaring need to improve Indian administration led to a series of policy reconsiderations during the 1920s. The Meriam Report may be the best known, but each, including the conclusions of the Committee of One Hundred, provided a useful basis for the significant Indian reforms of the Depression and New Deal years. Developments gained pace under ex-IRA president Charles Rhoads as Hoover's commissioner, with Joseph Scattergood as assistant; but it was John Collier, after their resignations in 1933, who made the deeper inroads into American Indian problems. Parker's contribution to the process of change was valuable, if on paper limited. Yet his efforts were part of an essential development of factors agitating for reform, and they stand as a useful indicator of how far an educated Indian professional was able to direct change, even when he sacrificed so much of his time and attention to the interests of "the race."

When the Indian Citizenship Bill was finally passed on June 2, 1924, only a week after the nation had determined to curtail the availability of citizenship to certain immigrants through the restrictive quota system enshrined in the Immigration Act, Parker felt that his hard work within the SAI had been rewarded. There is little evidence that citizenship moved Indian assimilation ahead much, but the bill was at least evidence of a new desire to curb the power of the BIA. Back in

1923, the Committee of One Hundred had not felt able to take a position on citizenship, lest such action affect the status of Indians protected by the federal government. Parker nonetheless believed that he and his associations had helped bring the right to citizenship into being, something he registered in a signed archive note.[139]

We cannot deny Parker a role in fomenting change. He had indeed contributed to the push for some positive transformation of Indian affairs during the 1910s and 1920s. Further, the SAI was unquestionably an important development within American Indian history with its attempt to exercise effective intertribal influence through accommodation. Yet, we must also acknowledge that it was a failure both as a reform organization and as a context for Parker's strenuous and enthusiastic efforts to secure Indian integration within the American cultural mainstream. Essentially, the SAI achieved nothing in terms of practical legislative change, and both its sphere of influence and its constituency were limited and ill-defined from the outset. Since neither its "active" membership of "Indian blood" nor its primarily white "associate" membership ever collectively numbered over a few hundred, and since in over a decade of operation individual tribes never came to be specifically represented, it is difficult even to award it the accolade of being a viable example of pan-Indian action. It was run by and for the emerging educated Indian middle-class, and they were unable to garner either the funds or the broad-based support needed to renegotiate the Indian position within American society.

Parker's involvement had made him more comfortable with his Indian and biracial credentials, but in the end, the depth of his commitment to the SAI and the racial significance he awarded it made its eventual disintegration all the more painful. He had hoped to become part of a vanguard of Indian middle-class professionals achieving full integration, but his years as a prominent SAI leader showed him that Indian self-help in this form would not achieve that integration. He also learned that tribal concerns militated against sustained, concerted Indian political action. He was forced to realize that "race leadership," on the terms of SAI members, was neither wanted or understood by most Indians nor desired by the dominant society.

From this point onward, Parker used his Iroquois or Indian identity selectively to serve his own agenda—success within the non-Indian world. In one sense, this had always been his vision within the SAI, that is, for "Indianness" to function as an inner quality that gave special valency to a fully integrated position. Sadly, it was the "show-Indian" image, rather than the respectable middle-class professional identity so carefully put forward by Parker, that won the day. That representation of Indian culture had much greater currency as an anti-modern trope than the more complex understanding needed to facilitate full Indian integration. Even when significant legislative reform did eventually come in the mid-1930s with the onset of Roosevelt's New Deal, it would be based on a primitive model of Indian culture.

In a very real sense, America was not ready for the reevaluation of Indian capabilities that Parker and the SAI wanted. Consequently, his complaints about America's need for show-Indians, its need to connect feathers, paint, and savagery with anything Indian, were as pertinent before the SAI began as after it finally lost coherence. Parker expressed his frustration at this abiding problem perhaps most eloquently in 1920, when he spoke at the opening session of the New York Indian Welfare Society:

> To the white man an Indian is only an Indian if dressed in feathers and buckskins. The white man is a queer mixture of inconsistencies and he likes to view men and things in the light of his preconceived notions. He may agree that everything in the world changes, but he does not want to know that the Indian changes with the world. Therefore, the vogue of the make believe "wild Indian."
>
> How would the white man like it if the Indians demanded that all white men who came upon their reservations must dress in Colonial uniforms and appear like the picture of Sir Walter Raleigh or of ancient Britain? Such white men want a show, a circus, a make believe Indian, and have but faint sympathy for the up to date Indian who living like a civilized man struggles in civilization for competence.[140]

There was, however, another forum within which Parker could be a progressive Indian, a modern professional successfully integrating with those he considered his peers, the non-Indian middle-class. This was the fraternal world, specifically, the Freemasonic lodge. He had joined the Masons back in 1907, when he was deeply engaged with the fieldwork that had helped make his name, but for many years had not advanced within it. It was not until the period of intense involvement with the SAI ended, after 1918, that he was able to turn his attention more fully to fraternal life. His fraternal relationship and fraternal discourse tell another story about how Parker tried to progress without sacrifice of his Indian identity.

Being Indian and Being a Mason: Parker and American Fraternalism

All Parker's hard work and earnest attempts to muster a united front to lead the "race" through the Society of American Indians brought him little obvious reward. He ended his period of sustained engagement with reform politics convinced that Indians were incapable of leading themselves toward inclusion within the American mainstream and disappointed with the enduring preeminence of the "show-Indian" image. The SAI had taught him that Indians were diverse, too diverse to be easily shepherded by an educated and select few. It was a hard lesson after so much sterling individual effort on his part. Yet great consolation was to be had from another source—his fraternal life, in particular, his Masonic involvement. The twilight world of the fraternity hall had a much firmer grasp of order, process, and unity of purpose than the SAI. There, he could easily be both Indian and respectable American without any awkward equivocation or burdensome administrative work. He could enjoy a satisfyingly secure position within its broad fellowship and benefit from the warm sense of inclusion generated both by membership and its associated ritual. With fraternal men he was, very probably, in his element. By nature Parker was friendly and approachable, able to talk to people at their own level, and very appreciative of what they had to say. He had the ability to make others feel special and to let them know that their ideas were important. The fraternal lodge was a convivial and pleasant context where his jocular good humor helped him to make useful and enjoyable contacts and to relax. As family members had done before him, he put real effort into being a fraternal figure of good standing, and in particular into being an excellent Mason. His reward, and the high point of his fraternal life came on September 16, 1924, not too long after the whole SAI debacle had been put to rest. He was awarded American Freemasonry's highest rank. This was the thirty-third degree, a specific honor conferred only on a select few from the pool of senior Masons.

It is difficult to assess the exact impact, both professionally and personally, of Parker's fraternal success, but it was certainly another ratiocinative focus in his struggle within the matrix of culture, ethnicity, class, and citizenship. Involvement represented a valuable avenue of integration for Parker, given that early-twentieth-century fraternal organizations were primarily white, middle-class, and exclusive. Typically, although their rhetoric stressed brotherhood, universality, equality, and cohesion around central themes of morality and good character, these clubs made constant reference to the "profane" or nonfraternal world, and they practiced fairly rigid de facto exclusion. As Parker put it himself in one article, secret fraternities were all about allowing men with common aims to gather "where they may promote their principles and engage in their ceremonies unmolested by those who have not been found worthy and well qualified."[1] Since fraternities positioned themselves as representatively American, in joining them Parker was too. Membership reinforced his middle-class status and allowed him to associate with those whites he considered his peers. Best of all, within the Masons there was no need for him to be obscure about his own nonwhite heritage. In fact, Masonry was one American hierarchy where Parker was able to excel without any sacrifice of his Indian identity whatsoever. Rather, because the Masons relied on the Indian to support some of their claims to legitimacy, he could use his Indian descent to help get himself into the Masonic world, and once inside could write for Masonic publications and work on better positioning his "race" within their discourse. Throughout his life, what he wrote for the Masons always tried to tie Indians and Masons ever more firmly together. If Masons were representative Americans, he very much wanted Indians to seem so too.

· · ·

Today it is easy to dismiss fraternalism and its ritual as ridiculous and irrelevant, especially since it has so often been mercilessly lampooned by the media. As soon as Freemasonry in particular lost its centrality in middle-class male American life during the 1930s, the American public started to ridicule the fraternities of previous generations. For example, television audiences laughed at the character Ralph Kramden, a member of the risible Loyal Order of Raccoons on the show *The Honeymooners*. What was being debunked was the Babbitt-like sentimentality, pomposity, and materialism with which such clubs had come to be associated, especially by intellectuals.[2] Such popular mockery may partly explain why social scientists and other academics have tended, until recently, to ignore fraternalism's role within the cultural and social life of the nation in the later decades of the nineteenth century and the first decades of the twentieth. In the words of revisionist historian Mark C. Carnes, "Scholars have understandably dismissed the notion that on the eve of the twentieth century between 15 and 40 percent of American men, including a majority of those categorized as middle-class, were transfixed by this hokum."[3]

Previous commentators have tended to think of fraternalism and other forms of voluntary association within the United States in much the same way as de Tocqueville did back in 1840. He explained the phenomenon as the citizen's defense against the anonymity and lack of protection offered by America as a nation-state.[4] However, new work published in the 1980s by Lynn Dumenil, by Mary Ann Clawson, and by Carnes has begun a reevaluation. While holding differing opinions about the nature and function of fraternalism, these writers agree that it must not continue to be overlooked. Clawson, for example, describes "the social metaphor of brotherhood" as a hitherto "unrecognized social fact" and finds it remarkable that the precise nature of fraternal identity has not received greater scholarly attention.[5]

All three writers have stressed how central fraternalism was to many Americans' social lives. Although the history of fraternalism stretches back to the colonial period, the last third of the nineteenth century was in fact the "Golden Age of Fraternity." In 1896, some five and a half million out of nineteen million adult American men belonged to some form of fraternal organization.[6] The most popular and prestigious of all the secret fraternal groups was the one to which Parker devoted most of his fraternal energies, the Ancient and Accepted Order of Freemasons. By the twentieth century, it had become the organizational model for hundreds of American social orders, trade unions, agricultural societies, nativist groups, and political movements across the ideological spectrum. Freemasonry also played a key role in other major fraternal orders, with the Knights of Pythias and the Odd Fellows being closest to it in organizational structure.

From over 55,000 members in 1879, the Masons had blossomed by 1900 and gained over 1 million adherents. After World War I, when there was a desire to "get ahead," Masonic participation boomed. According to Dumenil, "post-war, Masonic membership may have proved to be much more materially beneficial than in the past," and membership in a Masonic lodge "could well have been an expression of a desire for 'normalcy.'"[7] In any case, by 1925 there were over 3 million Masons, and Freemasonry "touched the lives of millions of American men."[8] It enjoyed an especially high profile throughout the 1920s, and many movie stars and famous figures such as Theodore Roosevelt, Henry Ford, and Charles Lindbergh were known to be members.[9]

Freemasonry has an interesting history and form. The fraternity probably originated in Scotland over three centuries ago as a stonemasons guild, and it retained an essentially reactionary, conservative nature in its crossover to the United States.[10] During the colonial period its tone very much reflected Enlightenment thought, with an emphasis on deism, rationalism, science, and the human relationship to nature. These characteristics persisted into the nineteenth and twentieth centuries as the nature of Masonic engagement became better known. Masons were required to progress through levels of initiation or "degrees," which were accompanied by "secret" and esoteric ritual, symbolic of greater knowledge of Freemasonry's central truths. These invoked charity, fraternity, morality, and a form of religiosity. Whatever the specifics of the Masonic tradition, generally speaking, the fraternity functioned as a "white, male, primarily native, Protestant society" that mirrored the values of middle-class America, with a commitment to self-improvement, temperance, piety, and industry.[11]

There were, of course, other aspects to Freemasonry and to fraternalism, in particular a financial side. At the turn of the century fraternal leaders and organizers made thousands of dollars out of the membership, which in a way conflicted with the fraternal ideals of mutuality and brotherhood. Clawson describes how "regalia manufacturers and merchants, job printers, physicians, and above all fraternal agents and leaders found in the fraternal order a source of material benefit and personal advance." Many fraternal organizations also ran fairly large-scale beneficial societies. By 1898, these societies had over two and a half million members, nearly half a million more policy holders than private U.S. companies.[12] But even without taking into account the insurance revenue, the income of the various Masonic bodies alone ran to the hundreds of millions.

However, financial matters were not primary to the fraternal experience of most members. Ritualism was central to the affairs of most lodges, and it was the central focus within Freemasonry when Parker first joined the organization in 1907. Within most clubs, each successive fraternal promotion achieved by each member was rewarded with initiation, new ritual, and fuller understanding of the earlier rites. Just why ritualism was so significant has been much discussed. Generally, fraternal orders are thought of as being "expressive"—that is, their purpose was to meet the social and personal needs of their members. This explains why fraternal rituals changed so significantly across region and over time. According to Clawson, the ritualism that took up so much of fraternal business "functioned as a form of entertainment that enlivened and gave purpose to the sociability it justified." Similarly, Carnes tells us that "the record shows that fraternal ritualists, through a maddeningly unpredictable process of trial and error, attempted to "give satisfaction" and "gratify the desires" of members."[13]

There may be some agreement as to what ritualism did for those who practiced it, but there is still little available information to help explain the exact fraternal significance and nature of the higher degrees that Parker was party to as a top-ranking Mason. Although there is now an extensive literature on Freemasonry, with perhaps fifty thousand items published as early as the 1950s, details such as these remain obscure. This is perhaps because secrecy has always been integral to Masonic rhetoric. Ritualistic admittance to each of the successive degrees or stages warned clearly of punishments should the applicant betray Masonic secrets to those outside the brotherhood—that is, to the "profane." For example, the first three degrees list as penalties having the tongue torn out, the heart torn from the breast, and the bowels being burned to ashes, respectively.[14] Ancient Charge Vl.4 of the Masonic Constitution advises, "You shall be cautious in your words and carriage, that the most penetrating stranger shall not be able to discover or find out what is not proper to be intimated; and sometimes you shall divert a discourse and manage it prudently for the honour of the worshipful fraternity."[15] Of course, the most likely punishment for the betrayal of Masonic secrets would have been the disapprobation of fellow Masons. However, even this has not prevented the initial three Masonic degree rituals, Entered Apprentice, Fellow Craft, and Master Mason, from becoming well documented since the nineteenth century.

When Parker joined, Masons were keen to be seen as individuals who were reinforcing all-American ideals and working to bring about social reform and social cohesion. Parker, of course, wanted to be seen in the same light, as all-American and as a positive factor in the struggle to maintain American values. As time progressed, Masons perhaps inevitably responded to perceived threats to national vitality—from radicalism, immigration, and Catholicism. Changes in the national political and social climate surrounding the United States entry into World War I, the aftermath of the 1919 Red Scare, and developing nativist concerns over immigration all caused Freemasonry to play down its commitment to the ideal of brotherhood and instead promote the organization's social conservatism and commitment to American democracy. Masonry did not create an overt policy of restricted membership, but in practice lodges during the 1920s became more obviously racially exclusive. Once, Masonic rhetoric had emphasized the principle of universality, defined as the association of good men without regard to religion, nationality, or class, with the additional proviso that prospective candidates had to be physically sound, free-born males who believed in God and lived a moral life.[16] However, by the 1920s, Masons, and Parker, were instead playing up their credentials as loyal and patriotic citizens and reasserting the dominance of old-stock, white American values. Anti-immigrant feeling was by this stage especially strong, a reflection of the national drive toward 100 percent Americanism. There was also an overall concern to modernize and bring the fraternity more firmly into the secular sphere.[17]

Overt racism was not expressed in official Masonic publications, since it would have obviously contravened the fraternity's central tenets of universality and brotherhood, but a set of biases and prejudices was evident nonetheless. For example, there seems to have been a strong connection between Masonry and the Ku Klux Klan. Dumenil is unable to provide statistics on this, but she does quote a Norman Frederick de Clifford, who in 1918 wrote *The Jew and Masonry* to "eradicate the hostile and Anti-Semitic feelings now existing in some of our Christian Masonic lodges toward the Jewish Brethren and the race in general."[18] In comparison, black brotherhood was almost completely unaccept-able to Freemasonry. In one instance, the fraternity resorted to legal-ism to exclude Prince Hall, a black Masonic order. Immigrants were also a target. Rather than disparage them directly in print, Masonic rhetoric forcefully stressed how essential it was for immigrants to fully assimilate.[19] Accompanying this was a discernible Masonic reaction against Catholicism. Masonic authors generally equated Protestantism with Americanism. The Catholic Church's long-held opposition to secret societies in general and to Masonry in particular allowed the Masons to maintain an essentially Protestant character. As early as 1738, Pope Clement XII had forbidden Catholics to join under threat of excommunication, and in 1884, Leo XIII brought out an encyclical that condemned the whole enterprise of European Masonry as politically subversive. Overall, as Dumenil explains, very quickly within modern Masonry, "ethnic qualifications and good citizenship, more than morality, became the primary standards for evaluating respectability."

Although Masonry was responding to changing times, the basic social purpose of the organization remained intact as the twentieth century progressed. "The motives for joining Masonry in the 1920s," Dumenil concludes, "seem to have been very much the same as they had always been: fraternity, sociability, personal gain, and status." Masonic fraternalism was about a shared sense of community; it gave its members a means of identifying with the values honored in the middle-class world. As a welcome sanctuary against an industrializing and changing America, the fraternity had "separate standards and concerns from the immoral, competitive, and commercial world beyond the temple," and it "provided a sacred asylum in which men could ignore the social, political, economic, and religious conflicts of the time while cultivating love of God, bonds of fellowship, and improvement of the individual."[20]

Clawson brings forward further complexities inherent in Masonry. "Its significance," she claims, "resides not only in the social networks it created, reinforced, or displayed, but in the meanings it articulated, the cultural context it provided for social action." While it offered an antidote to individualism in its facilitation of mutual aid and in its symbolic relationship to the artisan, at the same time it allowed a more powerful reaffirmation of it. It resolved some of the contradictions of progress, since it put forward "the vision of a society in which individual advancement and social solidarity were complementary rather than antagonistic—and attempted to create that society in miniature." Clawson argues that Freemasonry worked to deny class and instead offered "gender and race as appropriate categories for the organization of collective identity," its ritual being used to reconcile social difference.[21] She feels it attracted so many men in the decades surrounding the turn of century because it set up a separate reality. Like the street parades of the nineteenth century, its ritual acted out "dramas of social relations" in which "performers define who can be a social actor" and therefore "what society was or might be." Thus it went some way toward resolving awkward contemporary conflicts—over religion, gender, across generations, between wage workers and entrepreneurs. But at heart its function remained the same. It was "a cultural institution that maintained and idealized solidarity among white men."

Of course, the fact that fraternalism was a male pursuit cannot be ignored. Clawson recognizes this in her overall conclusion, explaining how fraternalism "defined manhood as an alternative reference point to a collective identity and critique based upon class difference and workplace identity." Carnes, too, is fascinated by fraternal ritual's symbolic relation to masculinity. He tells us how "these long and 'perilous' initiatory journeys facilitated the young man's transition to, and acceptance of, a remote and problematic conception of manhood in Victorian America." Gender, as "one of the most important tensions in Victorian American life," was an issue brotherhoods helped to assuage. When the young Victorian American male "left the home for the lodge several evenings a week, keeping his wife in the dark about what transpired there, he imparted to her a painful message about the marital relation. When he performed the roles of Old Testament fathers or Indian chiefs, he re-enacted paternal roles replete with gender significance. And when he ventured into the deepest recesses of fraternal secrets, he encountered ideas about gender expressed nowhere else in Victorian America."[22]

Masculinity must be salient within any analysis of an organization exclusive to men, but it seems that for Parker, Masonic membership was first and foremost a statement of commitment to the fraternity's moral system. It was a tangible and semipublic bond to middle-class American culture. To use Dumenil's language, Masonry "enunciated a moral code of self-improvement through self-restraint that harmonized with the prevailing Protestant middle-class culture," and this was what Parker was buying into. However, gender-focused scholars like Carnes and Clawson are unsatisfied with this argument. Carnes, for example, relegates Dumenil's idea that fraternal men were primarily bonding as middle-class individuals because of evidence that "the fraternal performance of so many long, repeated rituals left very little time for members to get to know each other." He insists that fraternal ritual had a great deal more to do with constructing manhood than it had to do with establishing social communities.[23]

Parker knew that fraternity touched something deep in the male psyche, but for him at least, the fraternal experience centered primarily on bonding with those in power rather than with reaffirming gender. Secret societies, he explained, allowed men to love their fellow men: "Because of this most normal men seek a fraternity and find in it the satisfaction of every fundamental desire in the male heart—the desire to be, to have, to rank, to know, to feel, to fit. Through the righteous satisfaction of these desires men grow in social and spiritual qualities."[24] He wanted, quite simply, a privileged position within a community at the apex of respectable American middle-class life.

Of course, Masonic organizational fervor may have served other functions for other people. Masonry was a men's group. It was also a spiritual retreat in an increasingly religiously diverse society. Its stress on brotherhood offered an alternative to the rugged individualism of the time, and it reaffirmed traditional values of self-restraint, industry, and morality. But above all this, it was a middle-class, predominantly white club. Progressive reform originated with such middle-class men, and most progressive leaders, of whatever gender, were "old stock" WASPs. This was the group at the forefront of change and the group with which

Parker needed to strongly affiliate. The lodge provided him with a place to make these powerful contacts, where he could work on repositioning American Indians within a discourse relevant to social change.

Aged twenty-six, Parker joined Sylvan Masonic Lodge No. 303, Sinclairville, New York, and was "raised" in November 1907.[25] Initial progression was slow. It took a further eleven years for him to achieve the second degree, Fellow Craft, on September 23, 1918.[26] It then took until he was forty-three for his years of fraternal duty to be rewarded with admission to the Royal Order of Scotland and the ne plus ultra of Masonic recognition—the thirty-third degree and with it the fraternal tag, Sovereign Grand Inspector General.[27] The thirty-third degree gave him access to Freemasonry's highest echelon. As with all degrees above the third, fraternal administration switched to the jurisdiction of a Supreme Council with headquarters in London, a building known within the fraternity as the Grand East. There is little supported information readily available about the thirty-third degree's purpose and operations, but it is reported to still exist today and to be restricted internationally to only seventy-five members.[28] What the thirty-third degree meant or means is perhaps less significant than the larger and more obvious truth about its bestowal upon Parker. Masonic membership conferred honorific status within middle-class America, what Dumenil calls "a badge of respectability," and in gaining promotion to the thirty-third degree, Parker had reached the pinnacle of success within that context.

One of the reasons Parker deserved his fraternal acclaim was that he had demonstrated his commitment, not just to Freemasonry, but to fraternalism in general. Like many men of the period, he belonged to more than one fraternal group at once. A long-term member of the Knights Templar, the Royal Order of Scotland, and the Sons of the American Revolution, he would also be feted by the Philalethes Society late in life. Such devotion was expensive. Members spent huge sums on initiation fees, annual dues, mutual assessment funds, and ritualistic paraphernalia.[29] In climbing up the Masonic rankings, Parker would have undergone repeated initiations and have absorbed all the associated costs. In addition to all the rituals and initiations accompanying the first three degrees of Freemasonry, known as Blue Lodge Masonry, there were ten additional degree sequences associated with Royal Arch, Royal and Select Master, and the Knights Templar organizations. On top of all this, office within the higher degrees, such as the thirty-third, was even more exclusive and more expensive.[30]

This did not seem to overly concern Parker. In fact, his correspondence makes no reference to the financial investment involved. Instead, as with the following reaction to the news of gaining the thirty-third degree, he simply expressed pleasure at being part of the fraternity and praised the group's caliber. "The honor is almost overwhelming and makes me feel that I must now do my utmost to justify the confidence that our beloved brethren of Buffalo have reposed in me," he wrote. "If I pass the probationary period and am eventually brought to the Great East of the H.E. to be crowned a S.G.I.G., honorary, I shall feel that I have received the highest honor that men and Masons can give—namely, the testimony of the greatest and truest fraternity the world has ever known." Almost overcome at his achievement, he went on: "I cannot express myself now, for I am filled with conflicting emotions. I am mighty happy and capable of doing all the undignified things that jubilant persons are, and yet the weight of honor awes me into discretion."

He was a little surprised to have received the award at all, since he felt he was at too far a remove from the thirty-third degree body to participate in its rituals. Still, he was not about to quibble with the Supreme Council since he deeply valued their "ardent friendship."[31] It may have been that his success imposed noblesse oblige and that Parker was a little nervous about the attendant financial and social obligations. Nevertheless, other Masons and friends regarded his selection as entirely beneficial, and none referred to costs or responsibilities. Many were quick to congratulate Parker on his new status, even if some, like his old boss John M. Clarke, had no idea what it meant. The anthropologist Alanson Skinner was especially effusive, telling Parker: "You certainly deserve it, for in you are more of the elements that go to make up greatness than any other person I know. I feel, as a Mason, that the Fraternity has honored itself as much as it has you by this act."[32] Parker's conferment carried its own social cachet, and the fact that he had achieved it as a respected figure of Indian extraction no doubt had its own significance to his peers.

It was not Freemasonry's rhetorical commitment to universality that allowed Parker to become a Mason. Rather, the fraternity's construction of itself as ancient, anti-modern, and noble allowed him access because of his ethnic identity. Being Indian was a plus to Parker as a Mason because Masonry chose to connect its arcane truths to the Indian past. Therefore, this connection was always the central theme of his Masonic writing. Through publishing articles that stressed correspondences between the Indian and Masonic worlds, he worked to bring the Indian ever closer to middle-class American life. Specifically, he did this through repeatedly comparing American Masonic ritual to aspects of Indian religious life.

His earliest Masonic article, "American Indian Freemasonry," maintained that, like Masons, Indians drew lessons and symbolism from a temple, the "Temple of Nature," and their "unwritten gospels" preached the same values cherished by Masons—"Fortitude, Loyalty, Patriotism, Tolerance, Fraternity, and Gratitude." Like Masons, they understood the significance of secrecy, because Indian societies had "possession of ritualistic words that belonged exclusively to the cult or fraternity" and were "jealously guarded." The Seneca Iroquois, he knew for certain, had "the thread of the legend of Osiris" that was integral to the third-degree Masonic ritual. It was evidence of their "inherent Freemasonry." In fact, a Masonic Museum of Archaeology and History should be set up because "every relic that is found on the sites where once lived the primitive peoples of the world is a lost letter syllable or word."[33]

Addressing the question of whether Indians might have been in possession of some proto-Masonic understanding was another way Parker connected Indians and Masons. The issue was the whole subject of his 1920 article "Freemasonry among the American Indians," which began, "One of the most frequent questions directed to the ethnologist who concerns himself with a study of the American aborigine is, 'Are Indians Masons?'" Parker's first concern was to firmly connect Indians of the past with contemporary Masonic Indians. "Today there are numerous Indians who are Free and Accepted Masons," he told his readership. "One can scarcely travel in Oklahoma, Nebraska, Kansas or the Dakotas without meeting Indians who belong to the ancient fraternity. Many of the most influential Indians of the Dakotas and especially of Oklahoma have full knowledge of the mysteries of Masonry and have sought further light in the concordant orders." He went on to explain how this firm bond between Indians and Masons had come about. Ancient Indians had possessed knowledge of some "extra-limital [sic] masonry, as if some uninstructed groups of mankind saw through a glass darkly,—and craved more light." Indians at one time had "the ability to construct an organization similar under the circumstances of forest and plains life to the freemasonry of the white man."

Warming to the theme, he pointed out that the Menominee Indians of Wisconsin had their own "fraternal or 'medicine' societies." Like Masonry, these had "several degrees culminating in the resurrection of the candidate who represents a slain hero." He also provided details of the Little Water Medicine Society ritual, the ritual of the Iroquois "Ancient Guards of Mystic Potence" or "Neh-Ho-noh-chee-noh-ga Nee-ga-hee-ga-aa" as further evidence of an ancient universal Freemasonry known to Indians. Again, his description of the ritual showed

You will notice Jake in the background.—He is re[hearsing for the 9th degree!]

Arthur Caswell Parker reservation photograph, which he captioned,
"You will notice Jake in the background—He is rehearsing for the 9th degree."

Personal Papers of Arthur Caswell Parker, in author's possession it to be very similar to "the rites of Osiris." Using Masonic allusions and keywords, he also pointed out similarities between the Indian ritual lodge and the Masonic temple: "The form of the lodge is an oblong and has two altars, one east and one west. Its ritual is sung or chanted by all the members, thereby rendering 'lost words' or forgotten sections next to impossible."[34]

Secrecy also connected Indians and Masons, as he argued in *Secrets of the Temple,* published in 1922, and "Why All This Secrecy?" published the following year.[35] In the former, he revealed that Indians had once had their own version of the Biblical Ark of the Covenant: "the various tribes of American Indians had their sacred arks or boxes and these were carried into battle just as was the ark of Yahwe Militant by the Jews, to give success in battle."[36] In the latter, he praised secrecy to the skies and claimed it as a specifically male virtue. It was a quality Indians particularly revered and would always, he said, be attractive to "normal American citizens of good character."[37] In 1924, Parker linked Indians and Masons yet again in "American Indian Freemasonry." It described initiation into Indian secret societies by white Freemasons. Parker was able to publish this kind of information because, sometime after his initial adoption into the Seneca Bear Clan during 1903, he had become a member of the Seneca Little Water Society, like his great-uncle Ely before him. He held the title "Deputy at Large of the Guards of Mystic Potence, or Little Water Society." He was also a member of two other religious Seneca fraternities, the Society of Mystic Animals and the Company of Whirlwinds, and was therefore in an excellent position to compare various tribal rituals with those practiced within the Masonic lodge. Furthermore, he was happy to act as fraternal intermediary, since he knew the topic interested his Masonic readership.[38] Masons could only have been charmed by his evidence. He showed that Indians, associated as they were with manliness, nature, and essential truth, were performing versions of Masonic activities. No doubt Masonic readers were further heartened by the knowledge that Seneca societies also shared the great virtue of secrecy.

In 1928, Parker reassured fellow Masons that, as an Indian, he shared with them an exclusively white vision of the true American character. He told in print a personal story that sought to strengthen the ties between Indians and Masons by using anti-black racism: "A short time ago a black Indian with a huge Masonic buttin [*sic*] rushed into my office and gave me what he thought was a grip, wanted to borrow five dollars and get my recommendation. His grip I knew not, neither did he get my recommendation or my five dollars. I told him what race he belonged to and that a police officer awaited him at the foot of the stairs. Oddly enough to avoid being thought of as a black he called himself "White Elk," but he was really a buck of another color, and one with which the Red Man does not mix."[39] Parker was using Masonry to distance his ethnic group from the group then suffering Jim Crow segregation in the South and racist aggression in the North. He wanted Indians to be associated instead with the ruling elite, of which a sizable chunk were Masons or at the very least social fraternal men of some sort.

Perhaps the best single example of him connecting Indians and Masons is an article he produced during the 1950s on his great-uncle, "Ely S. Parker—Man and Mason."[40] Parker described in depth the Seneca Little Water Society ritual, with all its striking similarities to what Masons would have known as the "traditional history"—the final ritual of the Masonic third degree. The parallel would have been obvious to his Masonic readership, but of course it was not a point Parker could ever make too explicit in print for fear of compromising Masonic secrecy. The Master Mason, or Royal Arch, ceremony mimed the murder "three thousand years after the creation of the world," by three Apprentice Masons, of Hiram Abiff, the principal architect of King Solomon's temple, because of his refusal to reveal Masonic secrets.[41] It then reenacts Abiff's subsequent resurrection and final reinstatement, going on to describe a crypt in the foundations of the ruined King Solomon's temple where the lost name of God, or the "omnibus word," is discovered.[42] Correspondences between this narrative and Parker's description of the Little Water Society ceremony, given below, are fairly clear. "It had three sections, and it was devoted to a ceremony taught by the hero who had resisted the blandish of three ruffians who demanded the secret of his power. He refused to divulge this or betray his trust and so was slain. When his forest friends, symbolized by various animals, found him, they sacrificed the vital sparks of their own bodies, while an aide collected them in an acorn cup, the contents of which were poured down the throat of the prostrate hero. He was then raised to his feet and to life by the powerful clasp of the Bear's claw."

Parker was keen to let fellow Masons know that this Little Water Society ritual had "exercised a profound influence on the Seneca people," concluding, "the writer has seen educated and well-to-do Indians from city homes return for the ceremony of this society, and several Freemasons, Indian and white, have been admitted.[43] If Clawson's analysis of the same Master Mason ritual is accurate, this was a symbolically powerful connection to make. She argues that the ritual was in itself "an idealized defense of individual private property," presenting "an idealized version of capitalist production and market relations."[44]

She then connects the ritual to Freemasonry's ability, through voluntary association, to mitigate against the reality of an individualistic, market-oriented society with its inevitable winners and losers. In linking Indian and Masonic ritual, Parker was tying the Indian to this reaction against modernity and at the same time binding Indians and Masons across generations on a deep and "secret" level.

The urge to connect the Indian past and Indian sensibilities to Freemasonry did not wane as Parker's professional life progressed. At age sixty-six, he would still be repeating his message that Indians and Masons shared common ground. The 1947 address he would deliver to a lodge in Vermont, entitled "The Age-Old Appeal of Universal Freemasonry," traced the Scottish and English origins of the "mighty fraternity" back to the sixteenth century. The overall premise was that "the deeper meaning of Freemasonry" was "ageless as well as ancient" and known to American Indian peoples. In fact, Parker claimed that recent research by then had confirmed that the Indian was of true Masonic caliber: "Only when these aborigines had been broken, confused and reduced to hunted animals did an awakening science find in them better values than had been dreamed." Perhaps, he wondered, historic conflicts over Indian lands could have been mitigated had civilized America "not only known but recognized the essential 'Brotherhood of Man.'"

By this stage, Parker had polished his arguments supporting the idea that the American Indian "could have qualified as a Freemason" and had isolated a total of five aspects of Indian belief with specific Masonic significance. First, like Masons, "higher groups of native people recognized a force in the universe that is beyond man," the "primal cause." Second, because they had an understanding of the soul, aboriginal Americans were able to recognize the central Masonic theme of immortality. "Since the soul acquired the substance of its immortality because of its earthly performance, another doctrine was held vitally essential." This other doctrine was morality, also central to Masonic thinking. The fourth piece of evidence was Indian pantheism, which, he argued, was itself a form of fraternal brotherhood. The fifth, Indian hospitality, was further proof of the Indian's understanding of charity and of the "idea of universal brotherhood." While acknowledging that Masonry was in itself unique, Parker once again suggested that the Indian possessed "a pre-Grand Lodge Masonic philosophy in a generative form." Therefore, he warned, Masons "must ever remember that behind the rite and ceremony, behind the letter-perfection of the catechist, the initiation and raising, the signs, grips and words, the symbols, the oaths and the lights, are deep meanings that are understood and have been understood for centuries by many diverse peoples of the earth." Masonry should protect itself against "diseased thinking that puts self above the common good." It was a bulwark against any threat to democracy, because Masonic morality was integral to the "defense of American character."[45]

Parker accepted requests to speak for various lodges, charters, and consistories fairly regularly throughout his Masonic life, although the task of connecting Indians and Masons was something he did mostly through Masonic publications. He also wrote and produced a total of twelve Masonic plays and from 1922 to 1924 was associate editor of the Masonic journal *The Builder*.[46] He spread the word about Indians and Masons to a lesser extent within other contexts.[47] For example, he would use his role as director of the Rochester Museum of Arts and Sciences to reinforce common correspondences between Indian and Masonic ritual through *Museum Service*, the Rochester museum's publication. Here, he again took the opportunity to underline in print the significance of the Masonic aspects to Iroquois Indian life: the common focus on ritual, rites of adoption, and the symbolic and spiritual significance of names, naming, and secrecy.

What allowed Parker to powerfully connect Masons and Indians was not really the fact that both groups appreciated secrecy or that they loved ritual, or even that the rituals they practiced shared a basic pattern. What actually bound the rhetoric of Freemasonry to Indians was the concept of antiquity. Indians and Masons occupied a similar space within the American imagination such that each reached beyond the concrete realities of the modern industrializing world. The idea of the Indian was simply not coeval with the present of the middle-class male Protestants who sought asylum within the Masonic lodge, and this was what made Indians attractive to them. They sought contact with the imagined glories of antiquity, and they used Indians, as they existed within their version of the mythologized past, to legitimate their own organizational message. Perhaps more interesting is that, in turn, Parker attempted to legitimate Indians as representative Americans through invoking Masonic rhetoric.[48] Nevertheless, what allowed him to do so was the appealing notion that Indians were connected to the shrouded mists of antiquity.

Of course, as a fraternity, Freemasons were not unique in being attracted to the obscure past. In fact, staking a claim to something connected with antiquity was almost prerequisite for a fraternal order. Characteristically, fraternities maintained that they had originated in the very distant past. Odd Fellows went so far as to claim Adam as the first member. The Knights of Pythias, founded in Washington, D.C., in 1864, claimed Pythagoras as the very first Pythian. The Improved Order of Red Men initially claimed descent from the Sons of Liberty of the American Revolution, and then at an 1864 committee meeting decided to trace their origins to the "discovery" of America by Columbus. Commentators suggest that the primary reason for all this reaching back into the mists of time was simply "to confer legitimacy upon institutions of recent origin."[49] Freemasonry also consistently tried to legitimate its claims to knowledge of universal truth by asserting archaic and esoteric origins. Its philosophic, religious, and ritualistic mix drew on a range of ancient sources—some, like the Isis-Osiris myth, which Parker referred to often in his Masonic writings, dating back to the dawn of history. Rosicrucianism, Gnosticism, the Kabbala, Hinduism, Theosophy, and traditional notions of the occult all have played a part, but the fraternity especially made claims to some original connection to groups such as the Knights Templar.[50] This had many benefits, not least that it allowed the costume of knighthood to be incorporated into higher-degree Masonic ritual. Even better, it connected Masonry with the ancient and mysterious wisdom of the Holy Land.[51]

A key factor in maintaining the fraternity's bond with antiquity was the repeated performance of ritual. Masonic ritual operated as a kind of theater that conjured a dislocated and mythical time for the membership. The gap, between real time and time as it was perceived within the Masonic world, has been usefully pinpointed by Carnes. He describes how "from the moment the lodge opened, a member's sense of time was blurred. Although meetings were always held in the evening, the ceremonies characteristically began at 'daybreak,' further distancing members from the outside world. While initiates were being prepared, the actors for the evening took off their clothes and put on robes, loincloths, or aprons. Others placed the scenery, lit the candles, and turned off the lights. Gradually the present dissolved, and a conjured sense of the past appeared before their eyes. After the initiations, the process was reversed."[52]

Carnes is convinced that Masons had a pressing need to commune with this "alternative past" and that at heart they were unconcerned about its authenticity. Modern men, who were building a new industrial order in a fast-developing country, at the same time chose to invent and perpetuate a ritualized fraternal past. They were reacting against their present, Carnes explains, a present that had "proven barren, devoid of emotional and intellectual sustenance," and they were invoking symbols that were in opposition to the existing hierarchies and rules. The phenomenon, Carnes tell us, is symptomatic of societies undergoing cultural change.[53] If he is correct, then Masons adopted the Indian as part of their project to articulate a reaction against turn-of-the-century industrializing America. As with all pasts posited as authentic, the Indian of antiquity served to denounce a present that Masons perceived as ruptured and inauthentic.

This was why American images of the Indian, as ritualistic, ancient, noble, and wise, fitted so well with Masonic identity. American Masons therefore claimed the Indian as a "natural Mason." As Philip Deloria has succinctly explained: "The Freemasons peopled their world with colorful historical figures—temple builders, crusader knights, and wise holy men—who had passed along the ancient secrets of Masonry. Indians inhabited this Masonic world as a curious primal branch of the brotherhood. If seemingly ancient Native American cultures possessed the same wisdom and ritual, Masons could claim that the great age of their origins had been confirmed."

Indians were a positive, legitimating force according to how the Masonic fraternity constructed itself and its history, and this allowed Parker purchase within the group. By comparison, another fraternity, the Improved Order of Red Men, denied membership to people like Parker. The Red Men's understanding necessitated that Indians occupy only the realms of myth and quasi-distant history. Their rhetoric constructed the Indian as an American cultural critic who was primarily a historical artifact. Consequently, in its heyday at the beginning of the century, the group denied membership to the material, progressive Indians. The existence of modern Indians, as living examples of a supposedly "vanished race," conflicted with the fraternity's idea of itself, which needed them only as symbols. Freemasonry, by comparison, acknowledged the Indian as a brother, in fact as a historical custodian of its own obscure and mystical "truths." Somehow in Masonic thinking, the Indians' connection with antiquity did not preclude their survival into modern age. Instead, Masons found it fitting that the mysterious wisdom possessed by Indians should continue to connect in the modern world with their own "secret" knowledge of essential verities.

Deloria tells us that this meant that Masons were "trapped in effect by their own discourse of legitimation" because their rhetoric necessitated that they conflate real and imagined Indians.[54] But this does not mean that Masonry was beneficial to Indians in any broad, inclusive sense. Masonry displayed an openness only to certain Indians—those adept at cultural mediation. Therefore the Indian Masons whom Deloria lists, Cherokees John Ross and Elias Boudinot, the Choctaw Peter Pitchlyn, the Creek Alexander McGillivray, are all illustrious and educated exemplars of cross-cultural exchange. Similarly, Parker's admission to fraternal groups and his Masonic success really cannot be separated from his cross-cultural heritage, from his good education, and his Masonic familial history. After all, two generations earlier his great-uncle Ely had been a respected Mason and had found the same sanctuary within the organization as Parker.

Ely had laid a bedrock of Masonic understanding and respect for fraternal involvement within the Parker family, which his great-nephew was able to build on. For example, in 1859, Ely had spoken with great eloquence to a Masonic audience at a convention in Chicago. His language encapsulated the warmth and respect he held for Masonry as a transcendent phenomenon operating outside of Indian culture. He asked his fellow Masonic brethren:

> Where shall I go when the last of my race shall have gone forever? Where shall I find home and sympathy when our last council-fire is extinguished? I said, I will knock at the door of MASONRY, and see if the white race will recognize me, as they had my ancestors, when we were strong and the white men weak. I knocked at the door of the *Blue Lodge*, and found brotherhood around its altar. I knelt before the Great Light in the Chapter, and found companionship beneath the Royal Arch. I entered the Encampment, and found valiant Sir Knights willing to shield me there without regard to race or nation. I went farther. I knelt at the cross of my Savior, and found Christian brotherhood, the crowning charity of the Masonic tie.
>
> I feel assured that when my glass is run out and I shall follow the footsteps of my departed race, Masonic sympathies will cluster round my coffin and drop in my grave the evergreen acacia, sweet emblem of a better meeting. If my race shall disappear from this continent, I shall have the consoling hope that our memory will not perish. If the deeds of my ancestors shall not live in story, their memories remain in the names of your great lakes and rivers, your towns and cities to call up memories otherwise forgotten.[55]

Parker was always proud to publicize this speech and Ely's Masonic history. He claimed Ely had first met Ulysses S. Grant at an Illinois lodge and wrote of him, "Two things this Indian never forgot—his Indian ancestry and his Masonic ties."[56] Ely, too, had been a "warrior in two camps." His entry into the fraternity had been an extension of a connection between Indian leadership and powerful Masons that stretched back at least to 1776 and Joseph Brant's adoption into the group during his visit to England. The famous Mohawk Brant had taken the opportunity to be initiated into the Falcon Lodge of the

Moderns on Princes Street in London while in England negotiating the Iroquois role in the Revolutionary War. It is even said that George III presented him with his apron.[57] Thus it becomes clear that no matter how Indians and Masonic rhetoric and legitimation connect, becoming a Masonic Indian was never something that operated outside of a wider historical context or a discernible set of power relations.

That said, being Indian carried an indisputable prestige within Masonry. This is affirmed and exemplified in Parker's "Indian" emphasis when he constructed a heritage for his entry within the *Masonic International Who's Who*.[58] Here, under "Notable facts in career of father, mother or earliest ancestors," Parker wrote: "Father descendent of the Sayen-Quaraughta line of Iroquois chiefs, also Jikonsaseh, compeer of Hiawatha. Mother descendent of line of Earl of Clarendon, (England). Father's family noted all through American history; great grandfather William Parker, (born King), turned Indians to friendly attitude to whites in War of 1812. Name Parker taken at Treaty of Niagara. General Ely Samuel Parker (Uncle), was Gen. U.S. Grant's military secretary." His entry is much more interesting because of what it says about the mores of Freemasonry than as a version of Parker's ancestry. He constructed a "noble" Indian ancestry and listed his mother as being related to English aristocracy. His "Indian" ancestry is patriotic, while his mother's relative, the Earl of Clarendon, is mentioned in the earliest histories of English Freemasonry. His religion is listed as Protestant (Presbyterian) and his politics as Independent Republican. He was therefore, an exemplary Mason. By comparison, the ancestry he provided in his application for membership to the National Society of Sons of the American Revolution contained no Indian names. In that context, Parker chose to trace his ancestors through his white mother, Geneva H. Griswold. Instead of listing his illustrious Indian descent, Parker omitted it completely and instead played up his maternal great-grandfather, Captain Abraham Batchellor, "4th Sutton Company 5th Worcester co., reg.," who, he said, had "marched to Providence on alarm."[59] Clearly, being Indian was a complex business within the fraternal world of modernizing America, but Parker could use his ethnicity to advantage in the right context.

Explaining Parker's engagement with Freemasonry depends on isolating the play of dependencies between his Masonic discourse and the larger political and social factors affecting his status as American Indian, as ethnic of dual heritage, and as American professional. A key benefit of his Masonic involvement, given that Freemasonry operated as a white, male, Protestant, and middle-class subsociety, was that he was able to work on bringing the idea of the Indian that little bit closer to the American mainstream. The fraternity's rhetoric facilitated this because of its own need to exist in an alternative past. To legitimate themselves, Masons needed to connect both with Indians and with the dislocated sense of long ago in which they operated within popular thinking.

All this allows us to see the integrative forces of the period operating from another perspective. Here was a determined American Indian attempting to be constitutive of integrative change, rather than being wholly subject to the forces deciding his opportunities within society. Powerful whites may have been mapping out the limitations of Indian integration and assimilation during this period, but as a Mason, Parker was at least going some way toward subverting those boundaries. Historian Frederick Hoxie tells us that during the early twentieth century, Indians as a group were asked to "remain on the periphery of American society, ruled by outsiders who promised to guide them toward "civilization" but who did not expect them "to participate in American life as the equal of their conquerors." But Parker had a radically different perspective from those outsiders who sought to structure his role. He wanted more than a subordinate and peripheral position, and Freemasonry was a way to do exactly what white society held was no longer a possibility for American Indians—participate in American life as equals.

Parker was swimming against the tide of national feeling that opposed any threat to the prevailing ethnic hierarchy. By the second decade of the twentieth century, a redefinition of Indian assimilation was firmly in progress, a reflection of fundamental shifts in social values. As Hoxie explains, "politicians and intellectuals rejected the notion that national institutions would dissolve cultural differences and foster equality and cohesion."[60] In place of that idea, American leaders wanted each group to preserve the existing social order. There was little support for Indians, middle-class or otherwise, who wished to alter it.

Nonetheless, as a Mason, Parker at least added his voice to the contemporary American debate on the proper nature of society. He tried to position the Indian positively using a rhetorical lie at the heart of Masonry as a social and political lever. His logic went something like this. If Freemasons were representatively American, as middle-class, white Protestants of good character; if he was a respected Freemason, and if "tribal" Indians were themselves inherent Freemasons; then there should be no hindrance to full Indian participation in American life. It was an argument and an approach to the limitations he experienced as an educated Indian that had its own coherence, but it could never adequately redress the great bulk of feeling within America demanding that Indians remain in the subordinate position they now shared with increasing numbers of immigrants and a burgeoning number of excluded poor.

Fraternalism, along with the quest to secure meaningful Indian reform, was a key theme of Parker's life. However, these themes simply give context to his life's work as a dedicated museum professional. It is to this central narrative that we now return. Parker, now aged forty-three, has bags under his eyes from all the late nights and hard work he has put into his professional concerns. He is wearing glasses, his dark hair is graying and receding, and he is often seen contemplating life over the curved stem of an aromatic pipe. He is about to have a long-awaited opportunity to advance his career and to implement his museum ideas.

Maturing as a Museum Man, 1924–1935

Parker was to serve for over forty years as a museum man, or "muse-ologist," to use his own neologism—from humble beginnings in 1903 as assistant field-worker on museum-sponsored archaeological surveys, through over eighteen years as archaeologist at the State Museum in Albany, to his final professional position as director of the Rochester Municipal Museum, New York, from 1924 to retirement in 1946.[1] During this time, the museum philosophy he expressed in his writings and the innovations he brought to museum practice made him a deservedly respected figure, nationally and even internationally, within a field that was undergoing considerable change and reorientation. As museums adjusted to a new social dynamic, as they went from being the loci of the anthropological discipline to being social and commu-nity institutions centrally concerned with popular education and leisure, he was a dynamic force within their transformation.

Much of Parker's approach and practice was well ahead of its time. Most notably, he tried to combine showmanship and entertainment with education—education being, to his mind, the museum's primary function within society. Since he saw museums as integral to American democracy because they encouraged good citizenship, he also advo-cated the very modern notion that they should be accessible at every level for all who might benefit from what they had to offer. To Parker, the museum was "the university of the common man"—a place where every individual could become part of the development and excellence that was the nation's project. Therefore, he promoted an interactive relationship between museum visitor and exhibits, and he insisted that museums cultivate a broad and inclusive set of concerns with which those visitors could connect. He carried forward the Progressive emphasis on service as a guiding tenet, and worked to bring standardized procedure to museum activities together with a new sense of professionalism. To his mind, the museum had a significant social role to play as the century progressed, as leisure time steadily increased and the need for some form of nationally unifying education continued to develop. He wanted museums to be in and of the modern world, for them to have a firm business awareness, and for each aspect of their success to allow them to expand so that they became an essential part of everyday life.

One of the great attractions of the museum field for Parker was that it provided him with opportunities to promote interests and ideas that were specific to his background and heritage. Specifically, museum work allowed him to visually display the narrative of social evolution well into the twentieth century, long after the approach had suffered serious attack within anthropology and after that discipline had itself become university based. The museum, rather than the university, was the institution that permitted him as assimilated Indian to be an intellectual, a professional, and Indian authority in a way that did not cause either intellectual or emotional conflict. Within its confines, he could successfully interpret Indian history so that it fit the triumphant optimism of early-twentieth-century modernity. He could reaffirm his own position as assimilated Indian through the display of social evolutionary schemata, while maintaining and developing his connections to contemporary Indian culture, especially his links with Indians in and around the reservations of his childhood.

Museums were one of the very few public contexts within American society where Parker could do all this. Here he could integrate, as assimilated Indian, as intellectual, and as professional because of the curious way in which museums worked to elide the more complex truths of Indian-white history and the messy reality of contemporary Indian accommodation and resistance to amalgamation with Euro-Americans. Instead, museums concerned themselves with exhibiting or representing Indians as "primitive" archetypes and with charting their evolution through time toward civilization. As institutions, museums presented themselves as the crystallization and apotheosis of civilization, a condition they demonstrated through their collection and display of America's past. All this involved a denial of Indian survival as Indians into the present; it required an elaborate recontextualization of Indian history that did not impinge on Americans' idea of themselves as the appropriate successors to a contained and strictly "primitive" past. Perhaps paradoxically, it was the constructed spectacle of social evolutionary museum display, where the colonized "other"

Arthur C. Parker engaged in his museum work with member of staff.

Courtesy of Rochester Museum & Science Center

was reproduced as both contained and ahistorical, that allowed Parker to shine as assimilated Indian.

His personal qualities of leadership, readiness to serve, and, most notably, his ability to motivate others were also very much part of his success. In particular, his influence over museum practice nationally must be connected to his steadfast service within professional museum organizations. He became the first president of the Society for American Archaeology; founded and for many years was elected president of the New York State Archaeological Society; served as president of the New York Historical Association; and, for over twelve years in total, was a vice president of the American Association of Museums.[2] Essentially, however, it was Parker's indomitable will to make his mark and his concern to promote the museum ideas he held with such certainty that explains his achievements as a New York museum man.

• • •

Getting the chance to really put his museum thinking into practice was a pressing problem for Parker during the early 1920s. The frustration he was feeling with Clarke's conservatism and the lack of scope for developing his ideas as archaeologist at the State Museum in Albany led him to seriously consider setting loyalty aside and moving on, especially once it had become clear that the Society of American Indians was never going to offer the opportunities he had once hoped. There was also the important issue of remuneration. Conditions at the State

Museum had already once occasioned his resignation, though his employer had ultimately managed to get him to stay through promising, but never delivering, an adequate salary. He had made a great push to get it raised to three thousand dollars, pointing out that this was "actually less than received by most members of his profession" and only equivalent to the amount then paid to an assistant geologist. He told the State Museum he had the backing not just of the museum's own officials, but of "a large and influential scientific society," "large tax payers," and congressmen. Apparently, his State Museum income met only one-third of his expenses, the rest coming from newspaper work on an ongoing basis. However, no one really listened to his case to better the approximately $1,600 he was paid, and gradually the idea of leaving Albany became more and more attractive.

By 1924, he had established contacts with several important men at various city museums, and toward the end of the year he was finally ready to make his move. He resigned on December 1, 1924, just before he was officially offered the museum position for which he would be best remembered, the directorship of the Rochester Museum, New York.

The fact that Parker was known to friends of Rochester's mayor, and that as far back as 1913 he had been employed by Mayor Edgerton as a consultant to help devise a development plan for the museum, no doubt helped him get the job.[3] Aside from this, he had connections with the local university. The University of Rochester had been so impressed with his scholarship that in 1922 it had awarded him an honorary M.S. degree after publication of his two-volume *Archeological History of New York*. He was able to add this accolade to the impressive curriculum vitae he had built up by this stage. By all accounts, he was a good catch for the Rochester institution. In addition to his extensive published work, which included six significant monographs and three more popular works for young people, he was an established lecturer and museum figure affiliated with a host of learned societies, especially within New York State. His innovations at the State Museum, where it was said he had collected over 100,000 specimens, had been well received within museum circles. The six large habitat groups he had devised for the State Education Building had made him a leading authority on group construction of this sort and had given him the beginnings of an international professional profile.[4] Overall, he had earned a deservedly secure reputation as an innovative museum worker with real potential to excel—and he knew it. Before leaving the State Museum job, he described himself as someone who was "regarded as one of the best known scientists connected with State work, and probably the most widely known member of the Science Division staff, frequently being called to various places from Washington to Denver for consultation on legal and political matters, and known and consulted by many university presidents and professors."[5]

A sizable amount of local press attention accompanied Parker's move to Rochester, some of which connected him to that other great Rochester scientist of another generation, Lewis Henry Morgan.[6] No doubt this pleased him, since he loved any suggestion that he was following in Morgan's footsteps or in any way excelling Morgan and his work. He may also have found it satisfying to note the amount of coverage devoted solely to the fact that when he resigned from the State Museum staff list on January 1, 1925, and moved to Rochester, he gained twice the salary and a much broader scope for research and writing. Aside from spelling out all the benefits and opportunities of his new post, the Rochester and Albany newspapers were full of regret at the loss from state education of such a qualified museum man. They bemoaned the fact that someone who was recognized as an author and authority on Indian lore was moving on simply because he could not reasonably be persuaded to stay due to the state's lack of funds.

This was true, but the fuss in the local press may have been just as much the result of the excellent working relationship that Parker had developed with them. As an ex-newspaper man, he knew exactly what information was most likely to interest them and in just what form they preferred to receive it. His press relationship would further blossom at Rochester, where he always very positively promoted himself and his work. His personal scrapbooks ended up crammed with his photographs on single and double-page features or attached to snippets either about him directly or some project of his. Indeed, Parker could not have secured more glowing press attention during his twenty years as museum head at Rochester had he carefully written and regularly supplied each piece himself.

The new director of Rochester's Municipal Museum let the press know he was preparing to leave his state job long before he tendered his resignation, and some of the copy produced in response suggested that something should be done about it. The *Knickerbocker Press* said Parker was "New York State's leading authority on Indians and archaeology and recognized throughout America as an expert on aboriginal affairs"; his departure was an example of political favoritism draining funds away from scientific state service. Parker's research would now be lost, work that "might have gone into books had the state appropriated sufficient money for it, but Dr. Parker was obliged to pay his own stenographer from his own slim salary." The paper concluded: "Parker, if he is allowed to go, is an irreparable loss. He cannot be replaced, and the state's investment in him is lost. What about it?"[7]

With his resignation, the son of his old boss John M. Clarke, director at the State Department of Education, got promoted from technical assistant into Parker's old job.[8] The appointment irritated Parker so much he hit back forcefully in print. He wrote a scathing letter to the *Albany Evening News* informing them that no trained archaeologist had been prepared to accept the post because the salary and working conditions were so poor. He ended with an artful put-down of everything connected with his replacement. It began with a description of the museum's predicament after he had left: "The only recourse seemed to be to reduce the requirements so that it was not necessary for candidates to know anything whatsoever about archeology in order to fill the state position. This made it possible for candidates so qualified to take the examination and without question the best man won the appointment. I have no comment to make other than to wish the present incumbent great success in his new field."[9] The politics of State Museum pay and conditions had left a sour taste. Rochester's Municipal Museum may not have had quite the same prestige as the State Museum, but at least the job of director offered him a much broader canvas.

Parker, as opposed to a career politician, got the $3,000-plus job on the recommendation of Alvin H. Dewey, head of the Lewis H. Morgan Chapter of the New York State Archaeological Association. Together with Earl Weller, Dewey put Parker's name forward to Mayor Clarence Van Zandt to replace the previous curator, Edward Putnam. Although no specific funds or plans for expansion existed at the time of his appointment, there were proposals for a fundamental reorganization of the museum's administration, which Parker knew would be to his advantage as director. Duly, on January 15, 1925, the Municipal Museum was designated as a city department and placed under the jurisdiction of an unpaid three-man Museum Board instead of under the Library Board trustees as had been the case. The idea was that Parker would have a free rein but would periodically report to the board, who were appointed by the mayor, an arrangement it was hoped would free the institution completely from city politics and facilitate growth.[10] It was a workable arrangement and one that certainly gave Parker much more immediate control over his working life than had been the case at the State Museum for all those years. He would soon win the three-, and later five-man, board's full support, and they would act very strongly as advocates to the city, encouraging increases in the museum's budget allotment.

According to Parker's ultimate successor at Rochester, Stephen Thomas, "Some people were surprised that a person of Dr. Parker's eminence in archeology and history should be willing to take over such a limited venture as the Municipal Museum appeared to be." Parker, however, never publicly expressed anything less than total confidence that Rochester's museum would ultimately compare with the best museums in the country. As he told the press just before he moved, "I have come to Rochester because I believe there is a field of real opportunity."[11] Even so, he was aware that there was a great deal of work to do. According to the newspaper condensed histories he carefully pasted into his scrapbooks at the time, "Dr. Parker found the Museum a more or less heterogeneous collection of objects and curiosities which had been built up in a hit-or-miss fashion in the years since former Mayor Hiram H. Edgerton had started it reputedly with an ancient ox yoke back in 1912." Over ten years later, the museum was still in the doldrums, but Parker arrived "flaming with revolutionary ideas," the press said, determined to bring order and to make the museum a place interwoven with Rochester's history and culture.[12] The Municipal Museum presented a dispiriting picture to some, but Parker was absolutely convinced that he and his team's hard work would allow for significant growth and eventually attract further support. His faith and effort were rewarded in time, but it was another fifteen years before he gained the connections and finance he needed to move the Rochester Museum from the cramped conditions he took on initially at Edgerton Park.

On arriving, all Parker had was the expectation of success and the certainty of a great deal of work ahead. He knew, however, that he would be able to control most of whatever development occurred and that this was a golden opportunity to put his museum ideas into practice. Those ideas were unique, but not everything about them was new. It is worth tracing the many elements within them that can be related directly to two figures whose thinking had an special currency with Parker, George Brown Goode (1851–96) and John Cotton Dana (1856–1929).[13]

First, George Brown Goode. Thought of today as the founder of museology, Goode was at the forefront of the museum movement of a generation before. Like Parker, he had felt that the caliber of museums was an indicator of the state of development of the people behind them, and so there was a civic duty for museums not only to exist but to be properly maintained. Goode had begun his career as an exhibit specialist at world's fairs and expositions. After studying natural sciences as a young man under Louis Agassiz at Harvard, by 1879 he had progressed to controlling the National Museum at the Smith-sonian Institution where he spent the bulk of his museum career. His vision for the National Museum of the United States was that it "show, arranged according to one consistent plan, the resources of the earth and the results of human activity in every direction." He felt it "should exhibit the physical characteristics, the history, the manners, past and present, of all peoples, civilized and savage, and should illustrate human culture and industry in all their phases." The institution was, in his scheme of museum classification, a museum of cultural history, that is, a museum that concerned itself with "the natural history of cult, or civilization, of man and his ideas and achievements."[14]

Parker admired Goode's approach and considered it a good basis for future development within the field. He described Goode's 1895 work, "The Principles of Museum Administration," as "a document marking the culmination of the old museum theory which has given direction and plan to the new," and he adopted several key elements of what Goode had to say.[15] In particular, most of his museum writings echoed Goode's stress on "enlightenment and education of the masses" and on system and classification. When it came to exhibition, Goode said, "the people's museum should be much more than a house full of specimens in glass cases. It should be a house full of ideas, arranged with the strictest attention to system." He was therefore keen on com-prehensive labeling so as to reveal those ideas and anxious that objects expressing the same idea should never be duplicated, all of which Parker took firmly to heart.[16]

Both men were indefatigable workers and excellent administrators. Someone who himself once suffered a form of temporary mental breakdown as a result of working fourteen-hour days for months, Goode may have influenced Parker in his exactitude about what was expected from museum personnel at all levels. Parker eventually char-acterized museum work as "evangelism" and advised his staff that "if they hope to become wealthy they might better seek positions in the commercial world but if they sought to emulate the missionary inter-ested in constructive good for society, the museum is a good institution to stay in for the enjoyment of poverty."[17] Of course, this kind of think-ing came not just from Goode. An ideal of disinterested service, of professional work as a vocation, was part of the Progressive movement. In fact, as professionalization developed into the twentieth century, it was invariably accompanied by this rhetoric of moral idealism.[18]

John Cotton Dana had a similar belief that professional service had the power to direct society. Even though he worked primarily within American libraries, his influence may have helped to make Parker open to innovation and progress within the museum profession. Dana served, across his career, as librarian of the Denver Public Library, the Springfield, Massachusetts, Public Library, and the Newark, New Jersey, Public Library, and only for a short period turned his attention specifically to museum management. Nevertheless, he was even more forceful than Goode in calling for reform because, like Parker, he feared what would happen if steps were not taken in American community institutions. He believed that the primary importance of the library for example, lay in its contribution to the social order. He even argued that poor libraries actually injured their communities.

Parker expressed the idea that institutions could ensure the continuity of democratic principles, in odd-sounding rallying phrases such as "History is the gun-sight of a safe future." These peppered much of his museum writing.[19] It was a way of thinking that justified the strenuous individual effort devoted to institutions by men like Goode, Dana, and Parker and that had the added benefit of making institutional endowment by the wealthy appear extremely edifying. Furthermore, if institutions were deemed capable of achieving so much, an emphasis could legitimately be placed on extending their influence so as to reach every level of society. Thus Dana and Parker advocated ease of use within institutions and specifically encouraged outreach and innovations such as adult education to foster mass participation.

Perhaps by the same reasoning, both valued the visual as a means of education. Dana specifically criticized lackluster "gazing museums," favoring instead a more dynamic and interpretative approach to display. He even half-eschewed the name museum itself, preferring instead the term "institute of visual instruction."[20] Aside from these kinds of connections, there were other, broader similarities of approach between the two men. Both acknowledged that institutions should have a regional emphasis and that they should cultivate commercial applications of their work, and both encapsulated their ideas on best practice in books that went into the very smallest details of institutional routine.[21] Both men had the opportunity to develop a museum more or less to their own taste, and Dana's hard work had ultimately been rewarded in just the way Parker hoped his would, with an enormous endowment for a museum building from an appreciative local merchant.[22] In sum, they were men of their time, caught up in the Progressive zeal for selfless moral input into the maelstrom of modernizing America and keen to bring system, method, and direction to their fields.

Goode and Dana influenced Parker's approach, but the hard work of developing Rochester's Municipal Museum lay at his feet alone. Undismayed by the challenge, he set about his new role with alacrity.

In fact, he seems to have quickly fallen in love with the job and with the city itself. He soon described Rochester as "the gateway of a garden valley that is without equal in America," and praised how it had grown from a single log cabin in 1812 to being the twenty-second city in size in America and the third most populous city in the state. He would rhapsodize in print that it was "the Flower City,—the Contented City, the City of Homes, the Power City, the Kodak City, the Optical City, the Citadel of the Genesee,—with a home life and a business life that make Rochester the City of Realized Dreams."[23] Its museum needed to reflect all of its glory, past and present. Unfortunately, the museum building was in a poor spot, there was only a low budget, the staff were untrained, and the Rochester public were unaccustomed to regularly visiting their museum or to thinking of it as a vibrant civic institution.

This did not deter Parker from drawing up an ambitious ten-year plan to ensure ongoing success. By the end of January 1925, he had created a blueprint whereby the museum would eventually reflect the anthropology, biology, cultural history, and the industrial arts of the whole Genesee Country. It was comparable to the four-field division he had advocated but never managed to achieve within the State Museum, and it gave Parker's new institution a basic project to display Rochester's history from prehistory to the present.[24] The emphasis was to be on the city itself, its industry and development over time. Any foreign material already owned by the museum was to be farmed out as portable dioramas or reserved as special exhibits. Loan materials were to be returned to their owners and henceforth only accepted for temporary shows.

Overall, it was a simple and practical framework for development, now that Parker finally had the chance to turn a museum into the kind of instrument for social progress he believed it should be. He told the people of Rochester that he would bring together "typical utinsels [sic] and implements of each stage of our historical development, thereby writing a record of the cultural progress that will bear comparison with the better types of ethnological exhibits."[25] History as told through local or regional artifacts was a concept to which he would always cling.[26]

The city of Rochester had center stage, but the real message of the museum's exhibits was to be social evolution according to Morgan. Indeed, the opportunity to pass on Morgan's legacy to another generation from Morgan's own hometown was to Parker one of the great advantages of achieving the directorship at Rochester. As he later admitted, at the Municipal Museum, as perhaps in life, he wanted "to complete the work commenced a century ago by another Rochesterarian, Lewis Henry Morgan."[27] Therefore, straight away he set about bringing order so that the exhibits could tell "a continuous story," a story of human evolution along Morgan's lines.[28] As a guiding theme, this became central to most of what the museum displayed. Whether it was cave men fighting woolly mastodons in the glacial period, Neanderthals fighting saber-toothed tigers, Egyptian boats, reproductions of Christmas a century prior, or displays of the new camera technology, Parker generally made sure of three things—that his exhibits received plenty of press attention and that they revealed human evolutionary development according to Morgan in a visually stimulating way. For example, when the museum's researches discovered what he termed a "prehistoric arms factory" in Rochester, Parker told the press, "These specimens will be used to illustrate the whole story of man's early struggles from savagery to civilization."[29] Order and sequence were essential to everything he did at Rochester because of Morgan and social evolution and because he was attempting to visually represent that near-impossible goal—objective, narrative history. The modern museum scheme was comparable to snapshot exposures, as he once pointed out in a speech before the American Association of Museums; therefore "the best practice is to arrange objects in such a manner that they tell a definite story or convey information about related things. Museums, therefore, deal with objective ideas. If these ideas are connected in a series, logically and purposively, so much the better."[30]

To give flesh to this vision, to support the dreams he was already developing for a hall of natural history, for loan exhibits for schools, for an industrial museum outlining Rochester's expansion, and for a children's museum, Parker needed exhibits. Therefore, he began drawing on his reservation contacts and prior experience. He had a Seneca log cabin shipped from Tonawanda, started acquiring various artifacts for period rooms, and began planning a Rochester version of the successful Indian groups he had created at the State Education Building in Albany.

Another source of exhibits lay in the soils surrounding Rochester itself, something Parker lost no time in exploiting. He began coordinating excavations at various locations in central and western New York, sometimes going on reconnoitering expeditions with his wife and then leaving his assistant William A. Ritchie to diligently get the most from the sites. By about one year after his arrival, Parker's museum had gained 15,000 new specimens, and he was able to hire two new assistants to aid Ritchie's colleague Henry Wardell and Ritchie himself, who was by then fully employed excavating for what had become the museum's archaeological section.[31] This work sponsored by the museum not only increased stock, but provided useful press opportunities for spreading the word about the museum's activities. The papers were full of gruesome photographs, for example, from the Lamoka excavation of a prehistoric Indian village. This was the first of the museum's archaeological expeditions to a site that Parker had discovered back in 1905, and it yielded two thousand separate exhibits.[32] Another excavation at Willow Point unearthed a "grotesque Indian witch woman," whose photograph was splashed over the local press. Digging yielded over thirty Indian skeletons, which would have been shipped immediately back to the museum had locals not been so interested that they stole some temporarily from the exhumation site.[33]

Parker settled into a very creative period, when his enthusiasm concerning his museum and the museum movement knew no bounds. He was never afraid to dream, and was forever discussing big plans for the Municipal Museum, especially in the new institutional magazine he developed called *Museum Service*. Later to be partially backed by the Rochester Museum Association, it was to go from strength to strength, evolving over a decade into a twenty-six-page illustrated journal dealing with all issues connected with museum administration and museum philosophy. Largely a vehicle for Parker's views, *Museum Service* would always bear the signs of his heavy editorial hand, just like his previous magazine publication for the Society of American Indians. But thankfully, there was no need to berate the readership over the shortcomings of the organization, and this time Parker was assured a good salary in return for the service promised by the title. Instead of subscription demands, readers were treated to laudatory write-ups of the institution's activities and snippets from Parker on a host of museum issues.

As early as May 1926, he used *Museum Service* to talk up the idea of a "million dollar museum" so that Rochester could hold its head up to the million and a quarter dollar museum in Buffalo. He argued that three things defined the soul of a city: its parks, its libraries, and its museum. To his mind, Rochester badly needed to invest in its museum and, by extension, to feed its own soul. War-ravaged European cities were just then devoting valuable resources to reestablishing their museums, he repeatedly pointed out, because they were aware of their great potential to aid business and increase civic spirit.[34] Surely Rochester should do the same?[35]

This was not just wishful thinking. After all, the social unrest of the 1870s in the wake of the Civil War had spurred earlier philanthropists to found America's great metropolitan museums in the first place. Now, as the 1920s progressed, the need for civic institutions to inculcate an appropriate national spirit seemed just as immediate. Population had soared from 30 million in 1860 to 105 million in 1920. A larger majority of Americans were now living in urban places, many of them in the very large cities where the foreign-born tended to congregate. Now an industrial nation rather than an agricultural one was steadily developing its role as a world power, America very much needed to educate its people to meet the challenges brought about by change. The Immigration Act of 1924 had restricted overall numbers entering the country and had stemmed the flow of immigrants from southern and eastern Europe that had prompted so much nativist ire, but the practical difficulties of integrating and assimilating generations of new Americans in the hypernationalist postwar era were still pressing. To Parker's mind, all this meant that the museums had a duty to expand.

Faith in the power and necessity of museum communication made Parker keen to find a way of connecting exhibits to the city's educational system. So during April 1926, he set up a School Service Division with circulating collections for the local schools. The idea was to use mobile museum exhibits to illustrate school curricula, a unique innovation within the national school system at the time and a direct application of John Dewey's philosophy of learning by doing. At the time, Parker was just about to publish the first of his Indian studies for children, *Skunny Wundy and Other Indian Tales,* which may have spurred him toward this emphasis on children's education. He was to publish three more children's books in the next four years and two more in retirement. But the educational mission of the museum was not to be limited to children. Education was to gradually permeate every aspect of its work. Therefore, when Parker inaugurated *Museum Service,* he assured his readership that the museum was dedicated "to the city of Rochester and to the cause of Education."[36] He wanted, first and foremost, to present to visitors "sequential ideas with a teaching value," a narrative model of museum education that made the communication of ideas, rather than the presentation of objects, primary.[37]

Museum education had to be available across class and age differences if the institution was to properly and democratically serve the community. The Rochester museum and museums like it were to fill the gaps in the nation's education provision through offering a different kind of educational experience to all. Parker wanted the Municipal Museum to function as a "poor man's university," able to offer a mass educational experience without requiring specific entry qualifications. He told *Museum Service* readers: "The modern museum is fitting into the accepted educational pattern. It has been called the poor man's university. Here the adult may study as deeply or as superficially as he wishes. He may study alone or join with others in an adult class. Children have the same privilege as adults and additional advantages of special programs, organized clubs, scheduled class visits escorted by teachers and definite instruction by museum guides and docents. On the other hand, the museum may visit the children through its extension service."[38] In the near future, he was sure, people would do more than briefly visit; they would stay in museums for indefinite periods. Families would come, "not for a few moments of passing fancy but for a day, a week, a month of zestful recreation and pleasurable instruction." The museum of the future would have hotels and recreation facilities and "forms of constructive amusement that are entertaining as well as instructive." It would be, Parker said, a place "where one can eat and sleep and learn by doing things."[39]

There would be a marriage of the activities traditionally associated with universities and those of museums. For its part, Rochester was to evolve a "university of visual instruction," which would "include every industry in the city so that it will have a vital meaning to the wage earners and the tax payers." It would succeed by being interesting and by having the power to educate not by books, but in a superior fashion, through exhibits. Parker was convinced that a visual means of receiving information and ideas would become an accepted and accredited mode of learning among modern educators.[40] Museums would excel because people could learn as learning was best done, "by doing" and through "actually handling and experimenting with the things they touch."[41] It was a philosophy bolstered by other contemporary currents in education, especially the fashion for manual training as an answer to the growing need for mass education.

Because he felt the museum had such vast potential as an instrument for social progress, the idea that it should be accessible in every sense was paramount to Parker. One of his best ideas was to encourage new groups to visit—for example, through making museum facilities available to amateur naturalists and hobbyists. But he knew that even once inside the museum, it was not always easy for people to connect with its exhibits. He therefore worked to reorient the institution around the visitor's experience. He carried over all the visitor-friendly innovations he had developed at the State Museum, including dramatic life groups and period settings, and tried to display material "from the angle of the visitor, rather than specialist." He later said he had figured out that "being a museum man is one thing and trying to do research is another," and had resolved, "I'll make *my* research talk. I'm going to make the smallest boy understand it."[42]

Good practice and proper museum management was also key to his overall museum message. True progress in realizing museum potential meant regularizing the roles and salaries of museum staff and giving them appropriate training, according to Parker. They needed clear statements of museum policy, so they could be in a position to closely identify with their work. He worked hard at this in Rochester, putting as much of himself as possible into staff projects. Eventually he cultivated a very motivated and hardworking team. Ritchie's success, in particular, testified to the benefits of his ideas about staff development. Having originally transferred Ritchie to archaeology from his post as part-time museum librarian, Parker encouraged him to obtain a bachelor's degree, master's degree, and finally, in 1943, a doctorate. In return, Ritchie seems to have had a very positive relationship with Parker as his boss, beginning his letters to him with "Dear Chief." Like other Rochester staff, he benefited from being able to publish readily within *Museum Service*, and he ended up winning awards for his work. He was finally poached to work for the State Museum in Albany, but Parker said this meant they could work in tandem on completing what Morgan had begun.[43]

After four years of Parker's directorship, staff numbers had expanded to thirty, including nine "museum professionals." By then he was itching to buy in more nonlocal trained museum personnel, having exhausted the local supply. He knew that the right staff were essential to success, even though he always maintained that any museum was really only "the materialized thought of its director."[44] He had overall control and responsibility for each aspect of what went on at the museum, but he was always looking for the right people to add to his team. These must have been difficult to find since so much was expected of them. The *Guide Bulletin* that Rochester eventually produced read, "When the Commission accepts an employee, it expects unswerving loyalty, honest effort and the acceptance of full responsibility for action on the part of the incumbent," accompanying the statement with forty staff regulations and a pledge of service for them to sign.

Yet, for what sounds like such an exacting boss, Parker seems to have had a positive, even fond relationship with those he generally referred to as "fellow workers," and he was continually able to commend their dedication and loyalty to the Board of Commissioners in his annual reports. This was appropriate, since they were prepared to work overtime without compensation, sometimes until midnight—as, for example, when the museum went through the fundamental reorganization initiated when Parker first arrived. Of course, Parker sought only the same kind of idealism and enthusiasm in his staff as he showed himself.[45] He seems to have found this kind of devotion at Rochester, for his successor said that he drew around him "a small but energetic and gifted staff of co-workers whom he trained and developed, inculcating in them the best principles of the 'museist.'"

Parker knew that theirs was a challenging profession, but as he put it, "The Life of a museum worker—well, it's the life, for it requires the exercises of all powers that go toward making every sort of man and sometimes requires hijacker nerve."[46] In return for their commitment, Parker was very proud of every member of the team at the Municipal Museum. He loved his own work and gloried unashamedly in their collective and individual achievements. Eventually, he would write a prose piece about it all for *Museum Service*, where he reflected: "I like immensely the group of which I am a part. I wonder if there are any better workers anywhere.[47]

Aside from promoting the gradual regularization of activities and working conditions within museums, Parker also wanted boundaries drawn around their field of operation. He was especially irritated by history societies muscling in on museums' traditional areas of expertise.[48] Probably, the proximity of the Rochester Historical Society in the same building as his museum prompted some of his irritation. He felt the Historical Society was just an unprofessional "mélange of arts, ethnology, civic records and travel souvenirs" whose purpose had been "unintentionally perverted by interested and well-meaning donors." He had no intention of letting it affect the Municipal Museum's work or reputation.[49]

Another issue of perennial concern to Parker was the need to curb interference with museum excavation work. This had irritated Parker as far back as 1917 when he had first joined the American Association of Museums. State's relics, as they were termed at the time, should, he said, remain in the soil or elsewhere until they could properly become the property of official museum representatives. Before coming to Rochester, Parker had already tried to do something legally about unregulated digging throughout the state. Back in 1923, the press reported, that he had been largely responsible for a pure relic bill being placed on the state's statute books prescribing imprisonment or a fine for "any person who willfully misrepresents a fake ethnological or archaeological specimen with intent to sell, or who gives false information about such a thing."[50] Parker felt that the nation had a duty to preserve its heritage intact, rather than to excavate material in a piecemeal and ad hoc fashion, and felt that that heritage by rights belonged to the nation's museums alone. To his mind, it was an affront that museums occasionally had to resort to buying artifacts from dealers, who often had excavated material in a totally unscientific manner.

As the years went by, Parker and his museum became ever stronger. After being closed from July 1 to August 30, 1926, to allow staff to redesign exhibits and rearrange displays, the museum's grand reopening was planned to coincide with Rochester's exposition to mark the sesquicentennial of the signing of the Declaration of Independence. Staff worked tirelessly on turning the tedious rows of "curios" and miscellaneous artifacts into what Parker called "chart" exhibits. These he described as "diagrammed exhibits that show objects in their relationship to time and space and upon a background that gives the display a real meaning," and they stood alongside the habitat groups created from the museum's rows of shelves laden with stuffed animals.[51]

With the museum up and running, he was able to focus on building the museum's research profile, including publishing his own new work, "An Analytical History of the Seneca Indians." Aside from all this, his ongoing campaigning for development money soon began to bear fruit. From his first year, funds, in the form of gifts and willed monies, had started flowing toward the museum, prompted in great part by a steady stream of local newspaper attention. As often as possible from November 1926, he told the local papers of the need for a new building, warning everyone who would listen that "a city without a museum is an amnesia victim. It may forge ahead in an era of great industrial activity, but it does not know who or what it is."[52]

Parker claimed that by 1927, 2,500 inches of publicity had been carried by the Rochester newspapers alone.[53] He made sure there was generally plenty to report. For example, the papers were able to cover Colonel Theodore Roosevelt, in Rochester for the Republican state convention, visiting the museum that year. During "Rochester-Made Products Week" that autumn, they were able to carry Parker's urgings that every man, woman, and child in the city visit the second floor of the museum where the whole floor had been transformed into a Hall of Industrial Science, showcasing Rochester commodities and their manufacture.[54] Another advance came in 1928 with the launch of *Research Records*, a published forum especially for the museum's scholarly output. The inaugural issue carried William Ritchie's 1927 fieldwork. Published only periodically, it did not interfere with the more populist *Museum Service*, which came out every month.[55]

Keen on finding out more about the best museum practices, the "Chief" managed to find time and funds of his own to tour Europe during the summer of 1928, visiting in total forty-seven museums and archaeological sites. Primarily in Europe as a guest of Denmark's Royal Archaeological Commission, he visited museums in Munich, Hamburg, Flensburg, Cologne, and London's British Museum, all of which powerfully affected his outlook. "I think we can gradually develop the industrial department of our museum along methods followed by the Deutches, in Munich, and in South Kensington, England," he later told the Rochester press, adding that his greatest single inspiration while abroad had been England's museum gardens. One other thing that had impressed him during his "Old World" travels was how legends from before the Roman occupation of Great Britain still survived as children's stories. "The most beautiful thing I found in my trip was the faith of the people in the rural districts of England in fairies," he said. "I hope that the time will come when we in the United States shall mark the sites where legendary spirits in tales of the Indians had their haunts." He was soon to publish *Rumbling Wings,* another of his fictional books for children and young adults incorporating Indian legend and myth.[56]

He returned to Rochester amazed at having seen the wonder that is Stonehenge, intent on the project of "Museizing the World," and, in a practical sense, especially hungry to find a way to relocate the museum away from the northwest of the city.[57] He knew that to truly succeed, the Municipal Museum had to move from the Edgerton extension it shared with the public library, to some better location either closer to the center of population or to one of the region's show parks.[58] He very much wanted a museum comparable to the much larger museums in Milwaukee and St. Louis, and so he began to forcefully talk up the idea of a more expansive, downtown site that could serve as "the epitome of Rochester." Already the museum's achievements made the idea seem more plausible. Rich industrial philanthropists knew about its work. For example, George Eastman, of Eastman-Kodak wealth, had shot a white rhinoceros while in the southern Sudan and brought it back especially for the museum of his hometown.

Possibly in order to make the museum even more attractive to the industrial benefactors of the region, or as a direct result of visiting European museums, beginning in 1929, Parker started promoting the idea of making the institution explicitly industrial. With all its varied industries, the city needed a "method of expressing its industrial soul," Parker felt; and even though he had created a museum Division of Industrial Science two years before, there was still scope for the city to more directly emulate places like Philadelphia and Chicago.[59] Keeping up his ongoing positive publicity offensive, Parker sent out five hundred cards to prominent Rochester citizens asking for their opinions and then shared their responses with the commissioners.[60]

Already the Municipal Museum was so developed that not a single old exhibit remained from when Parker first took over. The growth in collection size was now so strong that it was a real challenge to keep an adequate acquisitions record.[61] Parker was continually enlarging the museum's stock through archaeological expeditions to places such as Lamoka Lake, Schuyler County. By October 1929, he was able to extend the museum's hours to include Sunday afternoons and to stay open until 10 P.M. several days a week.

He was elected in 1929 as one of two representatives of the American Anthropological Association to the National Research Council.[62] As his professional status grew, his role as Indian spokesman began to take a back seat. That said, he was still known as a benevolent figure on the reservations, and he did allow the Society for the Propagation of Indian Welfare to hold its conference at the museum.[63] His expertise as an Iroquois specialist was also increasingly in demand. One example was the work he did with another museum professional, advising the American Scenic and Historic Preservation Society on how to organize their own "living exhibit" for the Letchworth State Park, New York. The park as "outdoor museum" was to include a Seneca Indian village flanked by a "typical Iroquois stockade." The idea was for a bark house to be constructed for "an Indian custodian and family who will live there under aboriginal conditions and cultivate the garden which is to contain the typical Indian food plants."[64]

Parker was doing too well to be seriously affected when some negative publicity connected with a colleague who had helped him with the life groups at the State Museum hit the regional papers that year. All the same, he found it difficult to ignore. At the time he had just completed a boy's book of fiction, *Gustango Gold,* which was set on the Cattaraugus Reservation to which the scandal was linked. The colleague was Henri Marchand, who had made the modeled figures with portrait busts for the Mohawk group.[65] A sculptor and artist of some renown, he had studied under Rodin and had left the State Museum a few months after Parker in 1925 to become chief preparator at the Buffalo Museum of Science. Just four years later the papers were full of news that his French wife Clotilde had been murdered, apparently at the hands of a sixty-six-year-old Seneca woman named Nancy Bowen at the instigation of Marchand's ex-lover and model, a thirty-five-year-old enrolled Cattaraugus Seneca woman named Lilac Jimerson. Mrs. Marchand had been beaten with a hammer and choked to death after a chloroform wad of paper had been stuffed down her throat. The papers claimed that Jimerson, using a Ouija board and Iroquois witchcraft, had motivated Nancy Bowen to commit the murder.

The unfolding investigation made for sensational copy. Parker was quoted in the press as an authority on Iroquois witchcraft, but he was careful to distance himself from any of the more sordid details.[66] It hardly mattered since Marchand, who during the investigation threatened to kill himself, was the really hot news. Parker carefully pasted into his scrapbook the story of how his lover, the handsome Lilac Jimerson, whom the papers said was "love-crazed and consumptive," had collapsed during her first trial but was eventually acquitted by the state supreme court. Nancy Bowen pleaded guilty to manslaughter, and not long after the case was concluded, Marchand made yet more headlines when he married an eighteen-year-old local beauty.[67] Parker's interest in the Marchand-Jimerson case was, of course, part of his long-term fascination with the secrets of witchcraft and Iroquois medicine. The interest had begun in childhood and was stimulated by fieldwork and successive contacts with reservation friends and relatives. The trial itself, as he darkly remarked to Keppler, "brought out many things" that piqued his interest, even if it also, to some small extent, connected him, and by extension his museum, to wrongdoing and supposed sorcery.[68]

No amount of scandal, however, was to get in the way of Parker's overall aim of planning and promoting an ever-better Municipal Museum. In 1930, in order to more firmly link it to education, Parker and the Museum Commission renamed the institution as the "Rochester Museum of Arts and Sciences." He intended that the new name would help the community "to see that modern museums are concerned more with education,—with the presentation of ideas, than with merely preserving things."[69] After all, a museum was about more than acquisition and display of the past; it was a gateway to civic understanding for the common man.[70]

With this fundamental reorientation in place, Parker was ready to broaden his search for new ways to expand and innovate. He told the press about his ideas for a game preserve in Genesee Country and for some form of state historical park to supplement the existing provision at Allegany and Letchworth.[71] Expanding parks and setting aside areas of national interest for popular use had been a concern of his for some time. Back in August 1923, while still at the State Museum, he had made a special push to get an area known as Indian Falls, near Tonawanda Reservation, made into a state-owned park.[72] Unfortunately, Parker never seems to have made much headway with these schemes, only managing to stir up interest and column inches in the local press. His other ideas for museum outreach, which eventually stretched to placing taster exhibits in hotel lobbies, enjoyed much greater success.

By this stage, however, it was clear to Parker that no amount of income that the museum could generate for itself would allow it to escape unscathed from the rethinking about public expenditure because of the Great Depression. During 1931, the museum's budget was slashed by almost 30 percent, and workloads became untenable as the number of even part-time professional staff was drastically cut. Besides the layoffs, salaries were reduced, opening hours restricted, and all acquisition, research, and exhibit development stopped.[73] The School Service Division also had to be let go since the museum could not afford to run its exhibit delivery truck. The "Chief" lamented the cutbacks in the press, highlighting that the collections amassed in the six years previous were of a value approaching that of the overall museum appropriation for that period, but his words had little effect.[74]

By the end of the year, there was a general fear that the museum might be closed. Teachers valiantly kept on using the museum's exhibits, transporting the materials themselves, but the outlook was grim. Then on September 23, 1932, the Board of Commissioners notified Parker with "profound regret" that he himself would have to be let go as of October 1, and the museum's maintenance income slashed even further. Public displeasure from various bodies was expressed in print, and a "Citizen's Committee" was set up to save the museum.[75] The hobby clubs that Parker had helped organize and on whose boards he had served also rallied to the museum's defense, as did the Museum Commission, which mounted a newspaper campaign. In the end the cut was partially restored in December 1932, with Parker being kept on as the only full-time employee. His salary went from $6,000 to $5,200.[76]

Life was tough, but tapping into the flow of government funding resulting from Roosevelt's New Deal meant Parker was able to begin a steady turnaround in the museum's fortunes during 1934. He secured funds from the Temporary Relief Administration (TERA), the Civil Works Administration, and the Works Progress Administration (WPA). He thought up a plan to allow the skilled unemployed to work in the museum, with the idea that, functioning as a university of the people with no entrance requirements, the museum would train and employ people interested in the cultural life of their area.[77] As a result, fifty new employees were taken on, including artists, geologists, designers, librarians, taxidermists, printer clerks, and anthropologists, in a public project the regional WPA director called "the most highly developed educational project in the country."[78]

At the time, drought was gripping the Midwest, there was a growing army of unemployed and displaced, and even Roosevelt's measured gravity and whirlwind of legislation seemed incapable of restoring confidence. Parker kept his focus and worked to make the museum an indispensable part of Rochester's relief and public support network.

He set up the Rochester Museum Hobby Council, which began mounting annual Hobby Shows to get people back using the museum. These were to become a real asset within the museum program, and the next year reportedly attracted 100,000 people in just six days. By the time Rochester celebrated its centenary that summer, the museum was once again in a position to make a well-received contribution. It arranged its activities and displays so that they synchronized with the exhibition laid on by the city called "A Century on Parade," reproducing a post office, a country store, a kitchen from a local home, and the first Western Union office with its original woodwork.[79]

The immediate funding crisis brought on by the depression having been averted, the following year Parker devoted much of his attention once again to publication. He found time to begin another museum bulletin, aside from the existing in-house *Museum Service* to which fellow workers were still expected to contribute. This was to further develop the level of professional communication available to his new cadre of staff, something he felt was of vital significance both to their personal progress and to the success of the museum. Thus *The Museologist,* essentially "a round robin of friendly letters from museum workers," was founded as an approximately fifteen-page mimeographed quarterly issue. Parker's newspaper flair made sure its format was engaging, and he periodically directed debate and adjusted the pace of discussion through asking questions of individuals about specific issues. *The Museologist* was his way of encouraging staff to adopt a professional outlook and of letting them gain a vital awareness of their role within the larger museum world. At a time when the effects of the depression made opportunities for funded travel hard to come by, it ensured that Rochester's museum workers had a cheap and immediate means of staying in touch.

The new quarterly, to which he would contribute over the next ten years, was not, however, Parker's greatest museum achievement during 1935.[80] This was his monograph *A Manual for History Museums,* a book that more or less encapsulated all his key ideas on museums, their purpose, and their management. Parker dedicated it to his friend Mark Harrington, now his sister's husband and, at the time, curator of the Southwest Museum, Los Angeles, describing him as the man "who lured the author into the world of museum work." Published as part of the New York State Historical Association Series, the 196-page work was partly subsidized by the Carnegie Corporation. It was edited by the distinguished Dixon Ryan Fox, a respected history professor at Columbia, later president of Union College, Schenectady, New York, and president of the New York State Historical Association. The two men's collaboration on the *Manual* was an example of the kind of close association between history museums and universities that Parker had always said he wanted to see. The men shared a commitment to a central educational role for museums, and both had the fundamental belief that scholarship must be brought closer to the people. Fox's credentials in this respect were at least as strong as Parker's. Having studied under Charles Beard and James Harvey Robinson, he was an important figure within the movement to write the history of ordinary life, having with Arthur M. Schlesinger, Sr., coedited one of the earlier examples of social and cultural history, the twelve-volume History of American Life Series.[81]

Parker's *Manual* was positively reviewed, though in essence it was a prescriptive bringing together of what he had been putting forward within other contexts for years. Although to a modern readership, the book seems larded with patronizingly obvious instruction, at the time Parker's basic exhibiting approach—to tell a simple story in a visually stimulating way—was new enough to merit detailed description. This was the first time a text of this kind had been devoted exclusively to history museums, and so Parker's advice was influential, especially on exhibition practice.[82]

So much of what Parker had to say in the *Manual* is today accepted as common knowledge that its significance is easy to overlook. For example, the good business practice that no modern museum today can dismiss was very much part of his message. Using Rochester as an example, he said that its museum visitors were in fact "museum consumers" and the institution itself really "a combination of a mail order and direct sales establishment." In essence, he suggested that what the successful modern museist needed to do was "to discover the simple principles that every good showman uses" while at the same time remembering to "manipulate his material so that it serves a highly useful end."[83] To meet the needs of its market, as well to maximize opportunities for publicity, museums needed to make themselves into special and visually seductive places, or "wonderworlds," as Parker put it, quoting his editor Fox.[84]

Parker saw the museum acting as a societal buffer, a pressure valve, helping to alleviate the problems of modernity, rather in the way Frederick Law Olmsted advocated large public parks as necessary institutions of democratic recreation to alleviate urban stress.[85] His earlier idea to "museuize" Letchworth Park and make it into an "out-of-door laboratory" had been an extrapolation of this type of thinking.[86] His very reform-oriented vision was always keen to position museums within the drive to make a better America. This was reflected in the use of the term "museum movement" throughout the *Manual,* so as to consistently connect museums to some larger syncretic drive toward national improvement. To an extent, this was boosterism, but it was also a heartfelt belief in the power of museum education to bring about desirable change.

Morgan's evolutionary ideas reverberated throughout Parker's *Manual.* The task of visualizing the narrative of cultural evolution should be the primary function of all museums, so that ideally every community could have its own "synoptic exhibits outlining the rise of civilization."[87] Parker felt museums had a duty to carry out this work since they were in themselves the apotheosis of the civilized condition and the preserve of the "evolved" races alone. Even the museum's "relics" were not as important as this message. Overall, the *Manual* made it very clear that there was really only a single "correct" approach to museum display. Any collection's purpose was strictly "to illustrate some pertinent fact in its proper place in the classification scheme," and its arrangement should always be "in as correct order as the books upon its library shelves."[88]

By 1935, Morgan's influence was undoubtedly fading within museum circles, and Parker's emphasis on the visual representation of cultural evolution was already behind the times. His *Manual* had a timely and productive message about accessibility and about how to successfully combine education and amusement, but there was little long-term value in its recommendation of an already compromised philosophy to underpin museum practice. Rather, it was Parker's interpretive innovations, his ideas about exhibit outreach, and his emphasis on the power of museums for universal education that had most currency. His ideas expressed the thinking of his class who felt, as T. J. Jackson Lears has succinctly described it, "that if only the proper educational balance could be struck, immigrants could be assimilated, angry workers calmed, and an incipient leisure class returned to productive life."[89]

Work continued at Rochester as the late 1930s progressed and then as America entered into the fray of World War II. For a municipal museum director in 1935, Parker was in a relatively good position. He had averted an immediate funding crisis through tapping government relief funds, he was still courting the local corporate community with a view to getting the museum endowed, and further funded schemes were still in the pipeline. Admittedly, he was giving a great deal to his job and sometimes doing so to the detriment of his health and his family life. He was, for example, regularly commuting from Rochester to his family home up in Seneca country in Naples, a village some 43 miles from the museum. This made him something of a weekend dad to his young daughter Martha, but the sacrifice seemed worth it as he steered the museum through the worst of the depression. Times were hard, but the "Chief's" unquenchable dynamism, innovation, and hard work had undoubtedly made the museum and its director into an impressive regional success. Further progress was just around the corner. He was soon to find himself in a position to fulfill some of his most cherished dreams, namely, expanding his museum, developing the work of Morgan, and having a tangible and practical impact on the lives of those he still knew as his own people, the Seneca.

CHAPTER 8

Success in the Indian New Deal Years and Beyond, 1935–1946

The Indian New Deal provided Parker with a series of opportunities. Especially beneficial was his central involvement with two government-funded schemes on the reservations of his childhood. They were known as the Tonawanda Community House and the Seneca Arts and Crafts Project. Both reflected well on Parker and the museum because they brought much-needed relief to the Seneca and because they were recognized as positive attempts to stimulate Indian integration. The Arts Project carried additional benefits, since it required those Senecas involved to reproduce the material past of previous generations, and everything made through the scheme remained the property of the Rochester Museum of Arts and Sciences. The artifacts, aside from their value as material replicated as a replacement for a lost collection compiled by Morgan, were valuable acquisitions and commodities with a definite trade value within the museum economy.

Each of the two schemes had a clear utility for Parker as a museum man, but at the same time they stand as instructive examples of the Indian New Deal in operation. Therefore, both need to be considered within the overall context of the sea change in the American government's approach to its native peoples that began in the 1920s and culminated in fundamental legislative reform during the mid-1930s. In fact, the schemes helped to fill a relief vacuum created through the Iroquois's specific rejection of the main plank of 1930s Indian reform, a rejection that in itself says something about the reform impulse of the time.

• • •

Change in national policy had begun with a series of governmental assessments of Indian conditions. In 1923, Secretary of the Interior

Hubert Work took steps to examine the Indian "problem." As mentioned in chapter 5, Work appointed a Committee of One Hundred "to review and advise on Indian policy." The group included civic leaders, reformers headed by John Collier, anthropologists Alfred A. Kroeber and Clark Wissler, and a delegation from the Society of American Indians (SAI). The SAI group included Thomas D. Sloan, Sherman Coolidge, and Henry Roe Cloud, with Parker acting as committee chair. Congress largely ignored the group's recommendations to improve health and educational provision on the reservations, to sponsor training to develop Indian leadership, to settle claims, and to investigate peyote use. The committee did not feel itself in a position to make any recommendation about citizenship. John Collier, who was keen to see effective reform, at the time described the group's achievements as "innocuous," and he was right. Nonetheless, the committee's deliberations signaled the beginning of significant Indian reform to come.

The following year Congress bestowed citizenship on all Indians born within the boundaries of the United States. This in itself did not universally guarantee Indians the vote or other civil rights, particularly in the West, and the need for fundamental reform remained. Nationally, Indians had suffered a massive erosion of their land base since the 1887 Dawes Act. A significant proportion of those living on allotted reservations were landless, and too much of the land Indians had been able to retain was arid and unproductive. Non-Indian humanitarians continued to voice grave concerns about health, education, and welfare on the reservations, where tuberculosis and trachoma were rife and infant mortality alarmingly high. The Indian Citizenship Act simplified that issue from the government's perspective and went some way toward satisfying a political desire to rein in the powers of the Department of the Interior and the Bureau of Indian Affairs (BIA), but it did almost nothing to economically or culturally integrate those it was supposedly designed to help.

The next important review of the Indian "problem" came in 1926, and was independently sponsored by John D. Rockefeller, Jr., through the Institute for Government Research.[1] Its conclusions were published in 1928 as *The Problem of Indian Administration,* informally referred to as the Meriam Report. Highlighting "deplorable conditions" on the reservations, it acknowledged that disproportionately high Indian mortality rates were a reflection of poor health provision, disease, malnutrition, low income, and unsanitary conditions. Clearly, the program of assimilation embodied by the Dawes Act of 1887 had failed. In response, the Meriam Report reiterated and extended many of the recommendations already made by the Committee of One Hundred. It called for a loan fund to stimulate business on the reservations, recommended that the policy of allotment be ended, and said "the fostering and development of the native arts" was "a wholesome thing in inter-racial relations." One of its basic tenets was that Indian integration should be achieved through education. Indians needed to be educated to help themselves "so that they may be absorbed into the prevailing civilization or be fitted to live in the presence of that civilization at least in accordance with a minimum standard of health and decency." The Meriam Report assumed, as the Dawes Act had before it, that this transformation could be achieved in a generation.[2]

The report also suggested that while Indians struggled to grasp Euro-American values, they should be allowed religious freedom and a degree of federal assistance and autonomy within their communities. They should be helped to retain and consolidate their property, their claims against the federal government should be investigated, the rule of law better enforced on the reservations, the BIA improved, and more Indians given jobs within it. All this may well have constituted a fundamental reappraisal of policy, but most Indian reform still required the support of an entrenched Republican Congress. It therefore took until 1932 and the election of Democrat Franklin Delano Roosevelt for significant legislative change to begin.

It came with the appointment by Roosevelt of John Collier, by then a well-connected reform figure in Washington as commissioner of Indian Affairs in 1933. He would hold the position longer than anyone else and have an enduring impact on twentieth-century Indian affairs. His twelve years in office saw dramatic new legislation, including the Indian Reorganization Act (IRA) and Johnson O'Malley Act of 1934, the Indian Arts and Crafts Board Act of 1935, the Oklahoma Indian Welfare Act of 1936, and the Alaska Reorganization Act of 1936. Even though debate has recently intensified over the achievements of both Collier and the Indian New Deal, certain developments stand out unequivocally as significant. During the New Deal, critically poor conditions on the reservations were eased, educational and conservation issues were addressed, and an attempt was made to begin rebuilding Indian self-determination and self-esteem. Even though a tribal structure was not how every group of Indian peoples was organized, tribal governments were nevertheless set up and granted "certain rights of home rule," together with eligibility for revolving credit loan funds. Just as significant, the Indian New Deal brought about the repeal of the land allotment dynamic of the Dawes Act of 1887, beginning an important reversal of the alienation of Indian land.

Whereas the Dawes Act had been fundamentally concerned with stimulating individualism and individual ownership of private property within tribal communities, the rhetoric of Collier's Indian New Deal was concerned with its opposite, tribal community and tribal ownership of communally held land. His was an overall approach to reform that rejected assimilationist ideals for both immigrants and Indians. This stemmed from Collier's work among immigrants in New York prior to World War I, which had given him access to ideas about community pluralism developed by people like Mary Follett and Eduard Lindeman. Such thinking saw community based on ethnicity as the foundation for an ultimate renovation of American society.[3] Collier's views were also symptomatic of a new kind of understanding of Indian culture informed by aspects of Boasian anthropology and by a pluralist view of cultures as self-sustaining, integrated wholes. The reform-minded like Collier and the intellectual elite had started to see unassimilated Indians as representative of an older and better form of society. This they increasingly contrasted with an alienated, materialistic, automated, and secular modernizing America. Social disintegration within the dominant culture was repeatedly and unfavorably compared with an idealized and generally ahistorical notion of community within tribal culture. In an individualistic and progressively urban United States, Indian community values took on a new significance.

This outlook made those Indian groups that were least assimilated, that were least like modern America, the ones most attractive to reformers and intellectuals. The agricultural Pueblo Indians of New Mexico were one example. They provided the backdrop for an artists' colony at Taos, New Mexico, run by an old friend of Collier's from New York. Collier visited it by chance in November 1920. With the Pueblo he found his dream of ideal society and a connection with heritage and community of deep personal significance. It was an epiphanal experience he later explained in his autobiography:

> The discovery that came to me there in that tiny group of a few hundred Indians, was of personality-forming institutions, even now weakened, which had survived repeated and immense historical shocks, and which were going right on in the production of states of mind, attitudes of mind, earth-loyalties and human-loyalties, amid a context of beauty which suffused all the life of the group. . . . It might be that only the Indians, among the peoples of this hemisphere at least, were still the possessors and users of the fundamental secret of life—the secret of building great personality through the instrumentality of social institutions.[4]

As Robert Berkhofer has succinctly put it, Collier "romanticized the heritage of these folk societies as part of his alienation from his own 'sick' times, and the Pueblos became his own personal countercultural utopia."[5]

Many of the most serious criticisms made of the Indian New Deal can be related to the limitations of this idealized picture of Indian society when it formed the basis of Indian reform. Change that was tailored to this vision and not to the diversity of Indian experience, which included interaction and accommodation to white culture, brought with it inevitable conflict. This was sensed by some within the anthropological discipline who chose not to give the Indian New Deal unmitigated support. Boas, for example, showed his characteristic fear of generalization when he wrote to Harold Ickes, secretary of the interior, in 1932, to oppose Collier's appointment, accusing him of being unnecessarily opinionated and emotional about Indian reform.[6] The great mentor of a generation of early-twentieth-century anthropologists shied away from any kind of synthesis that could be translated directly into policy, not least because his work was itself a reaction against older "armchair anthropologists" who had formulated generalizing laws based on limited fieldwork.[7] Ironically, from 1922 to 1933, Collier had attacked Indian land allotment and the drive for assimilation because it centered around a belief that all Americans should conform to one, homogenous cultural standard; yet his own New Deal reform ideas were open to criticism on similar grounds, this time for conceiving of all Indians as fitting into a single mold. As happens too often with American Indian policy, in this instance reform was based on a contemporary image of what mainstream America should be like, rather than on the existent realities of Indian life.

Scholars are still generally happy to acknowledge that Collier's intentions were extremely positive, but today there is a broader awareness of the limitations of his vision and its implementation. It is recognized that he wanted to actively promote Indian culture, rebuild tribal society and government, and develop and expand the Indian land base. His own and associated histories of the New Deal have presented the events of the period as being largely a fulfillment of this dream of Indian autonomy. However, especially since the late 1960s, Indian and non-Indian scholarship has highlighted that Collier always justified his reform in terms of the ultimate integration of the Indian into American society, albeit on Indian as well as white terms.[8]

The Indian Arts and Crafts Board is an excellent example of this. Collier saw the development of Indian arts and crafts as integral to successful Indian economic policy, which he believed would in turn lead to cultural preservation. Yet as Robert Fay Schrader has made clear, "the motivation behind the federal government's early role in Indian arts and crafts was a desire to industrialize the Indians" and therefore "to assimilate them into society."[9] This was also how Parker saw the Seneca Arts Project, and the Tonawanda Community House— as exercises in integrating Indians through industry. Regardless of Collier's rhetoric, overall, the Indian New Deal was primarily about incorporating the Indian into American life. Collier's vision, stemming as it did from the Progressive settlement house ethos, was essentially conservative. He wanted, through the restoration of community, to stimulate a reconnection with heritage that could better enable groups to cope successfully with economic and social change.

An important distinction has also been drawn between Collier's New Deal rhetoric, wider governmental aims, and the actual affect of legislative change on Indian communities. Undeniably, the original fifty-page proposal put forward by Collier in 1934 for an Indian New Deal was revolutionary in detailing a case for the restoration of Indian political and cultural self-determination. The document proposed to give Indians power over the selection and retention of government employees and to create a federal Indian court system. However, these proposals underwent major modification, such that, as D'Arcy McNickle has pointed out, "colonial rule was left intact." Ultimately, the Reorganization Act did not radically break with policies of the past. As Kelly and others have pointed out, it "sought not so much to reverse the nation's historic attitude toward the Indians as to freeze it where it was in 1934."[10]

The Iroquois voted to reject the Indian Reorganization Act of 1934, joining the one-third of Indian tribes who did so. They organized a coordinated campaign to block it primarily because they cherished a fundamental concept of their own sovereignty that conflicted with its application. The six separate nations of the Iroquois recognized a second level of pan-national organization in the Iroquois League. Even though the league was not and has never been recognized by the United States, it nonetheless represents all Iroquois tribes and bases a claim to sovereignty on three main eighteenth-century treaties: Fort Stanwix (1784), Jay (1794), and Canandaigua (1794). Repudiation of the Canandaigua treaty by the 1934 Indian Reorganization Act was a focal concern for the Iroquois, whom, as Hauptman has made clear, Collier simply did not understand. Legislation for tribal reorganization clashed by definition with the Iroquois's "overriding concern with legality as well as with the real and symbolic reaffirmation of treaty rights."[11] Many Iroquois had also rejected citizenship and the vote in

1924 because they saw themselves as already citizens of their own independent nations within the league, as guaranteed by treaty. Aside from this, conditions more generally would hardly make the Iroquois amenable to accepting the Reorganization Act. The Dawes Act had not been universally applied to New York, and the Iroquois were not generally receptive to federal officials. Furthermore, there was entrenched opposition to the BIA, something that Collier, before heading it, had added to himself.[12]

The real problem was that the Iroquois were not "Indian" in the same way as the seemingly quintessential Pueblos, who were Collier's standard. The Iroquois required specific and particular help during the New Deal period that did not correspond to policy formulated to preserve the cultures of the Southwest. In the end, Collier learned from his failure to achieve tribal reorganization in New York, and encouraged community projects instead. This was where Parker came in, by formulating, in the Seneca Arts Project and the Tonawanda Community House, schemes that provided a more acceptable form of government assistance for certain Iroquois than that offered through Collier's 1934 act. These were seen not as BIA interference, but as practical, community-based efforts at improvement of reservation life, having, in Parker, the backing and direction of a respected Indian figure known to the two reservations concerned. Collier, with whom he had a cordial working relationship, was happy to sanction Parker's ideas, since they gelled with his own overall project—to integrate the Indian into American society without sacrifice of native cultural traditions.

Of course, any form whatsoever of community uplift was sorely needed on New York reservations during the Great Depression, since New York Indians were sharing the same deficit in living standards as Indian peoples nationally. According to the National Resources Board, at the time it would have taken around $120 million to raise Indian living standards to that of their white neighbors, who were often themselves living in rural poverty.[13] Work was scarce at Tonawanda, apart from some part-time employment at the nearby gypsum mines at Akron. Many were on welfare, and there were sporadic outbreaks of pneumonia. At Cattaraugus, tuberculosis had reached epidemic proportions, and many had been reduced to surviving through subsistence agriculture because work in the region's factories and construction industries had dried up.[14] The reservation work-relief schemes that Parker helped initiate and coordinate may not have been exactly what everyone at Tonawanda and Cattaraugus wanted in terms of federal aid, but they were at least an alternative to deprivation and an enduring lack of opportunity.

The original idea for the Community House came from Parker, along with a small group of Seneca, but two women were primarily responsible for nursing the project toward completion. This is made clear in Lawrence M. Hauptman's able history of the project in his book *The Iroquois and the New Deal,* on which the following discussion is based.[15] The first woman was the wife of a minister who been a visiting clergyman at Tonawanda, Nameé Henricks, from Penn Yan, New York. She was appalled at the substandard facilities available to the Seneca at Tonawanda and had a number of useful contacts within women's organizations, particularly the Daughters of the American Revolution (DAR), that allowed her to do something about it. Working with Parker and the local library association, she began promoting the idea of a community center early in 1935. In all, she made eleven trips to Albany at her own expense and three trips to Washington to confer with Collier, prominent representatives, WPA personnel, and with the second woman essential to the project, First Lady Eleanor Roosevelt.[16]

Initially Parker, Henricks, and a Tonawanda Reservation committee headed by Elsina Doctor, May Spring, and Wyman Jemison held meetings to drum up community support. Parker then wrote a supporting letter to accompany a formal proposal and architectural plans for the building, which were submitted to the New York State Department of Social Welfare and to the BIA. He recommended the project because "the Tonawanda band of Senecas is the only group without an adequate building for gatherings."[17] April 1935 saw a DAR convention in Washington at which Henricks was able to network to great effect. As well as lobbying Collier, Elmer Thomas, chairman of the Senate Indian Affairs Committee, and W. Carson Ryan, Jr., the director of Indian Education, she managed to secure the all-important support of the president's wife.

Having been impressed by Henricks, Collier endorsed the project as something the WPA might sponsor and wrote to William N. Fenton, the reservation anthropologist, instructing him to assist Henricks and Parker with it. Fenton was at Tonawanda as part of Collier's wider plans to integrate anthropology into Indian New Deal reform, plans that had included the creation of an applied anthropology staff at the BIA the previous year. As resident anthropologist or community worker, Fenton was based at the reservation from February 1935 to August 1937. He did what he could to advance the project, which gathered pace.[18] By May of 1935, Elsina Doctor was at the head of a board of directors that became incorporated as the "Tonawanda Indian Community House Association" under state law. Henricks found herself invited to the White House, and as a result, Mrs. Roosevelt smoothed the project's way through various political and bureaucratic obstacles. Without her help, it is unlikely that the scheme would have reached a timely conclusion or even succeeded at all.

At this juncture, quick action was needed to avoid any entanglement with intertribal politics stemming in particular from the Council of Chiefs at Tonawanda. After all, the necessity under state law to have a sponsoring body or "holding agency" for the project could have been seen as oppositional to sovereignty. In the event, Parker calmed any brewing opposition through formally assuring the council that the association would "consult your honorable body whenever possible to secure the best advice," and the scheme won overall community support.[19] The association was able to raise $450 from people living on the reservation and used it to purchase a tract of land for the house just over the Akron side of the reservation boundary.

Parker and Henricks also had to be adroit at dealing with white bureaucrats. New York State Commissioner of Welfare David C. Adie raised a series of objections to the scheme, largely because he feared it might affect his budget and because of his rivalry with the WPA in New York. Parker responded to his criticisms point by point. He requested a full description of the land to be purchased with a signed option-to-buy statement from the Tonawanda Indian Community House Association, wrote a formal justification for the project to the WPA office, and forwarded a letter to Eleanor Roosevelt complaining about Adie. Henricks, too, responded to Adie's objections by getting approval for the building's maintenance and ongoing costs after completion directly from his superiors. She used her close ties to Mrs. Roosevelt and the commitment secured from the WPA to underwrite the complete construction costs of the Community House to such good effect that Adie ultimately had to give the project his support. In the end, the state agreed to service and maintain the building on the understanding that it could lease the tract of land, which was contiguous to the reservation boundary, from the association. This was an extremely positive but also remarkable example of intercultural interaction, since the arrangement required ongoing cooperation between the state and the reservation.

On May 15, 1936, a bill, largely drafted by Parker, was passed by the New York State Legislature that justified the scheme as a means of facilitating Indian integration through education. It required the state "to provide the maintenance of the Tonawanda Community House under the Supervision of the State Department of Social Welfare," after its erection by the WPA on lands acquired by the Tonawanda Indian Community House Association and leased to the state for ninety-nine years. Five thousand dollars was allotted for the center's maintenance, operation, and supervision. Perhaps unsurprisingly, Parker proposed that it contain what was for him the best indicator of civilization, a museum.[20]

Work began in November 1936, with the WPA spending $60,000 on construction, improving the surrounding grounds, and extending the water supply from Akron. The actual building work was done almost entirely by Tonawanda Seneca hired by the WPA with the intention of giving them transferable skills and construction experience. A two-story structure, the $45,000 building was designed along the same lines as a traditional Iroquois longhouse, using cypress logs and donated local stone. Four large wood-burning fireplaces were built in, along with clinic rooms, a workshop, laboratories, showers, a gymnasium, a game room, and a great number of books got together through Parker's auspices and those of the DAR.[21] Formally dedicated and opened by Eleanor Roosevelt on May 13, 1939, the Community House soon became an important social and educational focus for the reservation community, and it remains to this day exactly how Hauptman has described it, "a living legacy of the New Deal." It testifies to the ability of Parker and his project associates to organize a truly community effort that gained the cooperation of the state, the federal government, and the reservation. It is yet more evidence of Parker's ability to "get things done," the phrase that reverberated each time Parker was referred to during my own visit to the Community House in 1993.

Tonawanda was also the main site for Parker's other New Deal relief scheme, the Seneca Arts and Crafts Project, although work was also carried out to a lesser extent at Cattaraugus Reservation, which is about fifty miles away from Tonawanda and around one hundred miles from Rochester. With Parker's museum acting as a sponsor, funding came at first from the Temporary Emergency Relief Administration (TERA), and after 1935 from the Rochester City Council and the WPA. The project ultimately employed around one hundred Seneca. They produced over five thousand separate arts and crafts items, all of which were retained as the property of the museum. Overall, the scheme was an excellent way for Parker both to generate exchange currency within the internal museum economy and to raise the museum's profile during a time of economic cutbacks and uncertain visitor numbers. Even better, it also allowed him to engage with Morgan's anthropological legacy, because the materials produced were a deliberate attempt to replicate Morgan's collection from the early nineteenth century. Parker was able to ensure this because he had almost total executive control over the project from beginning to end. The Seneca Arts Project was his idea, he wrote the required proposals, he hired all the Indian and non-Indian personnel on the reservations and at the museum, and he was the professional generally in charge.

The project originated with a three-page proposal that Parker began circulating to New York State agencies in April 1934: "The Rochester Municipal Museum proposes a project by which the almost extinct arts and crafts of the New York Indians may be preserved and put on a production basis in order that such activity and products may contribute to the relief and self-support of the said Indian population." Instruction was to be by "native experts" under museum supervision, with the museum supplying all the necessary tools and basic materials. There was also a clear and unequivocal stipulation about what the institution was to gain in return. Everything the Senecas produced was to be "turned over to the said museum as its property," so that it could be used "for exchange or other distribution with other museums or the public."[22]

The Temporary Emergency Relief Administration had set up its program for artists in December 1932 in the wake of a general public interest in traditional crafts that was connected to the intellectual backlash against industrialization. A scheme that could use this fact to create ongoing work and income for Indians while fostering community on the reservations was clearly in keeping with the New Deal ethos. By July 1934, TERA had given the proposal its formal sanction and the project was off the ground with its own personnel. C. Carlton Perry was in charge of its coordination at the museum, while on the reservations Roy Jimerson and Arlene Doxtator at Cattaraugus and Robert Tahamont and Cephas Hill at Tonawanda were hired as native supervisors. Each person brought vital skills and abilities. Tahamont, for example, was educated, skilled in carpentry, and married to Parker's cousin, while Hill was an intelligent and well-respected reservation figure who, unlike Parker, understood and spoke Seneca very well. His communication skills and commitment to the project ensured that on a practical level it ran relatively smoothly.

Initial finances had materialized quite readily, but keeping up levels of ongoing funding was to prove a challenge over the six and a half years the project survived. Parker would be told several times that it would have to close, even though his efforts garnered support across the political spectrum at both municipal and ward level. He did everything he could to sell the project, using the press, the museum, and the radio program he broadcasted in Rochester.[23] At points he even stretched the truth a little—for example, telling the newspapers that Ernest Smith, an artist who later achieved national acclaim, had never painted before coming onto the project. He also gave influential whites status within Indian culture to gain their support. The governor of New York received a Seneca name that translated as "One who governs with justice." The New York WPA director also succumbed, receiving the name "Sa-Go-Ya-Da-Geh-Hus" or "He Helps All." In each case Parker presided over the welcoming ceremonies, with the actual adoption ritual being conducted by a project worker he knew well—"show Indian" and published author Jesse Cornplanter.[24] Perry also worked hard, defending the project in terms of its monetary value to the city administration. He wrote to convince them of what "very good business" it was to help fund it even in hard times, because the material produced was "easily worth three times its total cost."[25]

Parker also wrote an early detailed defense of the project, entitled "Museum Motives Behind the New York Arts Project" for *Indians at Work,* the Indian Service newsletter. The scheme, he wrote, would "capitalize the best in ancient art and to redevelop it as a racial contribution," allowing true "native creative ability" to at last shine through. He was sure that the creation of "manufactures for trade" that were "typical of the days when Indian art was original and pristine" would allow the Seneca to achieve their own salvation.[26] Clearly, despite Collier's New Deal rhetoric about the arts project, Parker himself was still thinking in terms of Morgan's scale of racial development as spelled out in *Ancient Society.*

As well as being another chance for the Seneca, the project, in Parker's mind, was exemplary museum practice. It fit not just with his concept of the museum as a vehicle for community service but also with his vision of the museist as a business entrepreneur who generated institutional assets. As he put it to readers of *Museum Service* in an article entitled "Museums Mean Business," "many a museum worker handles his funds in such a manner that he creates values far in excess of his recompense and does so year after year." Thus he made museums seem like places of business and productivity—two of the buzzwords of the age.[27]

All this meant that the art produced by the Seneca really had to be of good enough quality for successful exchange within the museum market. Parker needed to exercise great control so that only what had trade value was made by the project workers. His idea was to reproduce the valuable artifacts that Morgan had collected with the help of the Parker family and their reservation contacts in the early nineteenth century. To Parker's great chagrin, these had been destroyed by fire at the state capitol, but now there was a unique opportunity to replicate them on the same reservations where they had originally been collected. What Parker demanded from the project was ethnographic reproduction rather than contemporary Seneca art. As he put it in a letter to the president of the Tonawanda Council of Chiefs: "the workers are required to make duplicates of ancient patterns which the Rochester Museum supplies, suggests, or authorizes various persons to make" in order to "produce such material of any kind or sort as may be of use to the museum."[28]

At Tonawanda, the project operated from an abandoned district schoolhouse at the east end of the reservation amid an atmosphere described as "cooperation tempered with joking and good natured rivalry."[29] With the museum providing workbenches, carving tools, silversmith's tools, needles and thread, patterns, photographs, line drawings, and models, the Seneca involved set about producing a sizable body of material. It included wooden cradleboards, false face masks, flat carvings, benches, bowls, ladles, spoons, silver jewelry, "finger-woven" baskets, tump lines, bags and burden straps, embroidered beadwork and pine quillwork for costumes, pen sketches, oil paintings, and around a hundred watercolors. Few of the artists involved at either project site had had training, so there was little to get in the way of Parker's comprehensive artistic direction. He showed project workers illustrations he found from Morgan's writings for them to copy, and to inspire them he produced artifacts from digs carried out by him or his colleague Ritchie. Parker, Fenton, and Hill worked closely together, visiting and photographing from nearly all the museums, historical societies, and galleries in New York that had Iroquois ethnographic material, so as to provide models from which to work. They also found older Indians who still remembered traditional skills, such as how to weave baskets, burden straps, and sashes, and got them to pass on their knowledge. Parker would tell workers such as Ernest Smith which myth or legend to paint and therefore ended up creating, in part, the modern "Iroquois School of Art."[30]

A close arbiter of the standards of production at both project sites, Parker kept a careful eye on each. Quality and a particular concept of authenticity were paramount. Although it was now difficult to find "authentic" materials such as animal bones, beads, buckskins, black ash splint, and porcupine quills, Parker was still very firm about maintaining consistency in relation to the ethnographic record. For example, in one letter quoted by Hauptman, he complained that some finished costumes were "somewhat clownish rather than authentic Iroquois."[31] Perry therefore had to search far and wide for dress skins, even writing to an Oklahoma Indian trading post for samples.[32] In print, however, Parker played down his role as executive artistic director. "We allowed the workers to develop their own designs, take their own time and to create things as if for themselves," he told *Museum Service,* giving the impression that the idea to copy "designs found in Beauchamp and Morgan" had been the artists' own after they had been "encouraged . . . to employ correct ethnological patterns." Elsewhere he claimed that "only in extreme cases" had "any instruction been given, it being believed that our function is to assist in bringing out the innate ability of our Indian workers themselves."[33]

In his quest for the best, Parker was not above practicing some simple psychology on the workers at each site, claiming at the time that through his methods of "seeking to make each strive for the highest excellence and showing each the best work of the other (reservation) real standards are being set."[34] In truth, he tended to favor Tonawanda, which was the poorer reservation and much closer to Rochester. Even though the program at Cattaraugus established a tribal museum temporarily at the Thomas Indian School and Orphan Asylum and had the Beaux Arts-educated Indian painter Sanford Plummer, it was the first to fall to budgetary cuts.[35]

Parker thought of the Seneca Arts Project as a chance to repair some of the devastation caused by the fire of March 29, 1911, and as yet another opportunity to emulate Morgan's achievements—to "out-Morgan Morgan."[36] The project was, as Hauptman explains, Parker's "opportunity to come full circle in his romantic delusions of being the equal to the 'father of anthropology.'"[37] This is why the project was essentially an exercise in reproducing the material past, in creating replicas, as distinct from producing truly contemporary Indian art. Perhaps ironically, the collection Parker used as the model for the work his artists produced had itself, in part, also been created by Seneca under instruction. In 1848, Morgan had advised the New York State Museum to set up an Indian Cabinet where Iroquois arts and crafts could be preserved as the "unwritten history of their social existence."[38] He set about collecting Seneca objects that were in use at the time and simultaneously commissioned Tonawanda Seneca to make traditional items to be accompanied by records of how they were produced. It is entirely possible, therefore, that Parker in the 1930s was actually commissioning simulacra, or copies of copies, of Seneca material culture, that he was continuing a scientific project of salvaging what was, at least in part, a constructed past.[39]

All this made for inevitable difficulties when it came to categorizing the project work. After all, Parker was requiring the Seneca to create Seneca arts and crafts that were "correct" only when they exactly replicated the material culture of another time. What the Seneca produced was deemed authentic only when it resembled material from their less assimilated past. This made its ultimate value and status difficult to gauge, as Parker pointed out in "Art Reproductions of the Seneca Indians," produced for *Museum Service* toward the project's close. "We now possess hundreds of these recreated objects. . . . They are 'Indian made,' some are ethnologically correct but many are things that no ancestor would or could have produced. They are the product of the modern Seneca endeavoring to respond to the racial urge to create." Parker admitted he was a little confused about what would be an appropriate use for the material, inquiring of his readers, "Shall we pack it away, shall we display portions of the best as 'modern Seneca art,' shall we send the articles out to schools as reproductions made by the Indians themselves, shall we trade, exchange or give away what we do not want?" He was perplexed about "knowing just what to call these things" and wondered, "Shall it be '1935-1941 reproductions by Seneca Indians' presenting their own material culture; or, shall it be something else?"[40]

His difficulties stemmed from the nature of ethnographic collection itself. Were the Seneca at this stage still Indian and therefore producing something genuine, or were they simply reproducing the past and copying something once authentic but now lost? If their work was genuine, then so were they; they were still Indian and not assimilating Americans. If their work was not genuine, they were not Indians. So what were they? The problem was that ethnographic collection for museums required the gathering and selection of material that was traditional, that was, by definition, somehow in opposition to modernity. If 1930s Seneca art was to be acknowledged as historical and hybrid, this would problematize its status as authentic, traditional, and anti-modern, therefore detracting from its value as a museum commodity. The paradox Parker faced when classifying the project material was a reflection of the fundamental myth at the heart of twentieth-century salvage ethnography, because what was being saved—Seneca Indian culture—was actually indestructible, since it was subject to developmental change. The issue highlights how dependent institutional collection was on removing material from its historical context, and it reminds us of what James Clifford has so ably pointed out, that "cultural or artistic 'authenticity' has as much to do with an inventive present as with a past, its objectification, preservation, or revival."[41]

Nonetheless, the project overall must be considered a success. Certainly it was something from which Parker got enjoyment and satisfaction.[42] Although Hauptman has noted "grumblings from people excluded" and unease "from a few Longhouse people who objected to the secular carving of ceremonial false faces," overall the project instilled community pride and improved life on the reservations concerned. That said, worker pay was low, and the productivity Parker and the project supervisors encouraged was eroded by absenteeism.

Dissent about the project's operation existed from the beginning. To dampen criticism, Parker at the outset had prudently flagged the exact role and responsibilities of the museum as sponsor to the Tonawanda Council of Chiefs. He had suggested that responsibility really lay with TERA, who made the worker payments, rather than with the museum, and he made clear that "if any person on the project is not satisfied that he is making correct Seneca articles at the project he may manufacture them on his spare time for himself, or at any time he so desires." The respected reservation figure Jesse Cornplanter wasn't fooled. Cornplanter was very knowledgeable about Seneca culture, the son of a leader of the Longhouse, and a very talented artist and mask carver. He criticized Parker's work as inaccurate, suggested to him that the project was a sweatshop, and even told Parker's project director at Albany that what was created was all guesswork.[43] Customarily taciturn about such things, Parker was eventually reduced to complaining to Keppler that Cornplanter was a "high grade moron" whose chronic drunkenness had made him so manic on occasion that he had had to be laid off the project for days.[44] Such mudslinging aside, as the project's dynamic began to ebb and as funding became harder and harder to secure, Parker was still very glad, both professionally and personally, that he had worked so hard to make it happen.

During the course of the project, his professional status had grown, and the Rochester Museum of Arts and Sciences had slowly developed into an even more impressive institution. In 1936, Parker was honored by the Indian Council Fire of Chicago with their award to the "most famous person of Indian ancestry in the United States." It probably helped that Collier had been one of the judges, but even more pleasing to Parker, the announcement was made as part of Chicago's observance of American Indian Day, an anniversary that remained perhaps the only positive carryover from his years with the Society of American Indians.[45] The next year he was able to originate and promote yet another honor, the Rochester Civic Medal, conceived as a means of drumming up civic-mindedness among the city's men of wealth. He also managed to secure for the museum the 7,500 additional square feet of building space that had been occupied at Edgerton Park by the public library and, with it, WPA funds for its renovation.

Another boon for Parker was gaining the assistance of Mable S. Smith, his first qualified secretary. She helped Parker maintain his

Arthur Caswell Parker at his desk in 1936.

Courtesy of Rochester Museum & Science Center

strenuous work rate, and both regularly put in seven-day weeks. A highly respected local figure by this stage, Parker met with college presidents, industrial leaders, and scientists from across the region to discuss how to advance various mutual causes.[46] In 1938 the museum was selected by the World's Fair Commission to assist in creating a display to represent the Rochester area, yet another privilege that made him especially proud. Since he was extremely busy, he assigned the task to the man who had for some years been effectively serving as his assistant director after first being appointed in 1933, C. Carlton Perry.

By now Parker felt he had created one of the most advanced museum systems in the world, with large and valuable collections, worthy research publications, an adult education program, a Hobby Council and Show, and, despite setbacks, the country's largest school extension service directly geared to the classroom. Personally, the "Chief" was "in excellent health and in a good state of mind," and he felt he had "undergone an evolution" at Rochester.[47] Of course, keeping it all going in a coherent fashion was a challenge, but even this was something he relished. He wrote in 1939: "It takes all the skill of an old stage-coach driver who can control a 'Twenty Mule Team' to keep the horses running in the same direction. This may account for my lame shoulders. But it is a joyful task and I would not trade it for a single track museum and a lot of possible ease."[48]

The museum was now in its best-ever position to expand, but the Seneca Arts Project was facing inevitable decline. Since at least 1937, there had been a discernible erosion of the community ideal among intellectuals and reformers, and New Deal programs had become increasingly subject to a collectivist critique. The senator who had sponsored the Indian Reorganization Act at the outset, Burton K. Wheeler of Montana, revoked his support, spoke against Collier, and once again put forward assimilation as the answer to Indian problems. America's eventual formal entry into World War II during 1941 was approaching, and a conservative resurgence was afoot that bayed for New Deal projects to be either dropped or curtailed. When Pearl Harbor did bring war, the BIA soon found itself deemed a "nonessential" agency and was rehoused from Washington to Chicago, with the loss of vital funds and personnel. The community Indian New Deal would be in severe retreat by the time Collier eventually left the commissionership late in 1945, a point when Indian policy entered the doldrums.

The knife was drawn for the Arts Project in 1939 when the federal government started to seriously reduce WPA funding. Yet while there remained hope, every available promotion opportunity was taken up and the results of the scheme touted near and far.[49] Just then Parker was basking in the glory of yet another honor, this time membership in the British Royal Arts Society for his work in archaeology and museum administration.[50] Another coup was his appointment as a U.S. delegate to a 1939 Canadian conference on North American Indians, which was jointly hosted by the University of Toronto and Yale University. To his credit, along with the rest of the U.S. and Canadian delegates, Parker participated in a staged walkout from the conference on the last day. Although the event was masked by the big news of the day, Hitler's invasion of Poland, the group wanted to register that they were too acculturated to be truly representative of those surviving on land reserved for Indians. They went on record demanding an all-Indian conference on Indian welfare, restricted to "bona fide Indian leaders actually living among the Indian people of the reservations and reserves."[51] Having lived through the rise and fall of the SAI, Parker was only too aware of the dangers of assuming the right to speak on behalf of all Indians and of the gap in experience between himself and those he was expected to represent.

On reflection after his return from the conference, Parker could only be pleased by how both "his" New Deal projects had turned out. However, he was resigned to the fact that the Community House's general success had been marred by dissatisfaction over its management.[52] As

Portrait of Arthur Caswell Parker, 1941.

Courtesy of Rochester Museum & Science Center

for the Seneca Arts Project, aside from netting materials that Parker valued at $13,300, it had also, to his mind, fulfilled its original mission. He was happy to register that "the State W.P.A. authorities gave the Rochester Museum projects the highest rating in the State for productive results in material and in personal rehabilitation, all able special relief cases becoming fitted for positions in gainful work outside the museum."[53] But this was not strictly true, since the artists employed were not able to continue in the same trade after the project ended. When work on the reservation did begin to pick up in the early 1940s, it resulted directly from national preparation for war rather than from arts and crafts skills.

This lends weight to Alice Lee Jemison's contemporary criticism of the entire arts and craft aspect of the New Deal. Jemison was a Seneca activist of plural heritage who was consistently vociferous in her opposition to Collier and his policies. She complained to the 1937 Senate Indian Affairs Committee that he was educating Indian youth for

Arthur Caswell Parker and Kates during a hobby outing, 1938.

Personal Papers of Arthur Caswell Parker, in author's possession

nothing other than arts and crafts, that he was telling them "now we are fitting you for life on the reservation," but in fact only "arbitrarily making them supply arts and crafts for government controlled operatives."[54] Her complaint has even greater resonance given that the Seneca project's early success may have been used by Collier to justify the creation in August 1935 of the Indian Arts and Crafts Board by the Department of the Interior.[55]

In July 1941, a mysterious fire brought the project to a definitive close. This was the second to befall the project since 1937, when fire destroyed the project building and all the material owned by the museum up to that time. Undeterred, Parker had simply found another school, completely equipped it, and within forty-eight hours had got his people back to work, a recovery operation that could not be mounted for a second time.[56]

Clearly Parker used Collier's Indian New Deal to serve key elements of his own lifelong agenda: Indian integration into Euro-American culture, personal success within the museum world, and professional dialogue with the legacy of Morgan. We are left to wonder at the curious interplay of forces that caused a progressive, nonenrolled Indian to require his own people to reproduce commissioned material from the previous century so as to facilitate their contemporary integration into American society. Such circumstances came about because of non-Indian denial of the specifics of Indian history, a denial of the reality of Indian accommodative responses to the dominant culture caused by America's need to reconnect with some imagined and essentially primitive past. This denial gave commodity value to the art produced, and, if nothing else, it allowed for some alleviation of the poverty on the Tonawanda and Cattaraugus Reservations, while revitalizing the Seneca traditional skills that had by then fallen into disuse because of the tourist trade. Furthermore, Parker's cultivation of Seneca artists such as Ernest Smith and Sanford Plummer strongly influenced the careers of artists who followed, such as Mohawk John Fadden.[57] In sum, Parker's Indian New Deal projects were as complex and multivalent as many other aspects of his life.

Several years before the Seneca Arts Project drew to a close, circumstances had drawn Parker's attention firmly back to his main focus, the institution of which he was director. Year on year he had held fast to his vision of a truly industrial museum at Rochester, his dream that some day soon the city might begin the process of creating a more centrally located museum complex that could encompass all the facets of the museum movement he held dear. From his first days at Rochester, he had kept up an incessant, ever-optimistic drumbeat in every museum publication, promotional tool, and public forum he could think of in order to foster expansion. When support finally came, he was amazed by how spectacularly his fund-raising efforts paid off. Sometime around 1939 his pleas persuaded one of Rochester's men of industry, Dr. Edward Bausch, chairman of the board of the Bausch & Lomb Optical Company, to gift his substantial central residence and over half a million dollars for the construction of an additional wing. It was the crowning achievement of Parker's museum career.

According to Parker, it all came about because of a promotional booklet he had written called "Opportunity," which Bausch actually "came with in his hand to offer to build a new museum building." "Opportunity" was a fifteen-page illustrated brochure produced through the museum in 1936. It talked of "A Plan Enabling a Great City Through You to Serve Humanity" and left space for the future benefactor to fill in his or her name.[58] Several years later Parker told the story of how his endeavors had been unexpectedly rewarded. "One morning [in 1939]," he began, "without previous announcement, one of Rochester's eminent citizens knocked at the door of the Director's office. 'I feel that I should do more for my city,' said he. 'I have liked your program and approve of it. But that isn't enough, I know. How would you like a new building?' We gratefully answered that we would welcome one. 'Then,' demanded the visitor, 'you must have a plan for it. Let me see it.' Thus did Edward Bausch, the microscopist, challenge our sincerity and preparedness."[59] Bausch was one of a number of prominent local individuals Parker had been cultivating.[60] The same year he walked into Parker's office to make his sizable donation, he was awarded a newly inaugurated Rochester Museum Fellowship for his work in microscopy, one of six bestowed on individuals in the area.[61] Little is generally known about Parker's exact relationship with his financial patrons at this time except that he and Edward Bausch had a fairly long-standing acquaintance. Bausch was a member of the Lewis Henry Morgan Chapter of the New York State Archaeological Association to which Parker was closely affiliated, and he had helped Parker in connection with the New York State Indian Welfare Society in the early 1920s.[62] At the time of the donation, questions were being raised over the loyalty of the corporation originally founded by emigrants John Bausch and Henry Lomb, because it drew expertise directly from the Jena works in Germany and was supplying half the fire-control instruments for America's army and navy. Parker defended the firm's patriotism in *Museum Service,* but was more concerned about the benefits of moving the museum away from Edgerton Park and the old buildings of the Rochester State Industrial School. The Bauschs' offer was an extremely public-spirited arrangement. They agreed to gift their home at 663 East Avenue, between Oxford and Goodman Streets, deeding the residence and its grounds to the city for the museum on the understanding that they could remain living there during their lifetimes. In addition, they promised to pay to build the first unit of the museum's new home.[63]

This was wonderful news for the museum, but it brought immediate funding problems. Securing and maintaining adequate appropriations had been an uphill struggle at Rochester, but the combination of spending restraint due to the war and the need for enhanced support to move premises created a double bind. In November 1940, Parker had to tell *Museum Service* readers: "A difficult year faces our museum. The assurance of a new building brings into existence the dual problem of running the museum and its service in Edgerton Park and at the same time manufacturing larger cases and about fifty dioramas

How a Rochester Country Store looked in the 1850s.
Exhibit in Rochester Museum of Arts and Sciences produced
in connection with Rochester's centennial celebrations.
Also printed in *New York Sun,* August 25, 1934.

Personal Papers of Arthur Caswell Parker, in author's possession

to fit the planned-for spaces in the new structure on East Avenue. All this is manifestly impossible on our present budget."[64] Funding was slashed by one-sixth. Parker said in print that he felt like Moses unable to reach the promised land.[65]

All he could do was soldier on, let the press know, and point out the injustice of the funding decision given that the museum's collections alone had a value equal to the total expenditure up to that time by the city. His own personal achievements were just then being recognized formally by the academic establishment, with Union College conferring a doctorate in science on him in 1940, and three years later Keuka College bestowing the degree of Doctor of Humane Letters. The chairman of the citizen's Museum Commission said that were he to go, it would mean "certain death for the museum" given that "the genius of Dr. Parker is all that holds most of the technical staff together, in spite of their niggardly salaries."[66] The budget was still restricted the following year even though Rochester's schoolchildren joined in yet another crusade to increase it. Then, Parker finally managed to get the Board of Education to substantially contribute to the costs of the move.[67]

Parker was directly involved with the design of the new building and was determined that the new museum would give the public what it wanted "amply and effectively." He diligently set about filling the 1,100,000 cubic feet and two and one-fifth acres of floor space with new exhibits. He planned for visitors to enter the museum's great glass doors to see a Hall of Nature with natural-size habitat groups, dioramas, and a host of other material, all connected where possible with Rochester. The first floor was to house an auditorium for 275 people, with projection equipment and a loudspeaker system. The second floor was to dramatize human evolution in and around Rochester, with a predictable emphasis on the Iroquois from the Archaic period "to the last stages of their deculturation." The third floor was to have a hall of astronomy, a garden, and assembly rooms for clubs. There was also to be a basement and a mezzanine floor for the museum's school service activities and for docents' offices. The roof was to house a modern heating system, and the building was to have an air pressure heavier than normal atmosphere so as to keep away dust. Parker wrote enthusiastically: "The whole plan is a pageant of life from the conditions that made it possible to the ebbing influences of the Civil War period. There are, however, other exhibits and subjects of special importance to Rochester people."[68]

The building was dedicated in 1940, and the cornerstone of the new "ultra-modern" large granite and Indiana limestone $521,000 building laid in April 1941. The accompanying ceremony was spectacular and lavish. A thousand spectators watched the mayor and a scientist from the California Institute of Technology perform the honors, while Parker described events over the public address system for the radio.[69] He was by this stage no stranger to radio broadcasting and soon would write eighty-six scripts for the Rochester War Council Speaker's Bureau. War was raging in Europe, but Rochester folk were able to look on as a sealed copper box of modern artifacts was carefully stored within the cornerstone for the benefit of future generations. The Edward Bausch Hall of Science and History eventually opened on May 22–23, 1942, although the new wing was not fully completed until that autumn. Then another four years of "energetic planning and creation," as his successor later put it, were necessary before it was really up and running.[70] Parker did all he could to ensure that the new building had almost every available innovation. There was a self-contained "broadcast reception and recording room," a separate School Service Division on the mezzanine floor, solid glass doors, and concealed fluorescent

Arthur Caswell Parker with Naples Presbyterian minister, 1939.

Personal Papers of Arthur Caswell Parker, in author's possession

lighting so as to "give the effect of daylight." Better still, soon Mr. and Mrs. M. Herbert Eisenhart donated the Henry Bausch Auditorium in memory of Mrs. Eisenhart's father, and Mr. and Mrs. William Bausch gave funds for a wildflower diorama.

The building was such a marvel that it almost publicized itself. Around the same time, Parker accepted one of the city's streetcars as a museum exhibit, and this made the papers and helped bring in visitors. Also, very fortuitously, Parker was able to award lifelong membership in the Rochester Museum Association to the museum's two millionth visitor just as the new museum site was opening for business.[71] Of course, although Bausch Hall represented the fulfillment of a long-held ambition, he thought of it as simply the first stage in planned development. He pictured a vast complex of buildings or a university-type campus as the ultimate future expression of the civic museum. At Rochester he planned for more buildings, for an industrial wing, an auditorium, and a planetarium at the very least.[72] Bausch had allowed him to come closer to something like Munich's Deutsches Museum, but he was by no means there yet.

As war impinged further on every aspect of American life, Parker fought back in print to protect the museum's stipend. His basic thrust was that museums were a "morale-building line of defense and preeminently a front line attack upon every factor that seeks to pervert truth."[73] He kept up his own civic and patriotic profile during World

War II by serving as chairman of the Rochester War Council Speaker's Bureau from 1943 to 1945 and as officer of the New York State Committee for Conservation of Cultural Resources. He was also particularly prominent within the Rochester chapter of the Sons of the American Revolution, writing a history of the group on the occasion of its fiftieth anniversary in 1944. Having served as president from 1936 to 1938, Parker was proud of its wartime Minute Man work and of the way in which the chapter had kept a vigilant eye on the "subversive activities of foreign sympathizers since the rise of totalitarian powers."[74]

Parker also kept up *Museum Service* throughout the war, although it was smaller in size since he had less time to contribute. Even so, it carried several short essays by Parker on the topic of inherited characteristics. Now, while America was engaged in war to defeat Nazism, he used *Museum Service* to propagate even more strident eugenic ideas than he had put forward during the 1920s. In 1942, for example, he produced an emotional discussion of the probity of allowing "the mentally deficient and the physically unfit to propagate."[75]

As chapter 2 made clear, Parker was by no means unusual or alone in putting forward such views. In fact, according to J. David Smith, when Germany passed its own race hygiene law during 1933, it used an American model and was influenced by the American compulsory sterilization movement. As a result, in Germany between 1933 and 1945, 2 million people deemed defective were sterilized. It took many years for most U.S. eugenicists to begin to connect their work and thinking to the atrocities of the Nazi regime.[76] It is difficult to assess whether Parker ever made that connection or whether he ever began a fundamental reassessment of his deeply held assumptions about "race" and human development. Certainly, until his retirement in 1946, he kept mulling them over in print.

Although his experiences with the Society of American Indians had convinced him that there was no broadly homogenous Indian "race," he remained racist throughout his life. That is, he persistently connected genetic or innate factors within populations or groups that are not in fact linked. He connected physical traits, mental capacities, and civilization-building abilities where no connection really exists.[77] Throughout his life he remained broadly wedded to Morgan's racist classificatory scheme, even though it left only limited space for his own identity as Indian intellectual and even though it more or less condemned his "race" to the evolutionary past. During times of national crisis, he felt compelled to articulate the prejudiced fears of the American middle class. All of this produced inevitable confusions and frustrations evident in his writing. They stemmed essentially from

American Indians' status as an inferior caste within the United States, a situation that made it difficult for Parker to integrate the Indian and non-Indian aspects of his identity.

But he had found a professional niche where he could make a significant impact and achieve recognized success without having to abandon his Indian interests. Personal acclaim and honors were continuing to come his way. He had earned through achievement the doctorate whose title he had adopted but never actually studied for, he was president of the New York State Archaeological Association, and was on the State Museum Advisory Committee for the Regents of the University of the State of New York. Most important, by the close of the war, he had made "his" museum into something of which the whole city seemed to be proud. As one full-page advertisement sponsored by a local firm said in the *Rochester Democrat & Chronicle* just before Parker's retirement, the value of the museum's collections had increased over time and Rochester had become known as a center for museum excellence.[78] Parker had every reason to feel proud. He had succeeded through hard work, dedication, and clever use of his contacts and heritage in publishing an extensive and enduring body of literature and in reaching the top in American regional museum life.

Retirement, Pageantry, and Writing for Children: Retirement Years

At age sixty-five, Parker stepped down on January 1, 1946, after twenty-one years of service. The city's museum made every effort to show its appreciation for all his hard work. In the preceding years it had been trying to reorient away from anthropology and further toward science, especially the earth sciences. Parker's resistance had caused some acrimony, but it was all behind him now. At his retirement dinner, he was given a gold watch inscribed, "To our Director: With sincere appreciation for your untiring effort on our behalf—The Staff."[1] In May he was awarded one of the museum-sponsored Rochester Civic Medals that he himself had helped inaugurate.[2] The director of the Dallas Historical Society summed up the feelings of many within the regional museum community when he said after Parker's acceptance of the award, "just as truly as the modern high school is a monument to Horace Mann, so the modern museum is the creation of Arthur C. Parker."[3] It was high praise indeed. Nor was Parker quickly forgotten. In time, there was to be an oil portrait dedicated by the chairmen of the Museum Commission and the Museum Hobby Council, which now hangs in the renamed Rochester Museum & Science Center.[4]

The following year, Rochester's Sons of the American Revolution (SAR) also recognized his patriotism and industry with their 1947 Good Citizenship Medal Award. Although he had served as their chapter president during 1936 and for several years had edited their *Bulletin*, this was more than a perfunctory recognition of time served. It was a true acknowledgment of sterling community endeavor. The announcement that Parker was to receive the award was made at a Sesquicentennial Celebration of the Treaty of Big Tree, when the Seneca had been forced to sell most of their remaining land to the Holland Land

Company and the reservation system had begun along the Genesee River. A testimonial dinner followed at which this citation was read out to Parker: "The citizens of Rochester owe to you an undying debt of gratitude for the ardent, willing and self-sacrificing manner in which you have devoted nearly a quarter of a century of your life to their more abundant living and that of their children through the many and varied projects which you have fostered in their behalf . . . often forcing yourself beyond the limits of your physical strength."[5] It was a fitting commentary about a community figure who had made herculean efforts to advance the museum of his adopted city.

The nine remaining years of Parker's life were to be spent at the home he had bought on a hill in Naples, New York. There, perhaps unsurprisingly, he remained creative and deeply engaged with local events, with writing, with conservation, the outdoors, and with Indian matters generally. He had suffered a severe heart attack in 1945, which had persuaded him to seek uninterrupted relaxation at the leafy hideaway that previously he had been able to visit mostly only on weekends and holidays.[6] It remains a beautiful retreat 11,000 feet above sea level and some 500 feet above the head of Canandaigua Lake and Sunnyside. Parker seems to have bought the house because of its proximity to Clark's Gully on South Hill, an area he maintained contained the birthplace of the Seneca Nation at a village called Nundaweo. He judged that the Iroquois "mother of Nations" had chosen Clark's Gully as the site of the first Seneca town after the formation of the Iroquois League. Close to it was Bare Hill, which he also connected strongly to the Seneca past. There, according to legend, the Seneca had taken refuge against a giant serpent that two Seneca children had adopted in its infancy. When the serpent grew to man-eating size, the Seneca had been forced to flee to a stockade at Bare Hill, only to be devoured as they tried to escape. When the children were finally able to vanquish the serpent, it disgorged the heads of the Seneca it had eaten down the hill. It is said that these can still be found today in the form of head-shaped geometric stones. Parker said the story corresponded with aspects of the archaeological record, specifically, an Owasco and/or Seneca defeat on Bare Hill by the Massawomek, or "Great Serpent" peoples.

In retirement, Parker made much more of the connections between the Seneca and the area he had chosen as his home. Several times he explained in the local press that Clark's Gully was a sacred spot where fires had been built in honor of the Seneca ancestors, "the People of the Great Hill," or Nunda Waga. He resurrected the practice, which he said had fallen away only since the time of his own birth.[7] Although

Late portrait of Arthur Caswell Parker.

Courtesy of University of Rochester

Parker talked up the idea that Clark's Gully was a sacred Seneca site in his retirement, he had considered Bare Hill and South Hill to be special to the Seneca ever since his days doing archaeology for the state. He had had Bare Hill painted as the backdrop for one of his "magic window" displays at the State Museum, the Seneca Hunter Group Scene set at Canandaigua Lake. Perhaps the threat to the Seneca homeland at the time of his retirement made him keen to stamp an Indian identity more strongly on areas that he loved. Just then a flood of protest was being directed at ultimately successful plans to construct a dam at Kinzua, Pennsylvania. As a Six Nation resolution said at the time, effectively it was a plan to "confiscate all the lowlands of the Cornplanter Indian Reservation and the west end of the Allegany Reservation, both occupied by Seneca tribal Indians."[8] Although the project flew in the face of the 1794 treaty, in the 1960s the planners were to have their way. Nine thousand acres of Seneca land were put under water, causing one hundred and thirty families to relocate. The Seneca were awarded $15 million in direct damages and rehabilitation costs. Parker may never have gotten directly involved with the fight to protect and preserve the tribal land base, but at least in his old age he did all he could to resacralize the area around his home as indelibly Seneca.[9]

Time gradually allowed Parker to regain his health. Fortunately, his heart condition did not make his final years as arduous as his father Frederick's had been before his death in 1929. In fact, he found retirement surprisingly pleasant. He had feared he would be robbed of intellectual stimulus, but he need not have worried. His peers could not forget him, and a great many made their way up the winding hill to his home to consult. Even more wrote letters, to which Parker dutifully composed two- and three-page replies. Generous with information and energy even at this late stage in his life, his only complaint was that people did not supply envelopes and stamps. Such details had to be considered now that he and his family were living on a limited stipend.

He did have his organizational and fraternal life to keep him occupied. There was more time to meet with his local Masonic group, the John Hodge Lodge No. 815, F. & A.M., of Naples. He was also a member of over thirty state, national, and local societies, which, along with a range of other organizations and groups, periodically asked him to lecture. His public-speaking style was as robust and expressive as ever.[10] Photographs of Parker in retirement often show him with his pipe, smartly dressed as usual, with now silver hair and discreet chrome glasses, looking in the pink of health.

Being permanently at home in Naples gave Parker more opportunity to be with his wife. A Daughter of the American Revolution and

Arthur Caswell Parker at the medical academy.

Courtesy of Rochester Museum & Science Center

a respected local figure in her own right, Anne had a passion for the outdoors like his own. She was a dynamic sportswoman, who had been the local swimming instructor and, with her husband, had helped found the hiking clubs at Mohawk Valley and Genesee Valley. Just before World War II, she had developed cross-country ski trails across the region's High Tor. She was Parker's much-loved helper and confidante in his declining years, just as she had been while he worked at the museum. Well-educated and community-minded, she liked playing piano and singing in local church choirs. She had even performed for the early 1920s broadcasts from pioneer radio stations WGY, Schenectady, and WHAZ, the Rensselaer Polytechnic Institute in Troy. When Parker retired, she was working in personnel for a Geneva canning company not far from Naples, having had an interesting war working as an industrial personnel counselor at Bell Aircraft and at the U.S. Employment Service doing special placements for the Manhattan

Project. Ever since their marriage in 1917, the couple had enjoyed working together. Whether it was assisting on a dig, helping with installation of the Iroquois dioramas at the State Museum Building, or with design of the Fashion Hall at Edgerton Park, Anne was always a cherished companion and helpmate to her husband.[11]

Now they had leisure to explore the woods and valleys around the area they loved so well, Genesee Valley. It held the key sites of Parker's archaeological and anthropological career. He was much respected locally for what his successor at the museum called social service work in history, raising awareness about sites of historical interest. Back in 1938, he had been instrumental in reviving the Genesee Country Historical Federation, which brought together around thirty western New York local history societies. He had encouraged it to sponsor pilgrimages and trips, to set up a quarterly newsheet, and, in 1940, to make a special effort to celebrate the centennial of the Genesee Valley Canal. Genesee, he knew, was important as home of "the Chautauqua movement, Fourierism, Mormonism, spiritualism, the women's suffrage movement, the movement for male attire for females as sponsored by Amelia Bloomer, the preachings and religion of the Seneca prophet, Handsome Lake, and the Free Methodist Church." It was "the Garden of the Gods," named, Parker would say, by "the red men who lived here and understood the voices of the glen as they spoke in wind and waterfall." He traveled around it many years, but he still confessed, "were I to live two centuries I could not complete all the investigations that might be made or write all the books that crowd to mind as worthy of publication. I have only produced ten or a dozen and not one is all that I would like to make it."[12]

With his daughter Martha away at college in the city, there was time to indulge all the interests that museum work had tended to push to one side. Mostly these involved time spent in the outdoors. Hiking with Anne was still an option, even if Parker did have to take things more slowly. Gone were the days when he could organize all-day trips through the Tonawanda Reservation so the Genesee Valley Hiking Club could witness the annual Strawberry Festival council dance, as they had in 1902.[13] But there was time to study mushrooms again and time to rekindle one of his earliest boyhood passions, ornithology. Along with archaeology, it had enticed him, he used to say, "into a maze of alluring bypaths of knowledge and experience."[14] Now old age gave him time to remember scampering around collecting birds' eggs at Cattaraugus, time to notice buzzards moving as far north as Bergen Swamp, and time to talk about it all to local friends such as old-time farmer and trapper Joe Schultz. Joe and he once caught a snapping

Arthur Caswell Parker relaxing as he approached retirement.

Personal Papers of Arthur Caswell Parker, in author's possession

turtle together and brought it home to eat, but mostly they just spent hours sitting talking about trapping and the great outdoors.[15] It is not surprising that Parker, a self-directed learner and doer all his life, found a lot to occupy himself. After all, everyone knew he was a keen hobbyist who kept at least a dozen going at any one time. In middle age he had dubbed himself a polyhobbyist who sought "to infect everyone with the disease" because it was such a positive psychological tonic.[16]

His time spent on hobbies, on life outdoors, and on the quiet pleasures to be had from the local community was interrupted periodically by honors awarded by Indian, professional, and fraternal groups. The Akwesasne Mohawk Counselor Organization made him a surprise gift in 1954 at Ticonderoga of a replica of the wampum belt commemorating the founding of the Iroquois League. Then on his birthday that year, April 5, the museum held a luncheon for him, and a special cachet sponsored by the Six Nations was stamped on the mail at the post office at Fishers, New York. It read: "Dr Arthur C. Parker, 'Gawaso Waneh,' Archaeologist, Historian, Author, Humanitarian: He Honored His People and Is Honored by Them, the Six Nations."[17]

The Cold War made Parker want to get across to the public a message about the imperative for defense. He also wanted to raise the area's historical profile; so in 1954 he initiated one final organization, the Nundawaga Society for History and Folklore. It staged pageants during 1954, 1955, and 1956, bringing over three hundred people together. Parker was their moving spirit until his death. As chairman of its board of trustees, he helped secure a permanent charter from the Board of Regents of the University of the State of New York. Members were mostly from the Finger Lakes area, although a few joined from elsewhere in the United States and from abroad.[18] On September 4, 1954, the society staged its first pageant, scripted by Parker, at Parish Glen near his Naples home. It was held at a sycamore grove on land owned by Rochester attorney J. Allen Willis, in the shadow of South Hill and beside the West River in Middlesex Valley. It told the story of the birth of the Seneca Nation at Nundawao, their struggle with a tribe known as the Massawomek, or Great Snakes, and the accompanying legend.[19]

There was much preparation, with the Parkers acting as "keepers of authenticity" for the costumes and accoutrements. Parker did everything he could to sell the event. "We are trying," he told the local press, "to awaken interest in our region. . . . We are trying to show that the Finger Lakes Country has real history and real folklore and in reality is a Land of Legends."[20] Every effort was made to ensure the pageant was a positive Indian-American occasion, and the site was ritualistically dedicated beforehand by Seneca from Akron who made an offering of tobacco.[21] The sun shone, and the spectacle was a resounding success over the Labor Day weekend. According to the *Geneva Daily Times,* the "Nundawao, the Coming of the Senecas" pageant, had more than a hundred in its cast and over four thousand spectators. After the performance firmly identified the area as the site of the first Seneca town and night gradually drew in, Canandaigua Lake was encircled with flares in a "Festival of Fire." For one day at least Parker had succeeded in making the Seneca presence felt once again in their ancestral heartland.

As the papers pointed out, the pageant was a pro-Indian history lesson that made a number of symbolic points about present-day America. One obvious theme was that the Iroquois had influenced the founders of the government of the United States. Another was that they had helped America into being through facilitating expansion west. And yet another was that their own history was instructive. The trusting Seneca had been infiltrated by aggressive tribes from other areas, and their overtrustfulness meant many lives were sacrificed. Parker hoped a parallel with the Cold War context of 1954 would be obvious. The pageant was also about counteracting negative stereotypes about Indians, and the Nundawaga Society invited several impressive, successful Indians along. Arleigh Hill, Parker's faithful chauffeur at the museum was there, as was the "Keeper of the Western Door" of the Iroquois League at the time, Freeman Johnson. Parker's old friend Ray Fadden came with a delegation from St. Regis, along with delegations from Brantford, Ontario, and from Cattaraugus. The St. Regis dancers danced in full costume and met the queue that formed afterward for Indian autographs.[22]

Since the pageant was such a hit, plans were drawn up to make it an annual event. By the next September the Nundawaga Society wanted to put the region on the map by creating a pageant center at the original site. Parker's idea for 1955 was to depict the true story of "Hiawatha and the Building of the Longhouse" on the one hundredth anniversary of Longfellow's famous poem.[23] Sadly, however, the 1954 pageant was the last public project he worked on before his death.

"The Amazing Iroquois" was a manuscript Parker worked on sporadically throughout his retirement. A complete history of the Iroquois peoples from prehistory right up to their conflicts with the American government in 1947, it was to be the crowning work of his career. The idea, as Parker put it in letters to the historian Paul A. W. Wallace of Lebanon Valley College, was to tell "the whole story from archaeology to the last council of Federal commissioners" and to publish for the first time a detailed history of the Iroquois reservations. It was a giant task, especially at a time in life when one is expected to take things easy.

Subdividing such a vast period proved enormously difficult, and as he wrote, the work became unmanageably long and structurally weak. At the beginning of November 1945, the manuscript was over two feet in height and still growing. His publishers were "bowled over with the size" and asked him to condense. Soon the manuscript mutated into three separate volumes. To add to his frustration, friends and acquaintances like Wallace and Dr. Frank Speck at the University of Pennsylvania were producing briefer, well-crafted surveys on the Iroquois against which his work would inevitably be compared. Parker needed "The Amazing Iroquois," or, to use the title his wife preferred, "The Iroquois Invincible," to net royalties, because since losing his museum salary, he was "having to look into such matters more than formerly."[24] He was an experienced writer, but he ended up envisaging one hundred and twenty separate chapters. His aim was to produce a comprehensive overview of Iroquois history from a unique perspective, that of an educated twentieth-century Iroquois rather than of a scholar or anthropologist. "I have tried to write," he told Wallace, "as an Iroquois might see history if he could do so impartially, though knowing his own pattern, and describing events in that light."[25] It was an approach similar to the one he had taken when documenting Iroquois myth and folklore and when writing anthropology, in that he was deliberately choosing a creative strategy that contrasted with accepted methodology.

Although he saw the work as potentially the definitive treatise on the Iroquois, it was a tall order for any publisher to gamble on. It was extremely detailed, containing several lengthy quotations from family records, but lacking in narrative structure and pace. Even so, there were points of interest. A persuasive case was made for Ely Parker's statesmanship and courage in winning out for the Seneca over the onslaughts of the Ogden Land Company, and Parker revealed a new kind of cynicism, pondering "whether or not our legislative bodies and our officials, not to mention every-day citizens, do not actually approve, covertly of course, the preying upon native owners who have what we want?"[26]

Eventually, in 1947, his publishers informed him that the public was unlikely to be interested in something so lengthy. He lost all inspiration and put it to one side in favor of another archaeological study entitled "Discovering America's Prehistory." At some point he began toiling with "The Amazing Iroquois" again, until he realized in the spring of 1949 that he had become overly involved. What he needed was a collaborator, but unfortunately Wallace was overcommitted.[27] Not all was lost, however, since in 1950 Parker gave a talk to over two hundred on "The Amazing Iroquois" at the reopening of the Onondaga Historical

Association. He painted a convincing picture of the Iroquois as "amazing" because of how they had resisted the influence of the white man's culture. Their longevity as a race, he claimed, was due to their stable form of government created by Hiawatha and the close ties between the Five Nations.[28]

A year later Parker was again toying with various titles for his Iroquois book and determinedly restructuring what he had already written. By then Wallace had published *The White Roots of Peace,* prompting Parker to write to him that he felt impelled to again "commence more serious work instead of handling literary productions for other writers."[29] Wallace asked him to help host a summer seminar on the Iroquois in nearby Cooperstown in February 1954, and he got back some inspiration.[30] He thought the manuscript would appear a year or two later under yet another title, "Forever the Iroquois, A Survey of the Five Nations and Their Way of Life." The project had developed into three separate volumes entitled "Blood for Beaver," "The Tornado and the Dust," and finally "Red Embers of the Longhouse," about "what became of the Iroquois and their stages of acculturation." Pleased at having reached the end stage, Parker told Wallace, "You see I have been busy and I hope correct."[31]

"The Amazing Iroquois" was never published. Regrettably, even though he published extensively throughout his career, the only significant royalties he ever received were from his museum manual with Columbia University Press and from the books he published for children and young adults with Doubleday Doran. Only one adapted excerpt from the manuscript made it into print, when *The Galleon,* the bulletin of the Society of Colonial History in Schenectady, New York, printed "The Role of Wampum in the Colonial Era."[32] The great irony was that to complete "The Amazing Iroquois," Parker was awarded a fellowship for five thousand dollars by the John Simon Guggenheim Foundation on Friday, December 31, 1954. The funds were to be paid as and when he requested them, and the foundation required no record of how they were used. It could have been just the spur for Parker to complete his text, were he not destined to die within twenty-four hours of the fellowship notification.[33] His wife, Anne, considered finishing it, but although there was much support for the idea, it was never to be.[34]

Before describing the unique circumstances surrounding Parker's death, it is appropriate to evaluate the two books for young adults that he did see published during his final years. To best understand them, we need to consider them in context, that is, to consider as a group the seven texts he produced on Indian folklore and juvenile themes. This task begins with commentary on what stimulated Parker toward developing the Indian folklore he inherited into popular books for the young.

Writing for children and young adults was a way Parker could positively connect all things Indian with American patriotism, with national vigor, and with the great outdoors. He wanted the public to think of Indians as simply the first Americans, that is, for Indians to be included in the popular understanding of national development up to and including the present. He felt that twentieth-century Indians might be better recognized as modern contributors to American life if they were clearly connected in the public eye with a noble and nature-loving tribal past.

Each of his books in this genre owed something to his first book-length study of Seneca tribal lore, published while he was still in Albany, *Seneca Myths and Folk Tales*.[35] This in turn owed much to stories collected by Harriet Maxwell Converse during her own long and close Seneca association. That said, each of his books for children had its own story to tell, not just in terms of plot, but in terms of how Parker wanted the Indian legacy to develop within American discourse. Of course, on a pragmatic level, such books were perhaps the only way Parker could capitalize on his specialist knowledge and secure the kind of royalties that would never be forthcoming from his professional published work.

He combined children's themes with folklore and myth, which he categorized as the beginnings of philosophy, as primitive "answers to the perplexing riddles of the cosmos." He did not consider myth and folklore to be static. Rather, they were living cultural assets that were plastic and capable of undergoing positive developmental change. As living Indian historicity, they needed broad exposure to ensure this happened. Therefore, he published versions of Iroquois myth, legend, and folklore in his own unique style. As far back as "Aunt Hattie's" *Myths and Legends of the New York Iroquois* in 1908, he showed an overarching commitment to preserving the "native beauty" of such material, even at the risk of compromising its "scientific" status.[36] It could, he felt, be translated and transformed by someone sufficiently imbued with its culture of origin into a literary English that could recreate the emotions once conjured by the original.[37]

The scouting movement linked many similar themes. "I am very much interested in the Boy Scout movement," Parker wrote in 1912, "and have followed it with more than the interest of an ordinary layman since its very beginning."[38] He also helped the YMCA and supported banquets and outings designed to bring fathers and sons together. In Albany, during the spring of 1920, he helped found the highly patriotic Mound Builders of America, a nature-oriented scouting fraternity for which he invented ritualistic degrees.[39] From 1928, he was on the Council of Boy Scouts of America, and in 1932 he made a push to enlist scouts in aiding archaeologists on digs.[40] Scouting invoked the same small-town values, like decency and brotherhood, that bound Parker and others of his class to fraternalism. It addressed the nation's need to reestablish community, to react against the city, and reconnect with the virtuous rural life and family relations many remembered from childhood.

Young adult movements had also been the ultimate refuge of another leading light of the Society of American Indians in his final years. Charles Eastman chose to dress up in traditional costume within the Boy Scouts and YMCA before his death in 1939. At the time he was living in a tepee outside Detroit, attempting, as Robert Warrior has put it, "to regain the sense of Native identity against which he had spent so much of his life fighting."[41] Parker, however, was doing something different when he supported youth movements and wrote for the young. He was attempting, yet again, to tie Indians, nature, and the tribal past to a mainstream literature of the American present, and to make money.

The following chronological discussion of each of his Indian books for a young audience is intended to give a sense of how his treatment of Indian legend, myth, and folklore developed over time. I begin this overview with the text that underpinned much of the Indian content within his books in this genre.

Seneca Myths and Folk Tales (1923) was well received outside of the academy. It was put forward by the press as a worthy addition to the existing scope of American literature and as an ample source for popular books for children. The *New York Times* said, "As fairy stories they are the equal of the folklore of Europe."[42] Parker heard the stories during his 1903 archaeological sojourn with Raymond Harrington at the Cattaraugus Reservation. Nearly eighteen years later, Parker had gone over his notes with Edward Cornplanter, who had also been his native consultant for *The Code of Handsome Lake* in 1913. He had then published them without extensive annotation under the auspices of the Buffalo Historical Society, writing up the myths and legends as what he called honest "free translations," designed "to awaken in the mind of the reader sensations similar to those aroused in the mind of the Indian auditor hearing it from the native raconteur."

These myths and folk tales retain a fascination and wealth of conceptual interest that makes reading them today still rewarding. One can understand why the Seneca found them a powerful distraction and restricted their being recounted to the winter, "when the year's work is over and all nature slumbers."[43] To set the scene, Parker gave his readers a highly evocative description of longhouse life in the snows of January 1799. Then he told tales of quilts made of men's eyes, of humans with bear mothers and bear wives. He wrote of human doubles who lived in identical lodges, of soul-selves that guard a man's life, of war clubs that talk, of the power of laughter over wizardry, and of Hadjoqda—dried human skins that may, when a hero gives it wampum, decide to speak and help overcome an evil sorcerer. He wrote of talking skulls enchanted by cannibal ogres and of witch-girls who make heroes diminish just by patting them gently until they can be easily put into baskets, like in a Lewis Carroll story.

In one narrative the hero falls over a cliff and then decides to fall not in human form but as an autumn leaf. In another a pursued hero is able to throw down holes in the path of a sorceress that expand in whichever direction she takes to avoid them. Readers are told of removable hearts that get stored under beds or suspended over pots of water, of fires that speak, and of evil spirits that cause the dead to eat off husbands' faces in the night so that their wives awake because they hear gnawing and feel warm pools of blood. One tale tells of a lazy young warrior who is persuaded by a mischief-maker "to whittle the meat off his shins so that the bone stood out sharp like a long knife." In another, the heroine gradually realizes she is actually living underwater in the lodge of a shape-shifting great serpent. In another, wives paddle canoes above the trees over the head of their gambling husband so as to his escape him.

Aside from having a connection with the social concerns of their time, several of the myths and folktales contained elements reminiscent of Greek myth and/or of the Christian Bible, something Parker made no analytical reference to. But he did point out recurrent themes that he considered uniquely Seneca, such as shape-shifting and the resurrection of skeletons that, in the confusion, end up having each other's limbs. Another was the motif of a child being given the injunction never to venture in one of the four cardinal directions, which they inevitably do, thus encountering sorcery and challenges to overcome before bringing events to a happy resolution. Several tales tell of brothers saving sisters from enchantment and capture and of hollow logs that give protection from ghosts and cause regenerative transformation.

Parker also devoted one whole section to tales of talking animals. Along with many other mythical explanations of animal characteristics, these explained how birds came to be handsomely colored after they did a favor for Wolf and how the chipmunk got its stripes escaping from a hungry bear that drew its four claws over the length of its body. Another section dealt with tales of giants, monster bears, and of pygmies—the "little people" who so appreciate it when humans leave them their fingernail parings because it gives them certain human powers. This section also described female stone giants who were able to unfasten their great stone coats before entering a lodge and the human finger they possessed that gave directions when required. There was also appendixed information on the practice of scalping and, of course, on the role of the much-discussed false faces within Iroquois mythology.

Overall, as William Fenton pointed out in the introduction to the 1989 edition, *Seneca Myths and Folk Tales* was not a rigorous piece of anthropology. If we seek a thorough and comparative evaluation of Seneca folklore, we should consult Parker's Tuscarora contemporary at the Smithsonian, John N. B. Hewitt, and his collaborator Jeremiah Curtin, along with Fenton's own work and the pages of the *Journal of American Folklore and Ethnohistory*.[44] In producing the text, Parker was simply donning the hat of Seneca myth teller and reinvigorating a cultural archive for a new audience.

Just three years later, he did so again, this time in a much more explicit and commercial way. He published a collection of stories entitled *Skunny Wundy and Other Indian Tales* (1926), accompanied by a series of charming illustrations by Will Crawford. It was the first of his Indian books for young adults and one of the best-selling over time.

He described how he had first heard the stories at his grandfather's fireside, from buckskin and feather-clad visitors who had traveled from the wilder parts of the reservation where the longhouse people lived. He explained to his young readership how very different they were from the Indians of the West and that he was a descendant of Je-gon-sa-seh, the friend of Hiawatha who had helped found the great Iroquois League of Peace. The stories themselves dealt with the same themes as the myths and folktales he had published in 1923, but this time Parker gave them the tone of a Euro-American fairy tale.

They were a compromised version of the oral tradition, but they powerfully communicated an important message about the essential breadth of the Iroquois social worldview. They described, as George Hamell put it in the introduction to the 1994 edition, the "other-than-human kinds of people" who lived at the wood's edge. The Iroquois live "in a *social* world comprised of real human man-beings, like themselves, and of other kinds of people, who occasionally take the guise of real human man-beings, but who most frequently appear in their primary animal and plant forms." "There are," he tells us, "other man-beings, who have as their normal form that of so-called—in our culture—inanimate objects, among them, Mother Earth, Grandmother Moon, Elder Brother Sun, and Grandfather Thunder."[45]

Mostly the *Skunny Wundy* stories described the activities of the animal sort of people, such as clever Fox and Raccoon, gullible Rabbit, the brave but slow-witted Bear, and the activities of Wolf, who is very bad indeed. Predictably, the character of the Turtle being was unique, since Iroquois myth holds that the world itself rests on the back of a giant turtle and that out of his back grew the Tree of Life. The reader was addressed as nephew, and the initial story suggested that the writer had gotten each narrative directly from the mythical Skunny Wundy after he had outwitted Fox, S'hojiosko or "Mischief Maker," and forced Fox to reveal how he had played all his tricks. Each told of animal beings with very human strengths and failings, speaking enigmatically and outwitting one another in a social world they shared with Indians and with beings such as Old Man Autumn, Flying Head, the mischievous Wind Boy, and the Jungies—"the little folk that live in the woods and know everything."[46] Each kind of being was able to understand the other and, as in *Seneca Myths and Folktales,* the stories gave mythical explanations for animal characteristics and natural phenomenon. They explained, for example, how the deciduous trees decided to gang up on Frost and Winter so that they could keep their leaves throughout the year. They also revealed more about mythical characters such as the Stone Giants, who readers now learned were vulnerable only in the soles of their feet. Many delivered a fairly unenigmatic underlying life-message, such as how one should never ask for what one has already given away, how tricky it can be to find oneself in debt to a clever enemy, and what a good thing it is to keep one's eyes open even when asleep. Parker had made Seneca myth and folklore more obviously didactic and developed in terms of plot, and at times his animal characters spoke a rather pretentious high-born English.

The Indian How Book (1927) was Parker's next commercial publication on a native theme, pitched as a simple access book for those who understood the importance of "going back to nature and trying to live in its sweet embrace, just as the red man did." Parker envisaged a whole series of books detailing the Why, Who, When, Where, and What of Indian life. These were never to be, but certainly, in an age that revered the practical and that elevated the idea of learning through doing, it was appropriate to begin any attempt to educate non-Indians about Indians by explaining how they did things. Thus Parker combined a healthy dose of factual information about Indians with some practical advice about surviving outdoors.

One of the most pleasant things about the book was the way Parker shared his enthusiasm for all things Indian. "Some day," he confided, "I expect to find a secluded spot in a beautiful forest clearing where I may rebuild a complete Iroquois town and plant an Indian garden of maize, squashes, beans and tobacco." Overall he took a pan-Indian approach to the explanation of various Indian activities, interspersing his descriptions with Iroquois examples and personal anecdotes. In his section on "How Indians Found Food in the Forest," for instance, he shared with his readers his experiences when he tried to live off the land. Out in the wilderness with little clothing, he had gone hungry, but he and his camp mate had nonetheless found a new strength and vigor. "We swam in the streams," he wrote, "we roamed the hills, far from the sight of a critical civilization and we grew hard and brown."[47]

In large part his mission was to educate his readership away from some of the more insidious racial stereotypes. He was keen to disabuse them of the idea that all Indians were nomadic and lived solely by hunting and fishing. He described the legend connected to the three Iroquois staple food plants—maize, beans, and squash—and reminded his readership that when the French invaded Iroquois country around 1650, they had destroyed vast and important fields of corn and farm produce. Elsewhere he dispelled notions that Indians had an adverse smell and explained how Indians were thought of as silent and humorless when in fact they had a sophisticated appreciation of a good joke. He even explained "How Indians Talked." To copy their speech, he told readers, an imagination mystified by nature was required and a "terse expression of logical argument" capable of covering stinging words with a coat of nectar.[48] Parker also pointed out Indian cultural practices he considered more enlightened than those of non-Indians. Indians, for example, taught their children not through fear and punishment, but through play and practical instruction.

He discussed how Indian headdress had become culturally devalued as a result of interaction with non-Indians. "Nowadays," he wrote, "the white man's fancy has become the Indian's fashion." He made points about Indian Asian origins, about America's debt to its first Americans, and about Indians' true capability for achieving civilization. To close, he listed the achievements of modern Indians, such as his friends from the days of the Society of American Indians, and showed with specific examples how "Indians of mixed white and Indian blood, instead of being degenerates, as dime novels say, have risen to high places in society."[49]

He had created a simple and highly readable primer that explained to non-Indians key aspects of Indian culture as he understood them.

It was a deserved, if minor, success, reprinted again a year before his death and once again in 1975. It is still in print.

Rumbling Wings (1928) had a noticeably non-Indian tone and syntax. It was dedicated to "The Scouts of Old Fort Orange who hailed me as Grand Councillor of the Lodge of Hahnowa, the Turtle, and who listened to my tales of the ancient days of the Nunda Waga Tribe when the world was fresh from the kind hand of the Master of Life." At the time they were close to his heart. He had even dreamed up a secret society based on Indian lore for the older boys, which he dubbed the Mound Builders. He had written out rituals for them to follow, helped them get hold of suitable costumes, and given them a marvelous place to meet—the New York State Museum amid the exhibits and the full-size replica longhouse. According to one scout who experienced it, while there "one had the feeling of being among living people."[50]

Skunny Wundy reappears in this text, and his uncle is the genial Rumbling Wings, "Sachem of the Nunda Waga and story-teller of Onagee." After his father departs to the far east, Skunny Wundy goes to his uncle's lodge to learn his wisdom, which is revealed to the reader. With intricate artistic illustrations and a range of ethnological detail, the book was more complex and descriptive than *Skunny Wundy* but with the same sort of magic realist plot. There were injunctions against laziness, admonitions against judging books by their cover, and tips on how to outwit foes and rise above challenges. There were also elements of the positive thinking ethos that had dominated Parker's adolescent years and one noticeable departure—a character named Waynie Aanie, Skunny Wundy's little sister for whom he showed every affection and did all he could to please.

Another character of specific interest was Whooping Crane, who had recorded Rumbling Wings's tales on "sheets of bark" before stowing them away in a chest, an incident similar to one in *Skunny Wundy.* Toward the conclusion of *Rumbling Wings,* Whooping Crane learns an important lesson—to put his faith in "work, work, ceaseless work" rather than in charms and soothsayers.[51] Afterward, he wants to teach all mankind this lesson, but he is sagely reminded that the world is not interested in being taught, only in being amused. With such obvious messages about the true path to success and the nature of the modern world, it is perhaps unsurprising that *Rumbling Wings* was less popular than some of Parker's other juvenile books. There was not enough concrete description to hold the reader's interest, too many sudden plot departures, and somehow, although all the old characters were there—the Jungies, the stone giants, and so on—Parker had lost much of that sense of a separate social order that had given so much to his previous work of this sort.

The mystery action adventure *Gustango Gold* (1930) appeared just two years later. It was a charming book "for older boys," which sported a beautifully illustrated cover of boyhood Indian-style derring-do taken from the pages within. This time Parker had polished up his narrative technique and had a new approach. Indian signifiers now were secondary to the central story about David Barton, the young non-Indian son of the head of the Secret Service in the Third District of New York. David ends up in the north of the state in "Treasure Valley," where he pals up with an Indian character named "Bottle" Mulk and some reservation boys who help him solve two critical criminal mysteries involving cocaine smuggling and fraud.

As for the heroes of so many important American children's stories, David's adventures unfold in three parts. He is separated from his parents and guardian, just like Tom Sawyer, Dorothy Gale, Pollyanna, Toby Tyler, Tarzan, Little Lord Fauntleroy, Huckleberry Finn, and Rebecca of Sunnybrook Farm. Thus he is exposed to new experiences and undertakes a journey that helps him appreciate another way of living. Just like Huck, who escapes from "smothery" homes on the river shore, he is destined for the great outdoors. There, he is taken in by a second family, as was Tom Sawyer, Pollyanna, and Fauntleroy. Like Huck and Tarzan and Rebecca, he finds surrogate parents of a different social rank—Indians, in this case. Tom Sawyer is persecuted by an adult antagonist of the same sex, and David, too, is persecuted by a reprobate non-Indian thug. Fortunately, like Huck Finn who has Nigger Jim, David has a helper who is an outsider, a noble Indian chief named Deepwood who initially is wrongly imprisoned for the mystery crimes. David in time triumphs over his antagonist and emerges the savior of the situation. Finally, he makes a return to the non-Indian world, having facilitated a resolution of the confusions over identity that have to that point driven the plot. He is acknowledged by his father as a chip off the old block, and there is an accommodation of the two ways of living he has experienced.

Parker's transition to writing children's fiction set in Indian country, as opposed to simply writing up folklore and myth in ways that could appeal to a youth market, was perhaps predictable. After all, some of the greatest and most distinctively American literature up to that time had been written for children, and after the "golden age" of children's writing from 1865 to 1914, there was still a healthy market for it. According to Jerry Griswold, who has fleshed out the three-part ur-story applied to *Gustango Gold* above, this was partly because children's books addressed vital concerns about national identity. The recurring story of maturation that they embodied connected directly to America's vision of itself "as a young country, always making itself anew, rebelling against authority, coming into its own, and establishing its own identity."[52]

Gustango Gold is a convoluted but gripping boy's tale, with a white hero surrounded by capable and admirable Indian friends who are not completely stereotypical. They live very closely with nature but are also assimilated and teach David a great deal. As the plot develops he becomes utterly enthralled by Indian country, and the reader is educated about modern Indian life. David is warned to distrust "bunk history" that claims Indians are well cared for by Uncle Sam, and he learns how sincerely patriotic his Indian friends are. Deepwood, who is forced into social banditry, has all the exceptional outdoor talents of the modern trapper hero and a pet bear, Nee-yah-gwa, who smells the breeze above his ancient Indian bark lodge "amidst the countless birds and capering fawns."[53] But at the same time he is an urbane old college buddy of David's uncle, who is able to use such ploys as sending a telegram to decoy his pursuers. He even has letters in his cabin signed by Henry David Thoreau.

The storyline is set around Cattaraugus and echoes aspects of Parker's own family history. The Indian family home into which David is accepted sounds like Parker's grandfather's house, and David, like Parker, has an uncle named Spencer who makes inappropriate decisions about leases and Indian land. The ultimate villain turns out to be president of the Gustango Gold Corporation, James Chestering Bock, a respected town businessman with his eye on oil and gas leases belonging to the Nunda Waga. Ironically, he turns out to be David's own agent because Uncle Spencer had secured a damage release for David on Deepwood's farm and interests in a mine. Bock ends up being sunk at sea by a fellow reprobate while making his escape. David receives a reward, which he uses to build a fraternal longhouse for the boys of Gustango Valley. It is designed by Deepwood, who becomes the new vice president of the local bank. Incidentally, by the intricacies of the plot, the Gustango boys also end up with a pirate ship all of their own.

It is difficult to assess how well *Gustango Gold* sold, but likely it had only limited success because it was such a laborious read. Even so, it managed to combine many of the elements of a ripping boy's adventure yarn with a message about ancient Indian tradition and modern Indian patriotism and ability.

Four years after his retirement Parker once again resumed his children's writing on Indian themes. By the spring of 1950 he was able to impress Wallace with a copy of his latest "juvenile" by Children's Press, which he hoped would be a supplement for children to Wallace's own *The White Roots of Peace.*

Told from the perspective of a noble young warrior, *Red Streak* was highly commercial in form and written with the hope "that ideas of the brotherhood of man implanted in the minds of children and an example linked to the Hiawatha story might be of some use to the world."[54] His primary message after the inhuman events of World War II was global peace, and he hoped to inspire another Red Streak to bring it about. He told his young readers: "You may discover great truths in our tale that remind you of the world today. For instance the Iroquois wanted peace and succeeded to become ferocious warriors that peace might not be challenged." The way Parker had developed as a writer by this stage helped him get this message across. When compared with the much earlier *Rumbling Wings* and *Gustango Gold*, *Red Streak* is an easier and in this sense more enjoyable read. Plot developments are more comprehensible and not so jarringly sudden, and there is a more consistent register and tone.

It is set in the area full of "raccoons, deer and foxes, and ever so many friendly birds" he saw from his library study window in Naples.[55] A kind of scouting version of the story of the formation of the Iroquois League, it is bereft of much reference to any of the harsher historical and ethnographic detail that Parker was familiar with, including the acute warfare and torture practiced by the Iroquois around the time and the impact on their culture of biological exchange with non-Indians. The title hero's mother lives with the Erie, but she continues to secretly pine for her own people, the Seneca. Red Streak, in the course of the story, is taken captive by the Seneca and is separated from his mother. He is adopted by Peace Woman, a figure famous for helping to broker the formation of the League, and grows very fond of a new adopted sister, Blue Flower. He pals about with new young Seneca warrior companions, and together they behave a little like exemplary scouts. Red Streak reunites his mother with her people and helps Hayowentha/Hiawatha make his case for peace before the League through overcoming the handiwork of a young misguided rival, Weasel. Finally, he is honored when Hayowentha publicly acknowledges that it was Red Steak who provided him with the ideas that made the League and peace possible.

Red Streak was more appropriately pitched and executed, but Parker's main aims had not changed. He wanted his readers to learn about ancient Iroquois practices and for them to comprehend the true Iroquois character.

Parker published his last book for juveniles, *Red Jacket: Last of the Senecas,* in 1952 as part of a biographical series for McGraw-Hill in New York. Dedicated to his daughter Martha Anne, "who roamed the Red Jacket trail and drank from the bubbling spring at Canoga," Parker created an easy-reading history. Its sister books had titles such as *Alexander Hamilton: Nation Builder* and *Stephen Austin: Father of Texas.* Writing it turned out to be quite frustrating because he knew he was publishing a less than scholarly version of the great Seneca orator's life, something he made clear to Wallace after Wallace had delighted him by writing it a positive review in the *New York Historical Society Quarterly.* It almost seemed an insult to write the history of such a significant Seneca leader and Mason as a book for the young. After all, the presidential medal from George Washington, which Red Jacket had once so highly prized, had been passed down to Ely Parker. But, he admitted, in the end he simply had to "salve my conscience by thinking the book treated in the way the editors wished might do some good."[56]

To his publishers, *Red Jacket* was a sales opportunity, but to Parker it was much more. It was an addition to Iroquois history and a record of a dying oral tradition that he was in a unique position to perpetuate before it was irretrievably lost. As he told Wallace, he had consulted the records of Asher Wright, who had been at the mission at Buffalo, interviewed "the descendants of the families that took care of the old chief in the late 1820s," and learned from notes left by Minnie Myrtle and from Laura Doctor and Mrs. Caswell. He also remembered his grandmother and grandfather, who "brought me up on Red Jacket stories." He put in numbered citations and photographs, and provided a bibliography for the final draft, all of which the publisher refused. At this, Parker said he was "more than depressed," a feeling that graduated to anger when he found errors in the map accompanying the text. The whole experience made him want to set the record straight with another Red Jacket book "for more mature minds."[57] There was a gravity and deep cultural significance to Red Jacket that Parker knew he had not adequately expressed.

There was no sense of how or why Red Jacket's cultural nativism had solidified as he grew older, no reasoned discussion of his behavior in battle or his personal characteristics, and no developed explanation of his resistance to the Handsome Lake faith. Instead, Parker simply concluded: "Otetiani (Red Jacket), the always ready, had the misfortune of being always right. This hurt those who were often wrong." He had opposed Indian acceptance of white attitudes but had also "gradually seen that the best interests of his nation lay in the acceptance of the material blessings of white civilization." His fame, Parker told his young readers, stemmed not just from his eloquence but from the way he had "challenged the sincerity of our civilization." He had shown America to itself and asked it to study the distorted picture presented.[58] *Red Jacket* was therefore a simplistic picture of a complicated and contested figure. It was also the final installment in his long list of books for children about the glory and undisplaceable potency of an Iroquois tradition.

Old age and a weakening heart finally made Parker set writing aside altogether and turn his attention to his last public concern, another local pageant. He passed away on the afternoon of Saturday, January 1, 1955, at his home surrounded by his beloved Seneca country with its redbud trees, roaming red deer, partridge, and "chewinking" towhee birds. He was seventy-three.

The local and state city presses immediately carried formal obituaries that made much of his prolific literary output. Parker had died unexpectedly, leaving Anne and Martha in New York and, from his first marriage, Melvil in Texas and Bertha, now Mrs. Bertha Oscar Cody, in California. Friends were told to call to pay last respects at the Allen Funeral Home. That Monday evening, Ray Fadden, representing the Eastern Door of the Longhouse, brought men from the St. Regis Reservation to conduct ritual and sing songs, and they visited Parker's widow and his daughter at home.[59]

The ensuing ceremonies were reminiscent of those that had marked Ely's passing at the end of the previous century. When Ely died at Fairfield, Connecticut, and was buried, his Episcopalian funeral was attended, reports said, by "six full-blooded Indians, silent and stern," and by fellow comrades from the Loyal Legion, the Grand Army of the Republic, and the Society of Colonial Wars.[60] Similarly, the ceremonies at Parker's funeral testified both to a multiple heritage and to the range of groups within which he had influence and enjoyed respect. He was still in good standing both with his own lodge and the Masonic Consistory, having had many fraternal honors bestowed on him, including the Mason's Royal Order of Scotland and a fraternal knighthood. Twenty years prior, he had been elected one of the forty immortals of the Philalethes, a distinguished literary group that claimed Rudyard Kipling as a past member, and then in 1954 he had been elected one of the society's four life fellows.[61] Therefore, it was with sincere regret that on Tuesday, January 4, at 8 P.M., his fraternal brothers gathered to say good-bye to the man they knew as "Sir Arthur."

The Rochester Consistory held its service in Rochester's Masonic Temple, Cathedral Hall, and they were joined by the Rochester chapter of the SAR. The Masons spoke of their love for their departed brother, who "always stood ready to put his shoulder to the wheel."[62] The John Hodge conducted its own service the next afternoon in the local Presbyterian church. Afterward, according to the local paper, the chaplain from Cattaraugus Reservation, representing the Western Door of the Longhouse, recited an Indian version of the Twenty-third Psalm in English, accompanied by Seneca sign language. He then led a twelve-strong party of Akwesasne singers from the St. Regis Reservation in song and closed the service with a Seneca prayer. The fact that Indians from the Tonawanda Longhouse and Christian Indians from Cattaraugus shared amicably in the formal commemorations surprised some who attended. There were reports that Parker was to be buried at Mount Hope Cemetery in Rochester, but he was cremated and his ashes stand today in an urn on the mantel shelf of his home.

He was sadly missed, not least by his wife. Anne outlived her husband by thirty years, living on surrounded by the beautiful countryside her husband had stamped as the ancestral homeland of his people, the Seneca. The couple's mutual affection had only deepened with time. Just the year before, Parker had written a poem to Anne to mark almost forty years of marriage together.[63]

The letters of sympathy his family received attested to his many connections and, poignantly, to his ability to inspire others with a love of the outdoors and things Indian. Most expressed shock at the suddenness of Parker's passing, given that not long before he had seemed in relatively good health. Members of the Nundawaga Society, of which he was chairman, were especially saddened. The board member who spoke formally in memoriam was full of praise, describing him as "a man who loved the great and small alike, making for each a higher mark—yet never lowering his own. He turned the bitter word by gentle answer and found in each man that spark of human love so often lost by those with poorer vision."[64] Many individual fraternal brothers wrote to share their loss.[65] The SAR wanted to mark the grave and wrote to Anne of her husband's tremendous generosity with his time and talents. A letter also came from Albany, registering the sympathy of the Klan.

Heartfelt letters of condolence came from other sources too. From the New York State Library, from the Buffalo Museum of Science, from New Jersey's State Museum, from the state senate, and the state supervisor of Indian Affairs. The Council of the American Association of Museums passed a special resolution in silence in his memory to register their admiration for Parker as an individual and professional.[66] People who had known him through the New York State Historical Association and through smaller local organizations wrote thoughtful letters about his impact on their lives. Others wrote of long walks shared in the Keuka countryside and of how he had raised their horizons and belief in their own capabilities. Several wrote to say they had been inspired by his leadership and instruction at the museum. There were letters, too, from archaeological societies, natural history societies, the editors of Indian journals, from women's groups, religious bodies, business people, lawyers, from hobbyists, from academics, and people describing themselves simply as "one of Arthur's very devoted disciples." Some wrote in remembrance of his ardor for knowledge, his devotion to his fellow man, of how he had changed their lives. People wrote of his nobility of character, of his good humor, of the breadth and depth of his accomplishments, and the sincerity of his friendship. Some even composed poems. However people had encountered Parker, they came to appreciate his quiet depth of understanding, his patience, his modesty, and his innate generosity. To a great many, he was a man of brilliance who should be remembered forever.

Perhaps the warmest expressions of regret came from Indian sources, and perhaps the best example was from Ray Fadden, a good friend from the Akwesasne Mohawk Counselor Organization. He wrote to Martha to say that the Chief "was a great person, desiring nothing for himself, quiet, ever watching, and ever ready to do good for everyone, no matter who." To Ray, who went on to found the Six Nations Indian Museum in Onchiota, Parker was the greatest man he had ever known.[67]

· · ·

Arthur Parker had lived a life of complexity and achievement. "Work and achievement by careful planning," he once told an Indian journal, "are my secrets of accomplishment. Nothing ever came easy for me. My obstacles have been heavy and high. I had to overcome them or perish. I chose to overcome them."[68] This was true. Parker had crammed an inordinate amount of effort and determined endeavor into his life. He had overcome limitations placed on his potential achievement by the dominant culture while consistently educating Americans about their Indian heritage. Throughout his life he had striven to demonstrate how much of a national asset Indians were and could be. But he knew that transcending stereotype was an ongoing challenge. It required that Americans adopt a more informed understanding of the Indian character. They had to comprehend the essential diversity of native peoples living within and beyond American boundaries and allow for a nonvanishing Indian contribution to modern life. The fact that they generally did not was of the utmost concern, and irritation over the issue stayed with Parker until the very end. Not long before his death he had even written on the back of a photograph of himself taken at the Six Nations Reserve at Brantford, Ontario, "Dressed in Sioux costume at 500th anniversary of the founding of the League of the Iroquois. Indians to be recognized as such must 'play' Indian!"[69]

It is to be hoped that future generations, Indian and non-Indian alike, will make every effort to displace the need to "play Indian" in order to assert modern Indian identity.

Notes

PREFACE

1. See Campisi, "Iroquois and the Euro-American Concept of Tribe," 4.

2. See Dorothy R. Parker to William N. Fenton, 9 June 1987, ms. collection no. 20, series 1, Fenton Papers, APS.

3. Parker in 1923, from Fenton, introduction to Parker, *Parker on the Iroquois*, xi.

4. Mabel Smith, interview by Terry Zeller, 1986, RMSC.

5. Harwood B. Dryer to Anne Parker, 12 February 1955, Black Obituary Scrapbook, Personal Papers of Arthur Caswell Parker, a.p.

6. Oswalt and Neely, *This Land Was Theirs*, 428; Thomas, "Parker—Leader and Prophet," 18. "Arthur Caswell Parker: Resolution Adopted by the Board of Trustees of the New York State Historical Association," 12 February 1955, Black Obituary Scrapbook, Personal Papers of Arthur Caswell Parker, a.p.

7. Quoted in Hertzberg, *Search for an American Indian Identity*, 59.

8. "Susan Harjo Testifies before the U.S. Civil Rights Commission, 1988," in Hurtado and Iverson, eds., *Major Problems in American Indian History*, 543–44. For an introduction to contemporary Native American artists, see Abbott, *I Stand in the Center*.

9. Vine Deloria, Jr., quoted in Zimmerman, "Vine Deloria, Jr.," 121. Phil Deloria, *Playing Indian*, 191.

10. Thomas, "Parker: 1881–1955," and "Parker—Leader and Prophet"; Hertzberg, *Search for an American Indian Identity*, and "Nationality, Anthropology, and Pan-Indianism"; Zeller, "Parker: A Pioneer," and "Parker and the Educational Mission."

11. Hertzberg, "Nationality, Anthropology, and Pan-Indianism," 47. See also Hayes, "Published Writings of Arthur Caswell Parker."

12. Stephen Thomas, interview by author, Rochester, New York, March 1992; Ramona Charles, interview by author, Tonawanda Longhouse, Tonawanda Indian Reservation, New York, March 1992.

13. Hoxie, *Final Promise*.

INTRODUCTION

1. Seneca-English translation by Esther Blueye, Basom, New York, for author. See also correspondence between W. Stephen Thomas and Dr. William N. Fenton, 13, 15 July 1955, Fenton Papers, APS.

2. "Record of Arthur C. Parker," n.d., Arthur Caswell Parker Papers, UR.

3. See Hertzberg, "Nationality, Anthropology, and Pan-Indianism," 52. The University of Rochester records do contain, however, at least one affectionate letter from mother to son: Geneva H. Parker to Arthur C. Parker, 10 December 1900, Arthur Caswell Parker Papers, UR.

4. See Rickard, *Fighting Tuscarora*, 52, 135.

1. The Owasco cultural tradition was first defined by William Ritchie, who worked for Parker in Rochester in the first stages of his career. For an informed discussion of interpretations of this period, consult the initial chapters of Snow, *Iroquois*.

2. Parker has written about Iroquois legend and of how the three sisters can be heard talking to each other in the fields where they grow together (Parker, *Seneca Myths and Folk Tales* [1923], 14).

3. See Bakker, "Basque Etymology," 89; Snow, Iroquois, 2; and for the quotation, Richter, *Ordeal of the Longhouse*, 1.

4. See Snow, *Iroquois,* 100, 124.

5. White, *Middle Ground.*

6. Richter, *Ordeal of the Longhouse, 7.*

7. Snow puts the date of formal adoption of the Tuscarora into the Iroquois League at some time late in 1722 or early in 1723, prompted by conflict with Europeans and defeat in the Tuscarora Wars of 1711–13 (Snow, *Iroquois*, 138).

8. The Iroquois today claim individual tribal sovereignty and collective Iroquois League sovereignty operating from Onondaga near Syracuse, New York, and the Six Nations of the Grand River Reserve near Brantford, Ontario.

9. See Grinde, "Iroquois Political Theory," 228, 280; and Snow, *Iroquois,* 142, 154.

10. See Parker, *Life of General Ely S. Parker* (1919), 21; and "Parker Family: Biography of Frederick E. Parker," fol. 15, box V, Arthur Caswell Parker Papers, UR.

11. Parker, "The Amazing Iroquois," ch. 2, n.d., 4, Fenton Papers, APS.

12. Parker, *Life of General Ely S. Parker* (1919), 40–41.

13. Parker, "The Amazing Iroquois: "Building Fires under Bad Bargains: 1838–1848," n.d., 4, Fenton Papers, APS. There is little support for Parker's claim to be a direct descendant of Handsome Lake. Elizabeth Tooker suggests that the confusion may derive from the fact that in the Seneca system of kinship terminology, Parker would have called Handsome Lake "grandfather."

14. Parker, "Nature and Background of This Collection," n.d., series 1, ms. coll. no. 20, Fenton Papers, APS.

15. Parker, "Notes for the Biography of Ely S. Parker," 1919, Arthur C. Parker Papers, SEDA.

16. Parker, *Life of General Ely S. Parker* (1919), 53, 201, 88, 89.

17. Ibid., 195–95.

18. Parker, "Nature and Background of this Collection," n.d., series 1, ms. coll. no. 20, Fenton Papers, APS. Further information on Spencer Cone is to be found in Parker's unpublished manuscripts for "The Amazing Iroquois," especially "a Commissioner Listens to Legends," 12–14, and "Building Fires under Bad Bargains: 1838–1848," 24–25; "Buying Back the Homeland: 1848–1858," n.d., 6–7, series 1, ms. coll. no. 20, Fenton Papers, APS.

19. Parker, *Life of General Ely S. Parker* (1919), 191, 21; and "Parker Family: Biography of Frederick E. Parker," fol. 15, box V, Arthur Caswell Parker Papers, UR. Albany Normal School was a forerunner of the University of Albany.

20. There is some question regarding whether Nicholson ever worked as a "civil engineer," although his brother Ely certainly did. See William Fenton to Stephen Thomas, 13 July 1955, ms. coll. no. 20, series 1, Fenton Papers, APS.

21. Thomas, "Parker: 1881–1955," 2.

22. Parker, "A Brief History of the Parker Family," n.d., Arthur C. Parker Papers, SEDA.

23. Parker, *Life of General Ely S. Parker* (1919), 197–99.

24. For an excellent and readable discussion of Indian involvement in the Civil War, see Hauptman, *Between Two Fires.*

25. Hauptman, *Between Two Fires,* 163, 171.

26. Parker, *Constitution of the Five Nations,* appendix D (1916), 151, in Parker, *Parker on the Iroquois.*

27. Parker, *Life of General Ely S. Parker* (1919), 192–201.

28. "Parker Family: Biography of Frederick E. Parker," fol. 15, box V, Arthur Caswell Parker Papers, UR.

29. "Arthur Caswell Parker, ScD., L.H.D.," in *Naples (N.Y.) Record,* 5 January 1955; and Parker, "A Brief History of the Parker Family," Arthur C. Parker Papers, SEDA. According to the *New York Sun,* c. 1914, Parker's father was his mother's pupil at the Thomas Indian School and afterward they married. "Work of Ga-Wa-So-Wa-Neh," *New York Sun,* c. 1914, fol. 2, Keppler Collection, MAIL.

30. Edna P. Harrington died on 20 September 1948. See William Fenton to Mrs. A. Moorstain, 28 March 1968, Fenton Papers, APS.

31. "Asylum-geh" is derived from the name of the Thomas Indian School and Orphan Asylum.

32. See William Fenton's introduction to Parker, *Seneca Myths and Folktales* (1923), xii. Fenton argues that one of the reasons Parker's later folklore was so original was because "his vocabulary of Seneca terms and expressions was extraordinary; he understood but did not control the language."

33. Parker, *Life of General Ely S. Parker* (1919), 200.

34. See George R. Hamell's introduction to Parker, *Skunny Wundy* (1926). Elsewhere, "jon ge on," the little people who lived in rocky places.

35. Parker, *Life of General Ely S. Parker* (1919), 19; "Parker Family: Biography of Frederick E. Parker," fol. 15, box V, Arthur Caswell Parker Papers, UR.

36. Parker, *Life of General Ely S. Parker* (1919), 195.

37. Parker, *Skunny Wundy* (1926), 9.

38. Parker, *Life of General Ely S. Parker* (1919), 192.

39. Parker, *Indian How Book* (1927).

40. The Dawes Act stipulated under Section 6: "And every Indian both within the territorial limits of the United States to whom allotments shall have been made under the provisions of this act, or under any law or treaty, and every Indian born within the territorial limits of the United States who has voluntarily taken up, within said limits, his residence separate and apart from any tribe of Indians therein, and has adopted the habits of civilized life, is hereby declared to be a citizen of the United States, and is entitled to all the rights, privileges, and immunities of such citizens" (Prucha, *Documents,* 171).

41. See Hauptman, "Senecas and Subdividers," 86–99.

42. "Famous American Indians: Arthur C. Parker," 1; Parker "A Brief History of the Parker Family," Arthur C. Parker Papers, SEDA; Parker, "Parker Family: Biography of Frederick E. Parker," fol. 15, box V, Arthur Caswell Parker Papers, UR; "Edna P. Harrington," *Naples (N.Y.) Record,* Personal Papers of Arthur Caswell Parker, a.p.

43. Parker, *Life of General Ely S. Parker* (1919), 196.

44. Parker, *Indian How Book* (1927), 192, 216.

45. Frederick Parker's patriotic endeavors brought him the honor of being the first man to raise the American flag over a public school in New York City ("Famous American Indians: Frederick Ely Parker," *Chemawa American* 6, 28 November 1928, Arthur Caswell Parker Personal Scrapbook, "Miscellaneous," Personal Papers of Arthur Caswell Parker, a.p.).

46. A. C. Parker to General R. H. Pratt, 7 August 1915, SAI Papers. See also A. C. Parker to R. H. Pratt, 24 August 1916; and R. H. Pratt to Dennison Wheelock, 24 October 1914, SAI Papers.

47. Fenton, introduction to Parker, *Parker on the Iroquois,* 7.

48. Parker, *Life of General Ely S. Parker* (1919), 201.

49. Parker, *Skunny Wundy* (1926), 10.

50. Quoted in Thomas, "Parker: 1881–1955," 4, 3.

51. Rev. A. R. MaCombray, Pastor of the Presbyterian Church, White Plains, N.Y., to Whom It May Concern, 20 July 1896, Arthur Caswell Parker Papers, UR.

52. "Famous American Indians: Arthur C. Parker," 4.

53. "Record of Arthur C. Parker," n.d., Arthur Caswell Parker Papers, UR.

54. Parker, "Triumph of Woman's Wit" (1900).

55. Parker, "Making a Museologist" (1939)

56. See Zeller, "Arthur C. Parker," 42.

CHAPTER 2

1. Parker, *Life of General Ely S. Parker* (1919), 231, 7.

2. Turner, "Significance of the Frontier," 79–112.

3. House Executive Document no. 1, 51st Cong., 2d sess., serial 2841, clxvii, in Prucha, *Documents,* 181.

4. Zangwill, *Melting Pot,* act 1.

5. Theodore Roosevelt, 1906 New York Republican state convention at Saratoga, and *Metropolitan Magazine,* October 1915, 7.

6. Kevles, *In the Name of Eugenics,* 64.

7. Ludmerer, *Genetics and American Society,* 16.

8. Grant, *Passing of the Great Race,* 16, 76, 78.

9. Kevles, *In the Name of Eugenics,* 74, 85, 94; Roosevelt quoted in Gossett, *Race,* 238.

10. Kallen, *Culture and Democracy,* 11.

11. Kallen, *Culture and Democracy,* 68.

12. Gossett, *Race,* 426.

13. Although Boas may have focused his attack on the British anthropologist Edward Tylor, within American anthropology Tylor's thinking most closely corresponded to that of Morgan.

14. For a more detailed contextualization of Boas's early work with immigrants and of the strand of his thinking that predicted the progressive absorption of ethnic groups into a uniform American culture, see Williams, *Rethinking Race*.

15. Boas, *Race, Language and Culture*, 138–48.

16. Fenton, introduction to Morgan, *League of the Iroquois*, ii.

17. Parker, *Life of General Ely S. Parker* (1919), 80.

18. Leslie White, "How Morgan Came to Write," 3.

19. The name Skenandoah is known because it was the name of a fast friend of the Reverend Samuel Kirkland, the noted missionary to the Oneida.

20. Resek, *Lewis Henry Morgan*, 24.

21. See Trautmann, Morgan and the Invention of Kinship, 42.

22. Quoted in White, "How Morgan Came to Write," 4, 261.

23. Parker, *Life of General Ely S. Parker* (1919), 81. Morgan detailed the Ogden Land Company's attempts to defraud the Seneca in *League of the Ho-dé-no-sau-nee*, 33. The most influential voice raised in opposition to the actions of the Ogden Land Company was that of John Martindale, district attorney of Genesee County in 1842. For a fuller description of Morgan's limited role in the resolution of the Tonawanda question, see Tooker, *Morgan on Iroquois Material Culture*, ch. 3, and Hauptman, "Senecas and Subdividers," for a discussion of the longer-term impact of the Ogden claim. In "The Indian Education of Lewis Henry Morgan," David Oberweiser has also recorded Morgan's close relationship to the Iroquois and his championing of Iroquois rights.

24. Parker, *Life of General Ely S. Parker* (1919), 28–82, 86, 87.

25. Tooker, *Morgan on Iroquois Material Culture*, 74.

26. Quoted in Armstrong, *Warrior in Two Camps*, 10.

27. Parker, *Life of General Ely S. Parker* (1919), 88.

28. Tooker, *Morgan on Iroquois Material Culture*, 62, 87, 14.

29. Morgan, *League of the Ho-dé-no-sau-nee*, 351.

30. Quoted in White, "How Morgan Came to Write," 5.

31. Morgan, *League of the Ho-dé-no-sau-nee*, xi.

32. Letters between Ely Parker and Morgan have been published as appendices to Fenton, "Tonawanda Longhouse Ceremonies," 139–65. They reveal how much Morgan relied on Ely as his collaborator in the production of *The League*, a text that formed the basis of much of his later conclusions on human development in *Ancient Society*. Ely also points out, in these letters, that he could not remember the exact details and significance of certain Iroquois festivals and so on. For a review of the ethnographic information Morgan received from Ely, see the article cited above.

33. Fenton, "Iroquois Confederacy in the Twentieth Century," 251.

34. Fenton, introduction to Morgan, *League of the Iroquois*, xv, xviii.

35. Morgan, *League of the Ho-dé-no-sau-nee*, ix.

36. Quoted in Resek, *Lewis Henry Morgan*, 43.

37. Quoted in Stern, *Lewis Henry Morgan*, 50.

38. Quoted in Gossett, Race, 250.

39. Morgan later tried to bring his views on reform of Indian policy to a wider audience in the journal *The Nation*: "Hue and Cry against the Indians"; "Factory System for Indian Reservations," 23 (27 July 1876): 58–59; "The Indian Question in 1878" 27 (28 November 1878): 332–33.

40. Kosok, "Unknown Letter," 34–40.

41. According to Parker, by the time of his death on December 17, 1881, Morgan was worth $100,000, a sizable fortune (Parker, "Morgan, Social Philosopher" 1940, 14, Parker archives, RMSC).

42. Quoted in Gossett, *Race*, 250.

43. In *Systems*, Morgan came to puzzling conclusions on the results of Indian-white intermarriage. It is difficult to reconcile his views at this time with his respect for the Parker family. He wrote the following: "The Indian and European are at opposite poles in their physiological conditions. In the former there is very little animal passion, while with the latter it is superabundant. A pure-blooded Indian has very little animal passion, but in the half-blood it is sensibly augmented; and when the second generation is reached with a cross giving three quarters white blood, it becomes excessive and tends to indiscriminate licentiousness" (quoted in Stern, *Lewis Henry Morgan*, 71).

44. Although Morgan rigidly applied these "ethnical periods" in *Ancient Society* in 1887, he said they were "provisional." He had completed his subdivisions of human development just a few months before sending his manuscript to the Smithsonian for publication (quoted in Stern, *Lewis Henry Morgan*, 139).

45. Morgan, *Ancient Society*, 589.

46. Engels, *Origin of the Family*, 1, 71.

47. For further discussion of Marx's and Engels's manipulation and use of Morgan's research, see Resek, *Lewis Henry Morgan*; Trautmann, *Morgan and the Invention of Kinship*; and Bloch, *Marxism and Anthropology*. For a discussion of Morgan's connection to contemporary feminism, see Sayers, Evans, and Redclift, eds., *Engels Revisited*. Twentieth-century feminist connections to Morgan are appropriate, since he held progressive views on the position of women in society. On his death in 1881, he bequeathed a slice of his fortune to the development of American female education in Rochester, New York. As the scholars referred to above highlight, Morgan and Engels's lasting contribution to feminism lies primarily with the fact that they both placed the family, politically, within social history and made the institution an object of historical inquiry.

48. Morgan, *Ancient Society*, vi.

49. Ibid., 562, 12, 40

50. Ibid., 341; Kuper, *Invention of Primitive Society*, 71.

51. Parker, "Presentation and Unveiling of the Morgan Tablet" (1919), 23–26.

52. Parker, "Lewis Henry Morgan" speech, November 1928, Arthur Caswell Parker Papers, UR. Emphasis added.

53. Parker, "Iroquois Studies since Morgan's Investigations," September 1935, Arthur Caswell Parker Papers, UR.

54. Parker, "Morgan, Social Philosopher," 1940, 10–15, 5, Parker archives, RMSC.

55. Parker, *Life of General Ely S. Parker* (1919), 48.

56. Yeuell, "Ely Samuel Parker," 219. There is some confusion over Ely's time at Rensselaer, since his name does not appear on the institute records. See "Says Indian Penned Lee Surrender Terms," *New York Sun,* 27 April 1940, Arthur Caswell Parker Personal Scrapbook, "Seneca," Personal Papers of Arthur Caswell Parker, a.p. See also the version of Ely's young life within Parker's unpublished multivolume *The Amazing Iroquois: Building Fires under Bad Bargains* 1838–1848, 13, series 1, ms. coll. no. 20, Fenton Papers, APS.

57. Do-ne-ho-ga-wa was a name held by John Blacksmith.

58. Waltmann, "Ely Samuel Parker," 124

59. Parker, *Life of General Ely S. Parker* (1919), 129–41, 320; Hauptman, *Between Two Fires,* 182.

60. Waltmann, "Ely Samuel Parker," 129.

61. Quoted in ibid., 131.

62. Waltmann, "Ely Samuel Parker," 123.

63. Parker, *Life of General Ely S. Parker* (1919), 167.

64. Armstrong, *Warrior in Two Camps,* 165; Hauptman, *Between Two Fires,* 183.

65. Parker, *Life of General Ely S. Parker* (1919), 7, 323.

66. Parker to Joseph Keppler, 7 August 1907, fol. 1, P.2, no. 25, Keppler Collection, MAIL.

67. Parker, *Life of General Ely S. Parker* (1919), 10. Emphasis added.

68. Parker, *Life of General Ely S. Parker* (1919), 162–64, 172.

CHAPTER 3

1. Parker, "Making a Museologist" (1939).

2. See Arthur C. Parker Papers, series 1, NYSM; and F. W. Putnam to A. C. Parker, 25 November 1903, Arthur Caswell Parker Papers, UR.

3. John Fenton was the father of William N. Fenton, who in the 1930s was employed as anthropologist and community worker on Tonawanda Reservation where Parker was involved in two work-relief schemes. William Fenton has many connections to Parker and republished Parker's major anthropological texts in 1968 as *Parker on the Iroquois.* According to his son, John Fenton pointed Parker toward Ripley as a site for excavation. Ripley, in Chautauqua County, is remembered as Parker's most respected single archaeological study.

4. Parker to Harriet Converse, 30 January 1900, fol. 1, P.2, no. 1, Keppler Collection, MAIL.

5. Fenton, introduction to Parker, *Parker on the Iroquois,* 9–10.

6. For discussions of the life and work of early "armchair" ethnologists, see, for example, Green, ed., *Cushing at Zuni,* and Moses, *Indian Man.*

7. Dexter, "Frederick Ward Putnam," 316.

8. See Hinsley, "From Shell Heaps to Stelae," 49.

9. "Arthur C. Parker Dies: Former Museum Head," *Rochester Democrat & Chronicle* (n.d.), Black Obituary Scrapbook, Personal Papers of Arthur Caswell Parker, a.p.

10. See Fenton, introduction to Parker, *Parker on the Iroquois,* 10.

11. Parker, "Making a Museologist" (1939).

12. Thomas, "Parker—Leader and Prophet," 18.

13. Parker, *Manual for History Museums* (1935), 136.

14. Quoted in Thomas, "Parker—Leader and Prophet," 4.

15. See Fenton, introduction to Parker, *Parker on the Iroquois,* 10; and Parker, *Seneca Myths and Folk Tales* (1923), xx.

16. See Hauptman, "Senecas and Subdividers," 86–99.

17. Fenton, introduction to Parker, *Parker on the Iroquois,* 13. See also Hertzberg, "Nationality, Anthropology, and Pan-Indianism," 56, for a discussion of the problem of exactly when Parker was adopted. It seems likely that he was adopted during 1903 since Putnam wrote from the University of California on September 1, 1903, to congratulate him on being made a chief of the Seneca Bear Clan (Arthur Caswell Parker Papers, UR). Later, in 1909, Parker described for *American Anthropologist* the Seneca snowsnake game that bore his name (Parker, "Snow-Snake as Played by the Senecas" [1909], 250–56).

18. See Parker, ed., *Myths and Legends of the New York State Iroquois* (1908), 19–22.

19. "Among the Senecas," n.d.; "Governor Has High Praise for Indians in Ceremonial Talk," 6 August 1940, *Times-Mirror* (Warren, Pa.), Clippings Scrapbook, "Seneca, Onondaga, Six Nations, Western and Others," Personal Papers of Arthur Caswell Parker, a.p.

20. Frederick Ward Putnam to Parker, 1 September 1903, Arthur Caswell Parker Papers, UR.

21. Hertzberg, "Nationality, Anthropology, and Pan-Indianism," 54.

22. Parker, *Seneca Myths and Folktales* (1923), 456.

23. Parker, ed., *Myths and Legends of the New York State Iroquois* (1908). According to one of Parker's newspaper clippings, when Mrs. Converse took possession of a wampum in 1901, she did so to forward it to its ultimate custodian in perpetuity, Joseph Keppler, or Gyantwaka (the name Parker used in his letters to him), already an adopted Seneca chief ("A Historic Wampum Belt: Symbol of Algonquin Defeat 230 Years Ago," 8 August 1901, Indians Scrapbook, Personal Papers of Arthur Caswell Parker, a.p).

24. Frederick Ward Putnam to Parker, 1 September 1903, Arthur Caswell Parker Papers, UR.

25. For an overview of Boas's professional career, see Stocking, "Franz Boas."

26. Fenton, introduction to Parker, *Parker on the Iroquois,* 9–10.

27. Parker to Frederick Ward Putnam, 1907, fol. 1, box 1, vol. 1, Arthur Caswell Parker Papers, UR.

28. Fenton, introduction to Parker, *Parker on the Iroquois,* 10.

29. Hertzberg, "Nationality, Anthropology, and Pan-Indianism," 54.

30. Parker, "A Brief History of the Parker Family," Ely S. Parker Papers, BEHS; 1900–1901 newspaper, "Indians in Public School," Keppler Collection, MAIL.

31. Herskovits, quoted in Hertzberg, "Nationality, Anthropology, and Pan-Indianism," 55.

32. Hertzberg, "Nationality, Anthropology, and Pan-Indianism," 55.

33. Parker, "Where Questions Are Answered" (1953), 163.

34. Quoted in Dexter, "Putnam's Problems," 316–27. Yet Putnam was ever ready to defend what he felt were the Indian's best interests. He helped Navajo "exhibits" secure payment for their appearance at the exposition when the Colorado Board withheld their promised payment. A full-blood Apache, Antonio, was in charge of the Navajos brought to the exposition. He had been brought up by whites after being captured by the military in 1877, and Putnam employed him as an assistant. Putnam intervened in Antonio's favor when he was accused of improper conduct with certain of the female Navajo female "exhibits."

35. Stocking, "Franz Boas."

36. Boas, "Some Principles," 928.

37. Parker, "Making a Museologist" (1939).

38. Fenton, introduction to Parker, *Parker on the Iroquois*, 11. Refer also to the Fenton Papers, series 1, ms. coll. no. 20, New York State Museum, fol. 1, Papers on Appeal in the Appellate Division of the Supreme Court 1900, APS.

39. Fenton, introduction to Parker, *Parker on the Iroquois*, 11; and Andrew S. Draper, Commissioner of Education, 10 November 1904, "To the Indian People of the State of New York," box 1, Arthur C. Parker Papers, NYSM.

40. "Record of Arthur C. Parker: State Archaeologist and Ethnologist," n.d., Arthur Caswell Parker Papers, UR.

41. Parker to Joseph Keppler, 16 April 1905, fol. 1, P.2, no. 10, Keppler Collection, MAIL.

42. Parker to Joseph Keppler, 16 April, 12 March 1905, fol. 1, P.2, no. 10, Keppler Collection, MAIL.

43. Professor Emeritus William N. Fenton, interview by author, New York, 14 March 1992.

44. Parker, "Secret Medicine Societies of the Seneca" (1909), 163–81.

45. Parker to Joseph Keppler, 27 March 1905, fol. 1, P.2, no. 9, Keppler Collection, MAIL. Eventually, Parker became adroit at dealing with the new technology, telling Keppler he had become "an Edison" at the job (Parker to Keppler, 28 March 1906, fol. 1, P.2, no. 18, Keppler Collection, MAIL).

46. Parker to Melvil Dewey, Gowanda, 7 April 1906, quoted in Fenton, introduction to Parker, *Parker on the Iroquois*, 12–13.

47. Parker to Keppler, fol. 1, P.2, no. 9; and 25 February 1905, fol. 1, P.2, no. 6, Keppler Collection, MAIL.

48. Fenton, introduction to Parker, *Parker on the Iroquois*, 14–15.

49. Parker to Joseph Keppler, fol. 1, P.2, no. 21, Keppler Collection, MAIL.

50. Parker to Joseph Keppler, 31 May 1905, fol. 1, P.2, no. 14, Keppler Collection, MAIL.

51. Parker to Joseph Keppler, 24 November 1905, fol. 1, P.2, no. 17; Parker to Joseph Keppler, 27 July 1906, fol. 1, P.2, no. 20, Keppler Collection, MAIL.

52. Parker to Joseph Keppler, 6 October 1906, fol. 1, P.2, no. 21, Keppler Collection, MAIL.

53. Putnam to Parker, 26 October 1906, box 1, Arthur C. Parker Papers, NYSM.

54. Quoted in Zeller, "Parker and the Educational Mission," 106.

55. Parker, "Excavations in an Erie Indian Village and Burial Site at Ripley" (1907); "Archeological Investigations," 1 September 1907, Clippings Scrapbook, "N.Y. State Museum, Other Museums, N.Y. State Archeology, Archeology Material," Personal Papers of Arthur Caswell Parker, a.p.

56. See Burmaster, "World's Wonder Corner."

57. Parker to Keppler, 9, 27 July 1906, Keppler Collection, MAIL.

58. Fenton, introduction to Parker, *Parker on the Iroquois*, 17.

59. "Archaeological Investigations," *Statestown Times*, 1 September 1907, Arthur Caswell Parker Personal Scrapbook, "NY State Museum," Personal Papers of Arthur Caswell Parker, a.p.

60. Sullivan, "Parker's Contributions," 10.

61. "Record of Arthur C. Parker," n.d., Arthur Caswell Parker Papers, UR.

62. See Thomas, "Parker: 1881–1955," 7.

63. Willey and Sabloff, *History of American Archaeology*, 114.

64. Sullivan, "Parker's Contributions," 6.

65. Bender and Curtin, *Prehistoric Context for the Upper Hudson*, 10; Sullivan, "Parker's Contributions," 9.

66. Parker, "Method in Archeology" (1923), iv.

67. Parker, "Archeology Adopts a New Policy" (1937), 160.

68. Sullivan, "Parker's Contributions," 11–12.

69. Quoted in Zeller, "Parker and the Educational Mission," 122 n. 14.

70. Parker, *Manual for History Museums* (1935), 175, 180, 182.

71. Parker, *Indian How Book* (1927), 244–45.

72. Parker, "The Amazing Iroquois" (1927), 108.

73. Parker, "The Archaeological History of New York" (1920), 8.

74. Parker to Joseph Keppler, 10 October 1908, fol. 1, P.2, no. 29, Keppler Collection, MAIL.

75. Parker, "Excavations in an Erie Indian Village and Burial Site at Ripley" (1907), 461–66.

76. See Zeller, "Parker: Pioneer in American Museums," 44.

77. "Record of Arthur C. Parker," n.d., Arthur Caswell Parker Papers, UR; See also introduction by William N. Fenton to Parker, *Seneca Myths and Folk Tales* (1923), xiv; "Optional Release New York State Education Department" (1955), Black Obituary Scrapbook, Personal Papers of Arthur Caswell Parker, a.p.

78. Zeller, "Parker and the Educational Mission," 108, 111, 110.

79. Quoted in ibid., 107.

80. Parker to Clarke, 5 November 1905, 18 July 1906, Arthur C. Parker Papers, NYSM.

81. Parker to Muller & Sons, 3 October 1911; Parker to Kasper Mayer, 6 April and 4 December 1909; Parker to Letha Kenedy, 21 January 1909; Parker to Clarke, 13 June 1909 and 23 April 1910, Arthur C. Parker Papers, NYSM.

82. Quoted in Zeller, "Parker and the Educational Mission," 32.

83. Parker, "Habitat Groups in Wax and Plaster" (1918), 81–84.

84. Parker, "Making People Like Museums" (1943), 1.

85. Parker, "Habitat Groups in Wax and Plaster" (1918), 84.

86. Quoted in Jacknis, "Franz Boas and Exhibits," 102.

87. Parker, quoted in Zeller, "Parker and the Educational Mission," 108. Emphasis in original.

88. See, for example, Robinson, "Experimental Education in Museums," 5–8.

89. Quoted in Thomas, "Parker: 1881–1955," 5.

90. Parker, "Will Our Culture Survive?" (1939).

91. See Harris, *Cultural Excursions*; Weil, *Beauty and the Beasts*; Karp, Kreamer, and Lavine, eds., *Museums and Communities*; and, for a valuable compendium of perspectives on museums as contested sites of representation, Karp and Lavine, eds., *Exhibiting Cultures*.

92. Haraway, "Teddybear Patriarchy," 22.

CHAPTER 4

1. See Parker to Joseph Keppler, 31 October 1905, fol. 1, P.2, no. 16, and 24 November 1905, fol. 1, P.2, no. 17, Keppler Collection, MAIL.

2. Parker to Keppler, 1906–1907, fol. 1, P.2, no. 23, Keppler Collection, MAIL.

3. Parker to Keppler, 7 August 1907, fol. 1, P.2, no. 25, Keppler Collection, MAIL.

4. Fenton, introduction to Parker, *Parker on the Iroquois*, 23.

5. Parker to Keppler, 25 June 1908, fol. 1, P.2, no. 27, Keppler Collection, MAIL.

6. Parker, ed., *Myths and Legends of the New York State Iroquois* (1908), 12–13.

7. Fenton, introduction to Parker, *Parker on the Iroquois*, 24.

8. Refer to Fenton to Hamell, 18 August 1979, series 1, ms. coll. no. 20, Fenton Papers, APS.

9. Clarke to Parker, 19 October 1909, quoted in Fenton, introduction to Parker, *Parker on the Iroquois*, 25.

10. Parker to Clarke, 16 April 1909, quoted in Fenton, introduction to Parker, *Parker on the Iroquois*, 24.

11. Parker to Clarke, 16 June 1909, quoted in Fenton, introduction to Parker, *Parker on the Iroquois*, 25.

12. "Archaeologist Parker's Successful Quest . . .," 30 January 1910, 21, Arthur Caswell Parker Personal Scrapbook, Beauchamp Collection, NYSM.

13. Parker to E. Cornplanter, 17 October 1910, series 1, ms. coll. no. 20, Fenton Papers, APS.

14. Fenton, introduction to Parker, *Parker on the Iroquois*, 25.

15. Parker, *Iroquois Uses,* in Parker, *Parker on the Iroquois* (1968), 5, 34, 39, 62.

16. Morgan, *Ancient Society,* 125.

17. Parker, *Iroquois Uses,* in Parker, *Parker on the Iroquois* (1968), 86, 98, 103.For Parker's rendering of the legend surrounding the three sisters—bean, corn, and squash—see Parker, *Indian How Book* (1927), 201–202.

18. Parker, *Iroquois Uses,* in Parker, *Parker on the Iroquois* (1968), 13, 15, 64.

19. Speck, "*Iroquois Uses of Maize,*" 135–36.

20. Harrington, "Some Seneca Corn-foods"; Waugh, *Iroquois Foods and Food Preparation.*

21. Wissler, "Material Culture of North American Indians."

22. Fenton, introduction to Parker, *Parker on the Iroquois,* 28.

23. Parker, "Where Hiawatha's Laws Still Govern," 29 May 1910, 17, Arthur Caswell Parker Personal Scrapbook, Beauchamp Collection, NYSM.

24. Parker, "Archaeologist Writes of the Fire," Arthur Caswell Parker Personal Scrapbook, Beauchamp Collection, NYSM.

25. Parker to Joseph Keppler, 29 March 1911, Keppler Collection, MAIL.

26. Parker, "Fear for State Relics," Arthur Caswell Parker Personal Scrapbook, Beauchamp Collection, NYSM.

27. Fenton, introduction to Parker, *Parker on the Iroquois,* 43.

28. Parker to Joseph Keppler, 11 April 1911, fol. 1, P.2, no. 35, Keppler Collection, MAIL.

29. Parker to Joseph Keppler, 4 October 1911, fol. 1, P.2, no. 37; 5 November 1911, fol. 1, P.2, no. 39, Keppler Collection, MAIL.

30. Parker, "Report of the Archeology and Ethnology Section" (1913), 56.

31. Fenton, introduction to Parker, *Parker on the Iroquois,* 32.

32. See Wilson, *Magic and the Millennium,* 391.

33. Refer to Wallace, "Cultural Composition of the Handsome Lake Religion."

34. Parker to Joseph Keppler, 23 September 1911, fol. 1, P.2, no. 36, Keppler Collection, MAIL. Parker's familial relationship to Handsome Lake has been questioned by anthropologists.

35. Parker, *The Code,* in Parker, *Parker on the Iroquois* (1968), 8, 33.

36. Ibid., 56.

37. Ibid., 113, 114.

38. Ibid., 10, 11, 13, 14.

39. For details on Handsome Lake as a historical figure, see Wallace, *Death and Rebirth of the Seneca,* 256–60.

40. Parker, *The Code,* in Parker, *Parker on the Iroquois* (1968), 11.

41. See Deardorff, "Religion of Handsome Lake," 104.

42. Parker, *The Code,* in Parker, *Parker on the Iroquois* (1968), 68–74.

43. Lanternari, *Religions of the Oppressed*; Wallace, "Handsome Lake and the Great Revival," and *Death and Rebirth of the Seneca.*

44. Tooker's ideas imply that religious change can be directly related to changes in the economics of societies and, specifically, that agricultural

economies demand religions that suppress individual autonomy and produce settled conformity, whereas hunting economies do not.

45. Tooker, "On the New Religion of Handsome Lake," 187–95.

46. Parker, *The Code,* in Parker, *Parker on the Iroquois,* 10.

47. Wallace, *Death and Rebirth of the Seneca,* 271–72.

48. Ibid., 392, 387.

49. Skinner, review of *Code of Handsome Lake,* 182, 183.

50. Parker, *Constitution of the Five Nations,* in Parker, *Parker on the Iroquois* (1968), 8–13.

51. Refer to Parker to William N. Fenton, 10 November 1948, series 1, ms. coll. no. 20, Fenton Papers, APS.

52. Parker, *Constitution of the Five Nations,* in Parker, *Parker on the Iroquois* (1968), 7–13.

53. Further details on the ethnographic and Indian politics surrounding the Newhouse version were published in 1949 by Fenton, then senior ethnologist at the Smithsonian Institution's Bureau of Ethnology, under the title "Seth Newhouse's Traditional History and Constitution of the Iroquois Confederacy."

54. Hewitt, review of *Constitution of the Five Nations.*

55. Scott, "Traditional History of the Confederacy of the Six Nations."

56. Hewitt, review of *Constitution of the Five Nations.*

57. Goldenweiser, review of *Constitution of the Five Nations.*

58. Parker, "Constitution of the Five Nations, a Reply" (1918), 124.

59. Parker, *Parker on the Iroquois* (1968), 41–42.

60. Parker, "Constitution of the Five Nations, a Reply" (1918).

61. J. N. B. Hewitt to Jesse Cornplanter, 26 March 1934, series 1, ms. coll. no. 20, Fenton Papers, APS.

62. Fenton, "Seth Newhouse's Traditional History and Constitution," 158.

63. J. N. B. Hewitt to Jesse Cornplanter, 22 June 1934, series 1, ms. coll. no. 20, Fenton Papers, APS.

64. Parker to Fenton, 10 November 1948, series 1, ms. coll. no. 20, Fenton Papers, APS.

CHAPTER 5

1. The IRA began in Philadelphia in 1882, and the Lake Mohonk Conference of the Friends of the Indian began annual meetings the following year. The Lake Mohonk Conference occurred each autumn at the resort hotel at the expense of Albert K. Smiley, Quaker and member of the Board of Indian Commissioners.

2. "Report of the Executive Council on the Proceedings of the First Annual Conference of the Society of American Indians," Washington, D.C., 1912, 2, SAI Papers. See also Prucha, *American Indian Policy in Crisis,* for a full consideration of white reform groups in this period.

3. R. H. Pratt to Parker, 22 July 1915, SAI Papers.

4. Elaine Goodale Eastman to Parker, 8 February 1911, Amherst, Mass.; Parker to Mrs. Charles A. Eastman, 14 February 1911, Albany, N.Y., quoted in Hertzberg, "Nationality, Anthropology, and Pan-Indianism," 61.

5. *Argus,* 14 June 1911, Arthur Caswell Parker Personal Scrapbook, Beauchamp Collection, NYSM.

6. Executive Committee, American Indian Association [SAI], 11 July 1911, Arthur C. Parker Papers, NYSM.

7. "SAI Objects," series 1, Arthur C. Parker Papers, NYSM.

8. The letterhead read, "Memberships: Active and Associate Active: Persons of Indian Blood Only" (manuscript, Arthur C. Parker Papers, NYSM).

9. Parker to McKenzie, 1 April 1911, SAI Papers.

10. Parker to Charles E. Daganett, 22 September 1911, SAI Papers.

11. Clippings Scrapbook, Personal Papers of Arthur Caswell Parker, a.p.

12. Parker to Keppler, 23 September 1911, fol. 1, P.2, no. 36, Keppler Collection, MAIL.

13. "Educational Problems," manuscript, Arthur C. Parker Papers, NYSM.

14. Parker to Dr. Henry A. Bechtell, 13 June 1913, fol. 1, P.2, no. 36, Keppler Collection, MAIL.

15. See "The First National Conference of Indians," by F. A. McKenzie, *Red Man* 3, no. 4 (November 1911), SAI Papers.

16. See clippings, "Columbus Red Men Entertain Indians," Parker Scrapbook, SEDA.

17. Quoted in Philip Deloria, "White Sacheme and Indian Masons," 27.

18. Matthew Sniffen to Parker, 5 December 1911, series 1, Arthur C. Parker Papers, NYSM.

19. Quoted in Hertzberg, *Search for an American Indian Identity,* 72.

20. *New York Times,* 12 September 1912, Arthur Caswell Parker Personal Scrapbook, Beauchamp Collection, NYSM; and Parker to Emma Johnson, 20 November 1911, Arthur C. Parker Papers, NYSM; Parker to Joseph Keppler 5 November 1911, fol. 1, P.2, no. 39, Keppler Collection, MAIL.

21. See "The First National Conference of Indians," by F. A. McKenzie, *Red Man* 3, no. 4 (November 1911), SAI Papers.

22. "Indians to Demand End of Paternalism," press clipping, SAI Papers.

23. "Government Opposed to the Indian Congress; So Say Delegates Who Charge That Several Prominent Redskins Feared to Attend: Uncle Sam Is Scolded," 15 October 1911, Parker Scrapbook, SEDA.

24. See "Fails in Purpose: Braves Disagree"; "Indian Conference Splits on Politics; Government Party in the Saddle," 17 October 1911; and "Indians Prove Most Adept at Playing Politics; His Connection with Government Bars Charles E. Daganett from Presidency," 17 October 1911, Parker Scrapbook, SEDA.

25. Parker to Dr. F. A. McKenzie, 9 November 1911; Parker to Mr. Charles E. Daganett, 28 December 1911, SAI Papers.

26. Parker to Rosa B. LaFlesche, 27 November 1911, Arthur C. Parker Papers, NYSM.

27. Parker to Mr. S. M. Drosuis, 16 June 1913; Parker to Mr. Chas. E. Daganett, 4 December 1911, SAI Papers.

28. Parker to Mr. Charles E. Daganett, 28 December 1911, SAI Papers.

29. See Parker to Mr. Joe K. Griffis, 27 October 1911, and Parker to Dr. Sherman Coolidge, 20 November 1911. Parker feared that he might be subject

to the same criticism as Daganett (Parker to Dr. F. A. McKenzie, 9 November 1911, SAI Papers).

30. Parker to Mrs. Rosa B. LaFlesche, 12 January 1912, Arthur C. Parker Papers, NYSM.

31. Parker, "Why the Carter Indian Code Bill?" 1912, SAI Papers; Parker, "Occupations and Industry of the American Indian," *Indian Leader: A Periodical Printed by and for Indians,* 1912, SAI Papers.

32. Parker to Mr. C. E. Daganett, 4 January 1912, SAI Papers.

33. Parker to Dr. F. A. McKenzie, 14 January 1912; Parker to Dr. F. A. McKenzie, 20 January 1912, SAI Papers.

34. Parker to Joseph Keppler, 24 January 1912, fol. 1, P.2, no. 41, Keppler Collection, MAIL.

35. See Parker to Mr. Charles E. Daganett, 22 January 1912; Parker to Dr. Charles A. Eastman, 31 January 1912, SAI Papers.

36. Parker to Mr. Dennison Wheelock, 20 February 1912; Parker to Mr. Thomas L. Sloan, 22 February 1912; Parker to Mr. Henry Standing Bear, 28 February 1912; Rosa B. LaFlesche to Parker, 23 February 1912; Parker to Rev. Sherman Coolidge, 23 February 1912; Parker to Dr. F. A. McKenzie, 24 February 1912; Parker to Rev. Joseph K. Griffis, 26 February 1912, SAI Papers.

37. Parker to Mr. Henry Standing Bear, 5 March 1912; Parker to President, 5 March 1912; Parker to Mrs. Emma D. Goulette, 18 March 1918; Parker to Sloan, 19 March 1912, SAI Papers.

38. Parker to Professor F. W. McKenzie, 27 March 1912; Parker to Mrs. Emma D. Goulette, 18 March 1918; Parker to Fellow Indian, 2 April 1912, SAI Papers; Parker to Albert Hensley, 2 April 1912, Arthur C. Parker Papers, NYSM; Parker to Mr. Thomas L. Sloan, 7 April 1912; Parker to Mrs. Marie L. B. Baldwin, 12 April 1912, SAI Papers.

39. Parker to Prof. F. A. McKenzie, 21 April 1912; Parker to Fellow Member, 25 May 1912; Parker to Mrs. Orin J. Kellogg, 5 June 1912, SAI Papers.

40. "Proceedings of the SAI Conference," April 1912, 3–5, SAI Papers. Parker may have gotten the idea for an Indian Day from Harriet Maxwell Converse, who organized one on July 29, 1998, to mark the opening of the New York State Museum's Indian exhibits, which she had helped to bring into being. See "Indian Day at Albany: The Tribes of Five Nations Gathered Together by Mrs. Harriet M. Converse," Arthur Caswell Parker Personal Scrapbook, "Museums," Personal Papers of Arthur Caswell Parker, a.p.

41. Parker to Commissioner of Indian Affairs, 16 December 1914, SAI Papers; Thomas, "Parker: 1881–1955," 8.

42. Parker to Mr. J. N. B. Hewitt, 25 July 1912, SAI Papers.

43. Parker to Mrs. Laura Cornelius Kellogg, 12 August 1912, SAI Papers.

44. Parker to Mrs. Rosa B. LaFlesche, 3 September 1912; Parker to Rev. Sherman Coolidge, 6 September 1912, SAI Papers.

45. "Great Council of Modern Redskins," *New York Times,* 12 September 1912; Parker to Charles E. Daganett, 13 September 1912, SAI Papers.

46. Editorial, *Quarterly Journal of the Society of American Indians* 1, no. 1 (1913), 134, 126, 171.

47. Parker to William DuBois, 28 February 1913, Arthur C. Parker Papers, NYSM.

48. W. E. B. DuBois, *Souls of Black Folk,* 27.

49. See Taylor, "W. E. B. DuBois's Challenge to Scientific Racism."

50. Parker to Joseph Keppler, 12 June 1912, fol. 1, P.2, no. 41, Keppler Papers, MAIL.

51. Parker to Allen Albert, Edq., 1 August 1914, SAI Papers.

52. Parker to Mr. F. A. Abbott, 5 November 1912; Parker to Chief Alexander John, 17 October 1912, SAI Papers.

53. Parker to Hon. W. C. Pollock, 17 October 1912; Parker to Mr. J. E. Shields, 28 October 1912; Parker to Mrs. Emma D. Goulette, 18 October 1912; Parker to Mr. W. E. Johnson, 18 October 1912; Parker to Mr. J. E. Shields, 28 October 1912, SAI Papers.

54. Parker to Rev. J. Enory, 31 October 1912; Parker to Prof. F. A. McKenzie, 30 November 1912; Parker to Miss Ellen L. Bulfinch, 18 October 1912; Parker to Mrs. Emma D. Goulette, 29 October 1912; Parker to Mr. George Shawnee, 19 October 1912, SAI Papers.

55. Parker to Mr. J. E. Shields, 28 October 1912; Parker to Mrs. Emma D. Goulette, 29 October 1912; Parker to Mr. M. R. Harrington, 31 October 1912; Parker to Rev. J. Enory, 31 October 1912, SAI Papers.

56. Parker to Prof. F. A. McKenzie, 29 October 1912; Parker to Dr. Carlos Montezuma, 6 November 1912, SAI Papers.

57. Parker to Prof. F. A. McKenzie, 29 October 1912; Parker to Mr. Arnold D. Moore, 21 November 1912, SAI Papers.

58. Parker to Mrs. Laura C. Kellogg, 26 November 1912, SAI Papers. For a discussion of the "tragedy" of Laura Kellogg's life, refer to Laurence M. Hauptman's valuable study "Designing Woman, Minnie Kellogg, Iroquois Leader."

59. Parker to Mr. Wm. J. Kershaw, 6 January 1913, SAI Papers.

60. Parker to Mr. Charles Daganett, 5 December 1912; Parker to Mr. Wm. J. Kershaw, 6 January 1913; Parker to Prof. McKenzie, 28 January 1913, SAI Papers.

61. Parker to Joseph Keppler, 20 December 1912, fol. 1, P.2, no. 44, Keppler Collection, MAIL.

62. Parker to Joseph Keppler, 17 March 1913, fol. 1, P.2, no. 45, Keppler Collection, MAIL.

63. Parker to Joseph Keppler 17 March 1913, fol. 1, P.2, no. 45, Keppler Collection, MAIL; Parker to Miss Alice H. Denomie, 26 March 1912; Parker to General R. H. Pratt, 13 August 1913, SAI Papers.

64. Parker to Mr. Sho-Tha Joe Pate, 26 March 1913; Parker to Mr. Thomas L. Sloan, 27 March 1913; Parker to Dr. McKenzie, 14 April 1913, SAI Papers.

65. Parker to Coolidge, 24 April 1913; Parker to Rev. Sherman Coolidge, 1 May 1913, SAI Papers.

66. Parker to Prof. F. A. McKenzie, 6 May 1913; Parker to Gen. Pratt, 10 May 1913, SAI Papers. See Moses, *Wild West Shows,* ch. 9.

67. Parker to Mr. Sherman Coolidge, 1 July 1913; Parker to Dr. Geo. F. Kunz, 14 July 1913, SAI Papers.

68. J. N. B. Hewitt to Parker, 25 August 1913; Parker to J. N. B. Hewitt, 29 August 1913, SAI Papers.

69. Parker to Dr. Carlos Montezuma, 4 September 1913, SAI Papers; Parker, "Third National Conference of Indians and Their Friends: by Arthur C. Parker," *Red Man,* November 1913, SAI Papers; Parker to Dr. Carlos Montezuma, 16 September 1913; Parker to General R. H. Pratt, 24 September 1913, SAI Papers.

70. Hertzberg, *Search for an American Indian Identity,* 111. However, Parker wrote to Montezuma on 4 September 1913: "Our membership, to date, is associate—419; active—357, which is about one hundred per cent increase over last year" (Arthur C. Parker Papers, NYSM).

71. Editorial, *Quarterly Journal of the Society of American Indians* 1, no. 4 (1913): 405.

72. Editorial, *Quarterly Journal of the Society of American Indians* 1, no. 4 (1913): 411–12.

73. "Third National Conference of Indians and Their Friends: by Arthur C. Parker," Red Man, November 1913; Parker to Colonel J. S. Lockwood, 20 December 1913, SAI Papers.

74. "Rochester Portraits" by Jack Moranz, Thursday, 1 May 1930, Rochester, N.Y., Arthur Caswell Parker Personal Scrapbook, "Masonic," Personal Papers of Arthur Caswell Parker, a.p.; Parker to Dear Friend, 10 November 1913; Parker to Prof. F. A. McKenzie, 27 October 1913, SAI Papers.

75. Parker to Mr. Henry Roe-Cloud, 12 November 1913, SAI Papers; Parker to Joseph Keppler, no. 18, 1913, fol. 1, P.2, no. 46, Keppler Collection, MAIL; Parker to Prof. F. A. McKenzie, 15 December 1913; Parker to Henry Roe-Cloud, 19 December 1913, SAI Papers.

76. Parker to Mr. Wm. J. Kershaw, 10 January 1914; Parker to Rev. Sherman Coolidge, 14 January 1914; Parker to Dear Friend, 1 February 1914, SAI Papers.

77. Frank G. Speck to Parker, 25 February 1914; Parker to Frank G. Speck, 25 February 1914, Arthur C. Parker Papers, NYSM

78. Parker to Mr. Chas. E. Daganett, 4 March 1914, Parker to Miss Susan Janney Allen, 13 May 1915; Parker to Prof. F. A. McKenzie, 7 March 1914; Parker to General Pratt, 2 April 1914; Parker to Mr. Henry Roe-Cloud, 31 July 1914, SAI Papers.

79. Parker to Mr. C. E. Daganett, 29 June 1914; Parker to General R. H. Pratt, 29 August 1914; Parker to Every Member, 1 September 1914, SAI Papers.

80. Anna Theresa Cooke was born in Whitehall, New York, on 8 October 1897 to Inez Livingston Cooke and Dr. William T. Cooke. Obituary, Anna C. Parker, *Naples (N.Y.) Record,* 25 July 1985, p. 2. See Parker's marriage details within his *Masonic International Who's Who* entry, Arthur Caswell Parker Papers, UR. See also Anna C. Parker Adoption Certificate, Arthur Caswell Parker Papers, UR; "Obituaries, Anna C. Parker," *Naples (N.Y.) Record,* n.d., VFLH Biography—Parker, Arthur C., Parker archives, RMSC.

81. Parker to Professor McKenzie, 26 September 1914, SAI Papers; "Proceedings of the Fourth Annual Conference Society of American Indians," SAI Papers; editorial, *Quarterly Journal of the Society of American Indians* 2, no. 3 (1914): 165–66.

82. Parker to Chauncey Yellow Robe, 26 October 1914; Parker to Mr. Moorehead, 7 November 1914, SAI Papers.

83. Parker to Hon. Edgar A. Merritt, 9 December 1915; Parker to Mr. George Masquequa, 31 October 1914, SAI Papers.

84. Parker to Joseph Keppler, 16 December 1914, fol. 1, P.2, no. 51, Keppler Collection, MAIL.

85. Parker to Francis E. Leupp, 23 December 1914, SAI Papers.

86. Parker to Dr. Thomas C. Moffett, 29 January 1915; Parker to Mr. F. Red Fox James, 25 February 1915, SAI Papers.

87. Parker to Dr. Carlos Montezuma, 1 March, 9 March, 7 April 1915, SAI Papers.

88. Parker to Mr. Chas. E. Daganett, 8 April 1915, SAI Papers. See Schrader, *Indian Arts and Crafts Board,* 33, 37, and Schwartz, "Red Atlantis Revisited."

89. Parker to Mr. Chas. E. Daganett, 39 April 1915, SAI Papers; editorial, *Quarterly Journal of the Society of American Indians* 3, no. 2 (1915): 86–97.

90. Parker to Rev. Sherman Coolidge, 19 April 1915, SAI Papers; Parker to Rev. Ernest H. Abbott, August 1915, SEDA.

91. Parker to Rev. N. S. Elderkin, 30 April 1915, Parker archives, RMSC; Parker to Mr. Frank E. McIntyre, 11 May 1915, SAI Papers.

92. Parker to Mr. Henry Roman Nose, 16 June 1915, SAI Papers.

93. Parker to General R. H. Pratt, 10 September 1915, SAI Papers; Parker, *Quarterly Journal of the Society of American Indians* 3, no. 4 (1915): 261–63; Parker to General R. H. Pratt, 21 March 1916, SAI Papers.

94. Parker to Mr. Henry K. Phillips, 11 October 1915; Parker to Rev. Sherman Coolidge, 4 November 1915, SAI Papers.

95. Parker to Mr. A. F. MacColl, 13 November 13, 1915; Parker, "American Indian, the Government and the Country," *Quarterly Journal of the Society of American Indians* 4, no. 1 (1915): 45.

96. Parker to Mr. Edgar A. Allen, 15 October 1915, Arthur Caswell Parker Papers, UR.

97. Parker to General R. H. Pratt, 10 September 1915; Parker to Dr. Montezuma, 10 September 1915; Parker to Mr. Chas. E. Daganett, 12 October 1915, SAI Papers.

98. Editorial, *American Indian Magazine* 4, no. 2 (1916): 113.

99. Editorial, *American Indian Magazine* 4, no. 2 (1916): 60–65. Emphasis in original.

100. Parker to Dr. Thomas Moffett, 18 March 1916, SAI Papers. Parker was surprised at Montezuma's choice of name for his new publication since he had always been "so against everything aboriginal" (Parker to R. H. Pratt, 22 May 1916, SAI Papers).

101. Parker to Mr. Thomas Sloan, 15 May 1916, SAI Papers.

102. Parker to Mr. Big Spring, 28 May 1916, SAI Papers.

103. Morgan, *League,* 141.

104. Parker to General R. H. Pratt, 19 June 1916, SAI Papers.

105. "Attack on Bureau System Stirs Blood of Indians in Sessions of Tribes Here," 1916, SAI Papers.

106. *American Indian Magazine* 4, no. 2 (1916): 113.

107. Parker to Mrs. Gertrude Bonnin, 15 December 1916, SAI Papers.

108. Parker to Mrs. Gertrude Bonnin, 2 January 1917, SAI Papers.

109. Parker to Congress of the United States, 25 January 1917, SAI Papers.

110. Parker to Hon. Theodore Roosevelt, 25 January 1917, SAI Papers.

111. Parker to Gen. R. H. Pratt, 7 February 1917; Parker to Mrs. Gertrude Bonnin, 2 March 2, 1917; Parker to Rev. and Mrs. Sherman Coolidge, 7 March 1917, SAI Papers.

112. Parker to Mrs. Gertrude Bonnin, 7, 12 March 1917, SAI Papers.

113. Parker to Dear Sioux Secretary, 27 March 1917, SAI Papers.

114. Editorial, *American Indian Magazine* 5, no. 1 (1917): 13.

115. Parker, "Indian Medicine and Medicine Men" (1928), 8.

116. *American Indian Magazine* 5, no. 1 (1917), 152; Parker to Hon. Newton D. Baker, July 1917, SAI Papers.

117. Parker to Dear Sioux Secretary, 29 July 1917; Parker to Sherman Coolidge, 2 October 1917; Parker to Mrs. Marie L. Baldwin, 2 October 1917, SAI Papers.

118. "Record of Arthur C. Parker," n.d., Arthur Caswell Parker Papers, UR.

119. Parker to Hon. James W. Wadsworth, Jr., 24 January 1918; Parker to William C. Hoag, 1918, SAI Papers.

120. Parker, "Making Democracy Safe for the Indians," an address made before the Federated Conference of the Friends of the Indians, Philadelphia, 21 January 1918, UR.

121. Parker to General Pratt, 21 February 1918; Parker to Charles D. Carter, 12 March 1918, SAI Papers.

122. "NY Indians Exempted from Citizenship: Dr. Arthur C. Parker Tells Why They Do Not Come Under Provisions of Bill," 5 January 1920, *Rochester Times-Union*, Indians Scrapbook, Personal Papers of Arthur Caswell Parker, a.p.

123. Parker to Walter Kennedy, 5 August 1918, Arthur C. Parker Papers, NYSM; Parker to Mr. George Thomas, 10 August 1918, SAI Papers. The Onondagas also declared war on Germany on July 31, 1918, after seventeen Onondaga circus performers suffered four months of imprisonment and hardship in Germany at the outbreak of the war. "Onondaga Indians Will Make War against Huns," *Rochester Democrat & Chronicle*, 1 August 1918, Arthur Caswell Parker Personal Scrapbook, "Seneca," Personal Papers of Arthur Caswell Parker, a.p.

124. Parker to Rev. Thomas C. Moffett, 28 June 1918, SAI Papers.

125. Gertrude Bonnin to Parker, 3 October 1918, Arthur C. Parker Papers, NYSM; Parker to Gertrude Bonnin, 14 October 1918, SAI Papers.

126. Montezuma, editorial, *Wassaja*, October 1918, 1.

127. Parker to Joseph Keppler, 30 December 1919, fol. 1, P.2, no. 52, Keppler Collection, MAIL.

128. Parker to Dr. Thomas C. Moffett, 1 July 1919, SAI Papers.

129. James Irving to Parker, 14 January 1920, Arthur C. Parker Papers, NYSM; Parker to James Irving, 22 January 1920, Arthur C. Parker Papers, NYSM.

130. Parker to James Irving, 20 February 1920, SAI Papers.

131. Parker to Mr. Burns, 8 November 1920, SAI Papers. See also "Indians Plan for Pow-Wow in Rochester," 27 October 1920, Cayuga Clippings Scrapbook, Personal Papers of Arthur Caswell Parker, a.p.

132. Parker to Charles Daganett, 13 October 1921, Arthur C. Parker Papers, NYSM.

133. See John Higham, *Strangers in the Land.*

134. "America the Melting Pot of Nationalities," typescript, Arthur C. Parker Papers, NYSM. Paper delivered 18 January 1922.

135. "Record of Arthur C. Parker," n.d., Arthur Caswell Parker Papers, UR.

136. Parker to the editor of the *Christian Science Monitor,* 15 April 1923, SAI Papers.

137. Parker to M. A. Stanley, 6 August 1923, SAI Papers.

138. Meriam et al., *Problem of Indian Administration.*

139. Parker, note, n.d., Arthur Caswell Parker Papers, UR.

140. "Legal Action against the State Recommended by Archaeologist," *Rochester Democrat & Chronicle,* 13 November 1920, Arthur Caswell Parker Personal Scrapbook, "Seneca," Personal Papers of Arthur Caswell Parker, a.p.

CHAPTER 6

1. Brother Arthur C. Parker, "Why All This Secrecy?" *The Builder,* 9 December 1923, 361, Arthur Caswell Parker Personal Scrapbook, "Masonic," Personal Papers of Arthur Caswell Parker, a.p.

2. Lewis, *Babbitt.*

3. Carnes, *Secret Ritual,* 2.

4. Tocqueville, *Democracy in America,* 129.

5. Clawson, *Constructing Brotherhood,* 4.

6. Carnes, *Secret Ritual,* ix.

7. Dumenil, *Freemasonry,* 220, 152–53.

8. Ibid., xi; Carnes, *Secret Ritual,* 7.

9. George Washington (initiated 1752), eight signatories of the Declaration of Independence (including Benjamin Franklin), and seventeen presidents, including Ronald Reagan, have admitted to being, or been claimed by the fraternity as, Freemasons.

10. See Gould, *History of Freemasonry,* 6. However, Carnes insists that Freemasonry began in London in the early 1700s (*Secret Ritual,* 22–24).

11. Dumenil, *Freemasonry,* xi.

12. Clawson, *Constructing Brotherhood,* 213; Carnes, *Secret Ritual,* 10.

13. Clawson, *Constructing Brotherhood,* 228; Carnes, *Secret Ritual,* 105.

14. See Knight, *Brotherhood,* 15, 30.

15. Quoted in ibid., 7.

16. Dumenil, *Freemasonry,* 9. See Parker's Masonic drama *The First Grand Lodge* for a reiteration of the Masonic rhetorical commitment to universality and reference to "Dissenters, Jews, Catholics and Quakers who have suffered persecution" (*The First Grand Lodge: A Masonic Drama,* original text

dramatized by Rochester Consistory Players, n.d, Arthur Caswell Parker Papers, UR).

17. Dumenil, *Freemasonry,* xiv.

18. Quoted in ibid., 122.

19. Dumenil, *Freemasonry,* 10, 123.

20. Ibid., 126, 151, xiii.

21. Clawson, *Constructing Brotherhood,* 11, 14, 15, 18.

22. Quoted in ibid., 13; Carnes, *Secret Ritual,* 256, ix.

23. Dumenil, *Freemasonry,* 88; Carnes, *Secret Ritual,* 3.

24. Brother Arthur C. Parker, "Why All This Secrecy?" 1923, Arthur Caswell Parker Personal Scrapbook, "Masonic," Personal Papers of Arthur Caswell Parker, a.p.

25. I rely on the version of his Masonic degrees given in his personal correspondence record of his *Masonic International Who's Who* entry, and not William R. Denslow to Parker, 17 September 1953, Arthur Caswell Parker Papers, UR. I am presuming that the former, because in his own handwriting, is more accurate. Denslow, in his capacity as business manager of *The Royal Arch Mason: Official Publication of the General Grand Chapter,* wrote to Parker in an effort to identify Freemasons who were of Indian descent. He also wrote to him as part of his preliminary research for his text "Freemasonry and the American Indian."

26. Parker joined Master's Lodge, No. 5, at Albany, where he also became a member of Temple Chapter, No. 5, R.A.M., of which he was chapter historian. He also joined DeWitt Clinton Council, R. & S.M., Temple Commandery, No. 5, K.T., and Buffalo Consistory, A. & A.S.R. See "Arthur Caswell Parker," Arthur Caswell Parker Personal Scrapbook, "Masonic," Personal Papers of Arthur Caswell Parker, a.p.

27. See Parker to Lester W. Herzog, 13 September 1918, Arthur Caswell Parker Papers, UR. Parker received the thirty-third degree in the Northern Jurisdiction of the A.S.S.R.

28. Knight, *Brotherhood,* 45. All thirty-three degrees and their titles are listed in Carnes, *Secret Ritual,* appendix B. Recent popular writers on Freemasonry have argued that there were up to one hundred degrees (see Lawrence, *Freemasonry,* 37).

29. Dumenil, *Freemasonry,* 74; see Carnes, *Secret Ritual,* 5.

30. Clawson, *Constructing Brotherhood,* 78–83.

31. Parker to Mr. George L. Tucker, 22 September 1923, Arthur Caswell Parker Papers, UR.

32. Alanson Skinner to Parker, 26 September 1923, Arthur Caswell Parker Papers, UR. See also the congratulatory letter from John M. Clarke to Parker, 8 September 1924, Arthur Caswell Parker Papers, UR.

33. Parker, "American Indian Freemasonry" (1919), 13, 22, 16.

34. Parker, "Freemasonry among the American Indians" (1920), 297, 298. For comparison, consult another version of the Mystic Potence ritual in Parker, *Indian How Book* (1927), 226–29.

35. Parker, *Secrets of the Temple* (1922); Parker, "Why All This Secrecy?" (1923).

36. Parker, "TTGOTGAOTU: Secrets of the Temple" (1922), 42.

37. Parker, "Why All This Secrecy?" (1923).

38. See F. W. Putnam to Parker, 1 September 1903, Arthur Caswell Parker Papers, UR; Parker, "American Indian Freemasonry" (1924), 137; and Parker, "Secret Medicine Societies of the Seneca" (1909), 161–85.

39. Parker, "New York Indians and the Craft" (1928), 41.

40. Parker, "Ely S. Parker—Man and Mason" (1961).

41. See Lawrence, *Freemasonry,* appendix 1, 149–52.

42. Knight, *Brotherhood,* 30–54.

43. Parker, "New York Indians and the Craft" (1928), 234.

44. Clawson, *Constructing Brotherhood,* 82.

45. Parker on the occasion of the Sesquicentennial of Franklin Lodge, No. 4, F. & A.M. of St. Albans, Vermont, 15 October 1947, Arthur Caswell Parker Papers, UR.

46. "A. Caswell Parker," *Who's Who in America,* vol. 27, 1952–1953. An example survives: Parker, "The First Grand Lodge, a Masonic Drama," n.d., typewritten, Arthur Caswell Parker Papers, UR.

47. See "other Masonic data" in the entry on Parker in the *Masonic International Who's Who,* n.d [post-1924], Arthur Caswell Parker Papers, UR.

48. Consider Fabian, *Time and the Other.*

49. Carnes, *Secret Ritual,* 22.

50. Knight, *Brotherhood,* 15.

51. Clawson, *Constructing Brotherhood,* 78–83.

52. Carnes, *Secret Ritual,* 29. Parker explained the fraternal fondness for initiation, arguing that "men enjoy the experience of opening their eyes upon strange surroundings and of seeing the unfamiliar objects of another world, not for the novelty of it only but to discover for themselves how they react to unfamiliar conditions." Brother Arthur C. Parker, "Why All This Secrecy?" Arthur Caswell Parker Personal Scrapbook, "Masonic," Personal Papers of Arthur Caswell Parker, a.p.

53. See Carnes, invoking Turner, *Secret Ritual,* 30–33.

54. Deloria, "White Sacheme and Indian Masons," 28–36, 37.

55. Quoted in Armstrong, *Warrior in Two Camps,* 70.

56. Parker, "New York Indians and the Craft" (1928).

57. See "Ely S. Parker—Man and Mason," (1961), and Kelsay, *Joseph Brant,* 172.

58. "A. Caswell Parker," *Masonic International Who's Who,* n.d [post-1924], Arthur Caswell Parker Papers, UR.

59. Parker, "Application for Membership, The National Society of Sons of the American Revolution," Arthur Caswell Parker Papers, UR. Parker served as president of the Rochester chapter of the Empire State Society of the Sons of the American Revolution from 1936 to 1938. In 1944, aged sixty-three, he published *A Paragraph History of the Rochester Chapter Sons of the American Revolution,* which described the group as "a reservoir of men who pledge their lives to the promotion of the Americanism of the Constitution and who rally to the defense of the blessings that their fore-

fathers achieved during the Revolutionary struggle" (Arthur Caswell Parker Papers, UR).

60. Hoxie, *Final Promise*, 241.

CHAPTER **7**

1. "'Museology.' Coined by Rochester Museum Head, Grows in Dignity," *Rochester Democrat & Chronicle*, 18 August, n.d., Arthur Caswell Parker Personal Scrapbook, "Rochester Museum," Personal Papers of Arthur Caswell Parker, a.p. As a descriptive term, "museology" may well have originated with Parker in 1916. Eventually, it gained further sanction when the Buffalo Museum began offering a course on the topic.

2. Parker was elected president of the New York Historical Association on June 30, 1945, after the death of the much-respected previous president, Dixon Ryan Fox. An association trustee from 1925, he was also a fellow of the Royal Society of Arts and of the American Association for the Advancement of Science.

3. "Record of Arthur C. Parker," n.d., Arthur Caswell Parker Papers, UR.

4. "Museum Curator Assumes Duties," n.d., Arthur Caswell Parker Personal Scrapbook, "Masonic," Personal Papers of Arthur Caswell Parker, a.p.

5. "Record of Arthur C. Parker," n.d., Arthur Caswell Parker Papers, UR.

6. "Dr. Parker's Coming," 12 March 1924, *Rochester Democrat & Chronicle*, Arthur Caswell Parker Personal Scrapbook, "Masonic," Personal Papers of Arthur Caswell Parker, a.p.

7. "State Jobs and State Positions," 8 December 1924; "State Loses Authority on Ancient Life," 7 December 1924, *Knickerbocker Press*, Arthur Caswell Parker Personal Scrapbook, "Masonic," Personal Papers of Arthur Caswell Parker, a.p.

8. "Noah T. Clarke Made State Archaeologist," *Rochester Democrat & Chronicle*, 1925, Arthur Caswell Parker Personal Scrapbook, "Miscellaneous," Personal Papers of Arthur Caswell Parker, a.p.

9. Parker to City Editor, *Albany Evening News*, 1 April 1925, Arthur Caswell Parker Personal Scrapbook, "Miscellaneous," Personal Papers of Arthur Caswell Parker, a.p.

10. "Museum Policy to Be Continued by New Curator," *Rochester Democrat & Chronicle*, December 1925, Arthur Caswell Parker Personal Scrapbook, "Miscellaneous," Personal Papers of Arthur Caswell Parker, a.p.

11. Quoted in Thomas, "Parker: 1881–1955," 9.

12. "Director Plans Museum of Strong Teaching Value," *Rochester Democrat & Chronicle*, n.d., Arthur Caswell Parker Personal Scrapbook, "Masonic," Personal Papers of Arthur Caswell Parker, a.p.

13. Stephen Thomas, interview by author, Rochester, March 1992.

14. Brown Goode quoted in Alexander, *Museum Masters*, 283, 288, 289, 304.

15. Parker, *Manual for History Museums* (1935), 195.

16. Goode had begun in 1888 by criticizing America's early museums for being trivial and populist, but had at the same time begun a crusade to make

museums accessible to more than just scholars and connoisseurs. See Goode, "Museum-History and Museums of History."

17. Parker, "Museums in Taverns" (1939), 121, and Parker, *Museologist* 13 (1938): 10.

18. See Burnham, "Cultural Interpretation of the Progressive Movement."

19. Parker, *Manual for History Museums* (1935), 328.

20. Dana, *New Museum*, 19.

21. Johnson, "John Cotton Dana," 50–98.

22. See Parker, review of *John Cotton Dana, A Life* (1940).

23. "Rochester," *Museum Service* 3, no. 3: 21; 15 March 1928, Arthur Caswell Parker Personal Scrapbook, "Historical," Personal Papers of Arthur Caswell Parker, a.p.

24. Thomas, "Parker—Leader and Prophet," 25.

25. Parker quoted in Zeller, "Parker and the Educational Mission," 114.

26. Parker, "Financing Museums of History" (1950), 7.

27. Parker, "Dr. Ritchie Departs" (1949).

28. "Good Museum Civic Asset, Says Curator," *Rochester Herald,* 3 December 1924, Arthur Caswell Parker Personal Scrapbook, "Rochester Museum," Personal Papers of Arthur Caswell Parker, a.p.

29. "Prehistoric Arms Factory Found Here, Parker Says," *Rochester Times-Union,* 8 April 1925, Arthur Caswell Parker Personal Scrapbook, "Miscellaneous," Personal Papers of Arthur Caswell Parker, a.p.

30. Parker, speech before the American Association of Museums, 1928, Arthur Caswell Parker Papers, UR.

31. "Dr. Parker Plans Visual History in Museum Groups," 31 January 1925; "Director Parker Reports Progress at City Museum," 1927, Arthur Caswell Parker Personal Scrapbook, "Rochester Museum," Personal Papers of Arthur Caswell Parker, a.p.

32. "Museum to get 2,000 Relics of Ancient Indian Village Found By Field Expedition," *Rochester Democrat & Chronicle,* 10 November 1925, Arthur Caswell Parker Personal Scrapbook, "Rochester Museum," Personal Papers of Arthur Caswell Parker, a.p.

33. "Parker Leaves Willow Point to Study New Site," Arthur Caswell Parker Personal Scrapbook, "Rochester Museum," Personal Papers of Arthur Caswell Parker, a.p.

34. "Museum Here Held Need for City Records: Rochester Lacks One Vital Mark of a 'Soul,' Says Arthur C. Parker," Arthur Caswell Parker Personal Scrapbook, "Museums," Personal Papers of Arthur Caswell Parker, a.p.

35. Parker, "Museizing the World" (1929), 21.

36. Parker, "Greeting" (1926).

37. "Director Plans Museum of Strong Teaching Value: Dr. Parker Outlines Aims in Expansion of Institution," *Rochester Democrat & Chronicle,* n.d., Arthur Caswell Parker Personal Scrapbook, "Masonic," Personal Papers of Arthur Caswell Parker, a.p.

38. Parker, *Museum Service,* June 1937, quoted in Thomas, "Parker: 1881–1955," 10.

39. Parker, *Museum Service,* February–March 1939, quoted in Thomas, "Parker: 1881–1955," 11.

40. Parker, "Visual Instruction an Important Factor in Modern Education," *Business & Commerce,* 15 September 1932, Arthur Caswell Parker Personal Scrapbook, "R. M. Collections," Personal Papers of Arthur Caswell Parker, a.p.

41. Quoted in Zeller, "Parker and the Educational Mission," 116.

42. Parker, "Making a Museologist" (1939). Emphasis in original.

43. Annie O. Peet also benefited from Parker's professional encouragement. She took on museum training at the Buffalo Museum of Science around 1929, in time passed a civil service exam, and ended up as a full-time extension director at the RMSC. She was forced to leave the RMSC after the budget cuts of the early 1930s, but in time was able to carry on Parker's approach at the Boston Children's Museum. See anonymous dissertation, "Arthur C. Parker, Director of the Rochester Museum of Arts and Sciences," n.d., Parker archives, RMSC.

44. Parker, *Manual for History Museums* (1935), 36.

45. Parker, "Measure of a Museuist" (1935); Parker, "Staff Notes: 1," 25 August 1937, Parker archives, RMSC.

46. Quoted in Thomas, "Parker: 1881–1955," 12.

47. Parker, "Director Walks Around" (1937), 195–96.

48. Parker, "Set of Standards for US Museums Urged at Session: Rochester Director Says Time for Standardization Has Come"; "Parker Urges High Standard for Museums," 20 May 1925, Arthur Caswell Parker Personal Scrapbook, "NY State Museum," Personal Papers of Arthur Caswell Parker, a.p.; Parker, "The Museum of History" (1928).

49. Quoted in Zeller, "Parker: Pioneer in American Museums," 52.

50. "Capitol Observer," *Knickerbocker Press,* Tuesday, 10 April 1923, Arthur Caswell Parker Personal Scrapbook, "Masonic," Personal Papers of Arthur Caswell Parker, a.p.

51. See Zeller, "Parker: Pioneer in American Museums," 49; "Rochester Has Its Own 'Sesqui' Memorial," 2 September 1926, Arthur Caswell Parker Personal Scrapbook, "Museum," Personal Papers of Arthur Caswell Parker, a.p.

52. Parker, "An Analytical History of the Seneca Indians," (1926). "Parker Says Municipal Museum Has Outgrown Quarters," *Rochester Democrat & Chronicle,* 4 November 1926, quoted in Zeller, "Parker: Pioneer in American Museums," 46.

53. "Museum Has Gone Forward, Says Parker," 1927, Arthur Caswell Parker Personal Scrapbook, "Rochester Museum," Personal Papers of Arthur Caswell Parker, a.p.

54. "Roosevelt Visits Municipal Museum," 30 September 1927, "Edgerton Park Has Exhibit of Industries," 30 September 1927, Arthur Caswell Parker Personal Scrapbook, "RM Collections," Personal Papers of Arthur Caswell Parker, a.p.

55. "New Museum Pamphlet Treats Science Work," *Rochester Democrat & Chronicle,* 21 October 1938, Arthur Caswell Parker Personal Scrapbook, "Rochester Museum," Personal Papers of Arthur Caswell Parker, a.p.

56. "Curator Gets Museum Hints in Old World"; "Fairy Faith of England Cited," 14 August 1928, Rochester Museum Scrapbook, Personal Papers of Arthur Caswell Parker, a.p.

57. Parker considered Stonehenge the world's greatest surviving monument.

58. "Museums Reflect Civic Interest," *Torch Light,* July 1929, Arthur Caswell Parker Personal Scrapbook, "Museum," Personal Papers of Arthur Caswell Parker, a.p.

59. Quoted in Zeller, "Parker and the Educational Mission," 119.

60. Zeller, "Parker: Pioneer in American Museums," 45.

61. Parker, *Museum Service* 4, no. 3 (1929): 19, 20.

62. The same year Parker picked up yet another award, the Numismatic Medal, American Numismatic Association, Rochester Branch.

63. During 1933, Parker would also allow the museum to be the venue for the eighth annual conference of the Six Nations Association, a group with an approach to Indian "betterment" broadly similar to that the SAI once had ("Going Back a Few Centuries," *Rochester Journal,* 4 November 1933, Arthur Caswell Parker Personal Scrapbook, "Seneca," Personal Papers of Arthur Caswell Parker, a.p.). See also Parker, "Educational and Museum Program for Letchworth State Park" (1929).

64. Parker, "Educational and Museum Program for Letchworth State Park" (1929), 76. For further information on Parker's relationship with Letchworth, see Beale, *William P. Letchworth,* 196–99.

65. "Arthur C. Parker Inspired Indian Groups at State Museum: Henri Marchand Assisted," *Evening News,* 28 March 1930; "Iroquois Indians in Miniature Displayed in Museum in Buffalo," *Rochester Democrat & Chronicle,* 1930, Arthur Caswell Parker Personal Scrapbook, "Miscellaneous," Personal Papers of Arthur Caswell Parker, a.p.

66. "Witchcraft in Indian Graves Linked to Ouija Board Slaying," *Rochester Evening,* 17 March 1930, Arthur Caswell Parker Personal Scrapbook, "Myths," Personal Papers of Arthur Caswell Parker, a.p. Parker did write a laudatory chronicle of Marchand's life for a hobby publication: Parker, "Henri Marchand," *Hobbies,* Buffalo, New York, March 1929, Arthur Caswell Parker Personal Scrapbook, "Miscellaneous," Personal Papers of Arthur Caswell Parker, a.p.

67. "Nancy Bowen Freed After Her Sentence"; "Henri Marchand on Honeymoon with Troy Sister's Stepdaughter," 25 November 1930, Arthur Caswell Parker Personal Scrapbook, "Myths," Personal Papers of Arthur Caswell Parker, a.p.

68. Parker to Joseph Keppler, 18 April 1930, fol. 1, P.2, no. 53, Keppler Collection, MAIL.

69. Parker, "New Name" (1930).

70. "Museum Use in Education Placed High," *Rochester Democrat & Chronicle,* 10 December 1930, Arthur Caswell Parker Personal Scrapbook, "Miscellaneous," Personal Papers of Arthur Caswell Parker, a.p.

71. "Would Make Letchworth Park Real Outdoor Museum of State History," *Rochester Times-Union,* 2 May 1930; "State Archaeologist Urges Parks in Genesee Country to Mark Historical Spots," *Rochester Herald,* 17 June 1923;

"Game Preserve Is Now Contemplated: Parker Backs the Idea," *Perry Herald,* December 1933, Arthur Caswell Parker Personal Scrapbook, "Historical," Personal Papers of Arthur Caswell Parker, a.p.

72. "Conversion of Indian Falls Wilds into a Park Maintained by State Appears to Be Popular Project: Archaeologist's Scheme," 21 August 1923, Arthur Caswell Parker Personal Scrapbook, "Historical," Personal Papers of Arthur Caswell Parker, a.p.

73. Parker, "Meaning of the Budget Cut" (1931).

74. "Art Museum Slows Up to Meet Budget" by Roy Yerger, n.d.; "Arts Museum Costs City But $2000 Yearly," *Rochester Times-Union,* 3 December 1931, Arthur Caswell Parker Personal Scrapbook, "Rochester Museum," Personal Papers of Arthur Caswell Parker, a.p.

75. "City Could Support Museum on Reorganization Savings Comptroller Tells Meeting," n.d., Arthur Caswell Parker Personal Scrapbook, "Rochester Museum," Personal Papers of Arthur Caswell Parker, a.p.

76. See Thomas, "Parker: 1881–1955," 12, and "Appointments and Resignations," box V, Arthur Caswell Parker Papers, UR. Consider also the story of Parker's temporary resignation after the museum's finance was cut by almost two-thirds to $17,000 in "Arthur Parker Resigns," *Museum News* 10, no. 1 (December 1932).

77. "State to Get Museum Plan to Give Work," *Rochester Democrat & Chronicle,* 11 November 1934, Arthur Caswell Parker Personal Scrapbook, "Rochester Museum," Personal Papers of Arthur Caswell Parker, a.p.

78. Parker, *Municipal Museum Annual Report,* 1934, RMSC.

79. See Zeller, "Parker: Pioneer in American Museums," 50; "State Historical Association Emphasizes Viewpoint," by Charles Messer. Stow, 25 August 1934, Arthur Caswell Parker Personal Scrapbook, "Historical," Personal Papers of Arthur Caswell Parker, a.p.

80. *The Museologist* was issued from 1935 to 1945 and was then revived in 1950.See Zeller, "Parker: Pioneer in American Museums," 56.

81. Kulik, "Designing the Past," 19; Schlesinger, "Dixon Ryan Fox."

82. Kulik, "Designing the Past," 18.

83. Quoted in Thomas, "Parker: 1881–1955," 15.

84. Parker, *Manual for History Museums* (1935), xii.

85. See Fein, *Frederick Law Olmsted.*

86. "Museum Head Lauds Country Park Project," n.d, Arthur Caswell Parker Personal Scrapbook, "Masonic," Personal Papers of Arthur Caswell Parker, a.p.

87. Parker, *Manual for History Museums* (1935), 4, 6 n. 6.

88. Parker, *Manual for History Museums* (1935), 194.

89. Lears, *No Place of Grace,* 78.

CHAPTER 8

1. There were several other investigations of Indian policy carried out during the 1920s. Aside from the Committee of One Hundred, the Board of Indian Commissioners reported, followed four years later by the Preston-

Engle Report, the Meriam Report, and then, from 1928 to 1933, the Senate Committee on Indian Affairs.

2. Meriam et al., *Problem of Indian Administration*, 51.

3. See John Collier, *From Every Zenith*, 93–100, 230–34, for the genesis of Collier's social reform ideas. Collier reveals the major influences on his ideas about Indians, his concern to recover a sense of community in the cities in his early work at the Peoples Institute in New York City, and also his fascination with the British colonial system of indirect rule. See also Kunitz, "Social Philosophy of John Collier."

4. John Collier, *From Every Zenith*, 126.

5. Berkhofer, *White Man's Indian*, 178.

6. See Tylor, "Anthropologists, Reformers, and the Indian New Deal."

7. See Krupat, *Ethnocriticism*, 81–100, for a discussion of Boas's work and his relationship to modernism and irony.

8. These include Kelly, "Indian Reorganization Act"; Costo, quoted in Philp, *Indian Self-Rule*, 48–52; Parman, *Navajos and the New Deal*; and McNickle, "Indian New Deal."

9. Schrader, *Indian Arts and Crafts Board*. Schrader's book has a distinct regional bias and deals mostly with Plains tribes.

10. McNickle quoted in Kelly, "Indian Reorganization Act," 310; Berkhofer, *White Man's Indian*, 184.

11. Hauptman, *Iroquois and the New Deal*, 29.

12. For a discussion of organized Indian opposition to New Deal policies, see Hauptman, "American Indian Federation and the Indian New Deal."

13. See Koppes, "From New Deal to Termination."

14. Hauptman, *Iroquois and the New Deal*, 137.

15. Ibid., 126–35.

16. For a general discussion of the WPA from Parker's perspective in this period, see "We Like the WPA" (1938).

17. Quoted in Hauptman, *Iroquois and the New Deal*, 129.

18. Quoted in ibid., 108. Fenton was offered the role of director of the Tonawanda Indian Community Building, but turned it down. He did, however, negotiate the water line from Akron to the building (William N. Fenton to author, 22 April 1999; William N. Fenton to Dr. Louis Balsam, 6 April 1937, series 1, ms. coll. no. 20, Fenton Papers, APS). Although Hauptman claims that Fenton's success at Tonawanda can be attributed to "his keen ability to speak the Seneca language" (*Iroquois and the New Deal*, 106–35), when I discussed this with Professor Emeritus Fenton in March 1993, he denied ever being fluent in the Seneca language.

19. Quoted in Hauptman, *Iroquois and the New Deal*, 130.

20. Quoted in ibid., 132.

21. Parker to Mr. Joseph Keppler, 1 February 1937, Keppler Collection, MAIL. See also "Tonawanda Indian Community House," series 1, ms. coll. no. 20, Fenton Papers, APS.

22. Parker to Dr. Lewis A. Wilson, 18 April 1934, Indian Arts Project Correspondence, RMSC. The Indian Arts Project was originally combined with another proposal to make an extensive archaeological survey of the Genesee

Valley. Proposal extract quoted in Hauptman, "Iroquois School of Art," 292, and "Proposal: Indian Arts Project," 30 July 1934, Indian Arts Project Correspondence, RMSC.

23. Parker scripted *The Romance of Old Indian Days,* WHAM (Rochester) radio broadcasts sponsored by the Rochester Museum of Arts and Sciences, twenty-eight broadcasts, from 1937 to 1938, and *Radio Broadcasts,* sponsored by the Rochester War Council Speaker's Bureau, eighty-six broadcasts from 1942 to 1943, Arthur Caswell Parker Papers, UR.

24. Parker had a long-standing association with the Cornplanter extended family. Edward Cornplanter had been one of his most significant informants on Seneca rituals and for Parker's book *Code of Handsome Lake* (1913). As Fenton has noted, "the whole family was involved in rounding up informants and collecting relics for the museums with which Parker was affiliated." See Fenton, "'Aboriginally Yours,' Jesse J. Cornplanter, Hah-Yonh-Wonh-Ish, The Snipe Seneca, 1889–1957."

25. Quoted in Hauptman, *Iroquois and the New Deal,* 157.

26. Parker, "Museum Motives Behind the New York Arts Project" (1935), 11.

27. Parker, "Museums Mean Business" (1941).

28. Parker to President Jones, 21 November 1935, Arthur Caswell Parker Papers, UR.

29. Hill, Cephas, William Fenton, and A. C. Parker, "The Indian Arts Project on the Tonawanda Reservation," 1 May 1935, series 1, ms. coll. no. 20, Fenton Papers, APS.

30. Hauptman, "Iroquois School of Art," 297. N.B.: While I was on Tonawanda in March 1992, Ramona Charles, who now is in charge of the Tonawanda Community House, told me about when she took up her post. Smith's paintings were in disrepair, torn, and not on display, and she struggled to get them restored.

31. Hauptman, *Iroquois and the New Deal,* 155; C. Carleton Perry to Cephas Hill, 26 July 1939, Indian Arts Project Correspondence, RMSC.

32. Quoted in Hauptman, "Iroquois School of Art," 300–301.

33. Parker, "Art Reproductions of the Seneca Indians" (1941); Parker, "Museum Motives Behind the New York Arts Project" (1935), 11.

34. Parker, "Museum Motives Behind the New York Arts Project" (1935), 11.

35. See Hauptman, "Iroquois School of Art," 301

36. Parker, "Indian Arts Project" (1936).

37. Parker to John M. Clarke, 16 June 1909, Arthur C. Parker Papers, NYSM; Hauptman, *Iroquois and the New Deal,* 142.

38. Morgan, *Annual Report of the Regents of the State of New York* 2 (1849): 84, quoted in Rose, "Lewis Henry Morgan Collection at the Rochester Museum," 52.

39. For further detail on both the Morgan collection and the circumstances of its production, see Rose, "Lewis Henry Morgan Collection at the Rochester Museum."

40. Parker, "Art Reproductions of the Seneca Indians" (1941).

41. Clifford, *Predicament of Culture*, 222.

42. Parker to Joseph Keppler, 10 July 1935, fol. 1, P.2, no. 60, Keppler Collection, MAIL.

43. Parker to President Jones, 21 November 1935, Arthur Caswell Parker Papers, UR; Parker to Joseph Keppler, 23 May 1938, fol. 1, P.2, no. 60, Keppler Collection, MAIL.

44. Parker to Chief Cornplanter, 29 August 1938, series 1, ms. coll. no. 20, Fenton Papers, APS.

45. "Indian Council Pays Honor to Museum Head," n.d., Arthur Caswell Parker Personal Scrapbook, "Masonic," Personal Papers of Arthur Caswell Parker, a.p.

46. Mable S. Smith to author, 18 August 1993, a.p.

47. Parker to Joseph Keppler, 28 January 1939, fol. 1, P.2, no. 58; Parker to Joseph Keppler, 20 October 1939, fol. 1, P.2, no. 63, Keppler Collection, MAIL.

48. Parker, "Has a Twenty Mule Team," *Museologist* (1939), quoted in Thomas, "Parker: 1881–1955," 13.

49. "Notes and News," *Museum Service*, no. 8, October–November 1939, Parker archives, RMSC.

50. "City Shares His Honor," 24 May 1939, Arthur Caswell Parker Personal Scrapbook, "Masonic," Personal Papers of Arthur Caswell Parker, a.p.

51. See Dorothy Parker, *Singing an Indian Song*, 93.

52. Parker to Mr. Joseph Keppler, 1 May 1940, fol. 1, P.2, no. 64, Keppler Collection, MAIL.

53. "Professional Record of Arthur C. Parker," n.d., Arthur Caswell Parker Papers, UR.

54. Quoted in Schrader, *Indian Arts and Crafts Board*, 244.

55. Hauptman, *Iroquois and the New Deal*, 159.

56. "[A] mysterious fire destroyed the building and what remained of the equipment," in Parker, "Art Reproductions of the Seneca Indians" (1941); also Parker to Joseph Keppler, 1 February 1937, Keppler Collection, MAIL.

57. See Cooper, "Arthur C. Parker."

58. "Professional Record of Arthur C. Parker," n.d., Arthur Caswell Parker Papers, UR; Thomas, "Parker: 1881–1955," 17.

59. Parker, "Rochester Museum of Arts and Sciences" (1943).

60. "Museum Medal Honors Lovejoy," *Rochester Times-Union*, 2 March 1941, Arthur Caswell Parker Personal Scrapbook, "R.M. Collections," Personal Papers of Arthur Caswell Parker, a.p.

61. "Museum Plans Fellowships for 6 in Area," *Rochester Times-Union*, 2 May 1939, Arthur Caswell Parker Personal Scrapbook, "R.M. Collections," Personal Papers of Arthur Caswell Parker, a.p.

62. "Indian Welfare Society to Meet," n.d., Arthur Caswell Parker Personal Scrapbook, "Rochester Museum," Personal Papers of Arthur Caswell Parker, a.p.

63. "Culture Boon Seen for City By Site Donor: Bausch Says Gift Was Inspired by Visits," *Rochester Democrat & Chronicle*, n.d, Arthur Caswell

Parker Personal Scrapbook, "Masonic," Personal Papers of Arthur Caswell Parker, a.p. See also "Notes on the R.M.S.C.," Parker archives, RMSC; Parker, "Million Dollar Museum" (1940); Parker, "Fortune Smiles on B. & L." (1940).

64. Parker, "Problems Ahead" (1940).

65. Parker, "Doesn't Like Economy" (1940).

66. "Parker Says He'll Stick to Museum Job," *Rochester Times-Union*, 6 December 1940, Arthur Caswell Parker Personal Scrapbook, "Rochester Museum," Personal Papers of Arthur Caswell Parker, a.p.

67. "School Cash Okayed for Museum Aid: Board to Pay for Services Given to Pupils," *Rochester Democrat & Chronicle*, n.d., Arthur Caswell Parker Personal Scrapbook, "Masonic," Personal Papers of Arthur Caswell Parker, a.p. There is also reference to another "time chest," part of which was designed to be opened during 2001 and another part in 2041. For further details on the financial wranglings surrounding the museum move, see also "Museum Drops 5 Workers in Economy Step: $10,000 Slash in Budget Cuts Allowances," *Rochester Democrat & Chronicle*, n.d, Arthur Caswell Parker Personal Scrapbook, "Masonic," Personal Papers of Arthur Caswell Parker, a.p.

68. Parker, "We Survey Our Plans" (1942). See also Zeller, "Parker: Pioneer in American Museums," 58.

69. "For All the People—New Museum Gets Cornerstone," *Rochester Democrat & Chronicle*, 24 April 1941, Arthur Caswell Parker Personal Scrapbook, "Masonic," Personal Papers of Arthur Caswell Parker, a.p.

70. Thomas, "Parker—Leader and Prophet of the Museum World."

71. "New Home of Rochester Museum Is Ultra-Modern," *Syracuse Herald,* 18 October 1941.

72. Thomas, "Parker: 1881–1955," 17.

73. Parker, "Fabric of Culture Must Not Be Broken" (1942); Parker, "War and the Museum Program," (1942); Parker, "Museums in the World Crisis" (1943).

74. Parker, chapter editor, "A Paragraph History of the Rochester Chapter of the Sons of the American Revolution," 1944, Personal Papers of Arthur Caswell Parker, a.p.

75. Parker, "Looking Ahead in Anthropology" (1942), 62.

76. Smith, *Eugenic Assault on America*, 6.

77. After Montagu, *Man's Most Dangerous Myth*, 47.

78. Sibley, Lindsay & Curr Co., advertisement, *Rochester Democrat & Chronicle,* 6 November 1945, 24.

CHAPTER 9

1. "Farewell Dinner Tendered Parker by Museum Staff," *Rochester Democrat & Chronicle,* 28 December 1945, Black Obituary Scrapbook, Personal Papers of Arthur Caswell Parker, a.p.

2. See "Resolution, Rochester Museum Association," Black Obituary Scrapbook, Personal Papers of Arthur Caswell Parker, a.p.

3. Herbert Gambrell, fol. 8, 9, Arthur C. Parker Papers, NYSM; Thomas, "Parker: 1881–1955," 17.

4. Parker oil portrait dedicated September 8, 1959. This was painted by Stanley Jay Gordon and funded in large part through the auspices of the Genesee Valley Hiking Club. See "Arthur C. Parker: Master of Hobbies," *Museum Service* 32 (March 1959): 40. The museum took its new name in 1968.

5. "Rochester's S.A.R. Medal Citizen Award," *Empire State Minute Man* 1, no. 1, UR.

6. "A. C. Parker Dies: Former Museum Head," *Chronicle* 1–2, 1955, VFLH Biography, "Parker, Arthur C.," RMSC.

7. "Seneca Nation Birth to Be Re-Enacted," *Rochester Democrat & Chronicle*," 15 August 1954, Black Obituary Scrapbook, Personal Papers of Arthur Caswell Parker, a.p.; Parker, "Local Area Is Famed in Literature," *Naples (N.Y.) Record*, 9 June 1948, p. 1.

8. "Indians Protest Flood Control Dam Project," *Syracuse Herald*, Sunday, 12 May 1946, Cayuga Clippings Scrapbook, Personal Papers of Arthur Caswell Parker, a.p.

9. Powell, "Engineering of Forever."

10. "Arthur C. Parker Dies; Former Museum Head," *Rochester Democrat & Chronicle*, Rochester, 2 January 1955, Black Obituary Scrapbook, Personal Papers of Arthur Caswell Parker, a.p.

11. Obituary, Mrs. Anne C. Parker, 30 July 1985; *Naples (N.Y.) Shopping News*, Black Obituary Scrapbook, Personal Papers of Arthur Caswell Parker, a.p.

12. Quoted in Thomas, "Parker: 1881–1955," 16.

13. "White Hikers Guests of Red Men at Strawberry Festival," 27 June 1902, Masonic Scrapbook, Personal Papers of Arthur Caswell Parker, a.p.

14. "Dr. Parker, Hobbyist," *Rochester Democrat & Chronicle*, 1 March 1955, Black Obituary Scrapbook, Personal Papers of Arthur Caswell Parker, a.p.

15. Harwood B. Dryer to Anne Parker, 12 February 1955, Black Obituary Scrapbook, Personal Papers of Arthur Caswell Parker, a.p.

16. "Dr. Parker, Hobbyist," *Rochester Democrat & Chronicle*, 3 January 1955, Black Obituary Scrapbook, Personal Papers of Arthur Caswell Parker, a.p.; Thomas, "Arthur C. Parker: Master of Hobbies."

17. "Arthur Caswell Parker, Sc.D., L.H.D.," *Naples (N.Y.) Record*, 5 January 1955, Black Obituary Scrapbook, Personal Papers of Arthur Caswell Parker, a.p.

18. "Dr. Arthur C. Parker," *Rochester Times Union*, 4 January 1955, Black Obituary Scrapbook, Personal Papers of Arthur Caswell Parker, a.p.

19. "In conclusion," *Rochester Democrat & Chronicle*, 16 January 1955, Black Obituary Scrapbook, Personal Papers of Arthur Caswell Parker, a.p.; "Nundawaga Society Seeks Talent for Coming Pageant," *Naples (N.Y.) Record*, 14 July 1954, p. 5, Buff File 1, Personal Papers of Arthur Caswell Parker, a.p.

20. Parker quoted in "Seneca Nation Birth to Be Re-enacted," *Rochester Democrat & Chronicle*, 15 August 1954, Buff File 1, Personal Papers of Arthur Caswell Parker, a.p.

21. "Pageant Site Dedicated by Seneca Indians," *Chronicle-Express* (Penn Yan, N.Y.), 10 June 1954, Buff File 1, Personal Papers of Arthur Caswell Parker, a.p.

22. "Proud Senecas Return in Historical Pageant," *Naples (N.Y.) Record,* 8 September 1954, p. 1, Black Obituary Scrapbook, Personal Papers of Arthur Caswell Parker, a.p.

23. "Dr. Arthur C. Parker, Noted Iroquois Authority, Dies," *Geneva Daily Times,* 3 January 1955; "Hiawatha Was Here!"; *Naples (N.Y.) Record,* 20 October 1954, Black Obituary Scrapbook, Personal Papers of Arthur Caswell Parker, a.p.

24. Parker to Dr. Frank G. Speck, 10 November 1945, series 1, Fenton Papers, APS.

25. Parker to Professor Paul A. Wallace, 17 August 1945, series 1, ms. coll. no. 20, Fenton Papers, APS.

26. Parker, "The Amazing Iroquois," p. 29, series 1, ms. coll. no. 20, Fenton Papers, APS

27. Parker to Dr. Paul A. W. Wallace, 28 July 1947, 6 August 1947; Dr. Paul A. Wallace to Parker, 10 August 1947, series 1, ms. coll. no. 20, Fenton Papers, APS.

28. "200 Indian Lore Enthusiasts Hear 'Amazing Iroquois' Talk," *Syracuse Post Standard,* 11 November 1950, Cayuga Clippings Scrapbook, Personal Papers of Arthur Caswell Parker, a.p.

29. Parker to Dr. Paul A. W. Wallace, 24 May 1949, series 1, ms. coll. no. 20, Fenton Papers, APS.

30. Parker to Drs. John Witthoft and Paul A. Wallace, 23 February 1954, series 1, ms. coll. no. 20, Fenton Papers, APS.

31. Parker to Dr. Wallace, 19 July 1954, series 1, ms. coll. no. 20, Fenton Papers, APS.

32. Parker, "The Role of Wampum in the Colonial Era," *Galleon: Bulletin for the Society of Colonial History* (Schenectady, N.Y.), no. 14 (1954): 1–4, Buff File 1, Personal Papers of Arthur Caswell Parker, a.p.

33. Henry Allen Moe to Parker, 31 December 1954, Black Obituary Scrapbook, Personal Papers of Arthur Caswell Parker, a.p.

34. "Resolution: Lewis H. Morgan Chapter, New York State Archeological Association," Black Obituary Scrapbook, Personal Papers of Arthur Caswell Parker, a.p.

35. For a delineation of the main features of myth, legend, and folklore, see William Bascom, "Forms of Folklore."

36. Parker, "Myths Have Real Meaning," *Rochester Commerce,* 8 December 1930, Arthur Caswell Parker Papers, UR.

37. Parker, ed., *Myths and Legends of the New York State Iroquois* (1908), 12.

38. Parker to Dr. J. M. Vander Veer, 20 November 1912, SAI Papers.

39. "Mound Builders of America to Have Branch in Albany," 28 March 1920, *Knickerbocker Press,* Cayuga Clippings Scrapbook, Personal Papers of Arthur Caswell Parker, a.p.

40. "National Counselor Enlists Aid of Boy Scouts to Rescue Relics," 13 May 1932, *Rochester Democrat & Chronicle,* Cayuga Clippings Scrapbook, Personal Papers of Arthur Caswell Parker, a.p.; "Scouts May Save America's Pre-History," *Scouting* 20 (May 1932), 148.

41. Warrior, "Reading American Indian Intellectual Traditions."

42. "A Conserver of Myths," *New York Times,* 12 March 1924, Masonic Scrapbook, Personal Papers of Arthur Caswell Parker, a.p.

43. Parker, *Seneca Myths and Folktales* (1923), xxvi, xxviii, xxxii.

44. See Fenton, introduction to Parker, *Seneca Myths and Folktales* (1923), xvii, and Fenton, "This Island, the World on the Turtle's Back."

45. Hamell, introduction to Parker, *Skunny Wundy* (1926), xvii.

46. Parker, *Skunny Wundy* (1926), 60.

47. Parker, *Indian How Book* (1927), 14, 188.

48. Parker, *Indian How Book* (1927), 202, 132.

49. Parker, *Indian How Book* (1927), 333.

50. Lester Hochgraf to author, 9 May 1992, a.p.

51. Parker, *Rumbling Wings* (1928), 216–18.

52. Griswold, *Audacious Kids,* introduction, 242.

53. Parker, *Gustango Gold* (1930), 138.

54. Parker to Professor Wallace, 16 May 1950, ms. coll. no. 20, series 1, Fenton Papers, APS.

55. Parker, *Red Streak of the Iroquois* (1950), 10.

56. "Many Indians Distinguished Craft Members," *Masonic Tribune,* Seattle, Wash.), n.d., Indians Scrapbook, Personal Papers of Arthur Caswell Parker, a.p.

57. Parker to Dr. Paul A. W. Wallace, 28 July 1953, series 1, ms. coll. no. 20, Fenton Papers, APS.

58. Parker, *Red Jacket, Last of the Seneca* (1952), 80, 196, 210.

59. "Arthur Caswell Parker," *Naples (N.Y.) Record,* 5 January 1955, p. 1; "A. C. Parker Dies; Museum Expert," *New York Times,* 3 January 1955; "Dr. Parker Dies; Expert on Indians," *New York Herald Tribune,* 4 January 1955; "An Eminent Historian," *Geneva Daily Times,* 4 January 1955; "Dr. A. C. Parker, Expert on Indians," *New York World,* 3 January 1955, Black Obituary Scrapbook, Personal Papers of Arthur Caswell Parker, a.p.

60. See Yeuell, "Ely Samuel Parker."

61. Refer to Parker's letter of appreciation for his Philalethes Life Fellowship; Parker, "Meaning of Symbols" (1955).

62. "Personal Remarks Concerning Dr. Arthur C. Parker at his Funeral Service," Black Obituary Scrapbook, Personal Papers of Arthur Caswell Parker, a.p.

63. Parker to Mrs. A. Parker, poem, Personal Papers of Arthur Caswell Parker, a.p.

64. Paul V. Miller to Dear Friend, 10 March 1955, Black Obituary Scrapbook, Personal Papers of Arthur Caswell Parker, a.p.

65. It seems that Parker had in fact agreed to give a paper during 1955, at an Aurora meeting of the American Lodge of Research, on the Masonic involvement of his great-uncle Ely (Temple R. Hollcroft to Mrs. Parker, 3 January 1955, Second Black Obituary Scrapbook, Personal Papers of Arthur Caswell Parker, a.p.).

66. Laurence Vail Coleman to Mrs. Arthur C. Parker, 24 January 1955, Black Obituary Scrapbook, Personal Papers of Arthur Caswell Parker, a.p.

67. Ray Fadden to Anne Parker, 17 January 1955, Black Obituary Scrapbook, Personal Papers of Arthur Caswell Parker, a.p.; Ray Fadden, interview by author, Onchiota, New York, October 1997.

68. "Famous American Indians: Arthur C. Parker."

69. Quoted in Hertzberg, *Search for an American Indian Identity*, 57.

Selected Bibliography

I list here only writings that I have cited in this book. The list is in three sections: archival sources, Parker's writings, and other sources. Parker's writings are listed chronologically, but with those appearing in the same year ordered alphabetically. Among the archival sources are Parker's personal papers, which include his personal scrapbooks, associated folders, personal photographs, and other material. Parker's published and unpublished writings are too numerous to list in full. Readers seeking a bibliography of his complete works should consult the entry below under Catherine D. Hayes.

ARCHIVAL SOURCES AND ABBREVIATIONS

Joseph Keppler Collection, Huntington Free Library and Reading Room, Museum of the American Indian Library, Bronx, N.Y. (MAIL). Contains letters from Parker to Keppler from 1905 to 1940.

Arthur Caswell Parker archives and Indian Arts Project Correspondence at the Rochester Museum and Science Center, Rochester, N.Y. (RMSC).

Arthur C. Parker Papers, 1915–1953, and the Society of American Indians Records, 1911–1916, held at the New York State Museum (NYSM) and State Education Department, Albany, N.Y. (SEDA).

Arthur Caswell Parker Personal Scrapbook, William Beauchamp Collection, SC17369, filmed by New York State Library, July 1992, c/o New York State Museum, Cultural Education Center, Albany, N.Y. (NYSM).

Arthur Caswell Parker Papers, 1860–1952, Rush Rhees Library, University of Rochester, N.Y., donated by Parker in 1952 and 1953 (UR).

William N. Fenton Papers, American Philosophical Society, Philadelphia, Pa. (APS).

Ely S. Parker Papers at the Buffalo and Erie Historical Society, Buffalo, N.Y. (BEHS).

Papers of the Society of American Indians, ten microfilm reels, held at University of Rochester, N.Y. (SAI Papers).

Personal Papers of Arthur Caswell Parker, eleven scrapbooks and associated folders, author's possession (a.p.).

WRITINGS OF ARTHUR CASWELL PARKER

"The Triumph of Woman's Wit. A Dream, by Moonstone, pseudonym of Arthur Caswell Parker." *Dickinson Union* 6 (December 1900): 47–50.

"Excavations in an Erie Indian Village and Burial Site at Ripley, Chautauqua Co., N.Y." *New York State Museum Bulletin* 117 (1907): 459–554.

Ed., *Myths and Legends of the New York State Iroquois, By Harriet Maxwell Converse (Ya-ié-wa-noh). New York State Museum Bulletin* 125 (1908).

"Neh Ho-Noh-Ki-Noh-Gah, the Guardians of the Little Waters, a Seneca Medicine Society." In *Myths and Legends of the New York State Iroquois, By Harriet Maxwell Converse (Ya-ié-wa-noh),* edited by Arthur C. Parker. *New York State Museum Bulletin* 125 (1908): 149–76.

"Secret Medicine Societies of the Seneca." *American Anthropologist,* n.s., 11 (April–June 1909): 161–85.

"Snow-Snake as Played by the Senecas." *American Anthropologist* 11, no. 2 (1909): 250–56.

"Fate of the New York State Collections in Archeology and Ethnology in Capital Fire." *American Anthropologist* 13 (January–March 1911): 169–71.

"The Philosophy of Indian Education." *Proceedings* of the First Annual Conference of the Society of American Indians (1912): 68–76.

"Progress for the Indian." *Southern Workman* 41 (November 1912): 628–35.

"Congress and the Indian Problem." *Quarterly Journal of the Society of American Indians* 1 (April–June 1913): 95–97.

"A Plea for Social Survey." *Quarterly Journal of the Society of American Indians* 1 (April 1913): 107–14.

"The Real Tragedy of the Red Race." *Quarterly Journal of the Society of American Indians* 1 (October–December 1913): 345–50.

"The Real Value of Higher Education for the Indian." *Quarterly Journal of the Society of American Indians* 1 (July–September 1913): 278–84.

"Report of the Archeology and Ethnology Section." *New York State Museum Bulletin* 164 (October–December 1913): 45–57. Ninth report of the director.

"What Makes the Indian a Problem?" *Quarterly Journal of the Society of American Indians* 1 (April–June 1913): 103–14.

"The American Indian—What Is He?" *Quarterly Journal of the Society of American Indians* 2 (April–June 1914): 109–19.

"The Awakened American Indian." *Quarterly Journal of the Society of American Indians* 2 (October–December 1914): 269–74.

"Blood Mixture among Races." *Quarterly Journal of the Society of American Indians* 2 (October–December 1914): 262–65.

"The Discovery of America as an Incentive to Human Achievement." *Quarterly Journal of the Society of American Indians* 2 (October–December 1914): 265–68.

"Indian Blood." *Quarterly Journal of the Society of American Indians* 2 (October–December 1914): 261–62.

"The League of Peace." By Gawasa Wanneh (pseudonym of Arthur Caswell Parker). *Quarterly Journal of the Society of American Indians* 2 (July–September 1914): 191–95.

"The Legal Status of the American Indian." Lake Mohonk Conference on the Indian and Other Dependent Peoples. *Thirty-Second Annual Report* (1914): 77–82.

"The Legal Status of the American Indian." *Quarterly Journal of the Society of American Indians* 2 (July–September 1914): 213–18.

"Let Us Discover Human Elements of the Indian Problem." *Quarterly Journal of the Society of American Indians* 2 (July–September 1914): 183–84.

"My Race Shall Live Anew." A poem by Alnoba Waubunaki (pseudonym of Arthur Caswell Parker). *Quarterly Journal of the Society of American Indians* 2 (April–June 1914): 125.

"The Quaker City Meeting of the Society of American Indians." *Quarterly Journal of the Society of American Indians* 2 (January–March 1914): 56–59.

"Report of the Archeology and Ethnology Section." *New York State Museum Bulletin* 173 (April–June 1914): 93–102. Tenth report of the director.

"The Road to Competent Citizenship." *Quarterly Journal of the Society of American Indians* 2 (July–September 1914): 178–83.

"The Robins' Song." A poem by Alnoba Waubunaki (pseudonym of Arthur Caswell Parker). *Quarterly Journal of the Society of American Indians* 2 (July–September 1914): 190.

"The American Indian, the Government and the Country." *Quarterly Journal of the Society of American Indians* 4 (April–June 1915): 45.

"Industrial and Vocational Training in Indian Schools." *Quarterly Journal of the Society of American Indians* 3 (April–June 1915): 86–97.

"Problems of Race Assimilation in America, with Special Reference to the American Indian." *American Indian Magazine* 4 (October–December 1916): 285–304.

"The Social Elements of the Indian Problem." *American Journal of Sociology* 22 (September 1916): 252–67.

"Lewis Henry Morgan." *American Indian Magazine* 5 (spring 1917): 3.

"The Constitution of the Five Nations, a Reply." *American Anthropologist*, n.s., 20 (January–March 1918): 120–24.

"Habitat Groups in Wax and Plaster." *Museum Work* 1 (December 1918): 78–85.

"Making Democracy Safe for the Indians." *American Indian Magazine* 6 (spring 1918): 25–29.

"American Indian Freemasonry." *Buffalo Consistory* (Buffalo, N.Y.), A.A.S.R. N.M.J.U.S.A., 1919.

The Life of General Ely S. Parker, Last Grand Sachem of the Iroquois and General Grant's Military Secretary. Buffalo Historical Society Publications 23. Buffalo, N.Y.: Buffalo Historical Society, 1919.

"Presentation and Unveiling of the Morgan Tablet." The Morgan Centennial Celebration at Wells College, Aurora. New York State Archeological Association, Lewis H. Morgan Chapter. *Researches and Transactions* 1, no. 3 (1919): 23–27.

"Report of the Archeology and Ethnology Section." *New York State Museum Bulletin* 207–208 (October–December 1919): 69–73. Fourteenth report of the director.

"The Archeological History of New York." *New York State Museum Bulletin* 235–238 (July–October 1920).

"Freemasonry among the American Indians." *The Builder* 6 (November 1920): 295–298.

"Indian Tribal Government a Failure." *State Service* 4 (February 1920): 99–102.

Letchworth Memorial Address. William Pryor Letchworth Memorial Association. *Proceedings of the Seventh Annual Meeting,* 26 May 1920, 10–16.

"The New York Indian Complex and How to Solve It." New York State Archeological Association, Lewis H. Morgan Chapter. *Researches and Transactions* 2, no. 1 (1920): 20.

"Report of the Archeology and Ethnology Section." *New York State Museum Bulletin* 219–220 (1920): 99–120. Fifteenth report of the director.

"A Solution of the New York Indian Problem." Report to State Museum, State Education Department, 1920.

"New York Indians." *Southern Workman* 50 (April 1921): 155–60.

The Archeological History of New York. 2 vols. Albany: University of the State of New York, 1922. Originally published in *New York State Museum Bulletin* 235–238 (July–October 1920).

"Report of the Archeology and Ethnology Section." *New York State Museum Bulletin* 239–240 (1922): 41–49. Seventeenth report of the director.

TTGOTGAOTU: Secrets of the Temple. Buffalo, N.Y.: Buffalo Consistory, A.A.S.R., 1922.

"Method in Archeology." Ontario Provincial Museum, Toronto. *Thirty-third Annual Archeological Report,* 1923: 55–61.

Seneca Myths and Folk Tales. Buffalo Historical Society Publications 27. 1923. Reprint, Lincoln: University of Nebraska Press, 1989.

"Why All This Secrecy?" *The Builder* 9 (December 1923): 361.

"American Indian Masonry." *The Builder* 10 (May 1924): 137–38.

"Fundamental Factors in Seneca Folk Lore." *New York State Museum Bulletin* 253 (July 1924): 49–66. Reprinted from the nineteenth report of the director.

"Report of the Archeology and Ethnology Section." *New York State Museum Bulletin* 251 (1924): 38–44. Eighteenth report of the director.

"The Status of New York Indians." *New York State Museum Bulletin* 253 (July 1924): 67–82. Reprinted from the nineteenth report of the director.

"Unhistorical Museums." *Museum Work* 6, no. 5 (January–February 1924): 155–58.

"Unhistorical Museums or Museums of History, Which?" New York State Historical Association. *Quarterly Journal of the New York State Historical Association* 5 (July 1924): 256–63.

"Greeting." *Museum Service* 1, no. 1 (15 April 1926): 1.

"American Indian Freemasonry." *Masonic Outlook,* February 1926.

"An Analytical History of the Seneca Indians." New York State Archeological Association, Lewis H. Morgan Chapter. *Researches and Transactions* 6 (1926): 162.

"An Approach to a Plan for Historical Society Museums." *Museum Work* 8, no. 2 (July–August 1926): 47–56.

"The Museum Idea." *Museum Service* 1, no. 1 (15 April 1926): 3.

Skunny Wundy: Seneca Indian Tales. New York: George H. Doran, 1926. Reprint, Syracuse, N.Y.: Syracuse University Press, 1994.

"The Amazing Iroquois." *Art and Archeology* 23 (March 1927): 99–108.

The Indian How Book: Authentic Information on American Indian Crafts, Customs, Food and Clothing, Religion and Recreations. New York: George H. Doran, 1927. Reprint, New York: Dover, 1975.

"Government and Institutions of the Iroquois," by Lewis Henry Morgan. Introduction and editorial notes by Arthur Caswell Parker. New York State Archeological Association, Lewis H. Morgan Chapter. *Researches and Transactions* 7, no. 1 (1928).

"Indian Medicine and Medicine Men." *Archaeological Report of the Ontario Provincial Museum* 8 (1928): 3–11.

"Lewis Henry Morgan." Speech to Labor Forum, Rochester, New York, November 1928.

"A Museum for Rochester—?" *Museum News* 3, no. 7 (15 September 1928): 52–53.

"The Museum of History vs. the Historical Society Exhibit." *Museum Service* 3, no. 6 (15 June 1928): 43–46.

"New York Indians and the Craft." *Masonic Outlook,* October 1928, 10.

Rumbling Wings and Other Indian Tales. New York: Doubleday Doran, 1928.

"An Educational and Museum Program for Letchworth State Park." *New York State Museum Bulletin* 284 (December 1929): 73–79. Reprinted from the twenty-third report of the director.

"Modern Museums Stand for Commerce." *Rochester Commerce,* 24 June 1929, p. 5.

"Museizing the World." *Museum Service* 4, no. 3 (15 March 1929): 19–22.

"Solving the New York Indian Problem." *Six Nations* 3 (January 1929): 1–3.

(Gawaso Wanneh). *Gustango Gold.* Garden City, N.Y.: Doubleday Doran, 1930.

"Myths Have Real Meaning." *Rochester Commerce,* 8 December 1930, p. 6.

"A New Name." *Museum Service* 5, no. 1 (15 January 1930): 2.

"The Meaning of the Budget Cut." *Museum Service* 6, no. 3–10 (suppl.) (15 December 1931): 1–2.

"Scouts May Save America's Pre-History." *Scouting* 20 (May 1932): 148.

"The Place of the Small History Museum." Speech to American Association of Museums, Toronto, 1 June 1934.

"Iroquois Studies since Morgan's Investigations." Speech to Russian Academy of Science, September 1935.

"Lewis H. Morgan and the League of the Iroquois." Speech to Russian Academy of Science, 1935. UR.

A Manual for History Museums. New York State Historical Association Series, no. III. New York: Columbia University Press, 1935.

"The Measure of a Museuist." *Museum Service* 8, no. 3 (15 September 1935): 12–13.

"Museum Motives Behind the New York Arts Project." *Indians at Work* 2, no. 15 (June 1935): 11–12.

"The Small History Museum." *New York History* 16 (April 1935): 189–95.

"The Indian Arts Project." *Museum Service* 9, no. 1 (15 January 1936): 8–9.

"The Museum Moves Forward." *Museum Service* 9, no. 1 (15 January 1936): 3–4.

"A Museum Sponsors an Indian Arts Project." *Social Welfare Bulletin* 7 (January–February 1936): 12–14.

"Archeology Adopts a New Policy." *Museum Service* 10, no. 7 (15 September 1937): 160.

"The Director Walks Around, An Informal Talk to Those Who Work Together." *Museum Service* 10, no. 9 (15 November 1937): 195–96.

"Does Rochester Need a New Museum Building?" *Museum Service* 10, no. 9 (15 November 1937): 193.

"We Like W.P.A." *Museum Service* 11, no. 7 (15 September 1938): 146.

"A City with Vision and a Man." *Museum Service* 12, no. 5 (May–June 1939): 97.

"Has a Twenty Mule Team!" *Museologist,* no. 15 (22 March 1939): 9.

"Is There an Unmixed Race?" *Museum Service* 12, no. 2 (February–March 1939): 25.

"Making a Museologist." *Museum Service* 12, no. 5 (May–June 1939): 99.

"Making Mockery of Archeology." *Museum Service* 12, no. 3 (March–April 1939): 52.

"A Museum Is a Place in Which to Live!" *Museum Service* 12, no. 2 (February–March 1939): 27.

"Museums Are One Thing—Exhibits Are Another." *Museum Service* 12, no. 1 (January–February 1939): 3.

"Museums in Taverns." *Museum Service* 12, no. 6 (June–July 1939): 121.

"Museums Succeed Everywhere." *Museum Service* 12, no. 8 (October–November 1939): 192.

"Twentieth Century Time Chest." *Museum Service* 12, no. 7 (September–October 1939): 147.

"Will Our Culture Survive?" *Museum Service* 12, no. 4 (April–May 1939).

"Analyzing the Museum Worker." *Museum Service* 13, no. 8 (October 1940): 147.

"Doesn't Like Economy." *Museologist* 22 (22 December 1940): 11.

"Fortune Smiles on B. & L." *Museum Service* 13, no. 9 (November 1940): 170.

"The Genesee Country Historical Federation." *Museum Service* 13, no. 8 (October 1940): 151.

"Lewis Henry Morgan, Social Philosopher." Rochester Museum of Arts and Sciences. *Staff Lectures and Addresses.* 1940.

"A Million Dollar Museum." *Museum Service* 13 (November 1940): 3.

"The Museum a Complex Organization." *Museum Service* 13, no. 9 (November 1940): 169.

"The Museum and Science." *Museum Service* 13, no. 1 (January–February 1940): 1.

"Problems Ahead." *Museum Service* 13, no. 9 (November 1940): 170.

"The Realistic Idealism of Lotze: Being a Review of the Philosophy of Rudolph Hermann Lotze (1817–1881)." Rochester Museum of Arts and Sciences. *Staff Lectures and Addresses.* 1940.

Review of *John Cotton Dana, A Life. Museum Service* 13, no. 8 (July 1940): 167.

"Art Reproductions of the Seneca Indians." *Museum Service* 14, no. 9 (November 1941): 31–33.

"Bausch Hall of Science and History of the Rochester Museum." *Science Monthly* 53 (July 1941): 96–97.

"Edward Bausch Hall of Science and History. Rochester Museum of Arts and Sciences. *Guide Bulletin* 7 (1941): 4.

"Museums Mean Business." *Museum Service* 14, no. 9 (November 1941): 26.

"The Fabric of Culture Must Not Be Broken." *Museum Service* 15, no. 2 (February 1942): i.

"Looking Ahead in Anthropology." *Museum Service* 15, no. 3 (March 1942): 62–63.

"Museum Regulations." *Museum Regulations No. 9* (Rochester Museum of Arts and Sciences). 1942.

"War and the Museum Program." *Museum Service* 15, no. 2 (February 1942): 37–39.

"We Survey Our Plans." *Museum Service* 15, no. 1 (January 1942): 7–12.

"Making People Like Museums." *Museologist* 32 (22 June 1943): 1.

"Museums in the World Crisis." *Museum News* 21 (1 September 1943): 6–8.

"The Rochester Museum of Arts and Sciences." *Museum Journal* 43, no. 6 (September 1943): 81–84.

"Rochester (N.Y) Museum of Arts and Sciences" (description of new buildings and activities). *Museum Journal,* September 1943, 81–84.

"The Amazing Iroquois: Niagara the Keystone of the Continent." Speech, Cooperstown, New York, 1945.

"The Amazing Iroquois: Land of the Indians' Pride." Speech, Cooperstown, New York, 5 April 1946.

"Lewis Henry Morgan as Social Philosopher." *Union (College) Worthies* 1 (1946): 10–15.

"Dr. Ritchie Departs." *Museum Service* 2, no. 7 (September 1949): 77.

"Financing Museums of History: Analyze before You Ask." *Museum News* 28, no. 1 (1950): 6–8.

"The Museum Comes of Age." *Museum Service* 23, no. 4 (April 1950): 41.

Red Streak of the Iroquois. Chicago: Children's Press, 1950.

"Lewis Henry Morgan, 1818–1881." *Museum Service* 25, no. 9 (November 1952): 101.

Red Jacket, Last of the Seneca. New York: McGraw-Hill, 1952.

"Where Questions Are Answered." *Museum Service* 26, no. 10 (December 1953): 163.

"The Meaning of Symbols." *Philalethes* 42 (February 1955): 10.

"Ely S. Parker—Man & Mason." *Freemasons* 8, no. 2 (January–December 1961): 229–47.

Parker on the Iroquois: Iroquois Uses of Maize and Other Food Plants; The Code of Handsome Lake, the Seneca Prophet; The Constitution of the Five Nations, edited by William N. Fenton. Syracuse, N.Y.: Syracuse University Press, 1968.

OTHER SOURCES

Abbott, Lawrence, ed. *I Stand in the Center of the Good: Interviews with Contemporary Native American Artists.* Lincoln: University of Nebraska Press, 1994.

Alexander, Edward P. *Museum Masters: Their Museums and Their Influence.* Nashville: American Association for State and Local History, 1983.

Armstrong, William H. *Warrior in Two Camps: Ely S. Parker.* Syracuse, N.Y.: Syracuse University Press, 1978.

Baker, Will. *Backward: An Essay on Indians, Time & Photography.* Berkeley, Calif.: North Atlantic Books, 1983.

Bakker, P. "A Basque Etymology for the Word 'Iroquois.'" *Man in the Northeast* 40 (1990): 89.

Bascom, William. "The Forms of Folklore." *Journal of American Folklore* 78 (1965): 42–58.

Beale, Irene A. *William P. Letchworth: A Man for Others.* Geneseo, N.Y.: Chestnut Hill Press, 1982. Reprint, 1994.

Bender, Susan J., and Edward V. Curtin. *A Prehistoric Context for the Upper Hudson: Report of the Survey and Planning Project.* Skidmore College, Saratoga Springs, 1990.

Berkhofer, Robert F., Jr. *The White Man's Indian.* New York: Vintage Books, 1979.

Bloch, Maurice. *Marxism and Anthropology: The History of a Relationship.* Oxford: Clarendon Press, 1983.

Boas, Franz. *Race, Language and Culture.* New York: Macmillan, 1940.

———. "Some Principles of Museum Administration." *Science* 25 (1907): 921–33.

Bonte, Paul. "From Ethnology to Anthropology: On Critical Approaches to the Human Sciences." *Critique of Anthropology* 1 (autumn 1974): 36–67.

Burmaster, Everett R. "The World's Wonder Corner." Manuscript, Town of Hanover Historical Collections. Chautauqua County, New York, 1955.

Burnham, John C. "The Cultural Interpretation of the Progressive Movement." In *Conflict and Consensus in Modern American History,* edited by A. F. Davis and H. D. Woodman. Lexington, Mass.: D. C. Heath, 1992.

Campisi, Jack. "The Iroquois and the Euro-American Concept of Tribe." *New York History* 78 (October 1997): 455–72.

Carnes, Mark C. *Secret Ritual and Manhood in Victorian America.* New Haven, Conn.: Yale University Press, 1989.

Chafe, Wallace L. "Comment on Anthony F. C. Wallace's 'Cultural Composition of the Handsome Lake Religion.'" New York State Museum. Sixth Report of the Director of the Science Division. *Education Department Bulletin* 140 (June 1910).

Clawson, Mary Ann. *Constructing Brotherhood: Class, Gender, and Fraternalism.* Princeton, N.J.: Princeton University Press, 1989.

Clifford, James. *The Predicament of Culture: Twentienth-Century Ethnography, Literature, and Art.* Boston: Harvard University Press, 1988.

Collier, Donald. "Chicago Comes of Age: The World's Columbian Exposition and the Birth of the Field Museum." *Bulletin of the Field Museum of Natural History* 40, no. 5 (1969): 3–7.

Collier, John. *From Every Zenith: A Memoir.* Denver: Sage Books, 1963.

Cooper, Karen Coody. "Arthur C. Parker: From Cattaraugus Reservation Childhood to American Museum Leadership." *History News* 54, no. 3 (summer 1998): 9–11.

Dana, John Cotton. *The New Museum.* Woodstock, Vt.: Elm Tree Press, 1917.

Deardorff, Merle H. "The Religion of Handsome Lake: Its Origin and Development." *Bulletin of American Ethnology Bulletin* 149 (1951): 104.

Deloria, Philip J. *Playing Indian.* New Haven, Conn.: Yale University Press, 1998.

——. "White Sacheme and Indian Masons: American Indian Otherness and Nineteenth Century Fraternalism." *Democratic Vistas* 1, no. 2 (autumn 1993): 27–43.

Denslow, William R. "Freemasonry and the American Indian." *Transactions of the Missouri Lodge of Research,* vol. 13. Foreword by Carl H. Claudy. 1956: 25–50.

De Waal Malefijt, Anne Marie. *Images of Man: A History of Anthropological Thought.* New York: Knopf, 1974.

Dexter, Ralph W. "Frederick Ward Putnam and the Development of Museums of Natural History and Anthropology in America." *Curator* 42, no. 1 (1966): 151–55.

——. "Putnam's Problems Popularizing Anthropology." *American Scientist* 54, no. 3 (1966): 315–32.

Dixon, Roland. "Putnam, Frederick Ward." *Dictionary of American Biography,* edited by Dumas Malone. Vol. XV, 276–78. New York: Scribner, 1935.

DuBois, William E. B. *The Souls of Black Folk.* In *Three Negro Classics,* 23–207. New York: Avon Books, 1965.

Dumenil, Lynn. *Freemasonry and American Culture, 1880–1930.* Princeton, N.J.: Princeton University Press, 1984.

Dupuy, William A. "Looking for an Indian Booker T. Washington to Lead Their People." *New York Tribune,* 27 August 1911, sec. 3, p. 3.

"Ely Samuel Parker: From Sachem to Brigadier General." *New York State and the Civil War* 1, no. 4 (October 1961): 1–5.

Emberley, Julia V. "A Gift for Languages: Native Women and the Textual Economy of the Colonial Archive." *Cultural Critique* 17 (1990): 21–50.

Engels, Frederick. *The Origin of the Family, Private Property and the State: In the Light of the Researches of Lewis H. Morgan.* London: Lawrence & Wishart, 1884.

Fabian, Johannes. *Time and the Other: How Anthropology Makes Its Object.* New York: Columbia University Press, 1983.

"Famous American Indians: Arthur C. Parker." *Chemawa American* 30, no. 4 (14 November 1928).

Fein, Albert. *Frederick Law Olmsted and the American Environmental Tradition.* New York: Braziller, 1972.

Fenton, William N. "'Aboriginally Yours,' Jesse J. Cornplanter, Hah-Yonh-Wonh-Ish, The Snipe Seneca, 1889–1957." *American Indian Intellectuals.* 1976 Proceedings of the American Ethnological Society, edited by Margot Liberty, 177–95. St. Paul: West, 1978.

——. Introduction to *League of the Iroquois,* by Lewis Henry Morgan. New York: Corinth Books, 1962.

——. Introduction to *Parker on the Iroquois: Iroquois Uses of Maize and Other Food Plants; The Code of Handsome Lake, the Seneca Prophet; The Constitution of the Five Nations,* by Arthur C. Parker. Syracuse, N.Y.: Syracuse University Press, 1968.

————. Introduction to *Seneca Myths and Folk Tales,* by A. C. Parker. Lincoln: University of Nebraska Press, 1989.

————. "The Iroquois Confederacy in the Twentieth Century: A Case Study of the Theory of Lewis Henry Morgan in 'Ancient Society.'" *Ethnology* 4 (July 1965): 251–65.

————. "The Iroquois in History." In *North American Indians: In Historical Perspective,* edited by Eleanor Burke Leacock, 129–69. New York: Random House, 1971.

————. "Seth Newhouse's Traditional History and Constitution of the Iroquois Confederacy." *Proceedings, American Philosophical Society* 93 (1949): 141–58.

————. "This Island, the World on the Turtle's Back." *Journal of American Folklore* 75, no. 298 (1962): 283–300.

————, ed. "Tonawanda Longhouse Ceremonies: Ninety Years after Lewis Henry Morgan." *Smithsonian Institution Bureau of American Ethnology Bulletin* 128, nos. 13–18. Anthropological Papers. Washington, D.C.: U.S. Government Printing Office, 1941.

Fenton, William Nelson, and John Gulick, eds. *Symposium on Cherokee and Iroquois Culture* [papers]. Washington, D.C.: U.S. Government Printing Office, 1961.

Forbes, Jack D. *Africans and Native Americans: The Language of Race and the Evolution of Red-Black Peoples.* Urbana: University of Illinois Press, 1993.

Goldenweiser, Alexander A. Review of *The Constitution of the Five Nations* by Arthur C. Parker. *American Anthropologist* 18 (1916): 431–36.

Goode, George Brown. "Museum-History and Museums of History." In *Papers of the American Historical Association,* vol. 3, edited by Herbert Baxter Adams, 497–520. New York: Putnam, 1888.

Gossett, Thomas F. *Race: The History of an Idea in America.* Dallas: Southern Methodist University Press, 1963.

Gould, Robert Freke. *The History of Freemasonry: Its Antiquities, Symbols, Constitutions, Customs, etc. . . . Embracing an Investigation of the Records of the Organisations of the Fraternity in England, Scotland, Ireland, British Colonies, France, Germany and the United States.* Received from Official Sources. Edinburgh: T. C & E. C. Jack, Grange Publishing Works, 1852.

Grant, Madison. *The Passing of the Great Race; or, The Racial Basis of European History.* New York: Scribner, 1916.

Green, Jesse, ed. *Cushing at Zuni: The Correspondence and Journals of Frank Hamilton Cushing, 1879–1884.* Albuquerque: University of New Mexico Press, 1990.

Grinde, Donald A., Jr. "Iroquois Political Theory and the Roots of American Democracy." In *Exiled in the Land of the Free: Democracy, Indian Nations, and the U.S. Constitution.* Santa Fe, N.Mex.: Clear Light, 1992.

Griswold, Jerry. *Audacious Kids Coming of Age in America's Classic Children's Books.* Oxford: Oxford University Press, 1992.

Hamell, George R. Introduction to *Skunny Wundy: Seneca Indian Tales,* by Arthur Caswell Parker. Syracuse, N.Y.: Syracuse University Press, 1994.

Haraway, Donna. "Teddybear Patriarchy: Taxidermy in the Garden of Eden, New York City, 1908–1936." *Social Text,* no. 11 (winter 1984/1985): 19–64.

Harrington, Mark R. "Some Seneca Corn-foods and Their Preparation." *American Anthropologist* 10 (1912): 575–90.

Harris, Neil. *Cultural Excursions: Marketing Appetites and Cultural Tastes in Modern America.* Chicago: University of Chicago Press, 1990.

Hauptman, Laurence M. "The American Indian Federation and the Indian New Deal: A Reinterpretation." *Pacific Historical Review* 52 (1983): 378–402.

———. *Between Two Fires: American Indians in the Civil War.* New York: Free Press, 1995.

———. "Designing Woman: Minnie Kellogg, Iroquois Leader." In *Indian Lives: Essays on Nineteenth-and Twentieth-Century Native American Leaders,* edited by L. G. Moses and Raymond Wilson. Albuquerque: University of New Mexico Press, 1985.

———. *The Iroquois and the New Deal.* Syracuse, N.Y.: Syracuse University Press, 1981.

———. "The Iroquois School of Art: Arthur C. Parker and the Seneca Arts Project, 1935–1941." *New York History* 60 (July 1979): 253–312.

———. "Senecas and Subdividers: Resistance to Allotment of Indian Lands in New York, 1875–1906." *Prologue* 26 (1994): 86–99.

Hayes, Catherine D. "Published Writings of Arthur Caswell Parker 1900–1959: A Bibliography." Department of Special Collections, Rush Rhees Library, University of Rochester. June 1960.

Hertzberg, Hazel W. "Arthur C. Parker: Seneca, 1881–1955." In *American Indian Intellectuals.* 1976 Proceedings of the American Ethnological Society, edited by Margot Liberty. St. Paul: West, 1978.

———. "Nationality, Anthropology, and Pan-Indianism in the Life of Arthur C. Parker." *Proceedings of the American Philosophical Society* 123 (1979): 47–72.

———. *The Search for an American Indian Identity: Modern Pan-Indian Movements.* Syracuse, N.Y.: Syracuse University Press, 1971.

———. "Teaching a Pre-Columbian Culture: The Iroquois." University of the State of New York, State Education Department Bureau of Secondary Curriculum Development. Albany, 1966.

Hewitt, J. N. B. Review of *The Constitutions of the Five Nations* by Arthur C. Parker. *American Anthropologist* 19 (1917): 429–38.

Higham, John. *Strangers in the Land: Patterns of American Nativism, 1860–1925.* New Brunswick, N.J.: Rutgers University Press, 1955.

Hinsley, Curtis. M. "From Shell Heaps to Stelae: Early Anthropology at the Peabody Museum." *Objects and Others: Essays on Museums and Material Culture,* edited by George W. Stocking, Jr. History of Anthropology, vol. 3. Wisconsin: University of Wisconsin Press, 1985.

Hollcroft, Temple R. "Notes on: Ely S. Parker—Man & Mason." *Transactions of the American Lodge of Research, Free and Accepted Masons* 8, no. 2 (December–January 1961): 248–57.

Hoxie, Frederick E. *A Final Promise: The Campaign to Assimilate the Indians, 1880–1920.* Cambridge: Cambridge University Press, 1989.

Hurtado, Albert L., and Peter Iverson, eds. *Major Problems in American Indian History.* Lexington, Mass.: D. C. Heath, 1984.

Hymes, Dell, ed. *Reinventing Anthropology.* New York: Vintage Books, 1974.

Jacknis, Ira. "Franz Boas and Exhibits." *Objects and Others: Essays on Museums and Material Culture,* edited by George W. Stocking, Jr. History of Anthropology, vol. 3. Madison: University of Wisconsin Press, 1985.

Johnson, Hazel A. "John Cotton Dana." *Library Quarterly* 7, no. 1 (January 1937): 50–98.

Kallen, Horace M. *Culture and Democracy in the United States.* New York: Arno Press, 1970.

Karp, Ivan, Christine Mullen Kreamer, and Steven D. Lavine, eds. *Museums and Communities: The Politics of Public Culture.* Washington, D.C.: Smithsonian Institution Press, 1992.

Karp, Ivan, and Steven D. Lavine, eds. *Exhibiting Cultures: The Poetics and Politics of Museum Display.* Washington, D.C.: Smithsonian Institution Press, 1991.

Kelly, Lawrence C. "The Indian Reorganization Act: The Dream and the Reality." *Pacific Historical Review* 44 (August 1975): 291–312.

Kelsay, Isabel Thompson. *Joseph Brant, 1743–1807: Man of Two Worlds.* Syracuse, N.Y.: Syracuse University Press, 1984.

Kevles, Daniel J. *In the Name of Eugenics: Genetics and the Uses of Human Heredity.* Cambridge, Mass.: Harvard University Press, 1995.

Knight, Stephen. *The Brotherhood: The Secret World of the Freemasons.* London: Granada, 1984.

Koppes, Clayton R. "From New Deal to Termination: Liberalism and Indian Policy, 1933–1953." *Pacific Historical Review* 46 (1977): 543–66.

Kosok, Paul, ed. "An Unknown Letter from Lewis H. Morgan to Abraham Lincoln." *University of Rochester Library Bulletin* 6 (winter 1951): 34–40.

Krupat, Arnold. "Anthropology in the Ironic Mode: The Work of Franz Boas." *Social Text* 19/20 (1988): 105–18.

———. *Ethnocriticism: Ethnography, History, Literature.* Berkeley: University of California Press, 1992.

Kulik, Gary. "Designing the Past: History Museum Exhibitions from Peale to the Present." In *History Museums in the United States,* edited by Warren Leon and Roy Rosenzweig, 3–37. Urbana: University of Illinois Press, 1989.

Kunitz, Stephen J. "The Social Philosophy of John Collier." *Ethnohistory* 18 (summer 1971): 213–29.

Kuper, Adam. *The Invention of Primitive Society: Transformations of an Illusion.* London: Routledge, 1988.

Lanternari, Vittorio. *Religions of the Oppressed: A Study of Modern Messianic Cults.* London: MacGibbon & Kee, 1963.

Lawrence, John. *Freemasonry—A Religion?* Eastbourne, East Sussex: Kingsway, 1987.

Lears, T. Jackson. *No Place of Grace: Antimodernism and the Transformation of American Culture, 1880–1920.* New York, Pantheon Books, 1981.

Lewis, Sinclair. *Babbit.* New York: Harcourt, Brace, 1922. Reprint, New York: American Library, 1961.

Lowie, Robert H. "Lewis Henry Morgan in Historical Perspective." *Essays in Anthropology: Presented to A. L. Kroeber.* Berkeley, Calif.: University of California Press, 1936. Reprint, Freeport, N.Y.: Books for Libraries Press, 1968.

Ludmerer, Kenneth. *Genetics and American Society.* Baltimore: Johns Hopkins University Press, 1972.

Lyons, Oren, et al. *Exiled in the Land of the Free: Democracy, Indian Nations, and the U.S. Constitution.* Sante Fe, N.Mex.: Clear Light Publishers, 1992.

McNickle, Darcy. "The Indian New Deal as a Mirror of the Future." In *Political Organization of Native North Americans,* edited by Ernest Schusky, 107–19. Washington, D.C.: University Press of America, 1980.

Meriam, Lewis, et al. *The Problem of Indian Administration.* Baltimore: John Hopkins University Press, 1928.

Montagu, Ashley. *Man's Most Dangerous Myth: The Fallacy of Race.* New York: Columbia University Press, 1942. Reprint, Walnut Creek, Calif.: AltaMira Press, 1997.

Montezuma, Carlos. "Light on the Indian Situation." *Quarterly Journal of the Society of American Indians* 1, no. 1 (1913): 50–53.

Morgan, Lewis Henry. *The American Beaver and His Works.* Chicago: Charles H. Kerr, 1868. Reprint, *The American Beaver: A Classic of Natural History and Ecology.* New York: Dover, 1986.

———. *Ancient Society; or, Researches in the Lines of Human Progress from Savagery through Barbarism to Civilization.* Chicago: Charles H. Kerr, 1877.

———. *Houses and Houselife of the American Aborigines.* Chicago: Charles H. Kerr, 1881.

———. "Laws of Descent of the Iroquois." *Proceedings of the Advancement of Science* 11, no. 2 (1858): 132–48.

———. *The League of the Ho-dé-no-sau-nee or Iroquois.* 1851. Secaucus, N.J.: Citadel Press, 1975.

———. *Systems of Consanguinity and Affinity of the Human Family.* Chicago: Charles H. Kerr, 1871.

Moses, L. G. *The Indian Man: A Biography of James Mooney.* Urbana: University of Illinois Press, 1984.

———. *Wild West Shows and the Images of American Indians 1883–1933.* Albuquerque: University of New Mexico Press, 1996.

Murray, David. *Modern Indians.* British Association for American Studies. Tyne & Wear: Peterson Printers, 1982.

Oberweiser, David. "The Indian Education of Lewis Henry Morgan." *Indian Historian* 1 (winter 1979): 23–28.

Oswalt, Wendell H., and Sharlotte Neely. *This Land Was Theirs: A Study of North American Indians.* Mountain View, Calif.: Mayfield, 1996. Reprint, 1999.

"Parker, Arthur C." *Who's Who in America.* Buffalo Historical Society, Historical Volume 1, 1607–1896.

Parker, Dorothy. *Singing an Indian Song: A Biography of D'Arcy McNickle.* Lincoln: University of Nebraska Press, 1992.

Parker, Ely. "General Parker's Autobiography." *Publications of the Buffalo Historical Society* 8 (1905): 511–36.

"Parker, Ely Samuel." *Who's Who in America.* Buffalo Historical Society, Historical vol. 1, 1607–1896.

Parman, Donald L. *The Navajos and the New Deal.* New Haven, Conn.: Yale University Press, 1976.

Philp, Kenneth, ed. *Indian Self-Rule: First-hand Accounts of Indian-White Relations from Roosevelt to Reagan.* Salt Lake City: Howe Bros., 1986.

Powell, Aaron D. "The Engineering of Forever: Arthur E. Morgan, the Seneca Indians, and the Kinzua Dam." *New York History* 78, no. 3 (July 1997): 309–36.

Prucha, Francis Paul. *American Indian Policy in Crisis: Christian Reformers and the Indian, 1865–1900.* Norman, Okla.: University of Oklahoma Press, 1976.

————, ed. *Documents of United States Indian Policy.* 2d ed. Lincoln: University of Nebraska Press, 1990.

Resek, Carl. *Lewis Henry Morgan: American Scholar.* Chicago: University of Chicago Press, 1960.

Richter, Daniel. *The Ordeal of the Longhouse: The Peoples of the Iroquois League in the Era of European Colonization.* Chapel Hill: University of North Carolina Press, 1992.

Rickard, Chief Clinton. *Fighting Tuscarora: The Autobiography of Chief Clinton Rickard,* edited by Barbara Graymont. Syracuse, N.Y.: Syracuse University Press, 1973.

Ritchie, William A. "Arthur Caswell Parker, 1881–1955." *American Antiquity* 21 (1956): 293–95.

Robinson, Edward S. "Experimental Education in Museums—A Perpective." *Museum News* 10 (15 February 1933): 5–8.

Roosevelt, Theodore. Speech at New York Republican state convention at Saratoga, 1906, and *Metropolitan Magazine,* October 1915, p. 7.

Rose, Richard. "The Lewis Henry Morgan Collection at the Rochester Museum." In *Iroquois Studies: A Guide to Documentary and Ethnographic Resources from Western New York and the Genesee Valley,* edited by Russell A. Judkins. Department of Anthropology, State University of New York and Geneseo Foundation, 1987.

Sayers, Janet, Mary Evans, and Nanneke Redclift, eds. *Engels Revisited: New Feminist Essays.* London: Tavistock, 1987.

Schlesinger, Arthur, Jr. "Dixon Ryan Fox." *New York History* 79, no. 1 (January 1998): 57–60.

Schrader, Robert F. *The Indian Arts and Crafts Board: An Aspect of Indian New Deal Policy.* Albuquerque: University of New Mexico Press, 1983.

Schwartz, E. A. "Red Atlantis Revisited: Community and Culture in the Writings of John Collier." *American Indian Quarterly* 18, no. 4 (fall 1994): 518.

Scott, Duncan Campbell. "Traditional History of the Confederacy of the Six Nations: Prepared by a Committee of the Chiefs. Read May 16, 1911." *Royal Society of Canada, Proceedings and Transactions,* 3d. ser., sec. 11 (1912): 195–246.

Seymour, Flora Warren. *Indian Agents of the Old Frontier.* Millwood, N.Y.: Appleton-Century, 1941. Reprint, New York: Octagon Books, 1975

Skinner, Alanson. Review of *The Code of Handsome Lake, the Seneca Prophet,* by Arthur C. Parker. *American Anthropologist* 17 (1915): 180–581.

Smith, David J. *The Eugenic Assault on America: Scenes in Red, White and Black.* Fairfax, Va.: George Mason University Press, 1993.

Snow, Dean R. *The Iroquois.* Cambridge: Blackwell Publishers, 1994.

Speck, Frank G. "*Iroquois Uses of Maize and Other Food Plants.* By A. C. Parker." *American Anthropologist* 13 (1911): 135–36.

Stern, Bernhard J. *Lewis Henry Morgan: Social Evolutionist.* New York: Russell & Russell, 1931.

Stocking, George W., Jr. "Franz Boas." *Dictionary of American Biography,* suppl. 3, edited by Allen Johnson et al., 81–86. New York: Scribner, 1973.

———, ed. *Objects and Others: Essays on Museums and Material Culture.* History of Anthropology, vol. 3. Wisconsin: University of Wisconsin Press, 1985.

Sullivan, Lynne P. "Arthur C. Parker's Contributions to New York State Archaeology." Paper presented at the 75th annual meeting of the New York State Archaeological Association, Rochester, April 1991.

Sumner, William Graham. *Folkways: A Study of the Sociological Importance of Usages, Manners, Customs, Mores, and Morals.* Boston: Ginn, 1907.

Taylor, Carol. "W. E. B. DuBois's Challenge to Scientific Racism." *Journal of Black Studies* 11, no. 4 (1981): 449–60.

Thomas, W. Stephen. "Arthur Caswell Parker: 1881–1955: Anthropologist, Historian, and Museum Pioneer." *Rochester History* 17, no. 3 (July 1955): 1–20.

———. "Arthur Caswell Parker—Leader and Prophet of the Museum World." *Museum Service* 28, no. 2 (February 1955): 18, 25, 28.

———. "Arthur C. Parker: Master of Hobbies." Rochester: Rochester Museum of Arts and Sciences. Reprinted from Museum Service 32, no. 8 (October 1959): 134–35.

Tocqueville, Alexis de. *Democracy in America.* Translated by Henry Reeve. Vol. 2. 1840. Reprint, New York: Schocken, 1961.

Tooker, Elizabeth. *Lewis Henry Morgan on Iroquois Material Culture.* Tucson: University of Arizona Press, 1994.

———. "On the New Religion of Handsome Lake." *Anthropological Quarterly* 41 (1968): 187–200.

———. "The Structure of the Iroquois League: Lewis Henry Morgan's Research and Observations." *Ethnohistory* 30, no. 3 (1983): 141–54.

Trautmann, Thomas R. *Lewis Henry Morgan and the Invention of Kinship.* Berkeley: University of California Press, 1987.

Turner, Frederick Jackson. "The Significance of the Frontier in American History." *Proceedings of the Forty-First Annual Meeting of the State Historical Society of Wisconsin,* 79–112. Madison, Wis., 1894.

Tylor, Graham D. "Anthropologists, Reformers, and the Indian New Deal." *Prologue* 1 (fall 1975): 151–62.

Wallace, Anthony F. C. "Cultural Composition of the Handsome Lake Religion." Symposium on Cherokee and Iroquois Culture. *Smithsonian Institution Bureau of American Ethnology Bulletin* 180 (1961): 139–51.

———. *The Death and Rebirth of the Seneca.* New York: Knopf, 1969. Reprint, New York: Vintage Books, 1972.

———. "Handsome Lake and the Great Revival in the West." *American Quarterly,* summer 1952, 146–65.

———. "Revitalization Movements." *American Anthropologist* 58 (1956): 264–81.

Waltmann, Henry G. "Circumstantial Reformer: President Grant and the Indian Problem." *Arizona and the West* 31 (winter 1971): 323–42.

———. "Ely Samuel Parker, 1869–71." In *The Commissioners of Indian Affairs, 1824–1977,* edited by Robert M. Kvasnicka and Herman J. Viola. London: University of Nebraska Press, 1979.

Warrior, Robert Allen. "Reading American Indian Intellectual Traditions." *World Literature Today* 1 (spring 1992): 236–40.

Waugh, F. W. *Iroquois Foods and Food Preparation.* Memoir 86. Geological Survey of the Canada Department of Mines, 1916.

Weil, Stephen E. *Beauty and the Beasts: On Museums, Art, the Law, and the Market.* Washington, D.C.: Smithsonian Institution Press, 1983.

White, Leslie A. "How Morgan Came to Write Systems of Consanguinity and Affinity." *Papers of the Michigan Academy of Science, Arts, and Letters* 42 (1957): 257–68.

White, Richard. *The Middle Ground.* New York: Cambridge University Press, 1991.

Willey, Gordon R., and Jeremy A. Sabloff. *A History of American Archaeology.* San Francisco: W. H. Freeman, 1974.

Williams, Vernon, Jr. *Rethinking Race: Franz Boas and His Contemporaries.* Lexington: University Press of Kentucky, 1996.

Wilson, Bryan R. *Magic and the Millennium.* London: Heinemann, 1973.

Wilson, Edmund. *Apologies to the Iroquois.* New York: Farrar, Straus & Cudahy, 1960.

Wissler, Clark. "The Material Culture of North American Indians." *American Anthropologist* 16 (1917): 447–515.

Yeuell, Donovan. "Ely Samuel Parker." In *Dictionary of American Biography,* edited by Dumas Malone, vol. 772, 219–220. New York: Scribner, 1943.

Young, Robert. *White Mythologies: Writing History and the West.* London: Routledge, 1990.

Zangwill, Israel. *The Melting Pot: A Drama in Four Acts.* London: Heinemann, 1919.

Zeller, Terry "Arthur C. Parker: A Pioneer in American Museums." *Curator* 30, no. 1 (March 1987): 41–62.

———. "Arthur Parker and the Educational Mission of American Museums." *Curator* 32, no. 2 (June 1989): 104–22.

Zimmerman, Karen P. "Vine Deloria, Jr." In *Smoke Rising: The Native North American Literary Companion,* edited by Joseph Bruchac and Janet Witalec, with Sharon Malinowski. Detroit: Visible Ink Press, 1995.

Index

DuBois, W. E. B.: Descendants of American Aborigines and, 108; NAACP and, 92; the "talented tenth," 121

Eastman, Charles A.: Mrs. Bonnin and, 132–33; and Boy Scout movement, 229; and SAI, 93–94, 101 (departure from, 135; election as president, 134); support for peyote, 133;
Eastman, Elaine Goodale (wife Charles): SAI role, 95
Eastman, George: donations to American Eugenics Society, 30; and to Rochester Museum, 182
Edgerton, Hiram H., 171
Engels, Friedrich, 38–39
Eugenics: ACP's belief in, 4, 29–31, 137–38, 215–16; fashionable view, 29–32; Indians and, 30–31; Madison Grant's *The Passing of the Great Race*, 30; L. H. Morgan and, 30

Fadden, John (Mohawk), 210
Fadden, Ray, 225, 239, 241
Fenton, William N., 54, 197–98; ability to speak Seneca language, 270n.18
Fox, Dixon Ryan, 186–87
FREEMASONS: de Tocqueville's view of, 145; history and structure, 145–46, 158–61; hostility to Roman Catholics, 148; Indian assimilation and, 162–63; Indian connection, 152–60; Ku Klux Klan and, 148; as male pursuit, 149–50; racism and, 147–48; reevaluation, 145; ridicule of, 144–45; ritualism, 146–47; social purpose, 147, 148–49
  ACP and: the second degree (Fellow Craft), 151; the ninth degree, *154*; the thirty-third degree (Sovereign Grand Inspector General) (1924),

143–45, 152; expenses, 151–52; goodbye to "Sir Arthur," 239; Masonic pedigree, 162; perception of, 150–51; membership of other fraternities, 151; membership of Sylvan Masonic Lodge (1907), 151; in retirement, 220
ACP's masonic writings: "American Indian Freemasonry" (1919), 153–55; as editor of *The Builder*, 158; "Ely S. Parker— Man and Mason," 156; "Freemasonry among the American Indians" (1920), 153–54; *Secrets of the Temple* (1922), 155; "The Age-Old Appeal of Universal Freemasonry" (1947), 157; "Why All This Secrecy" (1923), 155

Galton Society, 30
Genesee Country Historical Federation, 222
Goldenweiser, Alexander A., 87
Goode, George Brown (1851–96), 171–72; *The Principles of Museum Administration* (1895), 172
Gordon, Father Philip: as SAI president, 139; sectarianism of, 126
Grand Order (or New Confederacy) of the Iroquois, 33–35; protection of Seneca lands, 34
Grant, Madison: *The Passing of the Great Race*, 30
Grant, Ulysses S.: corrupt administration, 43; EP and, 16, 43–44, 161; peace policy, 43–44
Griswold, Geneva Hortense (d. 1923): ACP's relations with, 5; family background, 7; marriage to Frederick Parker, 17

Handsome Lake (Skanyadariyoh): relationship to William Parker's wife and Ely Parker, 12, 78; shortcomings, 81–82; support for nuclear family, 11

Aborigines, 107–108; Improved Order of the Red Men (IORM), 100, 159 (memorialization of Indian ways, 100; "paleface" organization, 100, 160); Indian Arts and Crafts Board, 194–95; Indian Rights Association (IRA), 92, 100; Lake Mohonk Conference of the Friends of the Indian, 92, 98, 118, 122; Loyal Order of Tecumseh, 107–108; National Association for the Advancement of Colored People (NAACP), 92; National Congress of American Indians, 110; Ohio Daughters of Pocahontas, 100; Society for the Propagation of Indian Welfare conference at Rochester Museum, 183. *See also* Society of American Indians (SAI)

status: Carter Bill (1912), 99, 103, 114, 116; "resident aliens," 131; right to vote (1924), 99; U.S. citizenship, 5, 19, 132, 140–41, 191; rejection as compromise to sovereignty/rights, 5, 99, 195–96; SAI support for, 99; separate Indian regiment, 131; wardship, 5

See also Iroquois; Legislation affecting Indian rights; Meriam Report (*The Problem of Indian Administration*) (1926); Seneca; Society of American Indians (SAI); Treaties affecting Indian rights

Iroquois: anglicizing of, 64; *Apologies to the Iroquois* (Edmund Wilson) (1960), 78; as People of the Longhouse (Ho-dé-no-sau-nee), 7; collecting artifacts (flute and water drum, 73; L. H. Morgan, 34–35; race to preserve past, 64; *see also* Wampums); diseases introduced by Europeans, 8;

enlistment in the Union army, 16; food (*Iroquois Foods and Food Preparation* [F.W. Waugh], 75; *Iroquois Uses of Maize and Other Food Plants* [ACP] [1910], 73–75; "three sisters" [maize, beans, squash], 7, 73–75); France and the "Middle Ground," 8–9; headmen's role, 9; languages, 7; origins, 7–8; Owasco cultural tradition and, 7; rejection of Indian Reorganization Act (1934), 195–96; reservation system, effect on, 11; revolt at Six Nations Reserve, ACP's intervention, 75; sovereignty claims, 244n.8; translating myths, 72, 233

Iroquois League (Confederacy): and the British, 8, 10–11, 21; Grand Order of the Iroquois and, 33–34; "nations" constituting, 7; nature of organization (*The Constitution of the Five Nations* [ACP] [1916], 84–90; "oldest continuously functioning democratic constitution," 9–10; whether ritualistic or political social, 36); rise and decline, 8–10 (American Revolution and, 9; covering the council fire, 9; factionalism, 9; Seven Years War and, 9); status, 195–96; Tuscarora and, 9

Irving, James, 136

Jemison, Alice Lee (Seneca), 208–209
Jemison, Wyman, 197
Jimerson, Roy, 200
Johnson, Elizabeth (wife of William Parker), 12
Johnson, Freeman, 225

Kallen, Horace, 31
Kellogg, Laura: ACP corresponds with, 106, 110; charges of fraud

Civil War, 16; support for EP's brothers and sister, 34–35
publications: *Ancient Society, or Researches in the Lines of Human Progress from Savagery through Barbarism to Civilization* (1877), 38–39, 40 (impact on socialist and feminist writers, 38–39); *The League of the Ho-dé-no-sau-nee, or Iroquois* (1851), 13, 35–36, 40, 74; *Systems of Consanguinity and Affinity of the Human Family* (1871), 37–38
Morgan, Thomas J., 28
Museology developments, 48–49; J. C. Dana, 172–73; G. B. Goode, 171–72. *See also* Dioramas; Parker, Arthur Caswell, as museologist
Museums and learned societies: anthropology studies and, 48–49, 56–57, 166; the Indian as represented by, 166–67; as manifestation of U.S. global preeminence, 68–69; as "university of the common man," 3, 67–68, 165–66, 177–78, 184, 185, 188. *See also* American Association of Museums; American Museum of Natural History (AMNH); American Scenic and Historic Preservation Society; Buffalo Museum of Science; Genesee Country Historical Federation; National Research Council; New York Historical Association; New York State Archaeological Society; New York State Museum; Nundawaga Society for History and Folklore; Rochester Museum, New York; Seneca Arts and Crafts Project; Society for American Archaeology; State Museum Advisory Committee for the Regents of the University of the State of

New York; Tonawanda Community House
Myrtle, Minnie, 238
Myths, 71–72

National Association for the Advancement of Colored People (NAACP), 92
National Research Council, 183
New York Historical Association, 186, 241; ACP as president, 167
New York State Archaeological Society: ACP as president, 167, 216
New York State Museum, 57; ACP as archaeologist in Science Division, 60; ACP as curator of archaeology and ethnology, 115; ACP as ethnographic field worker, 57–58; ACP's exclusion of "foreign" and loan materials, 174; ACP's resignation, 167–68; fire (1911), 51, 76–77, 89, 97, 98, 201, 203; L. H. Morgan's collections for (1848–50), 35, 57–58; promotion of J. M. Clarke, Jr., 170; purchase of Iroquois wampum belts, 57, 65
Newhouse, Seth: *The Constitution of the Five Nations* and, 85–86
Nundawaga Society for History and Folklore, 224, 240; pageants, 224–25

Olmsted, Frederick Law, 187
Owasco cultural tradition, 7, 244n.1
Owen, Senator: relations with SAI, 116, 118, 119

Pageants, 224–25
Parker, Anna Theresa (ACP's second wife) (b. 1897): adoption into Seneca Bear Clan as "Yeiwano:t" (1928), 117; attendance at Lake Mohonk Conference (1915), 122; Daughter of the American Revolution,

Smith, Ernest, 200–201, 210
Smith, Mabel S., 205–206
Society for American Archaeology:
ACP as president, 167
SOCIETY OF AMERICAN INDIANS (SAI):
ACP and: arbiter and peacemaker, 101; attempt to prevent
factionalism at 1916 Con-
ference, 123; bailing out of,
104–105, 106, 111–21; decision
not to attend Madison Conference (1914), 117–18; defense
of, 138; detachment from,
135–37; effect on his philosophy, 91–92; importance of
SAI's "Indian" character, 96,
141–42; neglect of State
Museum duties, 116–17, 118,
119; *Quarterly Journal*, 111–12,
114, 115, 116, 120–21, 130, 132–33,
134, 136; visits to Washington
and Oklahoma, 111
ACP as holder of office: election
to executive committee, 100;
invitation to join permanent
committee, 97; lightening of
the workload, 120; president,
126–35; resignation from Advisory Board (1920), 136; role in
establishing, 77, 90; secretary-
treasurer, 102, 119, 124; permanent, salaried post, 109;
reelection, 118, 124; uncertainty
about long term, 104, 109
ACP's speeches and articles on:
"Albanian Working for
Betterment of Indians" (1911),
96; as source for "Looking for
an Indian Booker T.
Washington to Lead Their
People," 97; "Educational
Problems" (1911), 98–99;
"Making Democracy Safe for
Indians" (1917), 132; "Problems
of Race Assimilation in
America, with Special
Reference to the American
Indian," 127–29

beliefs and objectives: education
in Indian schools of the East as
unifying factor, 96–97; establishment of intertribal confed-
eration/race consciousness,
96–97; hostility to blacks, 92;
legal and political recognition
of Indian people, 92; "of
Indians, by Indians, and for
Indians," 92, 96; promotion of
"Indianness," 107–108; support
for Carter Bill (1912), 103, 114,
116; support for Indian citizenship, 99; "Supposition and
Reality," 93; thunderbird
(eagle) emblem, 100, 120
comparison with other groups:
Indian Rights Association
(IRA), 92; Lake Mohonk
Conference of the Friends of
the Indian, 92, 98; National
Association for the Advancement of Colored People
(NAACP), 92
conferences: 1911 (Columbus,
Ohio), 97–101 (ACP's publicity
for, 97; small attendance, 101;
success of, 99–100); 1912
(Columbus), 106–107; 1913
(Denver) (competition from
Buffalo Bill, 112–13; Denver
grant, 112; a success, 114–15);
1914 (Madison), 117 (ACP's
decision not to attend, 117–18);
1915 (Lawrence, Kans.) (ACP's
optimism, 121; factionalism at,
121–22; financing, 120); 1916
(Cedar Rapids, Iowa) (factionalism at, 123, 125–26; poor
attendance, 125–26); 1918
(Pierre, S.D.), 133 (ACP's
absence, 134; adoption of divisive policies, 134); 1919
(Minneapolis), 135–36; 1920
(St. Louis), 137; 1921 (Detroit),
137; 1923 (Chicago), 138–39
decline and fall, 134–39, 141;
financing, 104–105, 106, 110,

309

INDEX